THE DIPLOMATS

ALSO BY MARTIN MAYER:

THE MET
THE FATE OF THE DOLLAR
THE BUILDERS
THE BANKERS
ABOUT TELEVISION
BRICKS, MORTAR AND THE PERFORMING ARTS
NEW BREED ON WALL STREET (with Cornell Capa)
THE TEACHERS STRIKE
EMORY BUCKNER
DIPLOMA
ALL YOU KNOW IS FACTS
THE LAWYERS
SOCIAL STUDIES IN AMERICAN SCHOOLS
THE SCHOOLS
MADISON AVENUE USA
WALL STREET: MEN AND MONEY

Fiction

TRIGGER POINTS
A VOICE THAT FILLS THE HOUSE
THE EXPERTS

MARTIN MAYER

The Diplomats

DOUBLEDAY & COMPANY, INC.

GARDEN CITY, NEW YORK

1983

Portions of Chapter 5 originally appeared in a piece on the Foreign Agricultural Service in *Fortune*, May 19, 1980; and some of the material in Chapter 8 originally appeared in an article on the Regional Finance Center in *Forbes*, October 1981.

Library of Congress Cataloging in Publication Data
Mayer, Martin, 1928–
  The Diplomats.
  Includes bibliographical references and index.
  1. Diplomats. 2. Diplomatic and consular service.
I. Title.
JX1662.M36 1983   327.2
ISBN 0-385-14230-7
Library of Congress Catalog Card Number 80-2973

For Fredrica,
who never would have
come into existence
without this book

ACKNOWLEDGMENTS

This book was commissioned by Sam Vaughan of Doubleday in late summer 1977, for delivery in fall 1979. I think it is fair to say that we both underestimated the difficulty of the job. Diplomacy is a small profession—there are at most seventy-five thousand people working as Foreign Service Officers (FSOs) for all the nations of the world—but the diplomats' work cannot be understood outside the context of its subjects and its systems, and both subjects and systems are incomprehensible without their history. The literature of the field is vast, and a surprisingly high proportion of it is uninformative and undistinguished; the people you want to interview are all over the globe; and it's often difficult to get to see them after you travel to where they are. Because I was more concerned with the laborers in the vineyard than with the occupants of the seats of power, the untruthful habits and pomposity that cover what occupies such seats were offensive only in Washington, but one had to be wary everywhere.

During the course of the five years this book required, I visited foreign ministries, embassies, consulates and international agencies in (chronologically) the United States, New Zealand, Papua New Guinea, Australia, Singapore, Japan, Denmark, Italy, Hungary, Austria, Switzerland, Britain, West Germany, Mexico, Ivory Coast, Cameroon, Belgium, Israel, Egypt and France. In several of those countries, I visited the embassies of several of the others, with special concentration on those from the United States, Denmark and Israel; and I interviewed also ambassadors or deputies from Algeria, Ghana, Argentina, East Germany, Poland and the Soviet Union.

In all, there were something more than six hundred interviews. None was "off the record," a term of art I interpret to mean that the interviewer is forbidden to use the material (which makes an interview worthless and,

vii

incidentally, dishonest on both sides); a fair number were "on background," another term of art meaning that the material can be used but its source cannot be identified. I believe I have honored all requests for such protection. Where no request was made, I assumed the material from the interview was mine to use without restriction. I am grateful to all those who gave me their time, and I hope none finds in these pages cause to regret having done so. To those who do regret, let me offer the consolation that somebody else probably told me, too, but you said it best.

Quotes and information drawn from printed sources are credited in the Notes. Some of the books cited were both very helpful and very little known, and in hopes of repaying part of my debt to their authors (and recommending further reading), I should like to list a few of them:

Lamar Cecil, *The German Diplomatic Service, 1871–1914*
Walter V. Scholes and Marie V. Scholes, *The Foreign Policies of the Taft Administration*
John A. S. Grenville and George Berkeley Young, *Politics, Strategy and American Diplomacy*
Robert D. Schulzinger, *The Making of the Diplomatic Mind*
Phillip Jessup, *The Birth of Nations*
Richard K. Betts, *Soldiers, Statesmen and Cold War Crises*
John Franklin Campbell, *The Foreign Affairs Fudge Factory*
Foster Rhea Dulles, *Prelude to World Power*
Donald E. Queller, *The Office of Ambassador in the Middle Ages*
Edward W. Kolodziej, *French International Policy Under De Gaulle and Pompidou*
L. Ethan Ellis, *Republican Foreign Policy, 1921–1933*
Richard D. Challener, *Admirals, Generals and American Foreign Policy, 1898–1914*
Elmer Bendiner, *The Virgin Diplomats*
Robert Blum, *Drawing the Line*

No fewer than four FSOs assigned to the Bureau of Public Affairs were in charge of my case at the State Department at one time or another in the course of this work; all were courteous and more or less helpful; I grew especially fond of Mary Ann Yoden. Hodding Carter and William Dyess as assistant secretaries of this Bureau were highly supportive; their successors, so far as I could tell (I did not meet them), were not. Like most Americans who have reason to make repeated contact with the State Department (including those who work there), I came to regard the institution as a pain in the neck; but the individuals were almost without exception pleasant to visit with. So were the hundred-odd FSOs I met *en poste* in the various embassies and consulates. Among the ambassadors,

I am especially grateful to Warren Manshel in Denmark, Philip Kaiser in Hungary, Samuel Lewis in Israel and Mabel Smythe in Cameroon.

The Foreign Ministries of Denmark, Israel, Austria, Britain and New Zealand were especially hospitable, as was the Commission of the European Community. The Foreign Ministry in Japan proved surprisingly capable of adapting to a situation in which the Washington embassy had failed to notify (or the Tokyo press officer had failed to remember) that a visitor was coming.

Both in office as Under Secretary for Political Affairs and in private life at the Hoover Institution, Philip Habib was a wise and entertaining instructor. Dean Rusk, Frank Wisner, Francis J. Meehan, Ernest Koenig, Carol Laise, Deane Hinton, Thomas O. Enders, Anthony Lake, Sir Edward Youde, Hennings Gottlieb, Gunnar Riberholt, Frank Corner, Sir Michael Palliser, Kojo Debrah, Hanan Bar-On, Bernadette Lefort and Brian Urquhart offered insights of particular value. Sol M. Linowitz, a good friend of long standing, provided help, clarification and consolation on a number of occasions.

The New York Society Library, the New York Public Library, the library of the Council on Foreign Relations, the State Department library and the library at International House in Tokyo were all helpful in supplying material for my use. I am thankful, too, for a book distributor who went bankrupt not long before I started work on this project, forcing the nation's university presses to market their wares by direct mail, which enabled me to learn about and purchase a great number of books that might otherwise not have come to my attention. Among the periodicals, I found most useful the New York *Times, The Wall Street Journal, The Economist, International Security, Political Science Quarterly* and the *Annals of the American Academy of Political and Social Science.*

I am grateful to Betty Heller for her hard and (I hope) effective work on the manuscript, and for several imaginative suggestions on matters of organization, deletion and explication. Doubleday institutionally—read, Vaughan—was a brick about the delays in delivering the book, some of which were caused by my acceptance of other assignments during the six-year period, some by the course of events in my private life.

The late Ellen Moers accompanied me on most of the travels required by this book during the first eighteen months of work, denying an illness that in the end will not be denied. Her intelligence, powers of observation, good sense and linguistic abilities, her affections and her courage, were all placed in the service of this enterprise, at some cost to the progress of her own work.

Karin Lissakers, who was deputy director of the Policy Planning Staff at the State Department when we met, accompanied me on the travel involved in the last two years of work. In the time following our marriage, she gave her analytical talents and the resources of her training and experience, not to mention the joy of her presence, to help me find a frame for the scattered bits of mosaic that had to be assembled here.

My sons were continuously, affectionately, effectively supportive through all the time of my deepest need for them. My daughter, as indicated in the jacket photograph, contributed in her way to the resumed work, and the book is dedicated to her on the theory that you can't start too soon.

My thanks to all of them is beyond expression.

Martin Mayer

New York
May 1983

CONTENTS

I

Status

1

ISOLATIONS

> Prince Bismarck received me today, and after his usual complaints
> about the weary work imposed upon him by the obstinacy of his Im-
> perial Master, the incapacity of his Colleagues, the ignorance of Parlia-
> ment and the imbecility of mankind, he said that he was glad to rest
> his weary brain by talking over foreign affairs, which constituted the
> only recreation left him in his overworked existence.
>
> —British ambassador to Germany, in a report
> to Lord Granville, 1881

1

Grand personages and ordinary people enter foreign ministries in very
different ways. For the grand personage, the limousine rolls into a courtyard, escorted by roaring motorcycles, and the occupant of the limousine
disembarks to a cordial welcome, handshake or kissed cheeks according to
culture, from someone of suitable rank and station in the ministry. Flash-
guns pop and tape runs through the television cameras. If the visitor is important enough, hard-eyed men stand about with hands in pockets, their
gaze sweeping the scene high and low. The pace is brisk: personages must
not be kept waiting, and their exposure to public gaze must be controlled.
Presently, the reception area is emptied out, and the underlings of the
world reappear in the doorways to the courtyard, going about their business.

At the Quai d'Orsay in Paris, a sprawling palace on the Seine, the simple visitor, not a personage, is received in an anteroom about the size of a
living room in a private house. A high counter slashes across it halfway

back. On a platform behind the counter sit three male *fonctionnaires,* one gray, one mustachioed, one young. They search slowly through small piles of memoranda to confirm that the individual before them is in fact expected by someone. The flavor is that of an office in the front room of a small factory, with tourist posters on the dirty walls. The visitor waits, standing, until someone comes down the elevator and walks the long corridor to a door beside the counter, to provide an escort.

In Rome at the Foro Italico, the entrance area for the public is a long, narrow room with very high ceilings, a marble floor and a marble-topped counter running its length. Crowds of supplicants stand shabbily before the counter, clearly seeking some sort of redress or favor that probably will not be given them. Two *ufficiali* are talking to each other behind the counter; another scratches his head over some difficulty of an older woman wearing the Italian equivalent of a babushka. The visitor who is not a personage but has an appointment can call out this fact, and will be waved through the glass door behind the counter, out into the courtyard, where a carabiniere stops picking his teeth long enough to give general directions to the room the visitor seeks.

In Japan the Foreign Ministry is one of a row of nondescript mid-rise office buildings set back from a broad street a couple of blocks from the Imperial Gardens. A policeman sits in the nonofficial entrance area, which is virtually never used by anyone not a government employee, and when he sees a Western face he waves vaguely down a wide corridor. The doors are open from the corridors into large, crowded rooms. A step inside the first to the left produces a young woman who speaks English, who looks at the visitor's calling card and at the *meishi* the visitor acquired from the press attaché in the Japanese embassy in Washington, and who reads the four vertical rows of fast calligraphy on its back. She nods, and sends the visitor by himself to the fourth floor, to a door that opens onto an immense, windowed bullpen running almost the length of the building, with scores of apparent clerks (in fact, many are Foreign Service Officers of some seniority) bent over desks or chatting on the telephone. In the middle of the room is a small cleared space with two shabby vinyl-covered green couches, on one of which the visitor perches, quite ignored, until his host, a bureau chief with a small private office, comes out to welcome him.

At the State Department in Washington there is no wrought-iron vehicular gate through which the personage's limousine can be driven to avoid contact with the general public. Instead, the limousine containing the personage, accompanied by accessory vehicles and police cars, turns into the semicircular driveway before this immense, dull white-stone building, World War II recovery vintage and dead plain. Police briefly cordon off the area (including the street), obsequious myrmidons of the Secretary of

State perform welcoming ceremonies under the concrete canopy, and the party moves briskly through the glass doors in a glass wall, past the circular desk in the middle of the two-story-high reception room, past the guard who stands at the opening of the grille behind the desk (beside him the dingiest of little wooden tables to hold the briefcases and packages he examines), and off to the elevators that will carry them to the heroic figures of the Seventh Floor.

The routine visitor moves through the same space, but waits in line until the rather slow-moving receptionist inside the circular desk has verified his appointment, completed a blue paper form that must be handed to the guard, and drawn instructions on a map of the building—a most useful piece of paper, for the State Department is two city blocks long by one block wide, cut by a number of internal corridors with color-coded walls that do not give strangers (or even familiars) much hope of knowing where they are.

But the elevators up to the Seventh Floor are open to all. Just by getting lost, an ordinary visitor can wind up in the sweeping reception suite of the Secretary of State, ninety feet long, carpeted with oriental rugs, gracious furniture in colonial and federal style spotted through it, the walls hung with portraits of former Secretaries of State and genre scenes of the American nineteenth century. The area is broken into three sections by partial glass partitions, and the receptionist sits in solitary grandeur in the center section. She is likely to be someone out of an advertisement for a half-million-dollar retirement cottage—gray hair, modest glasses, a simple black dress, a single strand of pearls.

If the visitor has an appointment with someone in the inner precincts, he may proceed down the corridor that runs into the middle section of the triple reception area, to a narrower, interior corridor, wallpapered, lined with more portraits of Secretaries of State, widening out here and there into niches where deceptively amiable security men sit apparently casually at desks, leading to the rooms where the visitors to the Secretary and the Under Secretaries actually do their waiting. (The reception area merely receives: on several dozen trips through it, this observer never saw anybody sitting on any of the dozens of couches and chairs.) To his left as the visitor walks from the receptionist to the smaller corridor there is a large painting by Harold E. Bryant, a Western scene, snowy mountains in the distance, in the foreground a cowpuncher pushing a horse in some difficulty on a slick uphill path. The painting is entitled "A Slippery Push on a Slippery Trail." The Secretary of State walks past it on his way to his office, every day.

2

Diplomacy is an activity between two sovereign entities, neither of which can control the activities of the other. As such, it needs what the mathematicians call boundary conditions, narrow rules for a narrow game. The world watches uncomprehendingly, not knowing the rules, interested only in the purposes of the game, and often out-of-date on those. These purposes have been changing: "There was a time," said Sir Edward Youde, Chief Clerk of the British Foreign Office,* "when foreign policy was foreign policy—dealt with royal marriages, frontiers and wars. Now you deal with the size of lorries." Still the game itself remains not much different from what it was. As Henry Kissinger's memoirs illustrate, the tasks of international relations still permit a high official to devote his time to an amusing mix of abstraction and gossip, with relatively little attention to the grubbiness of everyday life.

Diplomacy is the profession *par excellence:* pure service, involving what the Middle Ages called a "Mystery," with the quality of performance utterly unmeasurable except by peer judgment. "We have an advantage," says the man in the State Department who must get the Office of Management and Budget to allocate funds for the nation's overseas consulates, "in that most of what *we* do produces a perceptible product—not like the rest of this building, where the product is bullshit." But these days, the least substantial of foreign policy decision memoranda can suddenly become frighteningly important. However hard he tries to escape—and Ronald Reagan struggled manfully—the President of the United States now must make foreign relations his first concern, the subject of his earliest meeting every morning (because the news arrives from both Europe and the Orient while congressmen are still asleep). It is the one area of national decision where the President is uniquely accountable. In his capacity as head of state and commander-in-chief, he is the sole source of authority for what the government does abroad. And nowhere else in government is power so circumscribed by the great truth that you can never change just one thing.

Nuclear warheads rest atop missiles that can deliver them anywhere on earth within half an hour. American forces are permanently stationed in

* At the time of the interview. Later, Governor of Hong Kong. This book took six years to write, and tours of duty in the world's foreign services average about thirty-six months. Relatively few of the people quoted in these pages will still be in the posts they held when their words were taken down for present purposes; titles are for identification and qualification only, not to be used as addresses.

Britain, Germany, Italy, Belgium, Portugal, Spain, Morocco, Greece, Turkey, Denmark (Greenland), Oman, Diego Garcia, the Sinai Desert, Iceland, Australia, Thailand, the Philippines, Japan, Panama, Micronesia, South Korea, New Zealand (under National Science Foundation supervision, for the Antarctic mission) and (to the great annoyance of the local sovereign) Cuba. American fleets are on or under all the world's oceans. "The first objective of the American ambassador to New Zealand," said Armistead Selden when he held that post, "is to make sure the nuclear subs can call in New Zealand ports."

About 10 percent of the American gross national product is now exported and nearly 12 percent of the gross national consumption is imported; something like 10 million jobs in the United States are directly affected by foreign trade. More than 10 percent of the total profits of American enterprise is earned abroad. Foreign governments hold about $100 billion of the national debt accounts, and uncounted billions more are held unofficially or by foreign private entities. Total dollar-denominated deposits in banks outside the United States, transferable to the domestic economy at the touch of a key, are greater than the total deposits of the domestic American banking system, including the savings banks. Every weekday morning, except for a surprisingly long hiatus while the Reagan Treasury struggled up the learning curve, the Federal Reserve Bank of New York talks with the Bundesbank in Bonn to analyze governmental interventions in the foreign exchange markets. Our textile mills operate under conditions set by the "multifiber agreement" in the context of the General Agreement on Tariffs and Trade; the income of American farmers is to a considerable degree at the mercy of decisions taken in Brussels by the Common Market (far greater in their impact than any decision in Washington to impose or remove a "grain embargo" on the Soviet Union); the prosperity of Seattle depends on Boeing's ability to sell American aircraft abroad, while that of Detroit is a function of Japan's ability to sell automobiles in America; the cost of U.S. defense procurement is profoundly affected by the economies of scale the arms manufacturers can achieve by selling their wares to foreigners. Films, recordings, television programs, the rootstock of contemporary American culture, are produced with a weather eye on projected foreign sales. Everybody knows about OPEC and the gas pump.

On a purely practical, daily, individual basis there is a constantly spreading collection of chores for diplomatic representatives to do. At the American embassy in Rome, for example, a staff of thirteen people processes "federal benefits" for almost 100,000 recipients in Italy, and correlates computer printout with the local social insurance agency to adjust payments to people who have qualified in both countries. The Rome consulate also needs Russian-speaking staff from the Justice Department, which controls immigration to the United States, to work with the Jewish emigrants from the Soviet Union who don't want to go to Israel and whose first prolonged stop is in and (especially) around Rome. Meanwhile, in Israel itself the U.S. consul general in Jerusalem is the only possible official link between the large community of Palestinians in the United States— 26,000 of them from the city of Ramallah alone—and their families at home.

Tourism and the consular chores associated with it spread like a stain across the globe. In Italy, again, in one recent year, Rome alone (one of eight consular offices in the country) had to deal with 155 American deaths, 3,000 cases of Americans robbed, 7,500 notary public certifications, and 5,000 miscellaneous "requests," ranging from Americans in jail or the hospital to calls from home as to someone's whereabouts. American narcotics agents help other countries sniff out local drug traffic (there was a staff of seven such, by Danish government request, at the U.S. embassy in Copenhagen). The Mexican consul general in Laredo, Texas, has a doctor on staff with diplomatic accreditation who does nothing but treat the arrested wetbacks held in camps pending deportation.

Trade and investment across national borders do not just happen. Tariff and customs treaties permit the necessary establishment of long-term relations between suppliers and purchasers. Tax treaties encourage or discourage investment by foreigners and the employment of foreign nationals. American inspectors work in Australia under the supervision of the U.S. agricultural attaché in the embassy to give USDA approval to Australian meat for export; Japanese pharmacologists inspect American fruit on American soil to certify the absence of pesticide residues. Patent and copyright protection by international agreement form a foundation for "transfer of technology."

The grandiose growth of the nation-state in this century has transferred much that was once private contract to diplomatic relations. "Westinghouse is building a nuclear plant for Yugoslavia," said Lucy Benson, Carter's Under Secretary of State for Everything Else, previously head of the League of Women Voters. "There were delays, I had to go to Pittsburgh, tell them they had to shape up."

"Before," said Arno Halusa, who was for years Austrian ambassador to the United States, "governments did not interfere with so many things in their own country."

Increasingly, nations as well as enterprises need established rules of the road. The United States is signatory to more than eight thousand treaties, and the State Department staffs delegations to more than eight hundred international conferences every year. Radio frequencies can be allocated only by international agreement; air travel requires flights over airspace and access to airports; the depletion of fishing grounds can be halted only if the big fishing nations agree; heavy industry in Germany and the United States drops acid rain on the lakes of Sweden and Canada; Antarctic wastes and the bottom of the sea can no longer simply be "claimed" by one sovereignty or another but must be allocated or reserved by international agreement; as the era of dollar hegemony wanes, international trade increasingly requires international institutions to enforce a monetary regime; epidemic diseases of humans, animals and plants cannot be satisfactorily attacked by purely national authority; eventually it will probably be necessary to establish worldwide rules for immense projects that could change the climate of the globe, like the Russian and Canadian schemes to divert north-flowing rivers from their Arctic mouths to irrigation or power use, and the Brazilian and Congolese drive to cut down the equatorial rain forests. Looming over all is the worldwide arms race, a cause of needless impoverishment and death, from which no nation can opt out alone.

"Interdependence," in short, is not just a slogan or something they teach in school. It is a condition of life for many people and all governments. This said, what next? Clearly, there are disputes between nations that are of great significance to the parties but cannot and should not interest most others. "Mr. Mayer," said Ebia Olewali, Foreign Minister of Papua New Guinea, a dark-skinned, smiling, round-faced man of about forty, formerly a high school teacher, sitting cross-legged in a leather skirt on a swivel chair behind a desk in an air-conditioned office tower on the edge of Port Moresby on the edge of a jungle. "Mr. Mayer, I have a terrible problem with which perhaps you can help me."

"I doubt it, but I can try. What is the problem?"

"Zionism."

"Why is that a problem for you?"

"I don't know what it is."

"Why should you know what it is?"

"Because we wish to be good citizens of the international organizations, and in all of them we are always being called on to vote on Zionism. . . ."

For the Papuans, the suppression of East Timor by the Indonesians is a horror story that haunts the dreams of the leaders of the state; what happens in Jerusalem or Chad or El Salvador is essentially meaningless. But East Timor, like Poland or Cyprus or Nicaragua, is at most a name on a map to the leaders of Sudan, who must worry every day about Eritrean refugees from Ethiopia and Bugandan refugees from Uganda, about Libyan control of Chad and starvation in the Sahel, about what the International Monetary Fund insists they must do with their budget. The government of Jamaica has a stake in Cuban–U.S. relations and the course of Central American revolutions, in the production of bauxite in Australia and coffee in Uganda; but the violation of Danish waters by East German warships, the invasion of Cambodia by Vietnam, the comparative taste for Indian as against Pakistani government in the Vale of Kashmir—real concern for such subjects is something to which Jamaica can only pretend.

David Stottlemyer at the International Organizations Bureau at the State Department remembered a New York meeting of the International Civil Aviation Organization that got hung up on a new scale of assessments: "I was talking to the Yemeni delegate, told him how important it was to get this right. He said, 'Mr. Stottlemyer, I can't get excited over this. We don't have any airplanes. Now, if you want to talk to me about *donkeys . . .'"

Maybe no man is an island, as Donne insisted, and each man's death diminishes me; as a practical matter it boots not, for the bell that tolls for him and thus for me will sound whatever I do. Anyone can find connections to one's own condition in any event or situation, like the exiled zoologists of Warsaw in the nineteenth century who were reputed to write papers on "The Elephant and the Polish Question," or the Israelis of the nightclub skits who ask whether hydroponic agriculture is good for the Jews.

Most countries have neighbors and a limited range of economic interests that must be dealt with here and now. Other than that, "interdependence" is a matter of a vague feeling that the national prosperity or even continued national existence requires some international "system" in which this state participates. Some days the feeling is strong, some days it is weak; the progress and stability of Taiwan (not to mention Switzerland) indicate that participation in the system is not necessary, while the history of Afghanistan and Cambodia and Uganda demonstrates that participation in the system is not sufficient. Still, the fact is that only one nation (Sukarno's Indonesia) has ever voluntarily left the United Nations. (Indonesia retained membership in the World Health Organization; an unkind observer noted that the wife of the Foreign Minister was a member of the WHO board, which gave her free trips to Geneva.) And every island wriggling out from under the heel of the imperial oppressor feels a need to send a chief of mission (at other people's expense: the UN pays) to speak in the "plenary" of the General Assembly and to supervise the celebration of the island's National Day in the delegates' lounge with its lovely view up the East River.

In the United States, the notion of "interdependence" comes as an overlay on a long tradition of proselytizing. Much of the nineteenth-century outreach from the United States was by missionaries. The American Board of Commissioners for Foreign Missions was founded in 1810, and by the end of the decade Americans were involved with foreign parts through their churches far more than through their government. In China, Dr. Peter Parker, founder of the Ophthalmological Hospital in Canton and of the Medical Missionary Society in China, negotiated the Wanghia Treaty that established diplomatic relations of a sort between the Celestial Throne and the White House in the 1840s, and later served as secretary of legation and eventually as commissioner to China. Having married a relative of Daniel Webster (who was Secretary of State at the time of the marriage), Parker also had considerable influence on whatever the then minuscule State Department thought about China.

In Africa and especially in Asia—in India, Burma, Korea, Japan and Turkey as well as China—American missionaries represented American life and thought much more pervasively than diplomats and consuls. The spread of American commercial interests made the presence of missionaries more important for American philanthropists: "Commerce is going everywhere," its president Samuel Capen told the Board for Foreign Missions in 1910, "and commerce without Christ is a curse. It means firearms and the slave trade and rum."

The American government itself could not do good in the world in the nineteenth century, because it was considered unconstitutional for the government to spend tax money on charity for either citizens or foreigners. During the Great Famine in Ireland in 1847, measures were introduced in Congress to appropriate funds to feed the starving in Ireland, and President James K. Polk, while announcing that he had personally contributed fifty dollars to an Irish relief fund, said he would veto any such bill on constitutional grounds. Not until after World War I, when Congress appropriated $4 million to help Herbert Hoover feed the hungry in the Soviet Union, was largesse from the taxpayers made available as a possible diplomatic tool—and then, considering the fact that the United States had no official relations with the Bolshevik government (in which Lenin had cast a vote "in favor of the acceptance of potatoes and arms from the bandits of Anglo-French imperialism," establishing a tradition that still survives), the foreign policy objectives were by no means clear.

As Secretary of State for Herbert Hoover, Henry Stimson regretted the prevalence of the opinion that "the world would overnight become good and clean and peaceful everywhere if only America would lead the way." But in the aftermath of World War II, when the United States with perhaps 6 percent of the world's population accounted for something like half its economic product, it came to seem natural for America to take an interest in the damnedest things all over the globe. Not a sparrow falls in Malawi but people in the State Department (and the Defense Department, the CIA, AID, ICA, the international affairs section of Treasury,

11

the National Security Council, the U.S. Trade Representative, the Foreign Agricultural Service, the Foreign Commercial Service) are supposed to know about it, with one copy of the memorandum marked for ACTION. India's control of Sikkim, the dispute between Argentina and Chile over the Beagle Straits, the attitudes of Baluchi and Kurdish tribes toward the nations in which they live, Morocco's war to hold the Western Sahara, the age-old hostility of Hutus and Tutsis, Greeks and Turks, Somalis and Ethiopians, Serbs, Croats, Albanians and Montenegrins, Hungarians and Romanians, Japanese and Koreans, Hausas and Yorubas and Ibos, Malays and Chinese—over such matters people work nights and Saturdays and fill pieces of paper and computer memory cores, *saecula saeculorum*, producing "a bloated mass of studies in every country and every problem," former UN Ambassador Charles Yost complained, which "only clogs the policy-making process, consumes interminable hours of the experts' time, and is almost always ignored."

Harlan Cleveland from inside the State Department wrote in 1966 that "we are not permitted for more than a few days at a time to ignore the raw conflicts among the new states of Africa, where the Somalis and the Ethiopians argue over an arid but precious piece of no man's land, the Algerians and Moroccans dispute a wedge of oil sand in the Sahara, and the Congo is periodically attacked by teen-age gangs led and equipped by other African nations." One's first reaction is that this was pretty good for 1966, truly prescient—but a little thought leads to the question of whether these situations would have been any different in 1983 if the United States *had* ignored them in 1966. Further thought may even raise the question of exactly who does not *permit* the government of the United States to tell these indefatigable disputants in distant Africa that their problems are their own concern, and we do not care to have anything to do with them.

It should be noted that 'twas not always so. Whatever the missionaries might think, American politicians until the second half of this century found a ready audience for arguments that the United States should steer clear of "foreign entanglements." When President Tyler urged the establishment of an official mission to China, Senator Thomas Hart Benton saw "no necessity for a treaty with China. . . . All things are going on well between us and the Chinese. Our relations are purely commercial, conducted on the simplest principles of trade, and unconnected with political views." China, Benton argued, "can have no designs upon us, or views in relation to us, and we have no need of a minister to watch and observe her conduct." The purpose of sending an official delegate to China, Benton said, was to give someone who enjoyed travel a chance to go to Asia "at the expense of the United States, and to write a book." But even those who wrote books did not inevitably stress their foreign adventures: Ronald

Reagan's hero Calvin Coolidge after leaving the presidency wrote an auto-biography "without devoting a single syllable to diplomatic matters."

Even American diplomats tended to lack a deep interest in the affairs that concerned foreigners—let alone any feeling that the United States had been born to set them right. "The United States stayed aloof from the international controversies of the 1890s," historians John Grenville and George Young write (alas!, I fear, censoriously). ". . . American dip-lomats in Europe avoided discussing in their reports home practically every major question of international diplomacy; ostrich-like they avoided even an intellectual entanglement with the Old World. Their dispatches were instead confined to reporting the progress made in negotiations of specific American interests, which were largely economic. At a time when the Anglo-French conflict in Siam posed the threat of war, the American minister devoted his dispatches to the prospects of increasing the export of American pork. The American ambassador in Berlin sent home a long dis-patch on the subject of the German prohibition of the importation of American beef cattle on May 9, 1896; he ignored the Kaiser's Kruger Telegram [a gaffe indicating German support for the Boers of South Africa, to the fury of Great Britain]. . . . In the early 1890s, Valparaiso and Honolulu figured more in American diplomacy than Berlin and Vienna. Santo Domingo was more important to the State Department than the whole continent of Africa. . . ."

As recently as 1961, according to Dean Rusk, both Britain and Spain came to the State Department for support in their dispute over Gibraltar, and "we told them to go away. They've had diplomacy since before we were born."

Now everything is important, everywhere and always. At the beginning of each winter, the regional bureaus of the State Department (with the advice and consent of the functional bureaus and the other departments of government) write up one-page letters of guidance to every American ambassador abroad. These are not very affectionately known as Goals and Objectives Review Memoranda, or GORMs, and they "task" the missions in every country on the globe. GORMs are of course classified if highly predictable documents, but every so often somebody becomes sick enough of the bureaucratic infighting that produces them to afford a visitor a glimpse.

At the height of the Carter administration's concern over human rights, for example, the GORM for the U.S. ambassador to Austria gave improve-ment of the treatment of that country's Slovene minority as the prime American goal. Vienna is home to the International Atomic Energy Agency, and it is a listening post for developments in OPEC (which has its headquarters there) as well as the entanglements of East-West trade (many multinationals with operations inside the Soviet bloc run them from Viennese offices) It is the site of the MBFR (Mutually Balanced Force Reductions) negotiations with the Soviet Union. It is the entropôt to the West for Jews permitted to leave the Soviet Union, whose debriefing is of considerable interest to students of Soviet society. And Austria is an agricultural nation with Common Market affiliations important to American agricultural exporters.

Everything considered, emphasis on the condition of the Slovenes might seem quirky. Seen from inside the machinery of American diplomacy, however (which is necessarily the viewpoint of the people who draw up the document), this memorandum served several purposes. It was an appreciated gift to H (for "Hill": the Bureau of Congressional Relations); as the Austrian embassy in Washington noted, "There are these two congressmen from Chicago." And at no cost with a little benefit, because American relations with Austria are placid and we enjoyed giving the needle to Socialist Chancellor Bruno Kreisky every once in a while, the blow for Slovenes was a sop to the strong feelings of HA (the Bureau of Human Rights and Humanitarian Affairs), which had to be restrained from making too many noises in countries where we swallow our distaste for domestic policies because we have real Goals and Objectives to be wheedled or dealed.

At the beginning of every summer, IO (the Bureau of International Organization Affairs) circulates through an enormous latticework of other bureaus and outside departments its analysis of the agenda for the fall meeting of the United Nations General Assembly and its laundry list of outcomes the United States would like to achieve when the delegates get down to voting. This list is a somewhat easier problem for its authors than the GORM, because there are no constraints on length, and because the same document will in the end be sent (by cable, of course) to every ambassador. With the cable goes an instruction to the ambassador (not a request) that he meet with the highest available level in the host government, usually the Foreign Minister, to go over these matters and get the right instructions sent to that government's representative at the UN. "I have to press them," an American ambassador to a major European country said disconsolately, "on how they are going to vote in the Second Committee on the motion to restructure the Committee of the Whole." Wesley Kriebel of the IO Bureau in Washington noted with irritation that "a surprising number of posts don't report back on their results."

There is a case to be made that these gestures are sometimes more important than the ambassadors realize. "In the 1960 Geneva Conference [on Law of the Sea]," Richard Gardner told the Murphy Commission on the Organization of the Government for the Conduct of Foreign Policy, "the United States lost by one vote in its efforts to achieve a six-mile territorial sea with an additional six-mile fishing limit. The day after the voting took place, the representatives of several developing countries indicated that they would have voted with the United States, had their instructions arrived in time. It was subsequently learned that the U.S. ambassadors in those countries had not considered the law of the sea as a subject important enough to take up on a priority basis at a high level of the host government."

Most of the time, however, these repeated calls on Foreign Ministries for help at the UN have created confusion rather than policy for the U.S. Government. And their effect is to stimulate still further the belief in a false, *political* interdependence. In this artificial "world order," nations relate to each other through refractions in the prism of American (and to a lesser degree, Soviet) attitudes. "Look," said S. Rajaratnam, then Foreign Minister of Singapore, a former journalist, a little world-weary, very savvy. "All I want to know is—if we vote this way, what are the consequences? If we vote that way, what are the consequences? This is how I make my policy. The rights and wrongs of the matter will make interesting reading, but not to decide my policy."

The consequences that most concern Rajaratnam, however, lack relation not only to the rights and wrongs of an issue but to the issue itself. The role of the Southwest African People's Organization in the government of Namibia is, after all, entirely irrelevant to any national interest of Singapore. Admission to the UN, writes Gideon Rafael, Israel's ambassador there, meant that Israel's "representatives would have to express Israel's views and cast its vote on issues ranging from the Kashmir dispute to South African apartheid, from diplomatic sanctions against Franco Spain to the determination of the future of the former Italian colony Libya." Rafael feels that having refused to vote for the British-Italian resolution that would have placed Libya under trusteeship for ten years (and the resolution failed by only one vote), Israel was entitled to less hostility later from Qaddafi & Co. But to the extent that any Libyan Government would have an institutional memory, one of the things that would stick most firmly in its craw would have to be the recollection of the day when a vote by Israel determined its national destiny. Why should the future of the Vale of Kashmir be influenced by the views of Israel or Bolivia or Gabon? Or, indeed, the United States or the Soviet Union?

In the modern system of international relations, then, a spurious "national interest" is forced by the United Nations in parts of the globe to which such an interest cannot remotely reach, and a highly abstract, political-science approach to the world's disputes is encouraged everywhere. The question of what any nation's *real* interests are in any given situation may not even be asked, for fear it will be answered, and the asserted or sought "world order" will simply evaporate, like Klingsor's garden. The leaders of East Africa stand shoulder to shoulder with the Arabs whose fathers enslaved their fathers and whose policies in OPEC are impoverishing their children.

The diplomat tends to define problems in the frame of reference of his culture, a culture that soon becomes that of the diplomatic community in which he lives. Charles Bohlen, describing Ambassador Joseph Grew's crusade to get Washington to let up on Japan in the years before Pearl Harbor, wrote that "the diplomat, being abroad and out from under the influence of American public opinion, tends always to look at problems as though they existed in a vacuum." But from the point of view of those in the field, the Washington home office is equally insulated from reality. The American legation in Abidjan, Ivory Coast, was extensively briefed on the Carter-Sadat-Begin negotiations at Camp David by a series of cables from Washington, because that fell into the box labeled "diplomacy"—but had to learn from the host country what position the United States was taking in the cocoa price stabilization talks. At home or abroad, the diplomat risks imprisonment in the box labeled "political relations."

"I call them the goldfish," said Eugene Douglas, a rotund, oratorical businessman (formerly in charge of the international division of Memorex), referring to the Foreign Service Officers he found in place when he took a job on the Policy Planning Staff of the State Department. "They know no life outside this building."

3

As more and more countries have joined the game, the arranged common ground of diplomacy has been lifted higher and higher into space, and the isolation of the diplomat from the rest of the population has become more extreme. He visits the village and smokes a hubble-bubble with the sheikh, but in fact he remains in his glass-walled carriage, projecting a deracinated expertise, a "generalist's" vanity, onto the world around him. Diplomats live essentially in compounds even when the housing situation at their post permits the embassy to send them out into the market to find their own accommodations. The diplomatic community as a whole is a compound. "The Chinese treated everyone equally badly," one of the Americans who opened the U.S. mission in Peking remembered from the Mao Zedong days. "Except maybe the North Koreans and the Romanians. The Russians were glad to see us—we traded rumors with them."

A diplomat will often be a newcomer to a place, but a familiar to some significant residents. "If I were to be posted to Cairo," said Barbara Angus, minister in the New Zealand embassy in Washington, "the first thing I would do would be to call their embassy here and ask to see the Cairo diplomatic list. Oh, yes—I knew so-and-so from Australia. And *there's* a familiar name from the U.S. You go in and say, 'What is this place *really* like?' "

Such contacts are of great importance on the job as well as off—and the more difficult the situation, the more comforting the contact. "They had never known each other before," Charles W. Thayer wrote, describing the work of the ambassadors during the crisis in Beirut just before the American military intervention in 1958, "but they had all shared similar experiences, worked on similar problems, and lived at similar posts. They had many friends and acquaintances in common and, as in every other profession, they not only spoke in the same terms but assigned the same meanings and values to them. . . . Finally, each had tucked away in his archives dossiers of his colleagues, prepared over the years by his fellow diplomats at posts where his colleagues had served. These contained a fairly full description of each of them: his major talents and weaknesses, his likes and dislikes, prejudices and hobbies, and above all estimates of his reliability."

The sense of uniqueness and isolation is worst, oddly, in the centers of international activity, where the international organizations have become excrescences on normal local life. When popular petition put on the ballot in Geneva a law to prohibit any expansion of that city's international agencies, the initiative carried the city over the massed opposition of the political parties (including the Communists), and only the votes of the farmers in the rural sections of the canton, concerned about possible loss of markets for milk and vegetables, prevented its adoption. One of the oddities of life in New York has been the invisibility of the United Nations community, whose members are occasional spectators but almost never participants in the life of what is the intellectual and cultural (far more than political) capital of the world. It is all very remote: the minions of and missions to the UN have (with some bitterness) adjusted to the fact that no newspaper, not even the New York *Times*, now finds their activities worth reporting on anything like a daily basis. What has driven the UNESCO effort to bring the world's news agencies under government control (in a "New World Information Order") has been less a resentment of reportorial unkindness to the Third World than a fury at the inability of the press to take the international organizations and their diplomatic attendants as seriously as they take themselves.

Starting with the police beating of the American vice-consul in Shanghai in 1949 ("he returned to the consulate," historian Robert Blum writes, "emotionally shattered, with 'soreness of all muscles and joints, twenty bruises, contusions, abrasions and some evidence of internal bleeding'"), and with the attack on the British embassy in Peking in 1950—both orchestrated by the modern genius of symbolism, Mao Zedong—the terrorist international has increasingly imposed its high-order abstractions and secret isolations on those of diplomacy. The job is less safe than it used to be, and thus considerably less pleasant.

And the work has become more difficult and time-consuming, especially for the junior staff, and especially in the parliamentary democracies, where the realities of economic interdependence have forced diplomats to become far more conversant than they ever were before with the operations of the local political machinery and administrative bureaucracy. Much of this working the halls of Congress or Parliament is for the purpose of selling one's country, its policies or its exports; but even more is for the purpose of surprise-reduction at home. All the democracies wish to know how the other democracies are likely to react to economic or political developments. But this absorption in the analysis of what the host country's politicians are thinking has a dark side when seen from the perspective of the politicians and the public back home, for it tends to worsen the conditions the State Department calls "clientitis" and "localitis."

Diplomats are necessarily more impressed with the concerns of their hosts than anyone can possibly be back home. Their sense of self-worth is enhanced or diminished according to the attention their home governments are willing to pay to those concerns. They invariably exaggerate the importance of the country to which they have been sent. "I never understood what an important world power Australia is," said a young Foreign Service Officer in the classic statement of localitis, "until I was assigned to New Zealand." Yitzak ben-Ari, Israeli ambassador to Copenhagen, said that "at this moment I really believe Denmark is the most important country—because I am here."

More significantly, diplomats become advocates for their hosts. "One of our functions," said Woodward Romine, political counselor at the U.S. embassy in Austria, a dapper, older man at work in a blue blazer with silver buttons, "is to say to Washington, 'Maybe these people have got a point here.'" Kingman Brewster, Carter's ambassador to Britain, a rumpled academic at the Court of St. James's, said that "the embassy performs an important task in informing visitors. I make congressmen understanding of and sympathetic to the British political process, spend a hell of a lot of time on that. But if you can send leaders of Congress back with a greater sense of what cannot be expected of the British, it's a great contribution." (One wonders what Brewster thought to be the function of the British embassy in Washington, which has people on Capitol Hill all day every day all year.) Perhaps the most spectacular demonstration of client-itis was Andrew Young's resignation statement as U.S. ambassador to the United Nations: "I have," he said, "sought to represent the less developed countries of the world to the people of the United States."

There is a long tradition of this sort of thing, too, especially affecting American emissaries. James Monroe as ambassador in 1796 went so far as to tell the French that most Americans did not agree with George Washington's policies of neutrality in the Anglo-French wars, that the Republicans would win the elections and that the new government would support the French. (The French, wisely, did not believe him.) Erasmus Peshine Smith as a legal adviser to the State Department was assigned to help the Japanese Foreign Ministry with organizational problems in 1871. He "did his best," British resident F. V. Dickins wrote, "to bring his employers into ridicule by going about in a Japanese split jacket and loose trousers with a couple of swords in his girdle and declaring in public that 'not one foreigner in ten in Japan was murdered who ought to have been murdered.'"†

Nobody can read J. K. Galbraith's memoir of his time as ambassador to India without noticing that he had two enemies in mind: the U.S. ambassador to Portugal (who urged support of Portuguese claims to Goa) and the U.S. ambassador to Pakistan (who was fighting for American recognition of Pakistani grievances over Kashmir). Intelligent discussion of American Middle East policy has been made more difficult by a succession of ambassadors to Saudi Arabia who insist on telling not just Washington but the public that the Saudis are forever sacrificing their own national interest because of their deep attachment to the United States.

Thomas F. Bayard as Grover Cleveland's ambassador to Britain spoke so strongly in favor of the British position on tariffs that he was formally censured by vote of the House of Representatives. Walter Hines Page as Woodrow Wilson's ambassador drew the wrath of Finley Peter Dunne's Mr. Dooley: "I am wondhrin' if we can't find some way f'r our ambass-dures to England to entertain th' English people without speakin' in public. . . . It makes me onaise to wake up in th' morning an larn that th' American Ambassdure in ordher to amuse th' annoyial meetin' iv th' Honorable Guild iv Deck Hands had offered to turn over Michigan to th' Canajen governmint because iv th' gratichood he feels toward William Shakespeare."

Occasionally, diplomats react against their hosts, with an anger heightened by their need to believe that what is happening where they are sta-

_____
† This coin has another side. The Japanese historian Chitoshi Yanaga wrote that Smith "was instrumental in bringing about the end of a humiliating period in Japan's foreign relations by initiating a positive, self-assertive policy."

tioned must be vital to the interests of their country. Unfortunately, impassioned negative advocacy is even less useful at home than the positive kind. General Stilwell was right about Chiang Kai-shek, and Spruille Braden had Perón's number, but no aspect of American policy with regard to wartime China or postwar Argentina was improved by their impatient reporting on the incompetence and evil of the local leadership. Bismarck insisted, Lamar Cecil reports, that "the correctly fashioned communiqué should avoid rumors and excessively piquant or critical remarks about another country, its statesmen, or its rulers, for these negative observations might make their way back, with disastrous results, to the capital from which they had emanated." The rule applies even to ex-ambassadors: U.S. relations with India, none too good at best, were ponderably damaged by the report that Daniel P. Moynihan, retired from his service as ambassador to a job at the Harvard Graduate School of Education, had told someone who had inquired in the corridors of that building about his prognosis for India that he was far from sanguine, because "the only thing those people are really good at is fucking."

Suffering under the weight of emotional reporting by his ambassadors in 1962, Kennedy commented that "Winston Churchill once said that the secret of the survival of the British Empire was that they never trusted the judgment of the men on the spot. I never understood that until recently." The traditional way of controlling the situation is to move people around, especially back home for tours of duty. Jefferson as Secretary of State urged Washington to make sure that no American spent more than six consecutive years abroad.

There is a story, which may be true, that Henry Kissinger instituted the GLOP (Global Orientation Program) after a meeting on Mexico in which, he said, he had heard his underlings talk of the interests of every other Latin American country, without anyone speaking of the interests of the United States. GLOP in effect prevents Foreign Service Officers from becoming full-time specialists in any one region of the globe, demanding that all FSOs take periodic tours of duty outside the area of their expertise to remind them that home is where the heart is. The Latin American specialist sent to, say, Burma is said to have been "glopped." He then becomes a spokesman for Burmese interests, *au courant* with the arguments about the impact of U.S. Burma-related decisions on the course of events in Thailand, China, Malaysia, India. . . .

4

The great change is that the work of a foreign service must now be judged in large part by the impact of the ministry—the State Department —on the policies and actions of its own government. The most important diplomacy today occurs within governments rather than between them. That is why the diplomats in the democracies must spend so much time with the legislators, at the trade ministries, agriculture departments, finance ministries, etc. If they wait until the departments of government have hammered out a nation's bargaining position, they have lost all chance of forcing their perspective to the attention of the decision-makers. For by then few perils in professional or personal life will frighten the committee members who initialed the talking papers so profoundly as the fear that they will have to reopen this subject and go through all those meetings, yet again. The diplomat at his post can do his job only by getting his country's position into the discussion before his hosts make their proposals—and among the first lessons he learns is that he cannot rely on the State Department, or the Foreign Ministry of his hosts, to carry the ball for him.

In 1975, the lawyer Adam Yarmolinsky, a former aide to Robert McNamara in the Defense Department and a participant in many think-tank conferences on foreign policy, wrote a paper on interdependence for the Aspen Institute, and concluded that "governmental decisions must be taken in the light of their anticipated consequences abroad as well as at home. . . . The decision-makers themselves must . . . seek out and give proper weight to the foreign policy 'input.'" But there was no one to enforce such a "must." What happened instead, as awareness of interdependence spread through the U.S. Government, was that the domestic departments put themselves in the foreign policy business.

The same year as Yarmolinsky's paper, a White House Commission on the Organization of the Government for the Conduct of Foreign Policy reported that most domestic departments had formed "Offices of International Affairs, some headed by Assistant Secretaries. Most carry on extensive contacts with foreign governments." In 1975, U.S. domestic agencies had 6,600 employees working full-time on international activities; 3,000 of them—a larger cadre than the Foreign Service—were "professionals." Through the postwar years, foreign affairs has become increasingly a handmaiden of domestic policy.

"The Secretary of State," said Dean Rusk, "runs on four engines—relations with the President, Congress, the State Department, and the press—

before he ever talks to foreigners." Indeed, it cuts deeper than that. "Anything affecting Saudi Arabia," Harold Saunders said when Assistant Secretary of State for Near Eastern Affairs (NE), "brings in Commerce, Treasury, Defense"—in consultations that must be carried through before Rusk's great engines make their entry. And Saunders' list was interestingly incomplete. "One phone call to the Department of Energy and I can change your mind about that," an experienced Saudi diplomat said not unkindly to close a discussion he was having with one of the new assistant secretaries who came in with Ronald Reagan.

"Summit" meetings of national leaders are scheduled not only because the individuals like the show and the spotlight (though of course they do: a summit meeting like an airplane hijacking is staged in large part for the publicity), but also because they give the leaders opportunities to impress upon their peers the degree to which resolution of international disagreements must stay on track with domestic political drives. "There is one international distress signal recognized by politicians all over the world," George Ball writes, "and that is the cry of another politician in trouble."

In one recent reckoning, the Department of State was represented in twenty-six nonsecret interagency groups, ranging from the National Security Council and the Committee on Foreign Investments to the Cabinet Committee to Combat Terrorism, the National Gallery of Art and the President's Council on Youth Opportunity. In the negotiations inside such committees, William Barreda of the Treasury Department sourly told a group of Foreign Service trainees, "the State Department represents foreign interests." Lacking a constituency that can vote, the Secretary and the assistant secretaries and their deputies are at a perpetual disadvantage in the meetings, and the diplomatic staffs working abroad are virtually out of the negotiations.

"During the fifties and sixties, when economies grew," said Erik Holm of the Danish Foreign Ministry, "there was a feeling that the future lay with economics, and a number of economists came in. The new generation of ambassadors came from economics." He was perched on the edge of a wondrously delicate eighteenth-century chair in the office of Hennings Gottlieb, an adviser to the Prime Minister on foreign affairs, in the grandeur of the third floor of Charlottenburgs Slott, gilded mirrors in the hallways, padded doors and spacious anterooms and intricately carved moldings on soaring walls that rise to distant, heavily ornamented ceilings. "Now the economic side is politicized. We know it can't run as a well-oiled machine. And now a number of international economic questions are settled by the Prime Minister, not the Foreign Minister. It creates a great deal of unrest among the diplomats."

22

The unrest problem is even greater in Washington, because Washington unlike Copenhagen can often control the outcome of an international meeting. One of the things the Carter administration *knew* it wanted to do on arrival was to control nuclear proliferation. The task of underpinning a policy was given to an Interagency Group chaired by Joseph Nye, Jr., in the State Department. But, political scientist Michael Brenner writes, "other participants—and they were legion—felt no qualms about procrastinating, insisting on organizational prerogatives, and resisting any effort to make the group behave as a policy task force rather than a study group. The President muddied the waters even further by intermittently offering advice or instruction to various parties, including junior staffers in his executive office, without bothering to pass the communications through a central clearinghouse. . . . In a poignant irony that was typical of life at the upper reaches of government, Carter's dramatic overture on nonproliferation was eventually authored by a team of holdovers from the Ford administration assembled by James Schlesinger, then Carter's energy secretary-designate. . . . None of them had been involved in the review laboriously undertaken by the interagency task force. None had seen it. . . ."

No "foreign policy" decision in the Carter or Reagan administration so strongly affected U.S. relations with other governments as the monetary policies pursued by the Federal Reserve System, mostly with Treasury Department approval—excessively easy (exporting inflation) in 1978–79; excessively tight (exporting recession) in 1981–82. Not until July 1982 did an American government admit that foreigners might have some stake in what the Fed was doing, and thus some right to get their opinions heard. Even then, at the Versailles summit, Reagan would agree only to send Treasury Department experts to a "study group": no diplomats need apply. When the "study group" reported critically in spring 1983, it was the Secretary of the Treasury who made the public response that American policy was not going to change.

In what is possibly the most important area of all, the diplomats speak in a feeble voice more likely to be heard by newspaper editorial writers than by the President. In Stewart Alsop's simple formulation, "The Defense Department has a great deal of impact on foreign policy, and State has very little impact on defense policy." Much was made of the matter in the press in 1981 when Secretary of State Haig was unable to deflect Secretary of Defense Weinberger from his announcement that the United States would start manufacturing neutron bombs whether the European powers liked it or not, but all the incident revealed was that the Reagan administration was proceeding along paths well traveled by its predecessors.

For the ambassador abroad and his staff the confusions and frustrations are unending. They are controlled not so much by the new communications technology as by the new concern in the home government that something said or done abroad will affect the course of events at home. They may be expert at horse-trading with the foreigners, but they are out of the bargaining that goes on inside their own government. The result is a severe loss of authority even in areas where nothing particularly complicated is on the table. "Our consuls general in Sydney and Melbourne know all about tourism," said Christopher Squire, deputy chief of mission in the U.S. embassy in Australia. "But when there's a need to negotiate a new civil aviation treaty, what happens? You send over some lunkhead from Washington to take charge."

5

Somehow, responsibility for national decisions that have international implications must be allocated among domestic experts, domestic politicians, home-office diplomats and diplomats *en poste*. This will never be easy. "You need someone," said P. W. Unwin of the British Foreign Office, "to keep the recognition that though the meeting may be about fish, it has a political purpose." Asked about this as a rule, Unwin's boss commented, "You also may have to remind the man that though the purpose of the meeting is political, he was chosen to attend because of his expertise on fish." All bureaucracies resist decisions on which any individual's name can be placed, and the United States suffers from a growing insistence that mistakes may be made only by the President himself, whose resources for getting others to take the blame are unlimited. We have been unable to avoid in America what Sir Edward Youde calls "the cork tendency of decisions to float to the highest possible level."

It seems fair to say that the State Department has less influence in American decision-making than it should, even when the subject matter is foreign relations. The key action in the alienation of Fidel Castro—the decision of the American owners of Cuba's refineries to refuse to process Soviet crude oil—was suggested to the companies by Eisenhower's Treasury Secretary Robert Anderson, who did not consult the Secretary of State. When Jimmy Carter decided to send the helicopters into the Iranian sandstorm to rescue the hostages, he scheduled the National Security Council meeting that would affirm the decision on a day when Secretary of State Vance was to be out of town. Secretary of State Haig was not in the National Security Council meeting at which Ronald Reagan, convinced by the idiot argument that "your credibility is at stake," imposed the self-defeating sanctions against European suppliers of components to the Soviet gas pipeline.

There is an overriding reason to want more influence by diplomats: their business, tautologically, is peace. War, Clausewitz wrote in a famous passage, is the continuation of diplomacy by other means—but from the diplomats' point of view the other means involve their exclusion from governmental process, the loss of their prestige and their inner confidence. History does offer examples of diplomats recommending bellicose action—George Kennan, for example, head of the Policy Planning Staff while Chiang Kai-shek's government was collapsing on the Chinese mainland, recommended an American seizure of Taiwan: "carried through with sufficient resolution, speed, ruthlessness and self-assurance, the way Theodore Roosevelt might have done it . . . [unilateral military action] would be not only successful but would have an electrifying effect in this country and throughout the Far East." But their experience has been that while war is merely hell for the soldiers, it is unemployment and degradation for the diplomats.

The historian Robert Schulzinger wrote of World War I days that "the Secretary of State was powerless to maintain the bureaucratic influence of the Foreign Service and the State Department during the American war effort or the peacemaking. Representatives of the War and Treasury Departments, such special wartime agencies as the War Trade Board, the War Industries Board, and the Shipping Board, and extraordinary presidential envoys handled the bulk of interallied negotiations during 1917 and 1918."

Dean Acheson remembered Pearl Harbor Day at the old State-War-Navy building beside the White House: "On the second floor south little groups stood about the corridor, talking almost in whispers, doing nothing. Mr. Hull was shut up with a few intimates, still, it was reported, in a towering rage. The Japanese ambassador, Admiral Kichisaburo Nomura, and their special ambassador, Saburo Kurusu, had left him only a couple of hours before. Each group added its bit of gossip. Mr. Hull had reportedly castigated the departing envoys in native Tennesseean as 'scoundrels and piss-ants.' War had or had not been declared. Germany would or would not join Japan. The Axis plan was or was not to involve us in the Pacific, leaving the European partners a free hand to finish the European war first; and so on. Our Petroleum Adviser, Max Thornburg, reported having seen terrifying telegraphed photographs of our shattered fleet. When no one seemed to have any use or orders for us, the groups dissolved and we went home.

"Although, happily, we did not know it, that Sunday afternoon's experience was an augury of the Department's coming role in the war years."

25

Ambassador Robert Murphy remembered that when Roosevelt sent him as a presidential representative to Africa (where he provoked one of the truly great domestic flaps of World War II by arranging to turn over captured Algiers to Admiral Darlan rather than to General De Gaulle), the President "said casually, 'If you learn anything in Africa of special interest, send it to me. Don't bother going through State Department channels.'" On the specifics of the African invasion plans, Roosevelt told Murphy, "Don't tell anybody in the State Department about this. That place is a sieve." There was a war on; in wartime, the judicious weighing of interests, the parceling out of bits of information for subtle purposes, carries a whiff of treachery.

Normal process—which means, in the context of international relations, the process of diplomacy—is what protects civilization. Felix Frankfurter liked to say that substantive law was extruded through the interstices of procedure; Dean Acheson, who had been Frankfurter's clerk at the Supreme Court, told Carol Laise that foreign policy was made at the interstices of daily operations. With due exception for dramatic events, that is the way it should be. The formal structure of diplomatic relations, created over centuries, serves as a shell protecting the activities of a mankind now subtly, confusingly, complexly interrelated. The periodical puncturing of that shell by terrorist activities disturbs far beyond its intrinsic importance, because the function the shell serves is indispensable. It is tautologically correct that the peace of the world is in the hands of those who conduct international relations. Historically, the expression of that truth has been in the trappings of diplomatic status. Today, when interdependence has further isolated the diplomatic function, the understanding and maintenance of that status have acquired a value of their own.

"The diplomats of the old school had such tact that they could always find a way out of a difficulty without ruffling anybody's feelings," Dmitri Abrikossow wrote in his old age in California after World War II, remembering his time in the Russian diplomatic service before World War I. "It is easy to write a stiff note, but it is likely to evoke an even stiffer one, to which you then reply in kind, one note leading to another, until the guns start booming. [Count Aleksandr] Benckendorff taught me that there was no situation out of which two gentlemen could not find a way without fighting. The great misfortune today is that there are so few gentlemen left in this world."

2

LIFE AMONG THE NATIVES

> Do you know why everybody wants to be an ambassador? It's because
> when an ambassador walks down the corridor of his embassy, *every-
> body* kisses his ass.
>
> —Philip Habib, while Under Secretary
> of State for Political Affairs

1

Service abroad as the head of a diplomatic mission was (still is) the most
luxurious job known to man. "It is hardly possible," writes John Ensor
Harr, "to exaggerate the status of an Ambassador. . . . In many countries
a high standard of living goes along with the status, and in fact is part of
it. Often it is of a nature—elegant residence, staff of servants, chauffeured
limousine, use of an air attaché's plane, and so on—that a man quite literally would have to be a millionaire to emulate at home." Some $65 billion
in debt to Western banks, Brazil in 1981 thought nothing of paying $4
million at auction for the Tree mansion on New York's Seventy-ninth
Street, to provide a suitable residence for its ambassador to the United Nations.

John Bright in the nineteenth century described the British Foreign
Office as "the outdoor relief department of the aristocracy." Franklin Roosevelt agreed: "You can get to be a Minister," he wrote to his Secretary of
State, "if (a) you are loyal to the Service, (b) you do nothing to offend
people, (c) you are not intoxicated at public functions." Peter Ustinov

27

once threw off the comment that "a diplomat is someone who is too ambitious and too lazy to be anything else."

Though an ambassador is theoretically on duty every moment of every day that he spends in the country to which he has been sent, the part of that duty which constitutes what other people would consider "work" was not (still isn't) either very time-consuming or very burdensome. "American diplomacy," Charles G. Dawes said while ambassador to London for Herbert Hoover, "is easy on the brain but hell on the feet." Dawes was talking about standing, of course, not about walking: ambassadors almost never walk out of doors, except in their gardens. The Ivory Coast has thirty-one embassies abroad, Konan N'da of its Foreign Ministry reported, with 288 employees, thirty-one of whom are chauffeurs.

Apart from the ceremonial tasks—ritual calls on foreign ministers, heads of state and other ambassadors, attendance at local political events and celebrations, parties, ribbon-cuttings, receptions for touring performers from one's own or others' national artistic enterprise—most of what the home government expects from its embassy could (still can) be performed by subordinates.

These subordinates, moreover, are subject to command to a degree unusual even in government, where senior officials quickly fall into a habit of regarding their juniors as essentially personal servants. Addressing an ambassador, his transnational interlocutors will say, "Your Excellency"; his underlings will say, "Mr. Ambassador." The essence of diplomatic relations among nations is that the accredited ambassador (E&P, Extraordinary and Plenipotentiary) represents in his person the chief of state of the nation that sends him. Cordell Hull as Secretary of State refused to travel abroad because his dignity was offended by the fact that at dinners and other ceremonial occasions he was necessarily outranked by the ambassador he had appointed. Henry Kissinger's penchant for informal visits—and his notorious rudeness to U.S. ambassadors in the countries he visited—doubtless grew from similar roots.

Not everybody can handle it: the literature sags with tales of ambassadors (and their wives) who tyrannize subordinates (and their wives). "Diplomatists," Harold Nicolson noted sourly, "especially those who are appointed to, and liable to remain in, smaller posts, are apt to pass by slow gradations from ordinary human vanity to an inordinate sense of their own importance. The whole apparatus of diplomatic life—the ceremonial, the court functions, the large houses, the lackeys and the food—induces an increasing sclerosis of personality." Lawrence Durrell's Mountolive, appointed ambassador to Egypt, "realized that now, as an Ambassador, he must forever renounce the friendship of ordinary human beings in exchange for their *deference*. . . . 'God,' he thought . . . 'I shall become like that dreadful parson in Sussex who always feebly swears in order to prove that he is really quite an ordinary human being despite the dog-collar.' "

The identity of the ambassador with the head of the state that sends him traces back to the beginnings of international discourse. The *nuncius* in medieval Europe was essentially a messenger: "he who takes the place of a letter," a Venetian historian wrote in 1594; "and he is just like a magpie, and an organ, and the voice of the principal sending him, and he recites the words of the principal." The language of that recitation, of course, was Latin, until the seventeenth century, when Don Juan Antonio de Vera, the author of the most widely used and most widely translated treatise on diplomacy, urged ambassadors to speak their native language—partly because "no one can be as eloquent in a stranger's as in his mother's tongue," partly because "it is an honour to a prince that his language should be heard in every land."

On the other side of that coin, the *nuncius* was entitled to the honors that would be paid his principal: Gregory VII demanded that "one see in the legate the pope's own face, and hear in his voice the living voice of the pope." In law, the *nuncius* had no person of his own: he could not sue or be sued; he carried his principal's immunity with him, and any harm done to him was a direct injury to his sovereign. Among the few items of discretion permitted him was the choice of who among his hosts should be bribed, and how heavily.

As private business expanded in the Renaissance, "procurators" for bankers and merchants were sent abroad with considerable discretion to make deals, and sovereigns cautiously began to adopt the same procedures. The procurator could be "plenipotentiary" within the bounds of his mandate, which he carried with him in writing, suitably sealed. Sometimes, of course, he carried two rather different mandates, and would decide which to show after he'd got the lay of the land. A procurator's signature on the treaty bound his sovereign: repudiation or even request for amendment, while it was known to happen, made a scandal.

This persists. Immediately after the Foreign Ministers in conference in Paris in 1947 had signed the treaty that established the terms of the temporary four-power occupation and eventual independence of Austria, Moscow decided the deal was unsatisfactory and ordered Andrei Vishinsky to secure further concessions. Incredibly, the telephone call from Moscow was made *en clair* (i.e., not in code), and the French eavesdropped, courteously inviting U.S. and British representatives to listen along with them. To avoid the unpleasantness of telling Vishinsky to his face that a deal is a deal, U.S. Secretary of State Dean Acheson and British Foreign Minister Ernest Bevin first made themselves scarce and then quietly left town—and the Russians ultimately honored the document their bumbling Foreign Minister had signed.

One of the most extraordinary and internationally troublesome aspects of the U.S. Constitution is that it makes impossible the role of procurator. Even the chief of state (who *is* bound by his representative's signature) cannot enter into binding treaties, but must gain the consent of two thirds of the Senate. As early as 1807, the Senate sent back to England unratified the Treaty of London negotiated for Jefferson. It was, Secretary of State for Foreign Affairs George Canning said, "a practice altogether unusual in the political transactions of States."

Over the years, such rejections have become much less unusual, though still virtually unique to the United States, a source of many and various disasters in American foreign relations, and of unfair leverage, excuses for irresponsibility and sharp practice in the conduct of American negotiators. Senator Frank Church remembered British Ambassador Peter Jay coming to him in 1977 after he had held his troops over the one-third threshold and blocked a tax treaty that would have limited the power of American states to tax foreign corporations. "With whom is one supposed to do business in this country?" Jay inquired. "Don't blame me," said Church, who had known Jay since the ambassador's days as a journalist covering Washington for *The Times* of London. "Blame George III."

When the Italian city-states began to embroil all of Europe in their quarrels, sovereigns began to appoint ambassadors to conferences rather than to countries. Such envoys, empowered to sign the treaties they negotiated, remained embodiments of the head of state who sent them. J. H. Plumb describes the surroundings of the ambassadors to the conference in 1559 that produced the peace of Cateau-Cambrésis: "As their coaches rattled down the long road to Cambrai, dashing horsemen in brilliant liveries led their cavalcades; fanfares of trumpets greeted their entrance to towns, mayor and aldermen turned up to meet them and waited humbly in the drenching rain, expecting nothing but a lofty greeting and a word of praise for the munificent hospitality that they dispensed. It was as if the kings and emperors themselves were passing by.

"At Cambrai, two years were spent in the examination and acceptance of credentials. Most of the time was taken up with the infinitely thorny question as to whether the Holy Roman Emperor could possibly, through his ambassador, address the King of Sardinia as 'Good Brother.' . . . Their excellencies whiled away the weeks and months with gigantic banquets, whose magnificence became a matter of national honor. The English Ambassador's health broke down under the strain and he was forced to request a separate table at his rivals' dinners so that he could keep to his diet. . . ."

Plus ça change. Gideon Rafael describes the Palestine Conciliation Commission of 1949 as having "scored a record of futility which is unsurpassed even in the annals of the United Nations. It failed to convene the delegations to the conference around the same table, and succeeded in uniting the Arab countries on a common denominator of extremism imposed by their most radical participants. For its diplomatic standstill the Commission made up with lively gastronomic activity. It organized a ceaseless round of dinner parties in honour of the various delegations, either individually or collectively. The guests would assiduously return the hospitality. After a short while the scoreboard looked like the tabulation of an international soccer competition: the United States entertaining Jordan, Syria dining France; all three Commissioners hosting Israel—in short it was a culinary merry-go-round. After three months of wining and dining around the Lake of Geneva, without a single meal being taken together by the Arab and Israeli delegates, I felt the time had come to call a halt to this festival which was so high in calories but so low in yields. I invited the members of the Conciliation Commission for a farewell dinner. My toast was short and factual: 'Never have so few consumed so much and done so little.'"

"In the poor countries," said Efraim Haran, director of Common Market relations in the Israeli Foreign Ministry, "being sent abroad is a plum. People like yourself cannot understand what it means. Even for me—when I am sent to Geneva, it is a change in my life-style." Explaining "that the intelligence business uses case officers harshly, burning them out at an early age," the renegade CIA agent John Stockwell notes that "most case officers work under official [State Department] cover, and circulate after hours in the world of cocktail and dinner parties. They become accustomed to a life-style of rich food, alcohol, and little exercise."

International meetings are luxurious beyond the dreams of domestic bureaucrats. The meetings may be boring but one does not, after all, have to attend all of them, and the ancillary activities are a chance to party on other people's money. After the first of the endless series of Law of the Sea conferences, in Venezuela in 1971, syphilis became known in Caracas as "Law of the Sea disease." (It should be noted that this particular meeting has gone into the UN history books as unusually disgraceful.) UNESCO conferences in Paris are the special prize, for Paris has been in this business longer than any other city, and no government expects anything useful to come from UNESCO exercises, anyway.

One source of delay and dispute at multinational meetings, however, has been resolved since Cambrai: order of precedence. As an embodiment of his sovereign, no ambassador could tolerate having one of his colleagues enter a ceremonial space before him, or occupy a more prized position.

Precedence, as Harold Nicolson has pointed out, was the eighteenth-century equivalent of the chimera now known as "national prestige" or "national honor." (Jefferson, incidentally, would have none of this nonsense, and refused to accept any order of precedence at presidential affairs, provoking outrage in a diplomatic corps already sullen from the nastiness of life in the unwholesome swamps of Washington.) Pope Julius II in 1504 had attempted to rank the countries once and for all—Holy Roman Empire first, France second, Spain third, etc., but by the 1700s the Pope no longer had the divisions to enforce such authority.

After unseemly scenes of violence in the streets of Vienna during the Congress that settled the hash of the Napoleonic wars—when coachmen pulled weapons on each other to gain what their masters considered their proper place in line—a deal was struck to make priority of place a personal rather than a national prerogative, the ambassadors to enter and sit according to their seniority in a post. The most senior becomes the spokesman for the diplomatic corps as a whole, in matters where the ambassadors have a protest or an appreciation to express. This can produce ludicrous results. For some years, the doyen of the diplomatic corps in Washington was the representative of Nicaragua's unspeakable Somoza, and in Canberra the man through whom diplomats in cohort had to communicate with the Australian Government was an amiable old Turk who had not in his twenty-odd years in that city managed to learn much English. In 1982, the Vietnamese ambassador became the doyen of the Peking diplomatic corps, through whom all formal relations between the government of China and the diplomats as a group had to be conducted; and he wasn't on speaking terms with either the government of China or any but a handful of the resident ambassadors. But it's better than swordplay in the avenues.

2

Permanent embassies with resident "ambassadors" (the term had died out after its use by Caesar in his account of the Gallic wars) began to appear in the fourteenth century. Garrett Mattingly found the first permanent "diplomatic agent" in the person of Luigi Gonzaga of Mantua at the Imperial Court of Louis the Bavarian, "before 1341." Ambassadors and their retinues were regarded with considerable suspicion as "nests of spies," to use the modern Iranian expression, and of course they were. Venetian law banished and fined any citizen who discussed public affairs with a foreign diplomat. In the English Commonwealth under Cromwell, a Member of Parliament seen speaking with a foreign ambassador would lose his seat. In nineteenth-century Japan, diplomats were shadowed by guards whenever they left their quarters, and among the prohibited activities was the purchase of lists of government officials. Nicolson denounced this "senseless custom" of forbidding contracts with ambassadors, but at the time secrecy must have seemed an entirely sensible precaution (as it still does in the Communist bloc and most of the Third World).

Early ambassadors routinely bribed members of the court to which they were assigned, both for information and for influence. The Venetians paid the Queen of Hungary in the fifteenth century to help maintain that kingdom's hostility to the Turks; Philippe de Commines as Louis XI's ambassador to the court of Edward IV was paymaster to the English nobility, and got receipts for the money. (In World War II, the German embassy supplied young men to the tastes of the homosexual King of Sweden.) Darker deeds were not entirely unknown: Venetian ambassadors put out a contract on prominent leaders of the Florentine republic, and the Spanish ambassador to England connived with persecuted Catholics to procure the murder of Elizabeth I. Meanwhile, Elizabeth's ambassador to Philip II, the poet Sir Thomas Wyatt, paid money to organize the assassination of England's leading exiled dissident, Reginald Pole, just as today's Libyan "people's representatives" earn their keep by plotting the murder of the folks from home.

From the point of view of host governments, there was a great difference between the reception of an ambassador on a specific mission and acceptance of a permanent representative. The first held out prospects of a mutually beneficial deal; the second offered certain nuisance for only speculative gain. Exchange of ambassadors—for of course these things are or soon become reciprocal—was something to be established by treaty, and each such was carefully negotiated. "It is not at all safe," de Commines wrote, "all this coming and going of Ambassadors." Still, over time, the belief grew that the value of learning what other powers were thinking and doing was so great that it warranted a sacrifice of one's own secrecy. And as the mercantile revolution of the seventeenth and eighteenth centuries made peace between nations a condition of domestic prosperity, the sovereigns began to explore what common interests they might have. In the eighteenth century, these relations amalgamated in an endless series of congresses at which the sovereigns were represented by ambassadors.

3

The title of "Ambassador" was not easily given: until 1860, Britain sent out only three such—to Paris, St. Petersburg and Constantinople. France had more; the United States until 1893 had none, preferring the civil title "Minister." Strongly held republican sentiments made Americans happier with a status that enabled an envoy to work with the host government but denied him participation in the rituals surrounding a royal court. Other representatives to foreign courts wore gaudy uniforms; American ministers by executive order wore "the simple dress of an American citizen." In London during the Civil War, Charles Francis Adams, next to Benjamin Franklin the greatest of American Ministers (soon after his departure, the House of Commons greeted the mention of his name with a standing ovation), took it upon himself to wear knee breeches and shoes with silver buckles. On his appearance, Queen Victoria commented, "I am thankful we shall have no more American funerals." As late as the 1910s, however, an American president tried to avoid appointing as ambassadors rich men who would run elaborate establishments. William Howard Taft felt the first job of an ambassador was to care for Americans abroad, and he "preferred men who would recognize an American when they saw him."

The first four U.S. ambassadors went in 1893 to Britain, France, Germany and Italy, and these countries of course simultaneously upgraded the rank of their chief of mission in Washington. Early in the next century, similar courtesies were exchanged with Turkey for reasons that interestingly illustrate one of many continuous threads in American foreign policy—and one of many perpetual sources of international tension and atrocity. The Turks were gradually exterminating their Armenian population, and American churchmen and editorial writers were calling on Washington to put the screws on the Porte for its abominations in the realm of human rights. But the Sultan would not grant audience to a mere minister. To express at the highest level America's horror at Turkish behavior, it was necessary to glorify the post in Constantinople.

Incidentally, the attachment to republican principles survived in two other countries long after it had been squelched in the United States. Until the 1950s, all foreign missions from Finland and Switzerland were headed by ministers rather than by ambassadors. When the State of Israel was founded in 1948, its leaders resolved to follow this model—but the United States automatically appointed an ambassador, so the wish for simplicity was frustrated at birth.

These protocol questions are still with us, especially on slightly lower levels. John Hoog, economics attaché at the American embassy in Singapore, found in the late 1970s that he could negotiate airline carrier rights with his hosts only by informal meetings, because he was merely an attaché: "I had to deal with a girl in the Minister's office; he couldn't deal with me directly if there was a third party present." For some years, the American agricultural attachés, who are employees of the Department of

Agriculture, banged fruitlessly on the doors of the State Department to get counselor status for themselves so they could meet officially with Agriculture Ministers in the more important countries, but the State Department insisted that only its own employees could hold such exalted titles. Finally, the arrival of a former congressional staffer as director of the Foreign Agricultural Service gave the attachés sufficient clout to get the Congress to pass a bill mandating the title of counselor for a dozen of the attachés.

Emerging nations have the most need for strong representation abroad, especially if they are in danger of being caught between the millstones of a great-power rivalry, as the United States was in the first twenty years of its independence. "The greatest of known diplomatic triumphs," Harold Nicolson wrote, "was when Benjamin Franklin arrived in Paris in December 1776, and managed, owing to the mesmeric quality of his simple friendliness and his beaming smile, to induce the bankrupt French Government to advance large sums to the thirteen colonies." (It should be noted, though, that Franklin did not equally please *everybody*: Louis XVI presented a lady of the court known to be a great admirer of the American with a chamber pot engraved on the inside with Franklin's portrait.) "I am interested in the ambassador of a small state," Albert Einstein said to Abba Eban, explaining his presence at the Israeli's lecture in Princeton. "Powerful states need no ambassadors. Their force speaks for themselves. For small states, it matters how they express themselves. What you are doing matters."

Of the first ten Presidents, three (Jefferson, Monroe and John Quincy Adams) had been both Ministers abroad and Secretaries of State; two (Madison and Van Buren) had been Secretaries of State; and one (John Adams) had represented the Revolutionary Congress in the Netherlands. (Franklin was not much impressed with Adams as a diplomat: "I am persuaded," he wrote when Adams turned up during the peace negotiations, ". . . that he means well for his country, is always an honest man, often a wise one, but sometimes, and in some things, absolutely out of his senses.") John Marshall, who invented the Supreme Court, was (ineffectively) American Minister to France and Secretary of State before becoming Chief Justice.

In the years since, only one President (James Buchanan, who did both) has either served abroad in a diplomatic post or been Secretary of State, though Taft worked overseas as the American proconsul in the Philippines (and a very good one); Hoover rose to prominence as the organizer of food relief for starving Europe after World War I; and Eisenhower, of course, ran a multinational military alliance from a base abroad. Buchanan's sense of his obligation to what might be considered American principles, incidentally, can be measured by his negotiation of a consular treaty with Czarist Russia, providing in part that U.S. Jews visiting Russia were to be treated as Jews rather than as American citizens. Organized Jewish political activity in the United States traces back to the fifty years of agitation, ultimately successful, to persuade Washington to renounce this treaty.

As embodiments of their monarch, European ambassadors were normally people in whom the King placed special trust—at first, flunkies (down to and including the King's barber); then companions in varying degrees (Ferdinand of Ferdinand and Isabella was represented in London for eighteen years by a converted Jew who had risen in the service of Aragon); finally, aristocrats. To this day, monarchical countries tend to be represented by people with connections to the nobility. This made it somewhat easier for the King on the other side to extend the often extraordinary courtesies ambassadors received (the protocol *maven* for Louis XIV noted that an "Ambassador Extraordinary" could wear his hat in the presence of the King)—and harder for the emissaries to bear the barbaric customs of oriental potentates like the Emperor of China and the Sultan of Turkey, who required foreign devils to kowtow (touch their heads to the floor) before addressing the throne. Similar indignities still occur in the Third World: Sékou Touré of Guinea likes to stage processions in which he rides in the state limousine while the corps of ambassadors walks behind in the equatorial sun. China and Turkey before the nineteenth century sent no ambassadors of their own: their potentates could see why others would seek to have relations with them, but not why they should care about anyone outside their realm. The symbols used for the word "diplomacy" in Chinese meant "barbarian control."

Even the American ambassadors, when they arrived on the scene, tended to be people of considerable station in the political world of Washington, which was where they won their appointments. In the 1920s, Ellis Briggs remembered, an American ambassador was "a pretty important fellow. The doorman at the Metropolitan Club knew his name. His credit was good at The Willard, and strolling back to the old State War Navy Building [now the Executive Office Building] through the unguarded White House grounds, Chief Usher Ike Hoover . . . not only recognized the Ambassador but usually remembered the name of the country he served in. . . . There were only thirteen American Ambassadors in the world when I entered the Foreign Service in 1925. . . ."

There were real reasons for aristocratic predominance in ambassadorial ranks. The aristocracy was the first international class: they knew each other, and that always helps, as much today as in earlier times. "I was seven years in New York at the UN," said Massimo Castaldo in the Italian

Foreign Ministry. "I got to know Gromyko very well. When I was as-signed to Moscow I found it much easier to get into offices because I knew these people—we called each other by our first names." Philip Kaiser re-called as a source of strength when he was deputy chief of mission for the United States in London the fact that he had been student body president at Balliol—"succeeded by Ted Heath, who was succeeded by Denis Hea-ley, who was succeeded by Roy Jenkins. I had known all these people a long time." On the day-to-day level, more casual matters can help. Asked how one got to know the leaders of an exotic society like Papua New Guinea, Russell Olson, political officer at the U.S. embassy, observed that "everybody of any importance in this government is a golfer."

Even more important, the aristocrat was or seemed to be a *personage* back home. What a sovereign receiving an ambassador wanted, after all, was assurance that the voice of the representative assigned to his court would be heard by the man who had sent him. Gondislavus de Villadiego noted in the Venetian Senate that "for important negotiations orators of excellent social standing should be sent, for the Holy Scriptures them-selves give an example in the Annunciation, not by a mere angel, but by an archangel." Lord George-Brown remembered that when he was nego-tiating with Egypt for revival of diplomatic relations between that country and Britain in 1967, Nasser wrote, "I don't want any striped-pants face-less diplomat transferred from some South American banana republic."

These desires, too, survive the transition to democracy. Though newspa-per editorial writers, opposition politicians and Foreign Service Officers in both sending and receiving countries are forever denouncing the appoint-ment of "political" ambassadors, the recipient governments are rarely dis-pleased if the politician in question looks important enough. Bronx County Democratic boss Ed Flynn got into trouble over the use of city-owned paving blocks in his private driveway, and Franklin Roosevelt ap-pointed him ambassador to Australia. The fuss kicked up in the press forced the withdrawal of the nomination, but there is no reason to believe the Australian Government objected. "The thing I want most in an ambas-sador," Australian Prime Minister Robert Menzies later told Harry Tru-man, "is that when he picks up the phone, you'll take the call." There was ample precedent for Roosevelt's appointment: Lincoln sent Secretary of War Simon Cameron off to St. Petersburg during the Civil War when the bloodhounds seemed to be closing in on corrupt practices in the Union Army.

Everyone at the United Nations was delighted in 1965 when Lyndon Johnson made Arthur Goldberg U.S. ambassador to the UN: even the Arab delegates felt that Goldberg's importance in the Washington scene, which he modestly conceded, would be a benefit greater than any cost imposed on them by dealing with a Jew. (Goldberg then demonstrated that the enthusiasts were right, using his influence in the White House to procure withdrawal of the long-standing American insistence that the Soviet Union and its friends pay their share of the costs of the UN Expeditionary Force in the Congo, which had threatened to bankrupt the institution.) Thinking back on his time as Roosevelt's wartime ambassador to the Soviet Union, Averell Harriman mused that "I am accustomed to taking responsibility when an unexpected situation comes up—a different position from a career officer."

This does not always work, of course. "The worst thing that can happen to you," said an FSO in the European Bureau, "is to work for a political appointee who doesn't really have connections." History is replete with egregiously unsuitable political appointees, from John Randolph (who presented his credentials to the Czar and said, "Howaya, Emperor? And how's the madam?") to the minister to Germany whose ceremonial presentation to the Kaiser had to be postponed because he was too drunk to stand, to General Daniel Sickles, a Civil War hero who enlivened his tour in Spain by conducting a public affair in Paris with the exiled nymphomaniac Queen, to . . . but let us spare the living.

The appointment of nonprofessionals inevitably leaves the country at the mercy of inexperience. Henry Wriston reported that "in 1914, Britain, France and the United States were represented in eleven world centers, the eleventh in each instance being the home country. In the ten nations where Britain was represented abroad its chiefs of mission had an average of 33 years of professional experience; the French chiefs of mission in the ten capitals had over 34; the American ambassadors and ministers had an average of a little less than one year of service in the field of diplomacy."

Like "President," "Senator," "Governor," "Judge" and (traditionally) "Colonel," "Ambassador" is a title people like to keep after their term in office has ended. Even today, when all matters of importance in foreign representation are supposedly kept under tight control by Washington, the move from the controlling post of Assistant Secretary of State to the controlled post abroad is generally considered a promotion by those who become ambassadors. Roy Atherton transferred happily from Assistant Secretary in charge of the Near East Bureau, direct boss of the embassy in Cairo, to the job of ambassador to Egypt; his friend and colleague Samuel Lewis was equally pleased to move from Assistant Secretary for International Organizations (though, strangely, he liked that awful job) to the embassy in Israel. When administrations changed in 1981, both men added to their ritual resignation a request for reappointment, and both were kept in post. Though the job required him to take instructions from Thomas Enders, his successor as ambassador to the European Communities now appointed Assistant Secretary for Inter-American Affairs (and a man he particularly disliked), Deane Hinton willingly left an Assistant Secretary post to become ambassador in war-torn El Salvador.

There are exceptions: someone sent from even a deputy assistant's job in Washington to Ouagadougou—capital of Upper Volta, the universal symbol of pitiable exile for everyone in the State Department—may feel himself invited to resign. (Distaste for Ouagadougou, incidentally, is not universal in all foreign services: Alexandre Guyomard of the French consulate general in New York remembered a happy week's inspection tour there: "It reminds you of home: the main street is called the Champs Élysées, the park is called the Bois de Boulogne . . .") But you never know when a post abroad may become important. Writing a book about the British Foreign Service, Geoffrey Moorhouse took Mogadishu in Somalia as his illustration of the back of beyond—and then the war in the Ogaden overheated the already broiling Horn of Africa. The United States began negotiating with the Communist Somalis for the use of a base the Russians had built and evacuated, and Mogadishu soon turned out to be a place from which dispatches were read by the highest authorities.

An embassy is extraterritorial, legally a piece of soil subject to the laws of its home country rather than those of the host country, and the local police may enter it only on invitation. The lives of many Latin American politicians, of both the left and the right persuasion, have been saved by the fact that a nation may grant asylum in its embassy as freely as within its borders. Cardinal Mindszenty lived for fifteen years in what had been and is again the U.S. ambassador's suite of offices in Budapest, overlooking one of the city's main squares. The flag on the pole is that of the ambassador's country, not that of the host. Acts that would be punishable outside the walls may be routinely practiced within: during the religious persecutions of the sixteenth century, the Dutch ambassadors held Calvinist services every Sunday in a France which denied the practice of Protestant religion to the Huguenots, and the Spanish ambassador to London flaunted his Catholic services in an England where saying mass was a capital crime.

Not only ambassadors but all accredited members of their staffs and their families have "diplomatic immunity" against prosecution for violations of the laws of the host country.* The problem these days arises

* Mattingly argues that in the fifteenth century, when notions of a single Roman-cum-canon law bound all of Christendom, ambassadors could be tried in the host country, though only in the court of the King himself, for "crimes of fraud and violence" or even "a whole list of political crimes, espionage, conspiracy, treason and the like." The later full immunity, Mattingly insists, was "a cynical rule . . . that a crime committed in the interests of one's country and in obedience to higher authority is not a crime at all." But he cites only two examples. In one, the envoy had betrayed his own master;

39

mostly in the great legal triangle of parking, traffic violations and automobile accidents. If you're hit by a duly licensed embassy vehicle driven by a member of the embassy staff you are out of luck: there's nobody you can sue. In general, stores in Washington and New York will not accept checks from diplomats, and displaying the State Department's ID card issued to all accredited personnel makes the merchant even less likely to oblige: if the check bounces, he is stuck, and he knows it.

This observer in 1980 took the cultural counselor of the Soviet embassy in Washington to lunch at the Cosmos Club. The Russian picked up an embassy car from the (legal) parking rank across Sixteenth Street, drove the few blocks to the club, and without troubling to look for a parking space pulled into the bus stop on Florida Avenue. When we emerged ninety minutes later there was a ticket on the windshield. The cultural counselor did not trouble to look at it; he tore it up and (out of a fastidious desire not to litter) stuffed the pieces in his overcoat. Incidentally, this story provides corroboration for the Soviet claim that Russian embassies run independently, with slight administrative direction from Moscow. In London, the Russians pay their parking fines: a 1981 British study of scofflaws found 3,542 unpaid parking tickets issued the previous year to cars from the Nigerian mission, 1,865 to cars from the French embassy, 1,867 to Saudi Arabian vehicles and 1,488 to Bulgarians. Americans failed to pay 187 tickets, but the Russians had an absolutely clean slate.

More serious crimes are equally beyond the reach of local law. In 1978, the U.S. *chargé d'affaires* in Equatorial Guinea murdered his staff assistant in the embassy vault (broadcasting the proceedings live via satellite to the State Department in Washington); the Equatorial Guineans turned him over to the U.S. Government for prosecution, which his lawyer long postponed by arguing about where in the United States he could fairly be tried. Early in 1981, the son of the Ghanaian ambassador to the United Nations raped a young matron in a Manhattan park, and was released by the police upon identification, in the clearly inadequate custody of his father. Similarly, the son of the Brazilian ambassador to the United States seriously assaulted a Floridian, who found that the U.S. criminal justice system wouldn't punish and the U.S. civil justice system wouldn't let him sue. The CBS news show *60 Minutes* found the offender quite unpunished in Brazil, too, taking his ease on the terrace of a luxury apartment at Ipanema.

The sticking point for those who tried to take the Iranian side of the hostage epsiode of 1979–81 was that in international law (and, incidentally, Koranic law) it didn't matter what the prisoners had done: they

---

and in the other, Wolsey released the accused ambassador from the Tower and sent him home with full honors when Charles V complained.

could by treaty be punished for it only by the government in whose service they had been sent. A recurring episode in international relations is the diplomat who is caught red-handed (these days, filmed or videotaped) in the act of paying money to secure secret information about the host country's defenses. The recipient of the money is thereupon put on trial; the payor is simply "PNG'ed"—declared "persona non grata"—and shipped home.

Until recently, dominant states asserted their control over client states by securing such immunities for their nationals resident in the lesser nations, whether or not they were diplomats. Such "capitulations," as they used to be called, might be justified in situations where the local ideas of law, legal process and punishment were (or are) a risk to which no nation would wish to subject its citizens. Even the rampant Turks, ravaging eastern Europe and the eastern Mediterranean in the sixteenth century, had seen that Venetian businessmen might have some worries about Turkish justice, and had permitted the Italian colony at Constantinople to set up its own court, at which the Venetian *bailo* was judge and where Italian rather than Turkish law was enforced. When Francis I of France negotiated a treaty with the Sultan in 1536, he secured the protection of French law and a French court for any and all of his subjects on Turkish lands.

Japan early on accepted the legitimacy of the Western demand to be free of its barons' *danyo* justice, sent legal experts to Britain to study how a criminal justice system ought to work, designed its first comprehensive criminal code, and by 1899 had put its own procedures in shape to meet European and even American objections and had won a new treaty with Britain (the others reluctantly followed) ending all exemptions for foreign nationals other than diplomats. China was unable to accept the implied cultural criticism or control the activities of its local *fonctionnaires*, and Western power kept foreign devils exempt from Chinese law (indeed, subjected Chinese who entered the "foreign settlements" to Western law) until Mao's revolution proclaimed that it would rather do without foreigners entirely. The incident that first put Ayatollah Ruhollah Khomeini into rebellion against the Shah was the passage by the *majlis* of a law which, in effect, extended diplomatic immunity to American military advisers and their households. Such a law, he said, would allow "any American servant or cook to terrorize pious religious leaders." But until Khomeini sought his revenge, it was understood that such privileges for diplomats were legitimate, if only because they were reciprocal.

Though they and their colleagues remain exempt from local criminal law, diplomats representing countries that send any number of tourists abroad do become fairly expert in local criminal codes and procedures because part of every embassy's job is advice to nationals who fall afoul of

41

the police. Movies like *Midnight Express* and horror stories from Mexican jails have testified to the relatively slight influence an embassy can wield in these matters (and to the guileless certainty of American youth that drug crimes, so indulgently regarded back home, are not really crimes at all). The attitude of diplomatic personnel called to a jail to visit a compatriot may leave the prisoner highly dissatisfied, partly because diplomats are drawn mostly from a rather square segment of the home society, partly because the embassy has no funds to pay lawyers to get people freed or to repatriate those whose release can be arranged. It is only the rare Lee Harvey Oswald whose passage home will be financed by the U.S. Government. When these arrangements are made, the money is provided as a loan, with interest; one of the grounds on which an American citizen may legally be refused a passport is, reasonably enough, failure to repay a prior repatriation loan. This happens.

Embassies can import goods, foodstuffs and booze without paying duty, and in countries where value-added tax is excused on exports an embassy can arrange to have the tax eliminated for its diplomatic personnel. In Germany—a considerable perk—diplomatic personnel buy gasoline for their private cars free of tax, which cuts the price about 50 percent; everywhere, those on the diplomatic list can bring their cars with them without paying duty.

The diplomatic courier's "pouch" (American; the British is "bag" and the French, "valise") may not be opened by customs authorities or local police, a privilege which has been fairly frequently abused. Perhaps the worst case in recent times was the North Korean use of the pouch to smuggle heroin to Sweden. The Swedes passed this problem to the Russians, who arrested and it is believed liquidated some North Korean diplomatic personnel changing planes in Moscow. (In general, diplomats and embassies from Eastern-bloc countries do not enjoy in the Soviet Union the privileges and immunities the Russians grudgingly accord to others. "The Russians treat Western diplomats like dogs," an East European ambassador to Japan admitted, thinking back on his own time in Moscow. "They treat *us* like shit.")

But if person and property are guaranteed against invasion, a price is paid in the almost total deprivation of privacy. Every host country spies on all significant embassies, and sometimes third countries find an embassy a useful source of information. The Israeli secret service (by common consent, the world's best) has on several occasions updated its information about United States policy by searching through communications files in American embassies in other countries. The Germans, in one of the most famous of all espionage episodes, planted a valet in the residence of the British ambassador to Turkey during World War II.

In the United States, the National Security Agency routinely monitors all radio communications between embassies in Washington and their home countries, and sweats to keep the code-breaking machinery up close to the state of the art of encoding. The Russians tend to be a little less subtle. In the office of the Deputy Assistant Secretary for Security in the State Department hangs a large and handsome wooden eagle presented to the ambassador's office in the U.S. embassy in Moscow in 1945 "in appreciation of American assistance" during the war; in 1952 it was discovered to be hollow and bugged. During the 1970s, the intensity of Soviet microwave bombardment of the U.S. embassy in Moscow was protested by the American government as a health hazard to its employees. Everyone serving in a diplomatic post abroad must expect that every telephone call is overheard, and that all elements of his private life and that of his staff are fully known in the Foreign Ministry to which he is accredited.

4

Housing, food and personal service are the great perks of being an ambassador. The chauffeured limousine is at his disposal, however poor his homeland, around the clock. (Indeed, the limousine is most needed between the hours of five and nine, when the ambassador will usually be expected to put in an appearance at several cocktail parties and at least one dinner.) The residence, normally some miles from the chancery in the case of the larger countries, is not merely the place where the ambassador puts his head on his pillow; it is the focus of the embassy's entertainment program.

Because the entire diplomatic colony of the place must be invited for major occasions (the National Day, arrivals and departures of ambassadors, visits by grand chams from home or a state-sponsored ballet, orchestra, drama company), the reception rooms must be large enough to hold considerably more than a hundred people. In the case of former colonies, the newly independent states allowed foreign governments to buy as ambassadors' residences the great mansions of evicted magnates. Sometimes the properties have an unsavory past: the U.S. residence in Copenhagen was Gestapo HQ during the war. In Washington, the embassies have been allowed to buy multi-acre properties in the fashionable outer reaches of Northwest as the entertainment needs of the ambassadors have outgrown the city's turn-of-the-century downtown mansions (and the downtown neighborhoods have decayed). Some residences include "private" gardens among the most magnificent in the world: the walled garden of Villa Taverna, the residence of the U.S. ambassador in Rome, is a park near the heart of the city, with splendid topiary work. Gardens come with gardeners. Staff and yardmen are usually supplied by the local secret police, though paid by the embassy.

Entertainment is paid for out of a "representation allowance," which may or may not be sufficient for the purpose. In the British Foreign Service, this allowance comes in two varieties: for the embassy—which approves its expenditure by counselors, first secretaries, etc., according to demonstrated need—and personal, as an extra emolument for the job. At the time of the so-called "think tank" report on the Foreign Service to Prime Minister Harold Wilson in the late 1970s, a counselor had a personal allowance of about $500 a year—which remained part of his perks when he was assigned home and put to work in the stately rabbit warren of Whitehall. The argument was that London was full of important foreign visitors whom a diplomat had known on post or would serve with in foreign parts at some later day, and should be encouraged to entertain. In most European foreign services, the representation allowances are quite large—a Swedish or Danish ambassador in Washington, London, Paris or Rome, for example, may have $100,000 a year to spend on entertaining. A French Foreign Service Officer is paid *en poste* about double his salary at home, and is expected to use about two fifths of the bonus for "representation."

The total representation allowance in the State Department budget for 1982 was about $3 million, which averages to $25,000 per post. No U.S. embassy has an allowance greater than $100,000, and from that sum must also be paid, for example, the expenses of the Fourth of July party to which all Americans in the area are welcomed. The expenditure of such funds, moreover, is controlled by law, sometimes down to the fine details: a 1980 act requires that representation appropriations "shall, to the maximum extent practicable, provide for the use of American products, including American wine." All the money goes to the ambassador and the Public Affairs Officer: in the absence of prior authorization by the ambassador, FSOs have to entertain out of their own pocket. An oddity of work on a book about diplomacy is that a visitor (a compatriot, after all, in a strange land) is virtually never asked whether he might be free for lunch or dinner or a drink. Denied access to his employer's deep pocket, the FSO is forever scared of being stuck with the check.

It's not quite so bad as it looks, because the cost of help to cook and pour and serve and clean comes out of another pocket in the budget. Warren Manshel reports that as U.S. ambassador to Copenhagen for Carter he came close to meeting his entertainment costs on the allocation though he was host to five hundred breakfast, lunch or dinner gatherings each year. But only truly frugal souls can carry the burden of an American ambassador's social responsibilities in most major capitals without dipping into their own pockets, which is one of the reasons posts in the more important cities go to businessmen and political contributors.

Sometimes the rich are not as welcome as they would like. Nixon's ambassador to London Walter Annenberg, for example, publisher of, among other things, the racing sheet *The Morning Telegraph* and the weekly *TV Guide*, didn't get invited to the nondiplomatic London parties he wanted to attend. He took care of that by donating a swimming pool to the Prime Minister's *dacha*, Chequers, to the great pleasure of Edward Heath, who loved to swim, and whose staff had taken the initiative in suggesting that the ambassador offer this *pourboire*. Thereafter the Tory lords and ladies included Annenberg on their lists. Those who snubbed the ambassador in London in 1969 suffered for it a little in 1981, when his wife, having donated $150,000 to defray the costs of refurbishing the White House, briefly became Chief of Protocol for Ronald Reagan and his State Department. In this capacity, she curtsied prettily to Prince Charles on his prenuptial visit to the United States, driving the Irish-American community straight up the wall.

Yet Annenberg in London could argue that he was only doing his job. "When Shirley Temple Black became ambassador to Ghana," Kojo Debrah said reminiscently, "she came to me, I was secretary of the Cabinet. She said, 'I brought my old films. May I show them? Would people like that?' I said, 'Of course.' The previous U.S. ambassador to Ghana had been a Catholic named Mahoney. He had ten children, he taught choir. Every Sunday at the Catholic church, he led the choir. Dealing with people is the first requirement of diplomacy. The problem of diplomacy today is lack of trust. As we lose our humanness, we lose our ability to communicate."

5

In May 1961, President Kennedy firmly proclaimed the U.S. ambassador to each nation as the boss of what was rather unfortunately called "the country team." "In regard to your personal authority and responsibility," he wrote, "I shall count on you to oversee and coordinate all the activities of the United States Government in _____. You are in charge of the entire United States Diplomatic Mission, and I shall expect you to supervise all its operations. The Mission includes not only the personnel of the Department of State and the Foreign Service, but also the representatives of all other United States agencies which have programs or activities in _____. . . . If in your judgment individual members of the Mission are not functioning effectively, you should take whatever action you feel may be required. . . . In case the departure from _____ of any individual member of the Mission is indicated in your judgment, I shall expect you to make the decision and see that it is carried into effect. . . ."

Though such powers seemed to be implied in the ambassador's status as the embodiment of the chief of state abroad, in fact only one previous ambassador had been given such universal authority—John Muccio, the American proconsul in South Korea in the late 1940s, who even had responsibility for the Military Assistance Group that tried (unsuccessfully) to prepare the South Koreans to defend themselves. Such special representatives of American power Kennedy's letter exempted: his ambassadors were not to command "United States military forces operating in the field." These of course were not part of a diplomatic mission; they came under a contract with the local armed services rather than by an agreement with the sovereign. But all those who were "accredited" to and by the host government—including the military attachés—were to be an ambassador's fiefdom.

The managerial responsibilities implied by this letter are enormous. Two dozen different departments of government and federal agencies send personnel abroad to the American embassies. Congress in its wisdom has made IDCA ("development") and USIA ("communications") independent of State Department direction, and has established separate foreign services for Agriculture, Commerce and Treasury. Health, Energy, Transportation, Education, Labor, Justice, even Housing and Interior have permanent representatives abroad, as do the CAB, FCC, FDA, EPA, NASA, IRS, Maritime Administration, Narcotics Bureau, NSF and others. All these people are to be found in the ambassador's "chancery," the official offices. The embassy in Brussels housed someone sent by the Bonneville Power Authority; "I could never," said Assistant Secretary for Administration Thomas Tracy, "figure out what he was doing there."

Ambassadors do not always *know* the full range of U.S. Government activities, even innocent activities, going on under their noses. Charles Frankel reported finding "tucked away, in a small corner of one of our embassies, an office of the National Science Foundation, administering a grant program which probably equalled or exceeded, in terms of the numbers of people involved, the regular exchange program with that country. Yet the existence of this office was hardly known to the rest of the embassy, and the statistical information regarding exchanges ignored its activities." Certainly, the ambassadors often don't want what they regard as superfluous people. Ellis Briggs when ambassador to Brazil replied to the news that a science attaché was being added to his staff with a despairing cable that his mission needed such a person "like a cigar-store Indian needs a brassiere"; he was informed that the program was dear to some important hearts in the White House, which was not amused. It is by no means clear, of course, that Briggs was right and the White House wrong.

CIA and Defense have foreign establishments that in several countries dwarf the Foreign Service component of the mission. (Moreover, contrary to all policy decisions, the two are sometimes mixed: CIA has got amiable Defense underlings to okay Defense attaché posts as covers for agents, sometimes against the express instructions of the Joint Chiefs.) Many embassies have "legal attachés" who are actually FBI agents. All such employees have career paths that have nothing to do with the ambassador: three quarters of the personnel in the U.S. missions do not work for the State Department.

Soon after the Kennedy letter was sent, John Franklin Campbell writes, " 'clarifying' messages, most of them classified, went out on the letterheads of the separate agencies addressed to *their* field representatives, listing 'exceptions' and revoking much of the purpose of the White House directive. In Washington, more by behavior than by words, the White House, Defense, CIA, Treasury and all the others soon made clear that they were not about to let a weakened State Department 'take charge.' The President had spoken, but he had neglected to give State the power and the practical means to carry out his mandate."

In the years immediately after the Kennedy directive, the departments could fairly easily run around State. In addition to their separate, independent budgets for their people abroad, they maintained their own communications facilities (or, in the case of Treasury, used U.S. Navy frequencies: the reports of the Treasury attachés were considered too secret to be run through the leaky pipes at State). Following what was a congressional enactment of Kennedy's letter in 1974, the Ford administration dropped the other shoe, requiring that all overseas communications (except certain intelligence reports on the so-called "Roger Channel" and Defense Department messages in the chain of command) move over State Department wires, passing the ambassador's desk en route to the cable room.

This is unquestionably important. "If you know and clear what everyone is saying to Washington," Galbraith writes, "you are in full control. Sometimes in exercise of authority, one is not sure where it is a matter of dignity, where a matter of discipline. But in control of communications, the requirements of the two happily coincide." There remains the telephone, especially when an attaché is trying to get something his ambassador (and the State Department) might oppose. "Even if the ambassador can control the people abroad," observed William Sherman, deputy chief of mission in Tokyo, "he has no control over the people at home." But

47

since the State Department cable net was made the sole approved highway for messages from the embassies to the U.S. Government, ambassadors who care have at least been able to get a much firmer grip on what the outriders of the embassy are doing.

But they remain outriders. In the parlance of bureaucracy, they are "attached" to the State Department and the embassy, not "seconded." They remain on the payroll of their home agencies, and owe a first loyalty there. "I serve two bosses," said Nicholas Thuroczy, agricultural attaché in Vienna: "the ambassador and the Department of Agriculture. Sometimes you have to be a diplomat." "We have to cajole them," said Robert Morris, a stout, pipe-smoking, fortyish economics counselor at the U.S. embassy in London, referring to the people from eight agencies over whom he was supposed to exercise the ambassador's delegated authority. "Show them the relevance of what we want them to do for the interests of their home agency." When David Bruce opened the Peking mission for Nixon, he insisted on a staff 100 percent State Department—no Defense attachés, no USIA people, no CIA—to make sure he could control it.

Elsewhere the situation may be even worse. "Historically," said an Australian who would not wish his name on the quote, "there has always been a suspicion of Foreign Affairs horning in on other people's business. Meat inspection is an excellent example. But our argument is that we have to know because there may be political implications in these technical questions. Some years ago as part of an inquiry we suggested a mega-department to coordinate. We didn't say it should be us, but everyone accused us of empire-building. In theory the ambassador sees the communications, but in fact when you have a problem of overlapping jurisdictions and ministerial jealousies the home department calls up the fellow in, say, Tokyo and gives him instructions of which there is no record. In times past, these things were carried to absurd lengths—a Ministry would not want an ambassador to know that its minister was coming to his country, so it wouldn't tell the Foreign Minister in Canberra about it." David Evans in the Australian Foreign Ministry's information office echoed the complaint: "Bureaucratically," he sighed, "one is always fighting to know what's going on."

The common practice in most countries *is* to "second" the attaché from his home department to the Foreign Ministry, which during his time abroad pays his salary and evaluates his performance. The other Ministries have no permanent "international" division, so the individual in the embassy has no turf to protect. Personally, moreover, he knows that he will return to purely domestic concerns when his tour is over, and he wants to do so. "In the Japanese bureaucracy," said Koreshige Anami of the Japanese embassy in Canberra, "if you are assigned out of your Ministry more than once it seems to mean they don't want you very much." In the Japanese system, moreover, the seconded attaché never reports to his home Ministry at all. Someone senior from the substantive Ministry is seconded to the Foreign Ministry in Tokyo, to hold temporarily a major administrative post (a division chief from the Finance Ministry, for example, headed a Second International Division in Economic Affairs at the Foreign Ministry), and the attaché abroad reports to him.

The status and job satisfaction of the various American attachés vary vastly according to their department, the nature of their work, and the posts to which they are sent. Treasury people are at only a handful of the most important commercial centers—London, Paris, Rome, Bonn, Brussels, Riyadh, Tokyo, Brasília. Their contacts are Finance Ministers, bankers, dealers in the foreign exchange markets. They serve long tours (upward of twenty years, for one man in Paris), they have no "action" responsibilities, their reports are read at home, they are well paid, they live in a world where something happens every day, they are considered important by those in the host country with whom they spend time, and they are a highly cheerful cadre. Almost as cheerful are the agricultural attachés, highly educated (about half of them have Ph.D.s), well plugged in at the local agriculture ministries and with local food processors, popular with the marketing cooperatives back home whom they help in selling efforts, proud of their part in the reporting network which is by far the world's most accepted source of information about crops, stocks and prospects.

At the other end of the cheerfulness scale are the commercial attachés, charged with selling American firms (not always convinced that export markets matter) on the idea that they should spend good money to promote American manufactures in countries where they will compete with local products to the discomfort of local producers. Commercial attachés tend to be young, without experience in business, shunned by whatever established American business colony may exist, forever disappointed by the going agley of the best-laid plans, socially isolated both in the embassy and in the host community. Somewhere in between are the labor attachés, officially members of the Foreign Service, often chosen by the Labor Department in a mostly acrimonious relationship with State, and subject to approval by the AFL-CIO, which maintains an international division.†

† This division, incidentally, was headed for two decades after World War II by Jay Lovestone, who in the later 1920s had been chairman of the U.S. Communist Party—until he was perceived to be on the wrong side of the fight between Stalin and Bukharin and was removed by orders from Moscow in 1929. (Except for a brief period after 1956, when the U.S. Communist leadership was appalled by the apparent truth of Khrushchev's speech about Stalin and attempted to assert its own authority, the U.S. Communist Party has always been closely controlled from Moscow. Theodore Draper

Because they have been conduits for CIA money, the labor attachés are often well acquainted with the local political as well as trade union scene and may or may not be considered assets in the embassy's political analysis work. But they are socially several cuts below their colleagues in the embassy, and they feel it. "Historically, the labor attaché had a horrible time fitting into our embassies," said Ed Woltman in Copenhagen, a small man with slicked-back hair and a neat mustache, wearing a gray checked suit. "A labor attaché has a peculiar clientele, which is not always understood." An FSO with academic training in labor matters, Woltman became committed to labor work while serving the special team operating to get elections held and U.S. Marines out of the Dominican Republic in 1965. "Our labor attaché, Harry Schlagerman, was the only man we had who could go into the city. . . ." George Anderson in Austria, an Iowa farm boy who became a labor attaché, says the attraction is that "in the labor field the Foreign Service leaves you alone to do your own work—and you make the most contacts with the public."

The State Department contingent at the embassy divides into four "cones"—political, economics, consular and administrative. The political officers—for good reasons, as we shall see—are the princely family, most likely to receive the eventual succession to ambassador's status. They are the people most likely to make the calls on the local Foreign Ministry and to be invited to diplomatic parties which the ambassador might but can't attend; in the parliamentary democracies they are the ones who know the host country politicians whose names are in the local (and sometimes the American) newspapers.

Since 1960 or so, the State Department has made major efforts to upgrade the economics "cone," and has required ambitious political officers to take courses in economics and serve tours in economics attaché posts as part of their career training. In general, economics attachés feel they know things their political colleagues don't, and they have been encouraged to believe that promotion policies now favor them. But their standing with the ambassadors, who are usually economic illiterates (this includes the businessmen, of course), tends to be less satisfying professionally unless they are in the international organizations (OECD, Common Market, en-

---

tells a story of John Pepper, U.S. delegate to the Comintern though he was always more at home in his native German, complaining to an interviewer about the downfall of his mentor Zinoviev at the Seventh Plenum in 1926: "Joe! Joe! *Eben habe entdeckt, dass ich sieben Jahre lang den falschen Arsch geküsst habe!*" [I've just learned that for seven long years I've been kissing the wrong ass!]) The experience left Lovestone firmly distrustful of the Russians, and only too happy to line up the AFL-CIO with the CIA, which had virtually free access to labor attaché posts as covers.

ergy, food, Geneva) where their expertise or asserted expertise seems crucial.

Until 1924, the consular service was separate from the Foreign Service, and part of the political spoils system. Consuls for a long time kept the fees locals had to pay for visas and commercial documents. ("Consul, *n.*," Ambrose Bierce wrote in *The Devil's Dictionary*. "In American politics, a person who having failed to secure an office from the people is given one by the Administration on condition that he leave the country.") Consulates were also the closest the U.S. Government got to the subvention of writers before the formation of the national endowments. Nathaniel Hawthorne lived three productive but not income-producing years in Italy on the proceeds of his four-year term as consul in Liverpool; Washington Irving learned about the Alhambra while consul in Spain. James Weldon Johnson, arguably the greatest of black American writers and later head of the NAACP, was consul in Nicaragua until Woodrow Wilson, always a Southerner at heart, became President. Consuls are much engaged with Americans abroad, an essential function. "Can you imagine," said Diego Asencio, Assistant Secretary for Consular Affairs, "that you've got an American in jail and you don't have anybody to send to hear his story?"

The Rogers Act of 1924 unified the Foreign Service, giving the political officers more money and the consular officers more status—in theory. Most entrants to the Foreign Service must now expect to take at least one tour on consular duty as part of their apprentice years. But in the capital cities a junior consul is a dogsbody stuck with routine chores most of the time, and his social status can be extremely low: he may not be invited to any parties at all except embassy get-togethers, and his contact with his opposite numbers in the other embassies is slight. Most smaller countries simply employ natives with no diplomatic status for consular jobs. A mid-career appointment as a consul general is very rarely—though we shall later have need to note an example to the contrary—a step on a path to ambassador. Young FSOs, said George Springsteen, director of the Foreign Service Institute, the State Department's in-house training program, "consider consular work a hurdle they have to get over to proceed on their careers."

This observer was in the State Department communications center a while ago, studying how people decided to route incoming cables around the government, when the screen came alive with the word URGENT. Feeling myself participant in history, I peered over the shoulder of the operator, and learned that the visa machine in Hamburg had broken down, that the cost of repair was $375, that the post could not commit more than $250 for *anything* without approval from Washington, and that a go-ahead was needed instanter. (Seven copies of this message were made and distributed, two of them to Archives.) I mentioned this apparent abuse of the URGENT classification to Warren Spurr, deputy chief of communications, a large man in shirtsleeves who kept good music playing in the background of his office to soothe his outrage at outraged visitors. Spurr made a *moue* at my innocence. "Of course it was urgent," he said; "the poor fellow's elbow was breaking"—he made a sidearm pumping gesture—"from stamping all those passports by hand."

Outside the capitals, however, the consul becomes the political officer on the scene as well as the notary public; he is on all counts a more important personage. Two consulates—in West Berlin and Jerusalem—are essentially political posts; the consul general in Jerusalem functions as the ambassador to the West Bank Palestinians, though neither the United States nor the Israeli Government would say that. He sets up shop (in two offices, one on each side of what used to be the dividing line through the city) as though he were representing Caterpillar Tractor, not requesting from the Israelis the traditional *exequatur* which would make his marryings and notarizings legal; he is in effect the heir to highly informal arrangements set up under the Turkish Empire as a service to religious pilgrims before World War I. The cable traffic to and from both Israel and Jordan comes over his desk, and his own cables stand a chance of being read on the highest levels.

At times, even rather obscure consular posts can become propellants to a career, given luck and skill. One Farsi-speaking young consul in Tabriz, for example, put himself on the fast track at the State Department with a report on the likely results within Iran after the Shah ceased his support of the Kurdish rising against Iraq. Another consul in the same post, a ham radio hobbyist, noted strange sounds on his speaker, deduced that they were the telemetry from the Soviet missile tests in Central Asia, and started in motion the chain of events which emplaced huge American electronic ears on the Iranian and Turkish (and later Chinese) borders with the Soviet Union.

What the consular cone offers is a degree of entrepreneurial challenge: a consulate is what a man makes it. Some young FSOs, John Ensor Harr reports, "speak of getting their 'own post' much as naval officers speak of getting their 'own ship.'" The alternative, after all, is not necessarily attractive: "I'd rather be number one here," said Charles Brown, American consul just across the border in Nuevo Laredo, Mexico, "than number-two economics reporting officer in Stockholm." As a kind of chief of mission, moreover, a consul general may have a representation allowance.

The "administrative" cone is ubiquitous, with more Foreign Service Officers slotted here than are allocated to the consulates. It is an interesting experiment in the assignment to what are essentially business-managerial jobs of highly selected people from liberal arts backgrounds with neither experience nor training in business. They do better than one might expect. Managing property and local personnel in foreign parts does, after all, require diplomatic skills and certainly employs language capabilities, and the bookkeeping has been centralized at regional offices in Paris and Thailand.

Inevitably, administrative officers live their working lives almost exclusively within the embassy community (which is not very restrictive in places like Tokyo, where the embassy has seven hundred employees). There is no reason for them to be invited to diplomatic parties. To ask whether they are happy raises echoes of Auden's poem to the bureaucratically controlled citizen: ". . . Don't be absurd/If anything had been wrong, we certainly would have heard." Every so often, though, one does hear: "It's like being a doorman in Las Vegas," said William Dyess, who served a tour as administrative officer in Moscow en route to Assistant Secretary for Public Affairs for Carter, and ambassador to the Netherlands for Reagan. "All the action is upstairs."

A great deal depends on the personality of the ambassador, on the post itself, and on the match between the individual and the place. There are people who love being in Moscow, for one of two reasons—because they are crazy about Russian language and culture, or because the walls around the diplomatic colony in that city are so strong that you make good friends among your fellow inmates in other embassies. For the others, Russia is quite properly a "hardship post," as it always has been. "This is a damned poor uninteresting place," William W. Rockhill wrote of St. Petersburg while U.S. ambassador there in 1909. "There is not a man in the diplomatic corps here who likes it, so far as I can learn. Don't you ever take it if it is offered to you."

Most embassies in the Third World are also "hardship posts," though some probably shouldn't be. "We like to say about Abidjan," said the desk officer in the State Department who handled relations with the Ivory Coast, "that it's a lovely city and very convenient to Africa." Hardship posts entitle the FSO to a pay bonus, 25 percent in some cases, 15 percent in others, offer additional home leave—and create a bias toward giving this fellow a break on his next assignment. "Buggins's turn," the British Foreign Office calls it: "Buggins's turn has come," its personnel director said thoughtfully. "If that's ignored too grossly, it hurts the organization."

Housing is crucial. Part of the problem of the Third World missions at the UN, one of the senior deputies there said, is that the home country acquires a luxurious residence for the ambassador and lets everyone else live in a slum. Most State Department employees abroad live in government-owned housing—about $3 *billion* worth of it. In London, where Parliament meets late at night and the political attachés are supposed to be hanging around the lobbies, the U.S. Government owns Mayfair and Belgravia flats for their use. In many countries—Germany, the Netherlands, Egypt, most of the Third World—the United States and the host government have agreed that it would be bad public relations for large American staffs to compete with locals for scarce housing, and apartment houses for the exclusive use of American diplomatic personnel have been built. (Soviet and Chinese missions, of course, live in "compounds.") Where the United States doesn't own, the administrative people in the embassy will probably do the renting for the staff; there is only a handful of cities where the arriving FSO is simply handed his housing allowance and told to fend for himself. Ideally, when a U.S. embassy rents it seeks a scattering of apartments around town, to encourage the diplomatic staff to mingle with the populace.

At bottom, the status of the less-than-ambassador diplomat abroad is that of "foreigner." As the New Zealand Overseas Staff Committee Report of 1966 put it, "The setting of overseas life, with its opportunities 'for travel,' for moving amongst interesting people and for what appears to be an interesting round of social activity disguises what is an unusually exacting way of life. The public servant overseas . . . has no settled background. He can expect to spend between half and two-thirds of his life away from New Zealand. He takes root nowhere. Friendships have to endure without the stimulus of frequent meeting. He and his family are left with little opportunity to enjoy the sympathy and help of their parents and close friends or to extend it to them when this is needed. He is obliged to make constant physical and psychological adjustment, adjustment to new climactic condition, to new types of food, to different hours of work and activity, to a new language, to different cultural and social conditions. The frequent moves coupled with the continuing need to adjust to foreign environments place unusual strain on his marriage. He will have less control over the education of his children. . . ."

John Le Carré's novel *A Small Town in Germany* is built around the disappearance of an employee of the British embassy in Bonn. London sends an intelligence officer to explore the situation, and one of his first contacts at the embassy says, "So far as I know, he has no close friends in the community. Few of us have. We have acquaintances, but few friends. That is the way of Embassies. With such an intensive social life, one learns to value privacy."

The great changes in life abroad are in transportation and communications—and entertainment. Obviously, home is less far away in the age of the jet than it used to be, and returning home on leave is considerably simpler. Reductions in international telephone rates have been a blessing, but the greatest blessing of all in recent years has been the advent of the videotape player, which allows the FSO in far places to see whatever it is (movies, football games, TV serials) that the home folks are watching. Nevertheless, for most of the day, the fact is that the FSO and his wife and children live in foreign parts with foreign customs. The great reform in international relations that has not been achieved, though diplomats of many countries are working at it, is a change in employment laws that would give wives (and, sometimes, husbands) a chance to continue their careers while their spouse is on overseas assignment.

At the Foreign Service Institute in an office building across the Potomac from the State Department, new FSOs in their first cycle of training heard a lecture from Fanchon Silberstein, an earnest, dressy former school-teacher exiled from special education to be coordinator of the Overseas Briefing Center and Family Workshop for the State Department: "Your culture is forever with you, especially the values. You tighten up and make judgments, and it's hard to discuss them. You'll experience a 'cycle of readjustment'—almost infant-like. What's true today will not be true in four weeks or two months. You have to be willing to accept help from other people." This is worse, of course, for wives: like the hills of West Virginia, the Foreign Service is great for men and horses but hell on women and dogs.

The temperamental fit between place and person can be overwhelmingly important. For many, Geneva is a dreadful city, divided into three communities that hate each other—the Genevois, the non-French Swiss and the international set. For many, Tokyo is a dream post, combining the excitement of a big, modern city with the challenge of a surviving culture that invites and repays constant study. William Culbert had spent five years in Geneva before he was assigned to Tokyo as economic affairs minister. A year later, William Walker, who had been appointed chief of a new U.S. negotiating team in Geneva, passed through Tokyo for meetings, saw Culbert, and inquired whether he might be available for return to Geneva as deputy chief of mission. "Do I have to leave this morning?" Culbert inquired anxiously. "Or can it wait till this afternoon? . . ."

Culture shock happens everywhere. Geoffrey Moorhouse tells of Sir Oliver Franks' arrival in Washington in the 1940s:

"He was rather taken aback by a telephone conversation he had with the local radio station before he had properly settled into his desk, a few days before Christmas. The man in the studio was welcoming him to the American capital, wishing him well during his time there, and seemed very anxious to know what Sir Oliver wanted for Christmas. Franks, not a man for small talk, spluttered a little as he groped for a seemly idea, and finally came up with something he thought might do. On Christmas morning the broadcaster came on the air, burbling goodwill across the District of Columbia. 'On this hallowed day,' crooned the announcer, 'we have a number of distinguished foreign residents in the capital city of the United States, and we thought it would be appropriate to ask some of them what *they* would like most of all for Christmas 1948. First of all, we asked His Excellency the French Ambassador what his choice would be . . . .' The broadcast cut into a tape recording of a Parisian voice, pregnant with sincerity: 'Pour Noël, I want peace through all thee world.' 'Then we asked the Ambassador of the Soviets, what he would like most of all today . . . .' A dogmatic voice on the tape this time: 'For Chressmas I want freedom for all the peoples enslaved by imperialism, wherever they may be.' 'Finally, folks, we asked Her Majesty the Queen's Ambassador from London, Sir Oliver Franks, what he would prefer this day . . . .' The diffident tones of Bristol Grammar School and Oxford came on the air: '. . . Well, as a matter of fact, it's very kind of you, I think I'd quite like a small box of candied fruit . . . .' "

Most of the stories, of course, run in the opposite direction, to the experience of Americans or other Westerners in Less Developed Countries. An ambassador from a small state that considers itself highly civilized talked about his time in Africa: "You make fifteen copies of every memo or invitation you send to a government official, so you can keep giving him new copies after you don't get a reply. Your wife gives a dinner for the Prime Minister. You prepare the tables, and an hour before, the Prime Minister calls, he cannot come. So you rearrange. Half an hour after the dinner starts, the Prime Minister comes, with three others. Or you have a dinner for the Foreign Minister, and he puts his hand on a delicate part of the ambassador's wife's anatomy. Or the Foreign Minister invites *you* to a dinner, asks to borrow two cases of whiskey, he's a little short; he will return them, of course. When you get there, he asks you to smuggle a camera for him. If you do, you may be in trouble. If you don't, you may be in trouble. . . ."

But more positive attitudes are not uncommon. Take Richard Cornish, U.S. political-economic counselor in Yaoundé, Cameroon: "My daughter, the big one, now twenty-one, started school in Togo, a native school in Togo, then had four years in Laos in a little school run by a Swiss missionary. The eighteen-year-old, born in Burma, is going to Mount Holyoke from a lycée in Addis Ababa. We loved Togo. There's never been a town that we haven't liked. We enjoy living overseas. Addis Ababa—talk about places delightful to live in! People were shooting each other in the streets —but if there was a pothole or a water-line problem out in that street, someone was there to fix it. The *fonctionnaires* worked—and everyone you dealt with spoke English."

6

In the end, it doesn't much matter whether an FSO likes a post or not: he has signed up to accept whatever may be his fate. The civil service is a job more or less like any other, but the Foreign Service really is a *service*, like the Army. Accepting his appointment—which is by the President, not by some personnel department—the FSO formally agrees to serve wherever he is sent, in whatever capacity. His salary and his rank in the service inhere in him, not in his post—an FSO-3 is an FSO-3, just as a colonel is a colonel, whether he is serving as a counselor or a minister or a deputy chief of mission.

What one always forgets, writing about the FSOs, is that they are patriots. It is a matter of nurture, not nature—unlike the army officer, the Foreign Service Officer usually does not start out with the instincts of a flag-waver. After a few years of living abroad, he grows sick of the way foreigners talk about his country, and he learns in his gut that however green other hills may be, they are not the hills of home. If clientitis makes him an advocate for the positions of the country in which he is stationed, the reason is not that he has shifted loyalties but that those positions, seen from his present perspective, seem clearly better for the interests of the United States.

The need to defend publicly positions with which one may privately disagree ultimately produces the deeper loyalty of shared identity. This loyalty can break, as it did for Frenchmen on both sides of the Algerian dispute, for Americans (though fewer in the Foreign Service than in other walks of life, perhaps fewer than in the military) over Vietnam. Accepting the decision of the nation though one feels it is wrong is not dishonest or even cynical: it should be seen, rather, as the secular equivalent of the leap of faith.

The angst of the Foreign Service is that this love of country is not reciprocated. "I've given 20 percent of my heart and 60 percent of my stomach to my country," said a senior FSO in Tokyo, "and occasionally I feel put upon." The reward is partly in the inherent interest of the life, partly in the satisfactions of service, partly in the glittering prize of an ambassador's post (which about 3 percent of career FSOs can expect to receive, as against about 1.5 percent in the case of military officers hoping to become generals‡). The burr under the saddle, then, is the politically appointed ambassador, who has not, in a very profound sense, paid his dues to his country. The great nonprofessional diplomats—a David Bruce, an Ellsworth Bunker, a Sol Linowitz—forever remind their interlocutors that they are not career people, they are amateurs. This asserts a cherished independence from the State Department and its machinery, but it also expresses a born diplomat's deference to the dedication of the cadre on whose shoulders he stands.

Working abroad, then, the FSO is first a foreigner, then a servant, only finally an officer. Apart from its utility in the procedures of diplomacy, the exaggerated status of the diplomat is a compensation for what may be a deeply disturbing situation. Of all the professions, diplomacy has succeeded best in retaining the popular envy and awe of the Mystery of the guild—nobody sues the diplomat for malpractice. But both in his work and in his psyche, the diplomat needs that deference; no one should begrudge it him.

‡ In some foreign services, the ratio is much better. Thanks to the very low intake in the MacArthur years and the very rapid rise in the number of countries eligible to receive ambassadors, the Japanese Foreign Ministry was for years able to find an ambassador's post for *every* entrant to the Foreign Service when his time came twenty-five years after the arrival of his class. "This year," the director of personnel in the Ministry said sadly in 1978, "is the first year we shall have to compel someone to voluntarily retire."

II

Function

3

INFORMING

> Bring out the machine guns. Let's liquidate the diplomats.
>
> —Stalin, in 1945, ending a dinner-
> party conversation about the
> future government of Poland

1

"An Ambassador," Sir Henry Wooton wrote in a royal comment book, attempting a witticism that got him fired by James II, "is an honest man sent to lie abroad for the good of his country." But what does he do once he has arrived? What do the members of his embassy do? What use, in what manner, will be made of their work by the government that sent them? What, in short, are the purposes of the enterprise?

Some embassies, of course, have special missions. The U.S. ambassador to Colombia works primarily on control of drug shipments to the United States, coordinating the efforts of four different domestic U.S. authorities that have sent narcotics agents to help him and do not coordinate with each other, trying to keep the Colombian Government in a proper state of shame and horror about a trade that produces probably half its country's foreign exchange earnings.

The Danish ambassador in Tokyo has a special assignment to maintain the privileges and earnings of the Danish cable company that long ago built and still owns the main communications link between Japan and Russia.

The U.S. ambassador to Israel spent much of his time for three years supervising the construction (by eight thousand Portuguese and Thai laborers) of more than $1 billion worth of air base, a gift from the people of the United States to the people of Israel on the occasion of the Camp David accords.

The Israeli ambassador in Uruguay cultivates a group of evangelical Christians who consider the return of the Hebrews to Jerusalem to be the first sign of the Second Coming.

Syrian ambassadors attempt to police compliance by local industry with the Arab League boycott against Israel.

French ambassadors are charged with the management of a huge cultural affairs output, including a worldwide system of *lycées* staffed by teachers from France who can meet their military service obligations by two years' labor in the surroundings of the Third World.

The Australian ambassador in Washington is supposed to keep up with and influence U.S. plans to purchase for or sell from stockpiles of the minerals Australia produces.

Ambassadors from big countries to little ones may be viceroys, communicating the instructions of their home governments to hosts who are willing (even eager) to take orders. In nations as sophisticated and rich as Japan and Italy, and through much of Latin America, the U.S. ambassador will have an influence on domestic policies: like it or not, he is part of the consensus process, and failure to secure his consent can doom governmental initiatives. To the heads of state in East Germany, Czechoslovakia, Mongolia, Afghanistan and Bulgaria, among others, the Soviet ambassador speaks as their master's voice. In the border countries where the Cold War is most vigorously fought, more sinister matters may emanate from the embassies. The Russian ambassador to the Shah's Iran commented wickedly on the appointment of Richard Helms to the American embassy by asking Prime Minister Amir Abbas Hoveyda why he thought the United States was sending to Tehran its number-one spy. "Because they are our friends," Hoveyda replied; "they do not send us their number-ten man."

But such situations are aberrations, both for the embassies and for the Foreign Ministries that send them. Normally, a Foreign Ministry is an information system specialized in the communication of judgments; both its authority and its ability to make decisions are narrowly circumscribed. Because its subject matter is *foreign* relations, it operates necessarily in an environment where no one government's policies can be controlling; in most cases, the reactions of several or many governments to events and to each other's decisions must be known (or if unknown, guessable) before the government of which this Ministry is a part can intelligently formulate its own plans. Its appendages abroad therefore are primarily reporting instruments, seeking to find—and more importantly, to analyze—information that would not necessarily be available or comprehensible at the home office without such help.

The Foreign Ministries of the larger countries are forever engaged in comparing impressions gained by their embassies. Thus, when President Carter was in Poland in 1977 the Japanese embassy in Washington had a man on all-day duty at the European Bureau of the State Department, hanging around the Polish desk to see what he could pick up about the incidents of the President's journey. His colleague in Poland, meanwhile, was relaying reports on the same events from a different perspective. And the U.S. ambassador to Tokyo was presenting the government there with daily reports on our pilgrim's progress, with injunctions to report back on any reactions. The women of the Hebrides, you may recall, were reputed to make their living by taking in each other's washing.

Still, one can on occasion pick up at the Foreign Ministry of a host country information of the greatest importance about what is happening in third and fourth countries. Perhaps the most spectacular example in American history was Rufus King's discovery at the British Foreign Office that the King of Spain had secretly ceded to Napoleon his country's holdings in the Mississippi and Missouri valleys, a piece of news that put in motion the process leading to the Louisiana Purchase.

There is a necessary symbiosis between diplomacy and journalism. "Most of the reporting of diplomats is what they read in the local newspapers," said Efraim Haran of the Israeli Foreign Ministry. "It's legitimate. You can't go every day and interview everybody. But if *all* of someone's reports come a day later in the *International Herald Tribune*, I know he isn't working very hard. When I was in Geneva, I made a practice of reading the *Neue Zürcher Zeitung*, and it was the basis of my reports. They did serious economic reporting. You cannot copy directly from the *Herald Tribune* or *The Economist* or the *Financial Times*, because it's in Jerusalem in two or three days. If you want to use those papers, you have to say, 'According to the *Financial Times*.' But the *Neue Zürcher Zeitung* . . . that you can make your own."

In posts like Moscow, Peking and most other Eastern-bloc capitals, an omnivorous approach to the local periodicals is required, because access to government officials is infrequent and usually unrewarding while access to private citizens is closely controlled by the secret police. By reading all the privincial papers, however, political analysts in the embassy can often get some kind of grip on the disputes that are agitating the populace and that will affect government policies. In the Israeli nexus, it is especially important to keep up with press reports from the Israeli embassy in Washington: "We have to get that back to Washington immediately," said Public

Affairs Officer David Hitchcock in Tel Aviv. "They must know what the embassy is leaking."

Everywhere that the press is state-controlled, of course, the newspapers tell the embassy what the government wants its citizens to believe. Not the least of the reasons why Foreign Ministries require (or should require) acquaintance with the local language before people are sent abroad is that without the language, they can't read the papers. If the panderers of UNESCO have their way, and governments are given by international treaty control of all the newspapers in all countries, it will be possible to find out anywhere exactly what lies each government insists that its citizens believe, and nothing else.

On the other hand, reporting from countries well covered by the wire services will often duplicate what is in the press in the home country, and invites rebuke from the budget controllers at some later time. England's Berrill Report pointed out that "when major events take place in public . . . missions should assume unless otherwise instructed that policy-makers in London can get the news from the media or the BBC Monitoring Service. . . ." Where American subjects are involved, the waste may be even more obvious: "It was unnecessary," the Report noted savagely, "for UKMIS [the British mission to the United Nations] to telegraph verbatim a speech by Secretary Kissinger when the text was simultaneously being distributed by the United States Embassy in London. . . ."

Contacts within the host government and local institutions are the cherished resource of an embassy. "I came here with the doors open," Ed Woltman, U.S. labor attaché in Denmark, said gratefully. "My predecessor gave a large cocktail party to which he invited his contacts. We are very different people temperamentally and ideologically, but we called together on the heads of the labor unions."

The "sources" whose hot recall of conversations or meetings bulk so large in every embassy's reports are real people with real careers and home lives, whose reasons for indiscretion are important. They must be stroked, admired, sometimes paid, never neglected or disparaged or made to feel insecure. Sources outside the government are even more precious over time, and even more difficult to cultivate from scratch. One of the common irritants of the U.S. embassies is a State Department assignment and transportation system that frequently requires incumbents in a post to leave for their new job before their successor arrives, making the new man start with a blank slate in establishing relations and discovering the levels of knowledge, sophistication and trustworthiness he will find represented by the names in the embassy's phone book. Sometimes the most useful names are in the attaché's personal phone book, and disappear with him.

Some contacts, of course, are too personal to be transferred: the higher the level of the contact, the more likely it is to be lost when the man moves. An obvious example was Averell Harriman, who was able to involve the Russians in the Vietnam negotiations in 1967 simply because as a former ambassador to the Soviet Union he had access to the gerontocracy of the Politburo; it did him no good, because the Russians could no more control the North Vietnamese than the United States could control the Israelis (indeed, rather less: this is the problem of arming one's presumed satellites beyond their need). Still, the "back-channels" Kissinger later had to cultivate with Dobrynin to get messages privately to the Vietnamese negotiators were operable for Harriman within the framework of the negotiations themselves, a condition that took Kissinger three years to establish after Harriman departed.

Philip Kaiser had met James Callaghan when he was ambassador to Senegal and participated with Callaghan in a conference on "The African Road to Socialism." As DCM in London, he found Callaghan Chancellor of the Exchequer, and the two men spent considerable time together. In 1966, as the British financial crisis came to a boil, Callaghan invited Kaiser for a bank holiday weekend on the Isle of Wight.

"He had a shack there," Kaiser recalled. "Really a shack. You pulled the chain on the toilet, the whole house shook. He poured out his heart, all weekend. I came back and wrote out a memo. Bruce [David Bruce, who spent the entire Kennedy and Johnson period as ambassador to Britain] read it and said, 'My God. You go to Washington. Never let this memo out of your sight. Show it to Rusk and to one person in the White House. And sit there while they read it.'

"Bruce was a great underreporter," Kaiser continued affectionately. (Some at the State Department felt less affectionate: when Bruce opened the American mission in Peking, weeks might pass without any word from him.) "Most of the time when I'd show him a cable, he would say, 'Well, Phil, was there any *need* for this?' Ambassadors should make more use of the telephone. As an ambassador, I will call Washington when I want to say things. . . ."

In the Communist countries and some of the Third World, protocol governs all: the embassy is supposed to receive its information from the desk in the Foreign Ministry that handles bilateral relations with its home country, and the level of contact within the Ministry is established for each member of the mission. Because such considerations can be brushed aside in the United States, Washington is just about every diplomat's favorite post, professionally if not socially. "There is an air of informality here," said Peter Asongwe, second counselor at the Cameroon embassy in Washington. "You work with the State Department on a person-to-person basis. People pick up the telephone. Elsewhere it's strict protocol, you communicate through verbal notes." A bespectacled head poked in the door of the office. "Good morning, chief," said Asongwe, and the head nodded and vanished. "In China," he continued, "they assign you a high government official on your arrival. In theory, he is your 'interpreter.' In fact, he gives you the answer to all your questions."

Small-country embassies to big countries will have a political attaché who keeps in touch with as much of the host government as he can, and an economics and commercial attaché who solicits business, picks up the local statistics, and tries to form a view of how meaningful they are. Large-country embassies to large countries will have a gaggle of attachés, counselors and ministers who divide up the labor in various exotic ways. John Franklin Campbell recalled from the glory days of U.S. representation in Bonn, in the spread-out assemblage of low glass-and-aluminum office buildings that looks like a 1950s suburban factory, an employee whose sole job was the purchase of toilet paper for the PXs of Central Europe.

In Britain, Americans are assigned to keep up with each of the more than twenty regional bureaus in Whitehall, sometimes to feed American views into British decision-making processes at the detail level, more often to keep informed on what British policy toward, say, Burma, is likely to be —and to exchange information and stories about the country in question. These tasks are usually doubled with domestic political reporting: the counselor assigned to monitor the East Asia division of Whitehall was also the embassy's liaison with the Conservative Party. It would be rare, however, to find economics attachés covering a beat in Parliament or political attachés nosing around to get details of export-credit schemes.

Commercial attachés put out trend reports, in some countries as often as once a week, with a big survey of the local economy, for publication by the Commerce Department, at least twice a year. Agricultural attachés supply their home office with monthly reports on the progress of crops and the prospects for exports. They are probably the most prolific reporters. "My first assignment was western Canada," Philip Habib remembered. "I wrote some of the great reports on the hops crop of western Canada. Not one report—*hundreds* of reports. An embassy can give you the best information on a company abroad, better than your bank, because the commercial attaché in the embassy goes and looks at the factory." But the State Department does not pay any attention to such matters or to what comes from the labor attaché, who tends to be socially downscale from the political officers. What he reports is easy to ignore, especially if he is a CIA man and is believed to keep the best stuff he finds for his own employers.

Public Affairs has its own officer, normally an employee of the U.S. Information Agency, though in the crucial posts an FSO may be detailed to the job. The PAO is the embassy's link with local journalists, and he is a bigger man in the embassy than outsiders are likely to realize. His influence is not reflected in his status: as a Foreign Service Information Officer, he is out of the State Department's chain of promotion and cannot hope to hold a post—ambassador, DCM, Assistant Secretary—that will grant him authority. In the embassy, he supervises the Cultural Affairs Officer, also a USIA employee, who arranges visits in both directions by academics, musicians, artists, writers, etc. Counting the culture operation, the PAO normally has the largest staff in the embassy, but the strength of his position rests on far more than brute numbers.

Washington keeps up with the size and texture and warmth of the treatment the United States and its embassy and its embassy's personnel receive in the local press. Even the evanescences of local broadcasts are caught, taped, translated and transcribed in a giant State Department operation that produces a thick daily mimeographed booklet from each region of the globe (the FBIS, for Foreign Broadcast Information Service). And, of course, what appears about America and its mission in the local press directly affects everybody's work on the spot. The PAO is the font of information for local reporters, which means he must know what is in the ambassador's instructions and on his mind in order to answer questions intelligently; except for the DCM, the PAO spends more time with the ambassador than anyone else at the post.

Moreover, the PAO is in a significant sense a reporting officer. In most countries, local journalists are prime sources of information about trends in the attitudes of the host government and population. The PAO is ideally placed to trade background information with reporters. What he gets is not always entirely reliable—but, then, neither is what he gives.

The PAO is also, of course, the conduit between the ambassador and whatever press from the home country may be stationed in or passing through the embassy's territory. What appears in the U.S. press about a foreign country—and especially about the ambassador—is a matter of prime concern in the embassy. American diplomats and businessmen, moreover, have a surprising faith in the acumen and accuracy of American journalists. Averell Harriman wrote of his first trip to Russia in the 1920s, when he was negotiating concessions to mine Soviet manganese, that "of all those I talked to, I found the best informed and the clearest analysts were the American and British correspondents then in Moscow. . . . I learned on my other travels, both as a businessman and a government representative, that our foreign correspondents were a most important source of information. I have, therefore, always made it a point to see them. . . ."

At all U.S. embassies and most others, reports for the home government go out over the signature of the ambassador himself, who may or may not have read them. Meanwhile, all instructions, replies to questions, information and gossip officially directed to the embassy from Washington arrive signed by the Secretary of State, who almost certainly hasn't seen them. When the ambassador is out of the country, the reports to Washington are signed by the DCM; when the Secretary is away, all communications to the embassy are signed by the Deputy Secretary. These rules are taken very seriously at the embassy, because when the ambassador is out of the country the DCM is entitled to "*chargé* pay," half the difference between his salary and the ambassador's, for every day of the big man's absence.

The ambassador himself is the primary reporting officer at the post. Like any knavish junior FSO, he writes or dictates "memcons" (memoranda of conversations) after all personal contacts with the host government. (Abba Eban noted that as Foreign Minister of Israel he never did "receive a dispatch from an ambassador about an encounter in which he came off second-best.") He will go home to Washington at least once every nine months, and will have the chance to convey his sense of the situation and his views at least to an Assistant Secretary, sometimes to an Under Secretary, *very* occasionally to the Secretary.

In other foreign services, the ambassador may have an even more direct reporting responsibility. British ambassadors are supposed to write (themselves) annual reviews of conditions in the country where they serve; recently they have been asked "to take a forward view." Danish ambassadors send back every *month* a classic "dispatch" in the form of a personal letter: "Mr. Foreign Minister, I humbly present my opinions. . . ." This goes to a list—the King, all Ministers, members of the Parliamentary Committee on Foreign Affairs. "It's a matter of discussion from time to time whether it's worth it," said Hennings Gottlieb of the Prime Minister's secretariat.

Most of an ambassador's information comes to him from others of his own nationality: the members of his staff, journalists, the bureaucracy back home, and—through whatever forwarding systems are employed—other ambassadors from his own country. A high proportion of the cable traffic at an American embassy is composed of copies of cables sent to Washington from other posts in the region. Where nations are organized into more or less formal groupings—the European Economic Community, the Association of South East Asian Nations, the Andean States in South America—ambassadors to all the countries involved will meet with each other in conference periodically. Similar meetings will bring together senior subordinates—the political counselors at one, the economics counselors at another. The problem with these, an economics counselor reports, is that "the team that comes out from Washington does all the talking; tells you how busy they are in Washington."

Other countries do this, too: Gideon Rafael reports on meetings of all Israeli ambassadors to Eastern Europe, in the days before the Six-Day War (when the Russians ordered their satellites to break contact with Tel Aviv, which all but the Romanians promptly did). One meeting was held in Poland, and a popular story in the Israeli Foreign Ministry relates that the Poles asked for it to be repeated because their bugging machinery had failed the first time.

What the ambassador sees of his colleagues' cables, and of the less urgent communications sent home by his own staff, is something he decides for himself. Most opt to be shown only a handful a day, selected by a young FSO assigned as a personal assistant, under general supervision of the DCM. Some ambassadors, like most Secretaries of State, prefer to see only summaries of cables, which are dutifully prepared. At nearly every embassy, the ambassador holds a morning meeting with his senior staff (junior staff in attendance perhaps once a week). Depending on the individual and the situation, these meetings may serve to relay Washington's attitudes to the myrmidons, or to fill in the ambassador on what his people believe is going on and what they think might be done about it.

Sometimes ambassadors are skilled at gathering information themselves. Armistead Selden had been a congressman, and retained his love of the lobby; in New Zealand, he hung around at Parliament a lot, came to know nearly all the MPs by their first names, and on those rare occasions when Washington wanted to know something about New Zealand, Selden could tell them.

Dean Acheson wrote a memorial tribute to William Herridge, Canadian Minister to the United States in 1931–35:

"Access to cabinet officers is easy for a diplomat of Herridge's ability and charm. His special achievement was to establish easy and friendly relations with the bureaucracy. . . . His luncheons were small, six or eight; his guests, of little cabinet rank, and never more than one from the same department or agency. He sat down promptly at 1:00, not waiting for later arrivals, and ended the lunch as promptly at 2:00. There were no cocktails, but an excellent white wine with the meal, which, in turn, was light, well chosen, well cooked, and served with flair by Horsely, the butler—as much of a character as the Minister.

"Herridge's part was to stimulate conversation. At this he was a past master. He would poke fun at himself, in a delightfully slow, clowning manner, for his inability to grasp the current crop of rumors and leaks, and make such gay nonsense of them, and of the rivalries between the cabinet prima donnas, that his guests would take over the talk and vie with one another to make all clear. Dawning understanding from Herridge and wholly erroneous guesses as to the future would bring forth further enlightenment. Sometimes he would speak hopelessly of some predicament which Canadian interests faced, often stimulating helpful suggestions. . . ."

A surprisingly high proportion of what an ambassador knows or believes comes from frequent conversations with other countries' ambassadors. That, after all, is his club, and the rules of the game keep him in its confines much of the time. Protocol requires considerable remote contact: the ritual of calling cards marked "p.f." (*pour féliciter*—to congratulate), "p.r." (*pour remercier*—to thank), "p.c." (*pour condoléance*—to offer condolences), "p.p.c." (*pour prendre congé*—to announce departure). If the card has been dog-eared, it means the ambassador came himself to leave it; if it is pristine, a flunky delivered it. But ambassadors are thrown directly into each other's company all the time, at official parties and receptions, private dinners and social events. They also pay purposive calls on each other, compare impressions of recent events, and discuss their colleagues.

"One of my first tasks," Charles Bohlen recalled from his days as U.S. ambassador to Moscow, "was to call on other ambassadors. These visits are time-consuming and frequently non-productive, but in Moscow they were of considerable interest because each ambassador had a different comment on the Soviet scene. While it required a year and a half to call on all the embassies, it was not long before I established close relations with the British and French Ambassadors." The United States has always been well informed about backstage happenings at Soviet party congresses, because the Italian Communist delegates always keep their embassy in touch, and the Italians share with the Americans.

Contacts between ambassadors from different countries to a third country are also media of communication about subjects that may have nothing to do with the host country. J. K. Galbraith remembered a lesson taught him during his first weeks in India by Polish ambassador Julius Katz-Suchy: "He advised me to be generous with information. 'In conversation with the American ambassador, I learned . . .' makes, he said, a fine beginning for another ambassador's cable."

Serious contact between the United States and China was initiated through conversations between their ambassadors to Poland. Walter Stoessel, later Deputy Secretary to Haig, liked to tell how he got this process started, by bearding the Chinese ambassador at the exit from a fashion show given at the Yugoslav embassy in Warsaw, when the puritanical Chinese left early in embarrassment at some see-through garments. It was, of course, only a start: Henry Kissinger later complained that "American ambassadors to Warsaw were generally not selected for their expertise in

Chinese affairs. . . . It all took time and got nowhere." The U.S. and Chinese ambassadors to Pakistan were the central intermediaries in setting up Kissinger's bombshell visit to Peking. In 1967–68, relations between Lyndon Johnson and Leonid Brezhnev were conducted mostly through the two countries' ambassadors to Denmark. Meetings of ambassadors of countries publicly hostile to each other go unremarked: they are part of the social life of a capital city.

Moreover, information of great importance about the host country can be acquired from other diplomats. In 1941, a Peruvian military attaché in Tokyo told the U.S. embassy there that a drunken Japanese naval officer at a cocktail party in his embassy had announced that if it came to war between Japan and the United States the Japanese would begin by destroying the fleet at Pearl Harbor. But such material has to be handled with great care. "I tell our ambassadors," said Alois Reitbauer, the avuncular, gray-mustached, paralyzingly smart "permanent head" of the Austrian Foreign Service, "that acquiring information from diplomats is the worst thing one can do. I am absolutely against it. Colleagues are unreliable. They get their information from their secretaries, and because of language, the secretaries come from a certain social situation. . . . In the East bloc, of course," he added, "you are forced to do it."

Often enough, the embassies simply don't know what is going on. "The real problems are qualitative," said Ben Read, the lean, athletic Philadelphia lawyer who was Under Secretary for Management in the Carter State Department (and head of the Executive Secretariat for Dean Rusk in the Kennedy and Johnson administrations, the real link, Mac Bundy reported, between Kennedy's National Security Council and Rusk's State Department). "You get a series of excited cables about a security problem, and then you have to start asking yourself, 'Has this fellow been out in the country? Or is this all lunch-table and cocktail party conversation?' There have been serious instances when we didn't know enough about what was going on—not a failure of covert intelligence, just a lack of good reporting."

In one-party states, the strength, views and prospects of the opposition are difficult to learn. It is all very well for the textbooks and the press to exhort diplomats to keep in touch with the outs as well as the ins, but host governments tend to protest when that is attempted—and, after all, a diplomat is present only thanks to an *agrément*. Among the benefits of having a human rights bureau in the State Department has been the sometimes bewildered recognition by foreigners that this bureau has the specific task of making contact with the opposition. Nearly half of all U.S. contacts with the opponents of the Shah in his last year were under the remote auspices of that office.

71

One always, of course, has to be careful. Spruille Braden's collaboration with the opponents of Juan Perón helped the Argentine dictator gain popularity as the man who pulled Uncle Sam's beard. In 1888, the British ambassador to the United States, Sir Lionel Sackville-West, allowed himself to be tricked by a Republican party worker into writing a letter expressing his belief that once the election was over President Cleveland would be very friendly to Britain; he had already demonstrated "a spirit of conciliation." This helped considerably to elect Benjamin Harrison.

Such conduct may be unpopular in the diplomat's home base, too. During World War I, the U.S. consul general in Zurich was a man with a daughter married to a German naval officer, who supplied information to him about the German war effort. A retired American clergyman in Zurich reported the consul general for "consorting with the enemy," and he was fired. The clergyman, incidentally, was the father of Noel Field, one of the Soviet Union's most successful spies, whose exposure in that role gave the CIA its greatest triumph: by allowing him to escape to Czechoslovakia and putting it about that he was a U.S. double agent, the CIA got the intelligence chiefs of four Soviet bloc countries imprisoned or killed, and thoroughly disrupted the Russian networks.

The CIA maintains and even publicizes an "operations" division that considers itself authorized to subvert governments in other countries, and uses embassies among its varied covers. Under these circumstances, governments are scarcely to be blamed for feeling a degree of itchiness when American diplomats are seen consorting with the overt or covert opposition. Salvador Allende had good reason to be concerned about contacts between the U.S. embassy and the Chilean military. Daniel P. Moynihan noted that as ambassador to India he had tried to find out the extent of CIA interference in Indian electoral life, and had uncovered only two instances when the agency had distributed money to a candidate. (He may not have found the whole truth, of course, or told it if he did find it.) "Both times," Moynihan wrote, "this was done in the face of a prospective Communist victory in a state election, once in Kerala and once in West Bengal, where Calcutta is located. Both times the money was given to the Congress Party, which had asked for it. Once it was given to Mrs. Gandhi herself, who was then a party official.

"Still, as we were no longer giving any money to her, it was understandable that she should wonder just to whom we were giving it. It is not a practice to be encouraged."

Sometimes the errors arise simply from the obscurity of the future always and everywhere. "On a Tuesday night in 1968, Soviet forces moved into Czechoslovakia," Dean Rusk said, recalling one of the worst moments of his incumbency as Secretary of State. "We learned later that they had made their decision the Saturday before. If we'd asked our intelligence community a week before, they couldn't have known. At press conferences, 80 percent of the time the right answer to a question could be, 'Damned if I know.'" It would not have been possible to predict the Liberian revolution, which began because some illiterate sergeants got drunk and angry and decided to tear apart a government that turned out to have all the resistance of tissue paper.

Still, it is probably fair to say that embassies—and especially ambassadors, which is what counts—tend to overestimate the tenure of the people with whom they are doing business. In the democracies, the embassies typically predict the reelection of incumbents: in Britain, the U.S. embassy was surprised by Heath's defeat of Wilson in 1970 and Thatcher's victory over Callaghan in 1979. In 1981, despite the public opinion polls, the U.S. embassy in Paris continued to predict the victory of Giscard in the runoff election, mouthing the old line that the French vote their hearts in the first round and their pocketbooks in the second. The result was that Reagan did not have a congratulatory message for President-elect Mitterrand until the day after the voting.

Even in places like Ethiopia and Nicaragua, where unspeakable governments were presiding over a starving populace, the U.S. embassies were unable to see big trouble ahead. In 1977, just as their movement was gathering what would be irresistible popular force, the Sandinistas were described by the embassy in Managua as a "small, pro-Castro, Marxist terrorist group." Visitors to the Philippines in 1981 were impressed by the intensity of the resentment of American support for President Ferdinand Marcos, at a time when the embassy was insisting the Marcos family had things well in hand, and the Vice-President of the United States was encouraged to hail the dictator's devotion to democracy at his inauguration ceremony.

Remembering the revolution in Ghana while he was labor attaché there, Edward Woltman said: "I turned on the radio at six in the morning of the day Colonel Acheampong took over. I called the ambassador, woke him up. 'There's been a coup,' I said.

"'Where?' he said. . . . Then Acheampong's people took over the telephone exchange and you couldn't make calls.

"Mrs. Nixon had just been there. They delayed the coup until she left. Government paid so much attention to that visit the coup must have been easy. . . . The chairman of the TUC [Trades Union Congress] stopped off at my house on his way to exile in Togo. . . ."

Certain kinds of misjudgment, moreover, are always with us. Dmitri Abrikossow told the story of an encounter in St. Petersburg during the Russo-Japanese War between the former military attaché in Tokyo who had reported that "the Japanese Army was no good" and a "high-ranking civilian who asked him . . . how he could have sent such reports. The General got angry and replied that he still felt the Japanese Army was no good. When the civilian asked how this could be in view of the fact that the Japanese were beating us at every step, the General shouted that what he had not known at the time of his reports was that our Army was even worse."

2

In the nature of things, embassies overreport. The man who bores his interlocutors in the home office gets occasional rebukes for wasting his masters' time; the man who has failed to alert the Ministry to a development that is about to make headlines and cause questions in the legislature will get thoroughly chewed out for it. Only a man with total personal and professional security—a David Bruce—can restrain himself from telling the home office all he thinks he knows. Some diplomats have risen through their detailed, closely reasoned, lengthy dispatches—George Kennan is perhaps the most notable example. Others have acquired a damaging reputation for longwindedness. Bismarck commented sourly about Count Max von Berchem's reports from Stockholm that "Berchem seems to believe he has discovered Sweden." Berchem never received another posting from the German Foreign Ministry.

"I had a good friend in Yemen who wrote incredibly detailed cables on what the tribes were doing along the border," said the young Arabist April Glaspie, who won the State Department's annual prize for political reporting when she was in Cairo in 1976. "I had lunch with him once in Beirut. I said, 'I say, old chap, don't you think that's a little much? What do you think you're doing?' He said, 'Keeping busy.' "

The cables arrive at the State Department slugged by their sender with his view of how rapidly they should come to the attention of the decision-makers. The first priority, overriding the queue in the communications center, is "CRITIC" (for critical); the second is "FLASH" (a hangover from journalism), followed by "IMMEDIATE," with "PRIORITY" a poor fourth. Even so, the diplomats in the field labor under an awful sense that nobody back home pays attention.

"I am rather vain about some of the political reports I made describing Hitler's earliest raucous efforts," Robert Murphy recalled from an early assignment in the Weimar Republic. "When I looked them up recently in the National Archives in Washington, they seemed reasonably perceptive. But while we were sending in our reports so earnestly, we never knew whether or not anybody in Washington read them. They were accepted in total silence." Asked by John F. Kennedy to serve as ambassador to NATO, Dean Acheson refused on the grounds that "I'm too old to go home every three months to answer my cables."

And the problem is much worse now. Arthur Schlesinger, Jr., noted that "in 1930 . . . the telegraphic traffic [of the State Department] for the whole year amounted to little more than two million words." But when Kennedy arrived, "every two months the telegraphic traffic was greater than in all 1930." In 1977, cable traffic at the State Department ran more than two million words *a day*, and the number is even larger now. It is physically impossible for one man to read the daily cable traffic from the U.S. embassy in Japan alone, even if he were to do nothing else all day. And there are more than 150 posts, almost all of them reporting *something* every day. Sometimes, moreover, the most important messages may be sent by attachés from the other departments of government, with the State Department acting simply as a conduit and nobody in the Foreign Service even reading the cable. The U.S. agricultural attaché in Moscow had reported on the disaster of the Soviet grain crop before the Russian purchases that discombobulated the U.S. markets in 1972—but nobody in the State Department or the White House had looked at the cable. ("If he'd sent it SECRET, EYES ONLY instead of routinely," Eugene Rostow said glumly, "history would have been different.")

Looked at from abroad, the State Department information system is a black hole that sucks in whatever passes by, and never releases anything but bursts of apparently random energy. Diplomats read newspaper stories from Washington, and receive summaries of policy decisions, that show no signs of contact with what has been crafted, edited and cabled at the mission. "Not a day goes by," Maynard Barnes, U.S. ambassador to Bulgaria, wrote in the aftermath of the Potsdam meetings in 1945, "that I do not envy my British colleague because of the prompt response he receives from his Government, while in my own case weeks go by with little or nothing to rely on except local possibilities for temporization." Two decades later, Galbraith wrote in fury to Kennedy that "when the Department does respond to telegrams it is invariably to recommend evasion of issues that cannot be evaded."

American ambassadors often are not told what their government's policy *is*. The most famous examples of this failure have come in public, in debates at the United Nations—once when Harry Truman recognized the State of Israel while Warren Austin and Phillip Jessup were arguing at the General Assembly for temporizing measures that would carry the Palestinian status quo past the end of the British mandate (Austin learned what the President had done by telephone call and simply went off to his hotel without telling his assistants, who thus had to continue the charade for another half hour); and again when Kennedy kept Adlai Stevenson in the dark about American involvement in the Bay of Pigs attack on Cuba and sent him off to lie with great sincerity in the Security Council.

Lyndon Johnson was always sparing with information to Sargent Shriver as his ambassador to Paris: a Kennedy in-law, Shriver was suspected of leaking to the domestic enemy anything that might be useful to Bobby. The entire Kissinger "back-channel" system implies that the ambassador on the scene is to be kept in ignorance of what his government proposes to do, and the admirable Gerard Smith testifies that in several stages of the first SALT negotiations Kissinger and Nixon without consulting their representatives significantly altered the American bargaining position. Jacob Beam, ambassador to Moscow in the Kissinger days, remembers trying to worm out of the Russians the news of what Kissinger and Soviet ambassador to Washington Dobrynin had been talking about. Nor was it only the ambassadors in the field who were kept in the dark. Richard Valeriani of NBC reports that when he returned from trips with Kissinger, "high-ranking State Department officials sometimes called me on the phone . . . to ask if Kissinger had talked about their area of responsibility, and if he had, would I mind telling them what he said."

"Hot lines" and summit conferences have exacerbated the situation. Correctly or otherwise, the American embassy in London in the Carter days felt that the fairly frequent conversations between the President and Prime Minister Callaghan simply soared over their heads. Ambassadorial ignorance was all the more resented because of the (correct) belief that the British ambassador in Washington was in fact routinely and completely briefed on all discussions between the two heads of state. The most humiliating moments came when the British Foreign Office gallantly shared its information about what the American President was saying with the representatives of that President in London. This situation deteriorated still further under Reagan, who appointed to the Court of St. James's a very rich man and large Republican contributor with no recorded accomplishments whatever. ("He's very well known," said the president of a company of which the new ambassador was nominal chairman, "for being able to write large checks.")

Such reports are commonplace: "Under Nixon in Bonn," says a mid-level FSO, "you'd find out from the Germans, routinely, what your own principals were doing, and often it was a surprise." On the other hand, Carter kept his ambassadors to Israel and Egypt closely in touch during his conversations with Begin and Sadat. Both ambassadors were at Camp David during the marathon negotiations, both felt that their views had been solicited, considered and significantly weighed.

It is by no means clear that ambassadors must *always* know what their government is planning. Bismarck once instructed Foreign Minister Friedrich von Holstein not to tell an ambassador something: "We would not," he said, "want to deprive the man of his naiveté." (His master Wilhelm II was even less likely to keep ambassadors—or, indeed, Foreign Ministers—fully informed. "I will tell you something," he once said to the head of the Political Division. "You diplomats are full of shit and the whole Wilhelmstrasse stinks.") But if an ambassador tells his hosts something that turns out not to be true, it must be because he has been ordered to do so, not because he didn't know.

Harold Nicolson quotes a book by De Callières, from 1716: "A lie always leaves in its wake a drop of poison. . . . The negotiator should recollect that he is likely for the rest of his life to be constantly engaged in diplomatic business, and that it is essential for him to establish a reputation for straight and honest dealing." Thayer in 1959 echoed the injunction: "A reputation for trickiness will follow a diplomat around the globe as tenaciously as the dossiers prepared by his diplomatic colleagues pursue him from post to post."

Foreign Ministers can get away with it: Henry Kissinger even fesses up to some little white lies in his memoirs. Speaking of Jozef Beck, Poland's prewar Foreign Minister, a French diplomat commented that "when Beck started to speak truthfully, it was immediately apparent." The Russians especially are under no constraint to be truthful, ever: writing of the first atomic weapons debate in the United Nations, in 1946, Herbert Feis described Andrei Gromyko as "the most unhesitant and bald-faced dissimulator—as well as liar—in the Communist company, which prized these diplomatic abilities." But Gromyko illustrates also the price that is paid: when the Russians in June 1982 pledged "no first use" of nuclear weapons, the force of the offer was much diminished by the fact that Gromyko was making it. He was, after all, the man who assured Kennedy that the Russians were sending Castro nothing but defensive counterinsurgency small arms the week the President got proof that the Russians were hurriedly assembling IRBMs in Cuba.

In any event, injunctions to honesty speak to person, not action. The fact is that governments are forever lying, all of them. Some are worse than others, for reasons of cultural tradition that endure through the most violent political changes. "Dealing with a government with whom mendacity is a science is an extremely difficult and delicate matter," Secretary of State John Hay wrote to President Theodore Roosevelt about the Czarist regime in Russia. And Willard Straight noted in 1905 from Seoul that "where the Japanese would fight and the Chinaman resist with his impassive obstinacy, the Korean will beg an issue by duplicity and double

77

dealing." The Israelis and Indians and Irish, among others, can cite chapter and verse about "perfidious Albion," and while it is quite impossible to work up any sympathy for Leopoldo Galtieri and his junta, the fact is that the Argentines had a case in the Falklands imbroglio.

Koreans remember that the United States ran out on what had looked like a pledge to maintain their independence, turning them over to the tender mercies of the Japanese in the Taft–Katsura agreement; and there are still some French around who recall that in the declining days of the war against Japan the United States while professing alliance refused to help the Free French fighters in Indochina with available air power because Franklin Roosevelt wanted to hasten the end of colonialism. ("Roosevelt was very strong that the French should not be allowed back in," Averell Harriman recalled somewhat wistfully. "We'd had good relations with Ho Chi Minh.")

George Washington said, "I hold the maxim no less applicable to public than to private life that honesty is always the best policy"—but his context was one of advocating only "temporary alliances for extraordinary emergencies" rather than long-term engagements of the kind with which the United States and most other countries are now saddled.

The problem is the ambassador who lies on his own hook, either to his hosts or (even more seriously) to his home government, as Itzhak Rabin is reported to have done when Israeli ambassador in Washington. (Rafael says Rabin continually cabled that the United States supported Israeli deep-penetration air raids on Egypt during the war of attrition along the Suez Canal in 1969–70, which was simply not true.) Most often in these cases, the lying is unconscious: incompletely informed by his own government and offered a sympathetic hearing by his hosts, the ambassador confidently projects his own opinion onto others, and communicates it as theirs.

Finally, there are some matters an ambassador arguably should not know. The most bureaucratically chauvinist FSO wants to learn only in general, not in detail, what the CIA is up to in the country to which he is assigned. The Secretary of State had better be told about it somehow, though, or the day will come when the well of relations between nations gets poisoned in ways his Department cannot cure. U.S.–Singapore relations were disturbed for years after the CIA foolishly offered Prime Minister Lee Kuan Yew a cash bribe to cover over its activities. (Rusk wrote a letter of apology, which Lee was then able to produce when Rogers' State Department later denied the incident.) Something of the same sort gave Nasser a propaganda coup.

3

"The great advantage of working for the government is that your information is so much better than what is available to the public," said Ernest Koenig, an avuncular, Viennese-born, Czech-and-French-trained *philosophe* who became chief economist for the Foreign Agricultural Service in the Department of Agriculture. This may be true in agricultural matters, where an extraordinary corps of trained attachés are out in the fields pinching the crops, but such a claim would not get much support in the State Department.

FSOs are schizophrenic about the government's own information system. Knowing what the ambassador is saying is one of the strengths of the Assistant Secretary for that region sitting in on the Secretary's meetings, and nothing is more important to an individual's status in the Department than his access to the "black book," the daily report of the National Intelligence Digest that goes to the President, the members of the National Security Council, and selected assistant secretaries of State and Defense. In the Executive Secretariat down the hall from the Secretary of State's splendid offices on the seventh floor, men work all night putting together a top-secret report for the Secretary to read before he comes in every morning.

Trusting outside sources of information has on occasion led the country down dangerous paths. The certainty that Mexico would readmit the Shah after his medical treatments—and that President Lopez Portillo sympathized with the Shah's desire to seek medical help in the United States—derived from a message, allegedly from the Mexican President to the Shah, relayed to the State Department by "[David] Rockefeller's office." Deputy Secretary of State Warren Christopher passed this information *to* the United States embassy in Mexico, which was not given any opportunity to confirm or deny; and the Mexican embassy in Washington, which denounced the message as fraudulent as soon as they saw it, some weeks later, was never consulted at all.

A daily press digest (plus copies of the Washington *Post* and the New York *Times*) is on the seat of the Secretary's limousine beside the intelligence report when he leaves home in the morning; and most secretaries, after they have worn into the office, tend to read the newspapers first. Most Foreign Service Officers have a habit of weighing what they find in the newspapers more heavily than what they find in the cables. William Culbert, deputy chief of mission for the U.S. team at the Multilateral Trade Negotiations in Geneva, reported the frequent irritation of his ambassador, a man brought to government service from management consulting, at the discovery that the FSOs on his staff typically accepted press reports of the progress of the negotiations even in areas where they had reason to know the newspapers had got it wrong. It is a conditioned reflex: over and over again, the Foreign Service Officer finds that congressmen, the White House staff, the assistant secretaries—all the people who are his bosses—look to the press to establish the parameters of policy and discussion.

"How do I decide what's most important for me to do when I come in in the morning?" said Charles William Maynes, Assistant Secretary for International Organizations in Carter's State Department, echoing a question he had just been asked. "That's easy. I read the Washington *Post*. Vance is reading the Washington *Post*; so is Carter. If it's in the *Post*, it's important to them, and that makes it important to me."

In part, this attitude represents a considered qualitative judgment. "Now and then," William Buckley reported from his time as a member of the U.S. delegation to the UN, "you would pick up from the cable something particularly illuminating, but far less often than one would expect. A careful reader of the Washington *Post* and the New York *Times* and *Time* and *Newsweek* and one or two of the foreign journals would be difficult to embarrass by leaning on knowledge that passed only under the eyes of the delegates reading the cables. What one does get is some idea of personal relations—what Ambassador X thinks about Foreign Minister Y; how Permanent Representative Z is spoken of at the staff meetings."

In larger part, however, willingness to accept press reports over the dispatches from the embassy and intelligence from the spies reflects the same bureaucratic syndrome that leads large corporations to follow their rivals in opening branches abroad. If you do what the other guy is doing, nobody can blame you for being wrong. In Washington this attitude, which need never be spoken, is part of the guiding philosophy compendiously subsumed under the designation CYA—Cover Your Ass. Moreover, the press (usually) does not have a policy to defend, which means that the evaluation of information is less likely to be infected with wishful thinking. Within the government itself, even the most apparently objective data—high-resolution photographs from satellites, for example—are likely to be "interpreted" in ways that support positions previously taken by the interpreters.

Throughout the foreign policy/security establishment in Washington, there has grown up a vicious game in which the counters are information. It is an atmosphere where information rather than knowledge is power. Information can be leaked at an appropriate moment, and everyone soon learns that the most effective way to get an argument to the attention of your boss or your opposite numbers in other agencies is to plant it in the press. Thus people who should be working toward a common purpose hoard information and release it reluctantly, only when it is most useful to promote what may be a more narrow purpose. The British Foreign Office finds that sharing secrets with the State Department not only risks leaks (which are what everybody worries about publicly) but may do no good, because the information remains in the sticky fingers of the bureau that first receives it and does not get shared with those who may have a more vital need to know. The crowded back-channels of Washington are not those that pass from the U.S. Government to other states but those that short-circuit the table of organization and get something directly to the attention of the Secretary of State or (oh, frabjous joy!) the President before the other members of the Department or the Interagency Group can perfect their defenses.

What is most surprising about the organization of the State Department, which we shall be considering in Part IV, is that it frustrates rather than facilitates the use of information from the field. The Department really ran U.S. foreign policy when Kissinger was Secretary, because Nixon was too distraught and Ford too insecure to fight him; and in 1982 George Shultz briefly made the Department the prime force in international affairs through a combination of intelligence, bureaucratic skill and Washington experience, aided by Reagan's sudden discovery that he really needed help. But institutionally the Department remained weak: when Reagan found he could get the help he wanted through Judge Clark—just as ignorant as this President and not quite so smart—the task of digesting the information that nourishes foreign policy decisions lodged once again in the bloated belly of the National Security Council. If the State Department is to increase its influence over time, the first step must be an improvement in the quality of embassy reporting and in the systems that move, preserve, analyze and use the information.

4

PERSUADING

Dr. Kissinger is expending this serious effort on behalf of the United States and many do not want his mission to succeed; and if this is not realized, the opportunities will be lost. Therefore, we want to be on record with the United States that we are more positive. . . . We are doing this in order to create favorable circumstances for the United States' efforts for peace. We appreciate the internal U.S. conditions also. We know if this did not succeed, it would be used to upset you in the United States. . . .

> Hafez el-Assad, President of Syria,
> to Henry Kissinger on the occasion
> of Syrian acceptance of truce lines
> after the 1973 war, as reported
> by Dr. Kissinger.

The dangers of vanity in a negotiator can scarcely be exaggerated. It tempts him to disregard the advice or opinions of those who may have had longer experience of a country, or of a problem, than he possesses himself. It renders him vulnerable to the flattery or the attacks of those with whom he is negotiating. It encourages him to take too personal a view of the nature and purposes of his functions and in extreme cases to prefer a brilliant but undesirable triumph to some unostentatious but more prudent compromise. It leads him to boast of his victories and thereby to incur the hatred of those whom he has vanquished. It may prevent him, at some crucial moment, from confessing to his government that his predictions or his information were incorrect. It prompts him to incur or to provoke unnecessary friction over matters which are of purely social importance. It may cause him to offend by ostentation or ordinary vulgarity. It is at the root of

82

all indiscretion and most tactlessness. It lures its addicts into displaying their own verbal brilliance, and into such fatal diplomatic indul-
gences as irony, epigrams, insinuations, and the barbed reply. . . .
And it may bring in its train those other vices of imprecision, excit-
ability, impatience, emotionalism and even untruthfulness. . . .

Harold Nicolson, *Diplomacy* (1939)

1

Among the great symbols of national history and unity, few were so re-
vered as the delicate two-part golden and jeweled Hungarian crown—its
top section a gift from Pope Sylvester II to the sainted Stephen I, first
King of Hungary, in the year 1000; its lower section given to King Geza I
around 1075 by the Byzantine Emperor Michael VII. Together with the
orb and scepter used by the Anjou Kings of Hungary in the fourteenth century, a fifteenth-century jeweled sword worn on ceremonial occasions by
the Hungarian Kings before and after the Turkish conquest, and corona-
tion robes that may indeed trace back to the handiwork of King Stephen's
wife Gizella, St. Stephen's crown was a holy object even into the days of
the twentieth-century republic, with a special cadre of "royal Hungarian
crown guards" on duty twenty-four hours a day to keep it safe, and a great
metal chest made in 1608, in which all the regalia were kept. Among the
items with which a Prime Minister was invested at the moment of his appointment was a key to the chest.

In November 1944, Ferenc Szalasi, the "National Leader" appointed by
the Germans after the more intelligent Hungarian fascists realized they
had backed the wrong horse in the war, absconded with the crown guards,
the crown and its appurtenances. In March 1945, they crossed the border
to Austria, heading for Berchtesgaden to join Hitler in the presumed last
redoubt, but the war ended before they could get there. Szalasi took the
crown to a castle near Ottersee, the home of a Baron Jeczenckesy, a
World War I calvary officer who had married an heiress from Montana.
They accepted the crown, the orb and the scepter, but not Szalasi, who
moved on to Matsee, near Salzburg, taking with him the chest with the
robes and the sword. On reconsideration, the baron and his wife turned
the crown and royal appurtenances over to the Bishop of Salzburg. Meanwhile, the American army unit that went out to Matsee from Salzburg was
approached by what Bela Herczeg, a Hungarian-American then working
for the OSS, describes as "forty men in shiny boots," who "wished to present the Hungarian National Leader Ferenc Szalasi." The sergeant in

charge called headquarters to find out whether the Hungarian National Leader was on our side or theirs. At first nobody knew, but eventually a lieutenant from Chicago whose father owned a shop in Budapest set everybody straight and came out to accept Szalasi's surrender.

Herczeg remembers that the bishop was reluctant to give up the crown, orb and scepter, but those were the days when the Americans were chlorinating the fresh water of the Salzkammergut: what the American Army wanted, the American Army got. Crown, orb, scepter, sword and robes were then transferred for safekeeping to the custody of Colonel Lionel Pereira, a foreign-exchange banker who was part of Allied Military Government in Germany. He stored it in the German National Bank.* Eventually, by means nobody seems to remember, the Hungarian relics were sent to the United States, to the vaults at Fort Knox, where they remained for more than thirty years.

From the beginning, the United States recognized that St. Stephen's crown was and had to be Hungarian property, but relations with Hungary were stormy. The first postwar elections in Hungary had given an absolute majority to one non-Communist party, which the Russians prevented from forming a government unless control of the police and Army were lodged in Communist hands. Purges followed, culminating in the execution of a Prime Minister and the elimination of all opposition to Soviet dominance. Though the United States had signed a peace treaty with Hungary in 1947, as part of a package deal that essentially recognized Russian suzerainty over Romania and Bulgaria but preserved the independence of Finland, there was no incentive for Washington to seek goodwill in Budapest.

No doubt the crown would have been returned to the government of Imre Nagy, who led a Hungarian revolt against Soviet oppression in 1956; but Nagy was ousted by Soviet tanks and presently executed (probably at the insistence of the Soviet ambassador, name of Yuri Andropov). The failed Hungarian revolution left a residue in the presence of Cardinal Mindszenty as a refugee in the U.S. embassy overlooking "Freedom Square" in the center of Budapest. "We'd always said we would return the crown," said Tom Longo, desk officer for Hungary at the State Department and formerly head of the consular section at the U.S. embassy in Budapest, "'when our relations had developed to an appropriate state.'" But the crown had been made for a saint, not just a king; it did not seem

---

* This story departs from the official version, which makes no mention of either Baron Jeczenckesy or the Bishop of Salzburg and claims that the treasure trove had been buried at Matsee. Herczeg was there, however, and the authors of the official version were not; and the U.S. Government of course would have reason to protect the Bishop of Salzburg.

appropriate to return it to godless butchers when the Cardinal of Hungary required asylum in the U.S. embassy.

In 1967, Martin Hillenbrand became ambassador to Hungary and began looking for ways to improve relations. Two years later, the embassy and the Foreign Ministry exchanged lists of thirty items, and at the very bottom of the Hungarian list was the return of the crown. "It was an awkward issue for them," said Herbert Wilgis, who was part of Hillenbrand's staff. "They couldn't decide whether to be nice about it or nasty—they could take us to the International Court of Justice, for example. But there wasn't much we could do about the crown. No U.S. President had anything to gain by returning it. And under Nixon a Hungarian refugee from 1956 was head of the ethnics division of the Republican National Committee."

Progress was made elsewhere on the list. In 1971, as part of Pope Paul VI's effort to renew the Church in the Communist states, Mindszenty was summoned to Rome. By then János Kádár, Nagy's successor, had become an authentic voice of Hungary to a degree that could not have been imagined fifteen years before, and the beneficial effects of his "goulash Socialism" had begun to impress even the still-bitter Hungarian exiles in the United States. As part of the general move toward détente, arm's-length negotiations reestablished consular services by each nation on the other's territory in 1973. ("Before then," Longo notes, "a U.S. citizen visiting Hungary could be in an automobile accident and spend a month in a hospital or in jail and nobody would know.")

Later in 1973, the two governments settled for $18.9 million the outstanding claims of the U.S. Government and American private interests for property nationalized, bonds unpaid, etc. Hungary threw into this pot its own claims for $3.3 million against the United States, including "Hungarian property lost as a result of World War II," which presumably left the United States a legitimate holder of the crown. In 1975–76, quiet negotiations resolved the emigration problem, which the State Department felt necessary—after being burned by congressional refusal to follow through on a deal with the Soviet Union unless the Russians permitted free exit from their country—before Hungary could receive the same trading status as all the other "most-favored nations." The other possible obstacle to such treatment was removed in 1976 when Hungary paid the United States the remaining $3 million of official debts assumed in the aftermath of World War I, joining Finland in that exclusive club. Shortly thereafter, embassy contacts at the Foreign Ministry began making discreet unofficial queries about the condition of the crown. It was part of the American hoard at Fort Knox, the embassy replied, and it was in fine shape: one of the duties of the Hungarian desk officer in Washington was an annual trek to Kentucky to look at it.

"In U.S.–Hungarian relations," said Janós Bartha, director of the Fifth Territorial Department in the Foreign Ministry (the bureau that manages relations with all the Western countries), "there was a long, long time— decades—when nothing happened. Then domestic situations in both countries changed in ways that made possible improved relations." As 1976 proceeded, however, both Kissinger and Gerald Ford had other things on their minds. Détente was a dirty word, and Ford got himself into horrible trouble in a televised debate by denying that Poland was under the thumb of the Soviet Union, a denial that reflected American policy and hopes more than it reflected the reality the inquiring journalist expressed with his incredulous follow-up question.

When Ambassador Eugene McAuliffe resigned the Hungarian post in the fall of 1976, Washington left the embassy to a *chargé d'affaires* for ten months. Among his other recommendations on departure, McAuliffe suggested that the United States return St. Stephen's crown to its rightful owners. The Bureau of European Affairs approved the recommendation, which was among the papers Zbigniew Brzezinski found on his desk when he became National Security Adviser. He put it aside to be part of a general review of relations with Eastern European countries.

Carter's choice for the Budapest embassy was Philip Kaiser, a labor economist, former university professor, Assistant Secretary of Labor for International Relations and special assistant to Averell Harriman when he was governor of New York State. Kaiser had served as ambassador to Senegal for Kennedy, and then as deputy chief of mission for David Bruce and Walter Annenberg in London. He had remained in London, first as head of Encyclopaedia Britannica there and then as a partner in the banking house of Guinness Mahon. Two of his sons had become outstanding newspapermen, one for the Washington *Post* and one for the New York *Times* in the great bipolar antagonism of American journalism (as perceived in Washington and New York). Kaiser had no particular need for an embassy, but he had organized Democrats abroad for Carter, with great skill, and he was something less than fascinated by the prospect of ending his days making deals in the private sector.

A Lincolnesque figure with a growling voice and the manner of an academic rogue uncle, Kaiser was also, unexpectedly, Jewish, something he called to the attention of the Hungarian authorities by attending High Holy Day services at the leading Budapest synagogue. ("The rabbi was so surprised, he almost dropped the Torah," Kaiser recalled cheerfully.) Among Kádár's accomplishments had been the restoration of religious freedom to Hungary, where the state helped support, among other things, the only Jewish seminary in the Eastern bloc. Billy Graham had made his first evangelical mission to a Communist country in Hungary, which is about one third Protestant, picking up there (and to some extent in Poland) the views that would later make him a laughingstock when he extended them to the Soviet Union itself. Participation in religious affairs was not a way to get ahead in Hungary, but it was not an absolute bar to advancement: the head of the Karl Marx Institute at the University of Budapest was a Catholic "believer" and a regular communicant. To people who cared about human rights, Hungary was clearly in the better half and maybe in the top quartile of the world's governments.

Harriman came to visit while Kaiser was settling down at the charming embassy residence, a mansion in the hills of suburban Budapest, with its own tennis court. Kádár, Kaiser and Harriman talked pluralism and religious freedom together. Kaiser looked around at what the United States could do for Hungary without spending any money, and immediately found the crown. "I thought that if I was going to have fun here—really have fun in this job—it would be great to return the crown while I was ambassador."

If ever there were an issue where the State Department did not have a domestic constituency on its side, this was it. More businesses were trading with Hungarian state farms and state corporations, but the crown had nothing to do with that. A considerable piece of the Hungarian refugee community was still unhappy with the notion of "rewarding" the Communists, and there was a key Hungarian in the Democratic ethnics division, too. Moreover, getting Washington's attention was no easy matter. Kaiser used Harriman to get to Vance, and Hubert Humphrey to get to Mondale. On a trip to Washington he sat down with Matthew Nimitz, then the Counselor of the Department, to discuss the situation in law. Nimitz found the question interesting, and determined that continued United States possession of the Hungarian crown, as a spoil of war, was not only unjust but unlawful. Vance listened, and agreed to bring the matter up at his regular Friday breakfast with the President, who asked for a "scenario." Wilgis, who had returned to Budapest as Kaiser's DCM, spent the weekend writing one. Kaiser took the results to Vance, who okayed it. Brzezinski gave a tentative approval—to be implemented as part of the general East European policy review. The review was completed in September, and the decision came down: return the crown, and complete the most-favored-nation agreement. An interdepartmental committee was formed to instruct the embassy, and Wilgis' scenario was accepted.

Everything took time. "This is a great example," Kaiser commented, "of how the tortoise really does beat the hare." The Foreign Ministry's Bartha analyzed the situation: "From the outside, this looked like a very simple question—just bring it back and put it here. But there might be side effects. Mr. Carter is not thinking of a one-term presidency. If he is running for election and bringing a crown to the Communist government of Hungary . . . this Kádár . . . It could have a negative effect. It would make an embarrassment in Congress. So they tried to minimize the emotional effect, and make the return a matter of people to people, not government to government [Wilgis' scenario]. A select delegation of Hungarians would receive the crown—church, trade union, military, party, all people rather than government. But everyone knows that people have a government."

The political considerations Bartha describes almost killed the project. Word that the crown was to be returned leaked from the National Security Adviser's office, and Carter saw a deputation of unhappy Hungarian-Americans—and told them (Carter was capable of this) that he was sorry but they were wrong.

Wilgis' scenario had called for hand-delivery by Vance or a special ambassador—Mrs. Carter or Averell Harriman. "You wouldn't have the crown of St. Stephen, the national symbol of Hungary, brought back by someone's deputy." Vance volunteered, then had to cancel because something blew up in the Middle East, and Kaiser postponed the ceremony. Vance grew more sensitive to the harm that might be done to Democratic interests by photographs of the Secretary of State handing the crown to János Kádár. Kaiser called on Kádár. "His ego control is so remarkable," Kaiser said. "He arranged to be on vacation the week Vance was here."

Negotiations were also necessary on the conditions in which the Hungarians would display the newly recovered crown and orb and scepter and sword and robes, and what would be said in the written material surrounding them. As excitement mounted over the recovery of what is not merely a national heirloom (which very few Hungarians had ever seen) but also one of the great examples of medieval Christian art, the Hungarian Government grew increasingly willing to thank the United States for preserving and returning it rather than grousing about its Babylonian captivity. The Hungarians, whose medieval museum in the bowels of the castle on the hill beside the Danube is perhaps the greatest such in the world, needed no lessons in how to display the crown and its accompaniments. But the wording of the signs that people would read as they waited to see their reclaimed treasure had to be hammered out word by word in three languages (including Russian; Russian is the official second language of Hungary, which every schoolchild must study; this is not the least of the reasons the Russians are so unpopular in Hungary).

Finally, the great day came. Cyrus Vance and his wife made a special trip to Hungary to escort the crown. In the presence of representatives of the three religions and assorted civic organizations, a presentation was made in the Budapest cathedral. The whole thing was telecast live, repeated in prime time, made available to Eurovision for dissemination through the continent (the crown would, after all, enhance Budapest's attractiveness to tourists). And the astonishing beauty of the artifacts, which had been lovingly restored in the United States for several months before their return (they had not been in fine shape: the desk officers had goofed), did the rest. Hungarians waited three and four hours in line, outside the city historical museum where the crown was housed, in the lobby, up the stairs to the very large gallery where the glass-enclosed relics were to be seen. And once they were in the building, they were surrounded by the signs that told not only about the crown and the paraphernalia but also about the fraternal feelings of Americans and Hungarians.

What's it worth? Who knows? "Diplomacy today," Bartha said, "differs from that before World War II, because of the tremendous high-ranking contacts. Heads of government, heads of state, ministers, special ambassadors deal with the important matters." And yet . . . The Danish Foreign Ministry likes to cite somebody's statement that "the ballet is good to sell the cheese." The little things really happen: the crown is returned, the ballet performs, the cheese is bought and paid for and eaten, people get used to visiting with each other, as they say in the Midwest.

Hungarian policy where vital Soviet interests are concerned is necessarily—though not permanently—controlled by the Soviet Union. But at a time when the Russians insisted that a ruble was worth $1.40, the Hungarians were giving 19 forints for a dollar and only 13 for a ruble; and four years later Hungary had joined the International Monetary Fund and was preparing for ever-increasing integration of its economy into the Western rather than the Comecon trading system, if the Reagan administration permits. When the commercial banks stopped lending to Eastern-bloc countries in the wake of Poland's flagellation, the European central banks, individually and collectively in the Bank for International Settlements, found half a billion dollars to help Hungary keep on track. Over time, it *does* matter how people of different nations think of each other.

2

Sol Linowitz observed of his experience representing the United States in the negotiations on the Panama Canal Treaty that "there's too little sense in the State Department of *why* things happened." Sir Edward Youde in the British Foreign Office went a cut deeper, stressing the difficulty people back home always have in understanding why—or even in realizing that—things didn't happen.

The focus changes. One can no longer quite imagine a society like that of eighteenth-century Russia, where "we find the Princess of Zerbst, mother of the Empress Catherine . . . writing to Frederick the Great advising him to choose as his Ambassador to St. Petersburg a handsome young man with a good complexion." One can, however, still feel sympathy with Count Anton Monts, who wrote after a thirty-one-year career in the German diplomatic service before World War I: "We diplomats of the old days who were trained by Bismarck lived by the maxim that the relation of courts to one another was of decisive importance. . . . Nowadays it is different. One usually obtains influence through the press, and that costs money, lots of money, or through the purchase of prominent . . . parliamentarians, for which one also needs a great deal of cash."

Whatever the method, the purposes are the same. In the appalling fake pagoda of the Japanese embassy in Canberra (no worse than the fake Williamsburg mansion of the U.S. embassy: the Australian capital is Disneyland), Koreshige Anami, a graduate of Harvard and Columbia, wearing a seersucker suit and a four-in-hand in the Australian summer, described a movie his embassy had just commissioned and supervised as part of the mission to shake off the last memories of World War II. "It's not a way of introducing Japan," he said. "It's about Australian-Japanese *relations*. The film has two Australian youngsters traveling in Japan and asking questions. Why are there so many people? Are they happy? There are no definite answers from our side. Finally the girl says, 'Do we *have* to understand this country?' I think it's very effective."

The task of the ambassador, everywhere, is to sell his country's positions and products, to improve the attitudes his hosts feel toward his government. Sometimes little things make the job miserably difficult. As part of the American feud with Ecuador over that country's 200-mile reserved fishing zone, Congress passed a law prohibiting the import of tuna from countries that made such claims. One of the few American investments in Papua New Guinea was a Starkist tuna plant, but Papua demanded a 200-mile zone. The United States has no fishing boats off New Guinea, and no quarrel with Papua—but the law was the law. Papua is not very important to the United States, both because it isn't very important to anybody except the Papuans and because the Australians carry the can in that part of the world. Still, this is one of very few Third World countries with multiparty parliaments, where governments change as the result of free elections: the embassy had a point when it urged Washington for some changes in the law that would have enabled an American company in Papua to sell its tuna in the United States.

A diplomat's problem is often in the home office, and usually he can do nothing about it at all. In dealing with the Japanese, for example, the prevailing school in Washington is usually what an attaché in Tokyo calls "the Black Ship syndrome: if you don't push you don't get anything. But when you push the Japanese too hard, they react emotionally." Something like the arrests of Hitachi and Mitsubishi executives on charges of industrial espionage may have an impact in Japan far beyond anything considered in the United States—particularly as it is common knowledge in the Japanese computer industry that similar practices could be and were not charged to many American manufacturers. "We occupy 85 percent of their foreign space," said William Sherman, DCM to Ambassador Mike Mansfield in Tokyo. "We have to keep explaining that fact, the importance of these relations and their fragility, to the people back home. If we don't hold up our end of the obligation, we destroy what the Japanese call the *giri*, the nature of the obligation; and it can do great damage to our position in Asia."

(There is also another view of the Japanese: "Tokyo speaks only the *langage economique, langage commercial*," said Brahim Ghafa, Algerian ambassador to Japan, after eight years in Tokyo. "If you talk politics, nobody listens. They don't want to hear about it. Even on China, South Korea, Southeast Asia. Even with the Russians: they forget the islands; all they want is the fish. It means that political problems here are very profound, not on the surface.")

Diplomats in the field feel that they get less help than they should from home simply because the State Department or Foreign Ministry doesn't know how to maneuver the craft through the shoals of its own government. "Very few desk officers and not many country directors," said Richard Dols, political officer at the U.S. embassy in New Zealand, "have Hill [congressional] connections. And they don't develop interagency connections, including the social connections they ought to have. An FSO abroad knows how to adjust; he's always making social connections with the bureaucracy of the host government that enable him to grease the wheels. You put the same man in Washington, it never occurs to him. He behaves like a suburbanite, goes home at the end of the day, never sees Jones from Commerce except when they get into a confrontation about something."

There are also times, of course, when the diplomat's job is simply to persuade the host government that what his government is doing is really legitimate and not to be changed by formal international proceedings. "When I arrived in London," Kingman Brewster recalled, "New York was refusing to let the Concorde land. There was a British presumption in favor of the American judicial process, and they had a kind of scornful patience—the Prime Minister would talk about it every time I saw him, but what he would say was, 'I hope you're doing all you can.' The French thought it was all crooked as a corkscrew—American protectionism. It was Arthur Hartman's dominant subject matter in Paris."

And sometimes you can't get help from home for rather special reasons. "When I arrived in Washington in 1967," said Frank Corner, who was later Permanent Undersecretary of the New Zealand Foreign Ministry, "we were in one of our economic problems. Those were the Vietnam years, and Lyndon Johnson was well disposed to us. He understood that our ability to be helpful to him was a function of our economic position. I began looking for things we could sell in the United States. Lamb was declining in the United States—the sheep population was going down a million a year. Johnson said we could go ahead and sell lamb, and he would hold the ring, see that nothing happened to us.

"Then Senator Bennett of Utah slipped a rider on a bill. I looked around to see who our natural allies were in the United States, businesses with New Zealand interests and the like. When Bennett introduced his rider, I thought of the Mormons—there was a large Mormon mission in New Zealand. I sent a message to the Prime Minister, asking for help in getting the Mormons of New Zealand to talk with their people in Utah. I got back a note: 'In New Zealand, we do not mix God and Mammon.'"

3

The man who goes abroad for his government must also be able on occasion to deal with situations for which he has no instructions and can't get any. Much of the most important work American diplomats have done, both before and after the improvement of telecommunications, has been one man's effort and one man's judgment. Kennedy sent Averell Harriman to Europe soon after his election "to talk," Harriman recalled, "with some of our more important associates. My relations with De Gaulle had been close. They were tremendously interested in this new personality. I was to inform people what the policies of this new administration were. I had no instructions—the President thought I knew enough about the situation." Sometimes people have to keep working though their instructions have in effect run out. "We used to get detailed instructions with some leeway," said Ernest Koenig, who was "project manager" in 1978 for the agricultural end of the Multilateral Trade Negotiations in Geneva. "Now we work quite independently, because of the confusion in Washington. Washington is preoccupied with a profoundly protectionist mood; there is even some sabotage. In the new economic climate, they are afraid." But the treaty was written, and approved.

Every so often, an ambassador must handle absolutely everything himself—even questions of peace and war. In summer 1958, the wheels came off the Eisenhower-Dulles treaty system for containing the Soviet Union on its southern borders. In Iraq, centerpiece of the U.S.-sponsored Baghdad Pact linking Turkey, Iraq and Pakistan, a military rebellion killed the pro-British King and his son and his Prime Minister and the ladies of the court, while a howling mob sacked the British embassy, robbed the ambassador and his staff of their watches and other valuables, and looted the buildings before setting fire to them. ("Boats were brought up the river," a subsequent British ambassador reported, "to take away the heavier pieces of furniture. . . . A book on Chinese jades was found by a Dutch engineer three years later on a rubbish heap a hundred miles south of Baghdad. Nothing else of the looted property was seen again.") A couple of American businessmen visiting Baghdad were lynched more or less by mistake (one of them may have been a CIA agent), and their bodies, together with those of the royal family and the Prime Minister, were dragged through the streets for photographers. Five years later, the severed head of the leader of this revolution was shown on television as a demonstration that his time, too, had come: the Iraqis have a kind of gift for political statement.

Lebanon had been in turmoil since that spring, with Nasser urging revolution from Egypt and Syria (then indissolubly linked as a United Arab Republic), infiltrating soldiers and supplies to help the Moslem and leftist tribes. The United States, considering all this a poor return for having taken Nasser's side in the Suez crisis of 1956, was willing to be of assistance to the highly pro-American, Christian-led government of Lebanon, and arms were supplied to the Lebanese Government forces. Meanwhile, Foreign Minister Charles Malik went to New York and secured a United Nations observer team to assure that the Syrians would stop helping the rebels. Secretary of State Dulles announced that if the UN couldn't help Lebanon, the United States would, with direct military intervention if necessary.

Following the revolution in Iraq, President Camille Chamoun of Lebanon cashed Dulles' chit. U.S. Ambassador Robert McClintock relayed the request on a Monday night, and early on Tuesday morning Washington informed him that the Sixth Fleet would be visible from Beirut by 2 P.M., with Marines to land at 3. He hustled to the presidential palace, where Chamoun was happy to see him but suggested that he should also talk with General Fuhad Chehab, commander in chief of the Army, who

93

had been less than ardent in seeking battle with the rebels for fear that his religiously divided force would split up.

"General Chehab," DCM Charles W. Thayer later reported, "was anything but happy. An armed foreign intervention, he told the ambassador, might well provoke his troops to join the rebels and resist the landing with force. Perhaps, he suggested, the ambassador would hold the fleet offshore until he could make sure of his own forces."

It then developed that McClintock had no radio contact with the fleet, and did not even know where the Marines would be landed. He guessed it would be Beirut harbor, and sent an attaché to the docks to tell the Marines to hold off on occupying the city for a while. But the Marines did not come in to the docks: they staged an amphibious landing on the beaches near Beirut airport, to the astonishment of large numbers of bikini-clad bathers and the joy of assorted soft-drink merchants, who were of course happy to accept dollars from these tourists, too. Meanwhile, the Lebanese Army massed on the road between the airport and Beirut—a road American television viewers would see often, in all its rubble-strewn devastation, in June 1982.

McClintock made contact with the navy captain commanding the task force, and urged him to come to the embassy for a consultation. The captain refused to leave his ship, and offered instead to send a helicopter for McClintock, who felt he could scarcely leave town at this juncture. He urged that no further steps be taken; the captain "answered that he was subject to the orders of the commander of the Sixth Fleet, who was under the instruction of CINCNELM, who was responsible to the Chief of Naval Operations, who in his turn was under the direction of the President of the United States. This sort of brass-bound answer torn from the naval regulations," McClintock added, "did not exactly fit the needs of an emergency situation."

The next morning the Marine brigadier general in charge of the ground forces showed up at the embassy. By then another problem had developed: President Chamoun badly (but, I mean, *badly*) wanted a Marine guard at the presidential palace. This was out of the question: no orders. McClintock then asked for a delay in the planned march to Beirut, to give General Chehab a chance to calm down his troops. This was reluctantly agreed upon by a nervous brigadier general (whose orders, cut far away, had said to advance at 10 A.M.). McClintock went to the palace, where he saw both Chamoun (who was convinced he would be abducted by the rebels if the Marines did not come quick) and Chehab (who said his forces stood ready to repel the invaders).

"It was an acutely awkward dilemma for the ambassador," Thayer wrote. "But it occurred to him that two could play the kidnapping game.

94

Later he admitted that it was a 'truly desperate expedient' but there seemed no other alternative. With all the diplomatic suasion he could muster he gravely suggested to the Lebanese Army's hero, Chehab, that it was his and the ambassador's duty to inject themselves personally between the opposing troops." Into the ambassador's Cadillac went Chehab, McClintock, the ambassador's personal bodyguard dressed in Turkish costume, and the ambassador's poodle. Between them, in effect, they persuaded the Lebanese Army to permit the "occupation" of Beirut by a battalion of Marines.

At no time during those twenty-four hours was McClintock in touch with Washington, except to ask for a message to be sent to the Sixth Fleet. There was virtually nothing Washington could do for him; and even if there had been, this was the kind of situation where the bureaucratic instinct is to hide. It is undoubtedly true that most of the positive work an ambassador does—especially a U.S. ambassador, probably an amateur, representing a country with an unlimited cable and telephone budget and a bloated government at home—must reflect policy decisions made by others far away, usually without consulting him. But in the lives of most ambassadors, there are going to be moments when what they say and do —and how they do it, and when, and sometimes why—can make a difference in the relations between nations. Of course, the situation in the Eastern Mediterranean in 1958 was such that the U.S. ambassador could speak with a voice of ultimate thunder; and perhaps one should note in passing that the Lebanese were a lot better off when that was true.

People far below the level of ambassador can make a difference. Kissinger tells of the invitation to visit China extended to the U.S. Ping-Pong team playing for the World Table Tennis Championship in Tokyo in 1971, before the National Security Adviser had made his trip to Peking: "Graham B. Steenhoven, president of the U.S. Table Tennis Association and manager of the American team, phoned the American embassy for advice. Without hesitation, the embassy's China specialist, William Cunningham, who knew nothing of our overtures to Peking . . . recommended that Steenhoven accept. Cunningham," Kissinger adds, "deserves much credit for his perception and initiative." Anybody who assumed such authority when Kissinger was Secretary of State, though, probably would have had his head handed to him.

Often, an ambassador is on his own because he can't rouse a response to a query, and this too has a long history in the annals of the State Department, tracing initially to the sheer difficulty of correspondence across the oceans and to the wildly inadequate staffing of the Department (in 1845, there were only five clerks to handle all diplomatic and consular correspondence for a major mercantile power). Robert Livingston purchased

Louisiana for Thomas Jefferson without the faintest shadow of authority to sign the contract. "For nearly a decade after the signing of the Treaty of Wanghia," Te-kong Tong writes, "the American commissioners to China were given no specific instructions. They were allowed to make their own decisions as they saw fit. Consequently, the United States commissioners to China were vested with 'large discretionary powers.' They were actually the policy-makers, although their decisions were subject to final approval from Washington. . . . It is interesting indeed to see that the dispatches submitted by the different commissioners were coincidentally based upon one common principle, which in later years was known as the 'Open Door' doctrine—that is, the territorial integrity of China and equal commercial privileges for all Western powers."

Townsend Harris as U.S. consul in Japan, in process of negotiating the treaty that really "opened up" that country to the West, went fifteen months without hearing a word from his government. A businessman, founder of New York's tuition-free City College and then a roaring alcoholic before he became a diplomat, Harris was to a later British consul in Nagasaki a hero of "marvelous tact and patience, of steady determination and courage, of straightforward uprightness in every respect." It is impossible to believe Harris would have done his job better under instruction from Washington.

In 1927, Henry Stimson was sent to Nicaragua during a civil war, with a general injunction from Calvin Coolidge to "straighten the matter out." Meeting with nearly all the sides, and there were many, he sold his "proposals of general amnesty and disarmament as a condition of American supervision of the election," a contingency which he had not cleared with Washington. Later that year, Coolidge sent his Amherst classmate Dwight Morrow to Mexico to resolve an ugly dispute between the two nations that had grown mostly out of the Mexican nationalization of American oil interests. A Morgan banker by background, Morrow was a sensational success as an ambassador:

"Speaking enthusiastically to all sorts of people in a version of Spanish peculiar to himself," L. Ethan Ellis writes, Morrow "endeared himself to the commoner by haunting the market places, to the wealthy by building a house at Cuernavaca, and to [President] Plutarco Elías Calles by trusting the President's own interpreter to moderate their early discussions. . . . Given *carte blanche* by his superiors, he flouted most of the rules, negotiating orally instead of relying on notes, using the telephone instead of the telegraph (sublimely indifferent to the knowledge that his wires were tapped), and trotting directly to any official, including the President, who he thought might be able to satisfy his insatiable curiosity.

"He entered his assignment convinced that threats would not divert

Mexico from her revolutionary course, already a decade old under the Constitution of 1917. Less apt to rely upon legal arguments than those more experienced in the Foreign Service, he sought by less formal means to balance Mexican exigencies and capitalist American desires. His personal charm thawed the somewhat suspicious Calles to a point where the President on their second breakfast engagement asked him point-blank for a lead into the thorny oil question. The Ambassador had a ready answer in the Texas Oil Company cases of 1921, in which the Mexican Supreme Court had held that later government action aimed at recovery of subsoil oil by private companies violated a prohibition on retroactive legislation contained in Article 14 of the Constitution. Cases attacking the Petroleum Law of 1925 on similar grounds were before the courts, and Morrow blandly suggested that he was 'expecting' confirmation of the Texas Company precedent.

"Offered this easy solution, Calles gave the judges their orders, and decisions emerged in less than a fortnight. . . . Calles was pleased, Morrow was pleased, Washington was pleased. [Secretary of State] Kellogg, indeed, suddenly discovered that 'it is best for Mexico if possible to deal with these matters on her own initiative without any pressure from the United States. . . .'"

The practical result of the deal was that the American oil companies kept the land on which they had already started drilling, but had to reapply for the rest. They sought further help from Washington, but Morrow was in charge, and he said, No. By then he was busily engaged in working out a compromise between the Mexican Government and the Roman Curia, which had closed all the Catholic churches in protest against government regulation (and economic expropriation of church holdings); he succeeded in that, too, temporarily—the churches reopened—without even discussing the matter in his dispatches to Washington.

In 1941, Ambassador William C. Bullitt negotiated out with the Germans the terms of the deal under which Paris was declared an "open city" —without instructions from the State Department (but probably with the okay of his friend Franklin Roosevelt, to whom he spoke fairly often on the telephone). Ellsworth Bunker was sent to Argentina by Dean Acheson after his retirement from the active direction of National Sugar Refining with instructions only to avoid reacting to provocations from Perón and Evita. (Writing of Bunker's accession to the embassy in Vietnam in 1967, Frances Fitzgerald described him as a "distinguished career diplomat," but in fact he was fifty-seven when he took his first diplomatic assignment; Acheson had known him from student days at Yale.) A taciturn Vermonter, who speaks only when necessary, Bunker "developed a program we called 'Masterful Inaction.'" Presently Perón lost the crutch previously supplied by his battle against the colossus of the North.

It should be added that these things do not always work right. Robert Klein, commercial counselor in Japan, remembered a negotiation in Thailand over the terms of some U.S. investments: "The Ambassador urged the Thais to give tariff protection to the resulting industry. The Thai delegates said that was thought to be contrary to U.S. policy. Which it was— but the Ambassador thought differently. . . ."

In London in 1944, Ambassador John Winant negotiated out with British and Russian representatives the terms of the subsequent four-power occupation of Berlin, and signed off on a piece of paper that omitted any mention of rights of access to the city. Robert Murphy, on roving assignment from Roosevelt, urged Winant to go back and get an access clause, and Winant blew up. As Murphy reported it, he said, "The September 12th agreement had become possible only because he had established close personal relationship with Ambassador Gusev, after months of patient effort, and had gained the Soviet envoy's confidence. In Winant's opinion, if we now belatedly raised the access question, this might upset the hard-won draft agreement and make further settlements impossible. . . . He would not do it. . . . A thorough check of the 1944 files has shown that Winant never communicated in writing with either the State or War Departments on this problem."

Ambassadors are most likely to go ahead on their own because they must do *something,* and Washington doesn't answer the query—sometimes because it is being processed through the endless round of consultations among the various bureaus and Interagency Groups, sometimes because it is being ignored. The desk officer may or may not know which of these polar opposites is the problem. In either case, the ambassador finds himself out on the limb, day after day, week after week. A common ploy in these circumstances is what the Navy calls a UNODIR—a cable proposing that the man on the spot will take certain actions or make certain statements "UNless Otherwise DIRected." Thomas Enders reports that as ambassador to Canada he made "an annual assessment with recommendations. I'd get back an informal comment, then go ahead and do what I thought ought to be done—always the best procedure in a large organization." But sometimes there is no way an ambassador *can* act without authorization from home.

Crucial opportunities may be missed because the Department's information system fails to flag queries from the field. Michael Samuels remembered from his time as ambassador to Sierra Leone the meeting of the Organization of African Unity which decided to declare the pro-Soviet Neto movement the only legitimate government of emerging Angola. Prior to that meeting, the OAU's position had been support for a triumvirate formed by Neto, the American candidate Holden Roberto (a not very adventurous adventurer based in the Congo, otherwise Zaire), and the highly independent leftist Jonas Savimbi. But Roberto had been observed too often living high off the hog of CIA subsidies—and Savimbi had accepted, presumably solicited, help from the South Africans. Nigeria moved the recognition of Neto, and the meeting split, 22–22. The Nigerians thereupon leaned on Sierra Leone to change its vote, and President Stevens, with whom Ambassador Samuels had become personally friendly, stopped by at the residence.

"I had done my Ph.D. dissertation on Angola," Samuels recalled. "I was the best-informed person on Angola in Sierra Leone—nobody could dispute that. So President Stevens consulted me. He didn't want to be out there supporting a nonviable option. What was the United States going to do?"

Samuels tried day after day to get some useful signal from Kissinger, who only a few months later would put his prestige on the line and lose in an effort to persuade the Congress that the United States should send arms to what were by then the rebels against a Neto government. No reply to Samuels' frantic cabling and telephoning was ever received, and presently Sierra Leone delivered its casting vote to the Nigerian resolution.

4

There is an unavoidable personal component in the relations between nations: a representative who is liked and trusted has a better chance of convincing his opposite number that what his government intends is acceptable.

Some people are hopeless, like Admiral Constant Juarés, sent by the Gambetta government of France to Czarist Russia in 1881: "Held in contempt by his own staff," George Kennan writes, "described in fact by Embassy Secretary Eugène de Vogüé as a 'farceur dangereux,' Admiral Juarés began his career as ambassador most inauspiciously. While marching down the corridors of the Winter Palace to present his credentials and observing on the walls portraits of earlier generations of imperial Romanovs, he inquired of the accompanying Russian chief of protocol, 'Qui sont ces magots?' [Who are these apes?]"

On the other side, a Neville Henderson by his anxiety to ingratiate himself with Hitler can destroy what small hopes there might have been of restraining the Nazis by words. Henderson had been British ambassador in Buenos Aires; he was chosen for Berlin, Telford Taylor points out, "incredibly casually, on the basis that Henderson was 'a good shot' and should 'have this reward' for doing his 'stint in South America.' " A localitis victim, an ambassador who does not faithfully represent the interests of his own country, can never close a deal.

The end result of diplomatic activity is highly impersonal, a document so carefully drafted—in more than one language—that everyone involved knows precisely what it means. Ernest Satow made the point that dealing with the Japanese was especially difficult because of "the absence of the definite article. . . . In English it makes a great deal of difference whether you say 'the treaties are sanctioned,' or simply, 'treaties are sanctioned,' but in Japanese the same form of expression does for both." UN Resolution 242, on what Israel should be expected to do to resolve the international conflicts growing out of the 1967 war, was fatally flawed from the start because the English version (accepted by the Israelis) spoke of withdrawal from "occupied territories" while the French version (accepted by the Arabs) spoke of "*the* occupied territories."

Kissinger, who could be cavalier about language—old-timers criticized him for his willingness to use Soviet translators in his conversations with Russian leaders—felt that negotiations could be endangered by too much precision; confronted with a disagreement, he might look for what he called "constructive ambiguity." This is the procedure by which legislation gets passed: as a member of the House Legislative Counsel Office once said when confronted with an impenetrable paragraph in a law, "It was one of those times when it was possible to get agreement on language but not on substance." But a legislative process implies a court that will ultimately decide in specific cases what the words mean, and the essence of diplomacy is that there is no such institution to rule between nations. "Understandings have to be very precise," said Averell Harriman. "You can't make a deal unless you can carry it out."

There are, then, two phases in a diplomatic negotiation: agreement and drafting. The latter requires control by the government, which will have to live with the results. The first simply cannot be achieved through either bureaucratic or political process. Dag Hammarskjöld defined quiet diplomacy as "diplomacy where you can nuance what you say with all the richness which is possible in a private talk, where you can retreat without any risk of losing face and where you can test out ideas, it being understood as only a testing out of ideas and not a putting forward of proposals." This is all but impossible to do with the Russians, for whom every suggestion of a compromise becomes an irrevocable proposal from which another concession can be extorted—deals can be struck with the Russians only when they have convinced themselves that they need it more than the other party to the negotiation. But it is the procedure that works when the end sought is mutual benefit rather than advantage for the next round.

"I never received an instruction that was worth reading," Lord Malmesbury once said. The moments of real despair for every diplomat engaged in a negotiation come when his Ministry finally does deliver itself of the positions he is to take—and he learns that they don't understand what the negotiation is about. Nobody can negotiate to a conclusion even in a bilateral relationship when every change of every detail must be approved by a committee back in the bowels of the government. An individual can keep asking himself about the purpose of the exercise (indeed, he must do so if he is not to go crazy); but the members of the committee inevitably have at least slightly different purposes.

"There is very little perspective," said Sol Linowitz, the gentle, shrewd lawyer who gave diplomacy a shot for Lyndon Johnson when he retired from Xerox and later returned to this fray to work on Latin American and Middle East matters for Jimmy Carter. (This second time around, however, he insisted on serving as a part-time dollar-a-year man, retaining an outside institutional base as senior partner in the Washington office of the New York law firm Coudert Brothers.) He was thinking of the anguished six months during which he and Bunker (who had been at it for years) put together the Panama Canal Treaty with a team of suspicious Panamanians. "The State Department gives you too many bits and pieces, too much compartmentalization. Craftsmen are not going to negotiate these treaties; you need designers. We grope for that. We have policy groups, the National Security Adviser. They're all trying to design. But what comes out is briefing papers and talking points—you shall say *this* to him. Whereas anybody who's really good knows you have to play it by ear, rely on your sensitivity.

"What worries me sometimes," Linowitz added, "is that I don't see the next generation of negotiators. Harriman is ninety, Bunker is in his upper eighties, Phil Habib has a heart condition, David Bruce is dead. Where is the next generation of negotiators, the ones who can look across the table and say, 'This you *must* do'—and it gets done, because you're known to be honest and you're their friend? We need these people, and I don't know where we're going to find them."

5

SPECIAL CASE I:
THE FOREIGN AGRICULTURAL SERVICE
OF THE UNITED STATES

> Nobody is qualified to become a statesman who is entirely ignorant of the problems of wheat.
>
> —Socrates

> I got a degree in agricultural economics from Montana State. I was from a wheat and cattle ranch in Montana before that. I worked one year for the state crop reporting service. I thought, there must be more to the world than Montana.
>
> —Fred W. Traeger, agricultural
> attaché, Copenhagen

1

In the endless war between the specialist and the generalist, the specialist has by no means won all the battles. Specialists in arms control have proved something less than useful, because they dance increasingly around a maypole of their impossible war, performing intricate and abstract steps that convey meaning only to those who have studied this subject so hard they have lost touch with everything else. If a deal is to be cut, generalists must elbow in and cut it. Similarly, the experts on environmental problems tend to become so absorbed in their language and their special solutions and their unlikely horror scenarios that they forget others will have to achieve the results they prescribe.

On the routine level, businessmen—who, in Milton Friedman's phrase, have their own money at risk—are likely to do more to promote trade between nations than the most active staff of commercial attachés. Still, a knowledgeable staff who feel good when a sale is made will generate the information that draws the businessman to the prospect.

Among this tourist's most vivid memories from five years in the bush is Gary Maybarduck, blond with a reddish-blond mustache, a graduate of MIT with a master's from the Fletcher School of International Relations at Tufts and a dissertation to write for a Ph.D. from the University of Minnesota. He was sitting with his wife in a guarded, rambling frame house with Somerset Maugham furniture in Port Moresby, Papua New Guinea, talking enthusiastically about his discovery that the Papuan airports needed new fire engines, about the cable to alert the American fire-engine manufacturers that got lost in transmission by the Commerce Department, about the consultant to the Papuan Government who found that several Australian airports were happy with their American fire engines but couldn't find how to reach the company and came to Maybarduck who had the information at his fingertips; and Oshkosh, Wisconsin, got $2.2 million of orders. . . . It may seem insufficient use of highly trained talent, and Maybarduck was indeed ready for other and better things to do; but it's real; and the people who don't find this sort of thing beneath their dignity do more service to the state than those who talk so elegantly about the abstractions of foreign policy and the personal quirks of political leaders.

2

One sector of specialized American representation abroad has been spectacularly successful: the Foreign Agricultural Service, which has changed not only the nature and substance of American trade relations but also the eating habits of hundreds of millions of people around the world. In 1970, the idea of eating a piece of chicken with the bone still in it would have been disgusting to a Japanese; German hausfraus shopping for cooking oil would have insisted on domestic vegetable products, and Danish cattle would have fattened just about entirely on good Danish grass. In the 1980s, Kentucky Fried Chicken flourishes in the Ginza and five hundred other locations in Japan, with bucketed drumsticks identical to those in America; a U.S. soybean oil product takes more than a quarter of the German cooking-oil market; and American feed grains give Danish cows a more interesting and nourishing cud to chew. They also give the United States, for the first time in history, a surplus in its balance of agricultural trade with Denmark.

Multiplied through the industrial world and the successfully developing countries, such changes produced an increase in United States agricultural exports from less than $7 billion in 1970 to about $42 billion in 1981. Since the early 1950s, the United States' share of world industrial and mineral exports has dropped from about 21 percent to about 10 percent; its share of world agricultural exports has risen from 12 percent to more than 18 percent. It is frightening to consider what the American trade balance would look like—or what would have happened to the American rural economy—without this burst of productive and marketing efficiency back on the farm and across the oceans. Indeed, the minor downward blip in the value of American farm exports in 1982 (to roughly $39 billion) was scary enough in its effects, not just on the farms but in the factories.

The expansion of agricultural sales is a triumph of American diplomacy. It has been accompanied by a vast improvement in the quality of worldwide agricultural statistics, now reported for the benefit of all by the U.S. Department of Agriculture in monthly bulletins that are the basic planning document for all governments everywhere. No one anywhere—including FAO headquarters in Rome—believes that the statistics compiled by the Food and Agriculture Organization are anything like as accurate as those from USDA. Fred Traeger, a blond, compact, neat agricultural attaché encountered in Copenhagen, remembered from his five years in Brazil that "the attaché reports and USDA publishes data quite different from what the Brazilians say or want us to say. They get upset, tell the ambassador—but we call it like we see it."

UN organizations are compelled to accept as true the statistics supplied by the governments of their member states, which are often guesses and even more often self-serving to a ludicrous degree. USDA statistics by contrast are gathered by the agricultural attachés at the U.S. embassies, who visit the farms, the trading companies and the processors, and put it together themselves. This improvement in the quality of the world's most vital information, as well as the growth in American agricultural exports, was made possible by a congressional decision in 1954 that a sizable Foreign Agricultural Service should be created, separate from the State Department, and that agricultural attachés in embassies should become employees of the Department of Agriculture rather than of State.

Congress reorganized American agricultural representation abroad as a by-product of "Food for Peace," Public Law 480, which established a program to dispose of the enormous surpluses that had come into government hands as a result of the anachronistic price-support programs postwar America had inherited from the Depression. Under the terms of P.L. 480, American food could be sold abroad for the local currency in the form of "counterpart funds" that could be used only by the U.S. Government to finance its activities (normally embassy activities, though the Fulbright

Scholars program was financed by these funds, and Lyndon Johnson once suggested to Indira Gandhi that India's immense debt for American grain could be put into a foundation—which would be administered by an American—for the support of higher education in India).*

Deciding which foodstuffs the poor nations of the world might need was clearly not a task that could be accomplished by FSOs, and because the rationale of the program was that the foreigners were really paying for the grain the personnel could not be housed in the aid agencies. The proper supervisor was clearly the agricultural attaché, and control of that cadre was transferred to the Secretary of Agriculture because he had responsibility for disposing of the surpluses. Serving attachés were given the option of moving their allegiance or taking a different kind of job in the State Department, and the overwhelming majority chose to remain FSOs.

All this had been to a degree anticipated. In 1951, the Agriculture Department created an Office of Foreign Agricultural Relations, basically an analytical service to process "agricultural intelligence." In 1953, a year before the passage of P.L. 480, the Department resurrected its Foreign Agricultural Service, a tiny institution Roosevelt had put to sleep in 1939, assigning its staff of nine to the State Department. Needing bodies, State began accepting people from the Office of Foreign Agricultural Relations as assistant attachés, and even as attachés, in the embassies. It was all pretty informal.

"I had a degree in animal husbandry from Virginia Tech," said William Rodman, a banker-like gentleman with long gray hair, who retired from FAS in 1980 after almost thirty years, the last seven of them as attaché (and counselor) in London. "I managed a purebred cattle farm for Admiral Lewis Strauss. There was an accident in the barn, I had a spinal fusion, and I couldn't be a farmer any more. I read in a little magazine called *Quick*, long dead, a section called 'Quick Predicts.' Said that the United States would be employing people to work abroad in agriculture.

"I drove to the Department of Agriculture and asked the receptionist who I was supposed to see about these jobs, wound up in the office of Eric Engling. He told me to write a letter, send a résumé, make an appointment, but I said it was a problem coming up from Virginia, I wanted to

---

* Some of this foreign currency holding was made convertible to other foreign currencies but not to dollars, a most peculiar arrangement because the only way one could get from Polish zlotys to Argentine pesos—a transaction that actually occurred in the 1960s—was to pass through dollars en route. At last report, in 1981, there was still something more than $75 million worth of convertible foreign currency at the Treasury earmarked for the use of the Foreign Agricultural Service, though virtually no one at the Department or in the Congress that authorized its budget knew that the funds FAS was expending were American taxpayers' money only by the most remote historical association, for the taxpayers had already spent it to buy surplus grain in the 1950s.

wait in his office and see him if he got free for a few minutes, and he saw me. We talked awhile, he said, 'You're on.' This was 1951.

"I left my wife and child on the farm and came to Washington wearing a blue suit and carrying a suitcase. The man I reported to said, 'You were wise to bring a suitcase. You're off to Canada on the eleven-thirty plane.' That night I went to a diplomatic reception in Ottawa. I was all alone. A white-haired man came over to me and said, 'Is something wrong?'

" 'Yes, sir,' I said. 'I'm the loneliest man in the world.' I told him what had happened to me, and he said, 'Well, my name is Louis St. Laurent.'

" 'My name is Bill Rodman,' I said. 'What do you do?'

"He said, 'I'm the Prime Minister of Canada.'

"I said, 'I'm the new assistant agricultural attaché. Sir.'

"The attaché was Francis Flood, the most senior man in the Foreign Agricultural Service. He left almost immediately, and I was the attaché. Fortunately, the first report was the annual livestock report—fortunately, because I knew something about livestock. Then Frank Bennett, the Canadian Agricultural Minister, came to my aid. Spent whole days with me, wrote my reports. One of the finest men I've ever known. Those were the days when you were flying the mail.

"You know," Rodman continued reminiscently, "I used to go with the ambassador, a great guy, Stanley Woodward, to meetings with St. Laurent. I'd be walking one step aside and two steps back, carrying the bag, as attachés do. St. Laurent would look up from his desk at us, and he'd say, 'Hi, Bill. Who's that fellow with you?' "

From Canada, Rodman went to Costa Rica, with a three-country assignment: Costa Rica, Panama and Nicaragua. He taught himself Spanish. "Our ambassador in Nicaragua was mad I was based in Costa Rica," Rodman recalled. "He demanded I come every three weeks. I went to the East Coast, flew to Bluefields. There were no roads. I took a dugout canoe up the rivers. The Indians were full of rice, had mountains of it. The ambassador asked me to sign off on a P.L. 480 rice sale to Nicaragua, and I wouldn't do it. Luis Somoza sent his Agricultural Minister with me to look at what I'd seen. He was amazed. He said, 'There's enough rice here to feed the whole army.' They got it out in DC-3s.

"The ambassador was pretty mad—he'd wanted the P.L. 480 sale on his record. . . ."

History: would Nicaragua have developed so violent a revolutionary potential if the Somozas hadn't found out about the Indians' rice and begun stealing it from them?

3

"When we were taken apart from State," said Jimmy Minyard, a Texas agricultural economist who became director of market development in FAS, "a lot of people stayed there, and we had to scour the hills. At first we got extension-service people who didn't understand international trade. The emphasis was on information-gathering, a lot of it for information's sake. There was an unbelievable number of people abroad who didn't understand how the size of the Argentine corn crop affected what the American farmer should do." But the authorizing legislation had listed among its purposes an aim "to stimulate and facilitate the expansion of foreign trade in agricultural commodities." As early as 1955, the new FAS had signed an agreement with the National Cotton Council "for research and development of global cotton markets," the first of what would become fifty agreements linking FAS with "farm-oriented nonprofit groups" representing the growers.

"When it started out," said David Hume, an egg and poultry man who served as attaché in Tokyo and London before becoming administrator from 1973 to 1977, "it wasn't all great. People were saying, 'Why are you doing this? How does this convey benefits to the farmers?' We had to have a disciplined, even an intellectual approach, and our disciplines came through contacts with the outside, the contacts with those who had something to sell and with potential buyers."

The turning point came with the arrival of Orville Freeman as Kennedy's Secretary of Agriculture. "I felt FAS should be a professional service," said Freeman, who remained in the trade world as head of the large consulting firm Business International. "I spent a lot of time on it, working in detail on contacts with the private sector. The thing I did early on was to give both sides confidence that they would have strong backing and, frankly, that the State Department wouldn't screw it up. The people at State had impressed on Kennedy that there had to be a unified political and economic Foreign Service. We had a meeting. I told Kennedy that the State Department had as much chance of getting this through Congress, through Wilbur Mills and Al Ellender and Richard Russell, as I had of being elected Pope. Kennedy turned to Rusk and said, 'There's your answer. Orville is right.'

"The first step," Freeman continued, "was to upgrade the attachés." To administer his expanded and improved FAS, Freeman chose Ray Ioanes, who had been in charge of food and agricultural matters for Lucius Clay in Allied Military Government in Germany and had later negotiated the deal by which Spain got wheat and the United States got permission to build air bases. Ioanes had been working on trade policy in the Department, looking for ways to put a spoke in the wheels of the Common Market's Common Agricultural Policy, which he correctly foresaw would become a source of barriers against American exports to Europe and subsidized competition against American exports to third countries. (The State Department was not worried about the CAP, partly because it was gung ho for European integration, partly because it thought the Europeans could never reach agreement on farm questions. Ernest Koenig, later chief economist for FAS, was then in Bonn as assistant agricultural attaché. "As often occurs," he said sourly, "the State Department people reported what they wanted to have happen, and I reported what was happening.")

Ioanes set himself three targets. The first was the recruitment of a cohort of attachés who would be both intellectually distinguished and "activist" as salesmen. "The attaché in a post like Germany or England or Japan," he said, "if he is a scholar, he must also be an outgoing person. He's dealing with jolly outgoing people, politicians and people who run farm organizations." But the scholarship came first. "We ran large public information campaigns about the jobs for attachés," Ioanes recalled. "We'd go to Texas A. & M. or the University of California at Davis, all the top staff, and make a speech. Freeman made himself available. Soon we had the professors and deans calling: 'We've got a good young guy here you ought to consider, and, by the way, he speaks Japanese. . . .'"

Second, Ioanes wanted money for the "cooperator" program, to pay some of the costs of direct sales promotion abroad and leverage other moneys from the farm groups themselves and from importers in foreign countries. The first appropriations for that purpose came in 1962.

Finally, Ioanes wanted an "educational" campaign to convince farmers "that there was more to agriculture than growing wheat and selling it to the government. High price supports had masked an efficiency that was always there. Farmers now understand—they had better understand—that their future rests on volume selling. It's been the biggest change in agriculture in my lifetime."

Under Ioanes and his successor David Hume, the agricultural attachés became the most highly educated corps of line officers employed by the United States. In the early 1980s, there were about one hundred and twenty of them, scattered in seventy-odd embassies, with a backup staff of six hundred analysts and programmers in Washington. The typical ag counselor in one of the larger countries was a farm boy in his forties or fifties, with a Ph.D. in agricultural economics, fluency in the local language, and a highly developed sense of marketing. "We are basically economists," said Larry Thomasson, who administered the attaché program after service in Brazil, Portugal and Japan. "Economists, and salesmen." Ag attachés are also people who are a little more comfortable out in the sticks pinching the produce and traveling in jeeps than they are riding in limousines to meetings and parties in the capital cities. "I visit the farms not only because I have to but because I like to," said Kenneth Murray in Ivory Coast. "Abidjan is unreal." The better ambassadors will go out in the jeep with the ag attaché every so often, to see what the country is really like.

In Vienna, covering Austria, Hungary and Czechoslovakia, the attaché was Nicholas Thuroczy, an energetic, white-haired man in a vested but racy checked suit. Born to Hungarian-speaking parents in a part of Czechoslovakia where the schools were taught in German, he spoke all three languages. He took a Ph.D. in agricultural economics at the University of California in 1953, and taught there before joining the Department of Agriculture in 1958.

On the day this observer visited him, Thuroczy had three things on his mind. One was the need to prepare his ambassador for a meeting with the Vice-Chancellor of Austria, to persuade him that a proposed subsidy to Austrian rapeseed-oil producers, to be financed through a tax on American soybean-meal imports, would not only violate the provisions of the General Agreement on Tariffs and Trade but would also be intrinsically a very bad idea. (The Vice-Chancellor was persuaded, at least temporarily.) Another was a two-day meeting in Linz for Austrian restaurateurs, who had been invited in Thuroczy's name to dine sumptuously off American turkey prepared by American chefs, both supplied by the U.S. Poultry and Egg Council, and to learn how they could profitably supply such goodies to their customers. The third was an impending visit from the Holstein-Friesian Association (based in Brattleboro, Vermont) as part of a continuing sales program for American breeding stock in Hungary.

"In agriculture," Thuroczy said, failing to anticipate the grain embargo Carter would impose fifteen months later, "East-West barriers are minimized. We are talking about food, which is such an important matter to the Eastern countries, they want to keep people well fed to keep them happy. They all have food priorities, need raw materials and technology, and can get them only from the West. Representing agriculture, I have easier access to people in these countries than my political colleagues do. And, of course, returning here after forty years—it comes in handy."

The FAS man in Brussels, at the Common Market, was Wayne Sharp, a round-faced, sandy-haired Texan who worked in white shirtsleeves and chain-smoked thin cigars. As a graduate student at Texas A. & M. in 1962, Sharp had won a national prize for the best master's thesis in econometrics. "A friend told me I ought to take a break between the master's and the Ph.D.," Sharp recalled, "and I said I'd do some research abroad if if was Argentina, Australia or New Zealand. Nowhere else—I was a Texan, didn't want to go anywhere else. In Argentina I met the ag attaché—I hadn't known there was such a thing. The program was six months abroad, six months back in Texas, then a research assignment briefly at the Agriculture Department. They said, keep on, we'll have a job for you. I got my Ph.D. at Michigan, did a study of trade relations between the EEC [European Economic Community, or Common Market] and Comecon [the Eastern-bloc equivalent]."

Sharp spent most of the seventies as agricultural attaché in France, where he felt he "made a contribution" to the progress of the Multilateral Trade Negotiations going on in Geneva: "I was involved in keeping the French from blowing the whole thing out of the water." Among the techniques employed was speechmaking to farmers' groups all over France—in French. Sharp's working languages are English, French, German, Spanish and Russian, which he needed for his dissertation, and which he does not like to see advertised around FAS, because he doesn't want to be sent to Moscow.

In Brussels, Sharp worked almost exclusively on "trade policy," which meant keeping up with everything that went on in the immense bureaucracy of an organization that, after all, devotes 70 percent of its revenues to agricultural subsidies. A couple of days a month he went to Strasbourg for meetings of the European Parliament, which has a large agricultural affairs committee. The phone rang incessantly. "It isn't like this all the time," he said pleasantly; "only weekdays." The issues with which he dealt were inherently difficult, because one man's export subsidy is another man's farm support program.

"The Europeans argue that we have our own subsidies," Sharp said, and shrugged his shoulders. "We have price supports for dairy, similar to theirs, tobacco programs, long-fibered cotton, peanuts. . . . We think our system is more neutral with respect to trade. We're going through a difficult period. Governments can agree on these lofty rules, but when it comes to implementing the rules, you touch people's lives. Everybody wants to test the rules. We're going to live up to them, use them when our trade rights are endangered. The Community is going to see how far they can go. We'll have to pick our cases carefully."

Actually, the United States gave up its challenge to the most significant of the Common Market rules in 1978, in the final phases of the Multilateral Trade Negotiations of the "Tokyo Round" to expand the General Agreement on Tariffs and Trade (GATT). The Common Market's basic device in controlling American agricultural imports was and is the so-called "variable levy," which in effect increased import duties on farm products to keep the price of imports at least as high as the average costs of producing such foodstuffs on the European continent (i.e., including Bulgaria as well as Germany). "I remember when I first heard about it," said Ernest Koenig in his Viennese accent. "I said, 'That sounds like the medieval notion of "a fair price."' They were *enthusiastic*; they said, 'That's right, you've got it.'"

This was a clear violation of the spirit (and in some instances, the letter) of existing GATT treaties, not to mention the economic principles of comparative advantage. Before the "Tokyo Round," the United States had never recognized the legitimacy of such arrangements, but in the protectionist climate of the late 1970s it wished to use similar devices itself in other areas (the "trigger price" system for determining tariffs on imported steel is spiritually if not in detail a "variable levy"). After fifteen years of fighting, the White House, if not the Department of Agriculture, was prepared to throw in the towel.

The battle had begun in the famous "chicken war" of 1962. Rapid development of feeding technology in the chicken coop had greatly reduced the costs of producing poultry in the United States, and exports of chickens to what were then the six nations of the European Community had risen from about ten million pounds in 1958 to more than a hundred and sixty million in 1962. Arguing that their chicken producers would gain the benefits of the new technology themselves in a very few years and had to be protected in the interim, the Germans persuaded their continental allies to triple, from 15 percent to almost 50 percent, the ad valorem duty on chickens imported to Europe. The announcement was made on a Wednesday, to be imposed at the dockside on Friday, which meant that chickens on the high seas, already contracted for by European importers, suddenly cost a third more than the contract price. "We saw our markets disappear," said Rolland Anderson, director of the Dairy, Livestock and Poultry Division of FAS. "Not only through the high prices, but also the uncertainty."

Under congressional prodding ("Senator Fulbright's state of Arkansas was a great chicken producer," Averell Harriman remembered with a sigh) and over State Department objections (was it really worth disrupting our relations with our most important allies?), the United States took the EC to the GATT court, a body empowered to assess damages and authorize an aggrieved plaintiff to raise *its* duties on products imported from the offender. GATT found injury to the United States and authorized $26 million of punitive tariffs, which the Americans could place on any items they bought from Western Europe. Lyndon Johnson's White House chose to slap the tax on European trucks, Volkswagen vans without seats, potato starch (to hit the Dutch) and cognac with a wholesale price of more than nine dollars a gallon. This last covered only 20 percent of cognac imports in the 1960s, but began to bite on the French in the 1970s, when inflation drove all cognac prices above the nine-dollar level.

Ever resourceful, the American exporters began shipping chicken parts instead of whole birds; and the Europeans responded by applying the levy to parts. Then the emphasis was placed on turkeys, which Europeans had eaten only at Easter and Christmas. Promotion campaigns in the European media, paid for in part by the U.S. taxpayer, made the *dindon* a dish for all seasons—building a better market for the European turkey farmer when the Common Market extended its levy to larger birds. Then the Americans sold turkey parts, which European processors began to use for new kinds of wurst—and again the bureaucrats in Brussels extended their levy. *Then* the Americans began shipping preseasoned poultry, hoping to escape European tariffs under the stronger GATT sanctions against interference with trade in industrial goods, and when that too was taxed at the border they went to *precooked* chicken and turkey parts, which was a considerably smaller market and which Brussels left alone.

Meanwhile, the protection of the variable levy led to overproduction of poultry in the EC, which began to subsidize exports to neighbors, especially Switzerland and Austria. The American share of exports to those markets had been about five eighths; by the late 1970s, it was down to one fifth.

In the "Tokyo Round" of GATT (actually negotiated in Geneva), the United States accepted the legitimacy of variable levies on fresh whole birds and seasoned chickens, presumably in return for concessions on other products; the Europeans agreed to exempt seasoned turkey parts and not to subsidize exports that "displace" the Americans from their existing markets. The duties on trucks, Volkswagen vans, potato starch and cognac over nine dollars a gallon were restored to their pre-1962 levels. This, in case the reader has been wondering, is the real substance of day-by-day international diplomacy. And the fundamental negotiations, clearly, were not in Geneva but in Washington, where the State Department, the Commerce Department, Treasury, the Special Trade Representative in the White House and the Department of Agriculture had to reach *their* agreement before any deals could be struck at GATT.

Among the problems of doing business this way is the fact that once the deal is made the peripheral players don't want to hear about this game, ever again. Two weeks after the treaties of the "Tokyo Round" came into effect, in early 1979, the Europeans introduced a new subsidy code imperiling American poultry sales in the Caribbean, Japan, Singapore and Hong Kong (where U.S. poultry producers had developed a good market in raw materials for *dim sum*, much of it then shipped back to San Francisco and New York). Nobody at the State Department wanted to hear about it, though what was at stake was a market totaling $165 million a year. When the subsidies reached out to seize Middle East markets, however—and Reaganauts succeeded Cartesians in the political jobs at the State Department—the American beast bestirred itself, and in the fall of 1981 the White House took the case to GATT, where it was still languishing more than eighteen months later.

4

The changes in American farm production and worldwide food consumption over the last twenty years have far outrun public perception of what's happening in the world. When American Military Government in Japan needed soybeans soon after the war, they could not be bought in the United States, which grew less than 300 million bushels a year and exported only about 10 percent of that. A triangular barter trade had to be arranged with Chiang Kai-shek's China, by which the United States supplied cotton to Chinese textile mills in return for soybeans shipped to Japan. By 1980, the United States was growing more than 2 billion bushels of soybeans a year, exporting more than 60 percent of the crop, and earning almost $8 billion a year from it. The biggest customer, incidentally, was the Netherlands, which took more than $1.25 billion worth of soybeans from the United States in 1979.

American selling efforts are exerted mostly through some scores of tripartite marketing schemes which bring together under an attaché's aegis the producer cooperatives back home and the foreign importers and processors of American farm output. Though plans and promotion budgets are formally proposed by the producer "cooperators" for approval by the Department of Agriculture, in fact the initiative for a specific project may come from some local importer, or from the attaché himself, who keeps an eye on the details of the local food markets—and stays in one post long enough to master them: normal terms are four years, with six and seven years considered a reasonable time at a post. Most often, the development work grows out of the Department's continuing intelligence operation on both supply and demand, at home and abroad.

"A guy calls up Washington," said Turner Oyloe, a tall, gray-maned, professorial South Dakotan (Ph.D. with a dissertation on integrated turkey production in Minnesota) who was agricultural counselor in Paris. "He wants to sell blueberries from New Jersey. The Department sends out word: blueberries are in supply, looks like prices are competitive. The blueberry guys come over, sometimes we pay their way, we can make travel money available. You tell them, 'Here are the users and the prices.' You go with them, send bilingual people, visit the process users, fresh users. You tell them about sanitary regulations, work out with them the key questions—should we fly over fresh, send by ship, can? Would it be best to send fresh and can here, because of taste factors? Is there a firm here with whom we can join in promotions? That's the way it happened with almonds. In 1970 we were net importers of almonds. In 1980, we exported $500 million worth of almonds from California."

More generally, it has been the agricultural attachés, living on the spot, who have sensed the political pressures on host governments to upgrade their citizens' diets—which means, less potatoes, corn and beans, and more meat; which means, in turn, feed grains, in which the United States has the dominant export position. They can also sense the extent to which changing socioeconomic conditions may change well-established dietary habits. It was the agricultural attachés in Tokyo, for example, who insisted that the Japanese were not so wedded to rice as the anthropologists and thus the diplomats thought, and would buy a lot of baked goods if the stuff was intelligently offered; today wheat, most of it from the United States, accounts for almost a third of the grain consumption in the Japanese diet—and Japanese warehouses are stuffed with price-supported surplus domestic rice.†

Activity is all but incessant. The Poultry and Egg Council alone stages about fifty tastings a year, all over the world, most of them for diners formally invited on embassy stationery by "The Agricultural Counselor of the United States and. . . ."

Fresh from the experience of a meeting attended by the Secretary of

---

† Selling off this rice is important to the Japanese, just as disposal of the "butter mountain" is important to the European Community—and selling off huge American commodity surpluses in the 1950s was important to the Congress that passed P.L. 480. In the late 1970s, the Japanese peddled rice at greatly reduced prices to Indonesia, infuriating American rice growers and troubling the State Department, which was concerned also about sales lost by Thailand, an important American ally. Protests about subsidized export of rice were folded into the general American complaint about Japanese trading habits in agricultural as well as industrial goods; Under Secretary of State Richard Cooper, a Yale economics professor when not practicing bureaucracy, once made a special trip to Japan to demand an end to unfair competition in rice sales. Meanwhile, in another part of the forest of American government, concern was growing about internal stability in Indonesia. Governmental and private corruption was eating into the living standards of the people; immense frauds at the state-owned oil company were reducing Indonesia's foreign exchange reserves. Soon after the Japanese had agreed to abandon their subsidized rice exports (which went especially to Indonesia), the United States offered Indonesia some hundreds of thousands of tons of rice on highly concessional terms, under Title I of the still viable P.L. 480. The effect on Japanese-American relations was considerable, but everybody was sufficiently embarrassed to keep the story out of the newspapers.

Agriculture himself, at which an $80-million-plus sale of 177,000 tons of beans to Mexico had been announced, John McGill, Jr., of the Michigan Bean Shippers Association (publishers of the *Michigan Dry Bean Digest*) explained that "when we sell to governments, just the agency's presence in or near a seller-buyer situation provides creature comfort to the customer. The attachés are very helpful. They aren't thinking beans all the time, but with our status as a 'cooperator' we can jog them out of their complacency, get them thinking about beans."

The cooperative program for soybean sales involves an annual budget of about $13 million, of which slightly less than $3 million is kicked in by FAS, with the rest evenly divided between the foreign importers and the American Soybean Association (which has ten offices of its own abroad, financed by special state taxes on farm output, each tax imposed with the approval of a farmers' referendum). Some of this money went to Unilever in Germany, for example, to help pay for the advertising programs that converted German cooks from domestic oils (and even olive oil) to the cheaper soybean product; some went to the travel expenses of a Japanese television crew that came to the United States to make a program on American soybean farms and farmers. Some went to events like the banquets for the Food Grains Club of England, which meets regularly in the ambassador's private dining rooms on Grosvenor Square, or the annual reception and seminar in Bonn for German swine feeders.

More aggressive partying may be done by host-country nationals on the FAS payroll: "When one of our locals goes to Hokkaido," Larry Thomasson said reminiscently, remembering early promotions of soybean-consuming feedlots in Japan, "he never gets to bed before 1 A.M.—he's out every night drinking sake with the boys. It's all work." Of the $81.7 *billion* value of the American soybean crop in the 1970s, no less than $43 billion was exported, at a promotion cost to the U.S. Government of $17.5 million.

"On wheat, which is one of the oldest programs," said Jimmy Minyard, head of market development, "we have the advantage of five different kinds of wheat that work with five different kinds of product. Our position is that if you can introduce doughnuts, introduce them—takes a lot of flour, some shortening, export products. And outside Europe it's usually governments that buy the wheat, which makes a joint government-industry program very useful—the government buyer relates to the embassy and the attaché, and the industry is there to sell." Some FAS programs flourish in countries where the United States has no other significant commercial or diplomatic relations—an FAS-sponsored training program for rice-grading (suitably, at Rice Institute in Houston) helped boost Iraqi imports of U.S. rice from 9,000 tons in 1973–74 to 148,000 tons in 1978–79.

Sometimes the initiative is highly personal. Between tours in Australia and London, William Rodman served as agricultural attaché in Mexico, a particularly free-form job because Mexico is not a signatory of the General Agreement on Tariffs and Trade and can manage its food imports and subsidize its food exports pretty much as it pleases. Rodman contributed technical assistance to the Mexican effort to introduce irrigated farming for fruits and vegetables, and lived through the first of what became a series of tomato wars, as Florida growers protested competition from south of the border. Among the major American exports to Mexico was breeding stock for cattle ranches, but it was all being done ad hoc. Rodman found that the United States had never taken a booth in the annual Mexican livestock show.

"I sent in a recommendation," he recalled, "one, that we take the biggest booth in the fair, and give Mexican importers CCC credit [low-interest loans] for breeding cattle; two, that Lyndon Johnson give President Díaz a prize bull from his own ranch. I never got a reply.

"We were selling a lot of nonfat dried milk to Mexico, and the purchaser wanted a week in Washington without his wife. I went up with him. There was a weekend in between, and I went to see my mother. I came back, found my mailbox stuffed with messages—the Department wants you, the President wants you. I'd been around too long for that; I ignored it. Came in at nine the next morning, and found somebody waiting for me, from the White House.

"When I got there, Pop Watson took me right into the Oval Office. Johnson said, 'You're the fellow who thinks I should give a bull to the President of Mexico?'

" 'Yes, sir.'

"He flicked the toggle switch on his desk that plugged him into his ranch, and he talked to Dale Malechek, who ran the place for him. 'Dale. Do we have a bull good enough to give to the President of Mexico?' Then he put his hand over the mouthpiece, and he said to me, 'If I give you one, can you sell five for me?'

"These are the things that happen," Rodman added, "in the life of a little farm boy who becomes an agricultural attaché. . . ."

5

Most FAS selling activity has been routinized. In Britain, FAS has an annual "flying circus" that sets up exhibits and tastings in hotel ballrooms in three cities every spring, three others every fall. The computer at the embassy has six and a half thousand names and addresses of significant

British importers of American foodstuffs (U.S. agricultural sales to Britain run almost $2 billion a year), and invitations to functions are sent out by the machine, breaking the lists into regions. Since 1978, FAS has operated "agricultural trade offices" in a steadily growing number of the larger centers to offer one-stop service, housing for the cooperator groups and a permanent Agriculture Department staff.

The most routine and at the same time most controversial activities relate to health-and-safety requirements, which can be manipulated to protect local farmers against American competition. Part of the agricultural attaché's job is to protest what seems to him the abuse of such regulations; another part may be to convince the American producer (who *always* sees discrimination at work) that the foreigners have a case. U.S. potatoes cannot be exported to Britain, for example, because there is an American potato blight that does not exist in the United Kingdom, and its importation cannot be risked. California citrus producers complained bitterly for years that Japanese tests for pesticide residues set tolerance levels lower than what was measurable. "I arranged," Larry Thomasson recalled from his days in Tokyo, "for a California chemist to come over and work in their labs for a week. He was very impressed: sophisticated equipment. Damn right they could measure to those tolerances—and they did."

When the Europeans alleged misgraded and contaminated wheat in American shipments in the mid-1970s, the agricultural attachés verified the validity of their complaints and saw to it that the argument became one between the Department of Agriculture and the U.S. shippers, rather than between governments. On the other hand, the Department got caught in the middle when Governor Jerry Brown decided (wrongly) that the environmentalists were more important than the farmers to his political future, and briefly prevented aerial spraying of a medfly infestation in California's Santa Clara County. When the infestation spread and the Japanese banned the importation of California citrus, the attachés found themselves protesting an action for which, professionally, they felt considerable sympathy.

The United States, too, of course, has health-and-safety standards for agricultural imports, which foreign farmers *always* consider an unfair means of protecting U.S. producers. Only three countries are now licensed to export poultry to the United States, and as part of the campaign against hoof-and-mouth disease there is an absolute ban against fresh, chilled or frozen meat from Africa, Asia, Latin America, and the Common Market. (Cooked meats are okay.) "If some way were found to cure hoof-and-mouth disease," said Ernest Koenig thoughtfully, "we would be highly embarrassed."

The worst dispute came to a head in 1967, with the passage of the

Wholesome Meat Act, which applied national inspection standards in what had been an area of state regulation, and virtually eliminated American imports of Australian beef. Rodman remembered arriving to take the post of agricultural attaché in Australia in the middle of this flap, and being greeted at the airport by a lady reporter from a Sydney newspaper whose first question was, "Why don't Americans like our meat?"

For years, the outcome of this confrontation looked like a triumph for both sides. Unable to change U.S. law and needing the export sales, the Australians modernized their meat-packing industry. (There are other places to sell, of course: the Soviet Union is always an eager buyer, but only at very low prices. Harold Sanden, who had come to diplomacy from meat-packing, ran into Russian purchasing agents while he was U.S. agricultural attaché in New Zealand, and recognized in them the lineaments of many cheap-jacks back home: "The New York market would call them gravediggers: they come and clean up the market when it becomes a case of sell-it-or-smell-it.") The United States, full of feedlots for the production of marbleized prime and choice meats, needed infusions of Australian "industrial grade" grass-finished beef for the burgeoning hamburger chains. Beef imports to America are controlled by quota rather than tariff, the U.S. advocating but not practicing free trade in agricultural produce, and the Australians quickly won 51 percent of the entire quota, which meant that 20 percent of their production crossed the Pacific. And they were able to advertise around the world that sanitary standards for Australian beef "exceeded U.S. requirements."

The United States policed the Australian meat-packing industry through the services of three inspectors, who worked for the U.S. agricultural attaché in Canberra and visited the meat-packing plants with their Australian opposite numbers, awarding the USDA seal on completion of the inspection. "There's a memo of agreement between the U.S. and Australian governments," said agricultural attaché Harlan Dirks. "It's not a 'diplomatic' matter—it's a relationship of meat inspection service to meat inspection service, a technical exchange. I've never even seen the agreement. We'd be pretty perturbed if we heard the Australian Government had complained about anything through diplomatic channels." At least on second thought, the ambassador is usually content. Speaking of Larry Thomasson's pesticide residue problem, William Sherman, DCM for Ambassador Mike Mansfield in Tokyo, noted that "Fred Dent when he was STR [Special Trade Representative] wanted the ambassador to raise hell. But diplomats don't terribly much enjoy this sort of thing. It requires learning a lot about things you don't particularly want to learn about."

Then the system went blooey in 1981, to the horror of both governments, both agriculture departments, both meat inspection services and the American fast-food chains. Horsemeat and kangaroo meat were found in shipments of Australian beef. Unlike the U.S. Department of Agriculture in Japan, the Australian Ministry did not fight the consequent temporary ban, but began grimly digging in to determine which meat packers were responsible, and whether they had corrupted one or two meat inspection services.

6

World trade in agricultural products long ago made national food policies and marketing practices into political matters of the greatest urgency and complexity. A threat of hunger, or of rapid increases in domestic food prices, concentrates a politician's mind wonderfully.

The international division of labor introduced in the colonial era produced a tendency toward the allocation of cropland in the warm climates away from local food needs and toward exportable commodities. Population, meanwhile, gravitated toward the entrepôt cities where metropolitan attractions were more or less available, a movement masked in its agricultural impact by the improvement in general health levels that created the "population explosion." The dominant political philosophy among the governments that succeeded the colonizers was Peronism, a doctrine that calls for cheap bread and rhetorical circuses for the shirtless ones in the cities (who can, after all, overthrow governments), paid for by squeezing the countryside.

In countries where a food product was the commanding height of the economy (Ghana's cocoa is the most obvious example), government seizure of the marketing rights and profits devastated the farms and reduced output; in countries where an effort was made to reduce dependence on an exported commodity and work toward agricultural self-sufficiency, governmental incompetence and counterproductive attitudes soon forced a return to export crops. The best statement of what went wrong is still Fidel Castro's famous three-hour speech on why the Cuban economy had collapsed under the burden of his policies.

The first food trade problem, then, is the sustenance of the cancerous cities of the Third World. Clearly, they should be fed by their own hinterlands—and they could be, if the average yield per acre in their countries' farms could be lifted to, say, one third the European level. This has happened along the Pacific littoral in the countries most heavily under American influence—Thailand, the Philippines, Taiwan, South Korea, not to mention Japan—and the political reverberation of their success is an untold story, the reason why the simplifications of Marxism have lost their appeal in the Third World though not (of course) among the well-fed academics of the industrial nations. From the panic of 1974, when shortfalls in grain production raised a specter of starvation through great swatches of the Third World, there survives a world grain reserve program administered by a small bureaucracy housed in Rome but kept separate from the monstrously overstaffed structure of the Food and Agriculture Organization in the same city. This "Food Bank," suggested by Henry Kissinger off the cuff without consulting the Department of Agriculture, limps along on a budget somewhat reduced by the failure of the OPEC nations to make the large contributions they committed to it. Efforts to get the intended beneficiaries to complain about OPEC's welshing have so far been unavailing.

In the aftermath of OPEC's success with oil, producers of various primary commodities—especially agricultural commodities—attempted to set up similar monopolistic alliances. Those were heady days for the world's intellectuals, consumed by the *Schadenfreude* of the Club of Rome, predicting the end of affluence for Western society. One after another, the cartels collapsed—sugar, coffee, cocoa, tea, tin, bauxite, copper—with enormous losses to the countries that had sought to organize them (and, incidentally, to the Japanese, deeply influenced by currents of opinion in Western intellectual life, who busily stockpiled years of supply of sugar and soybeans at the very top of the market.)

In this situation, however, the poor countries have a case. As long ago as 1956, Dag Hammarskjöld in his annual report to the United Nations stressed that "a change of only 5 percent in their average export prices is about equal to the entire annual inflow of private and public capital and government grants to underdeveloped countries." Excepting only the arms control discussions, the long-running negotiations on commodity price stabilization agreements are the most important venture in diplomacy in the late twentieth century. They have been disappointing in many ways. When commodities are rising in price, the producers hold out for unrealistically high floors (at which the stabilizing authority would purchase to clear the market); when prices are falling, the consuming nations demand unrealistically low ceilings to be maintained by sales from the stockpile.

The problem is intrinsically very difficult. Markets equilibrate supply and demand much more efficiently than governments or international bureaucracies. The effect of setting cocoa prices too high was to make it profitable for the Brazilians to plant this slow-yielding crop—and by the publication date of this book, Brazil will have passed Ivory Coast as the largest producer of cocoa. High sugar prices switched American soft-drink manufacturers to corn syrup. The big run-up in coffee prices in the mid-

1970s apparently changed American beverage habits permanently: half a dozen years later, with prices down two thirds from their peak, American coffee consumption still has not returned to its pre-1975 levels.

As both producers and consumers, *people* are not parties to these treaties, and governments cannot that closely control the economic behavior of mere people. If in fact a commodity can be grown and sold profitably in quantity at prices below the support price, commodity price stabilization agreements will collapse under the weight of accumulated surpluses. Julius Nyerere of bankrupt Tanzania has been complaining in every international forum that his country cannot pay its way because the price of cotton has fallen too low in the international markets—but American farms would be bankrupt, too, if they had stuck with cotton instead of shifting to soybeans. Nyerere's failure to understand that markets are information systems, and that the information they provide is crucial to the management of a rural economy, has crippled his people's efforts to improve their lot. It does neither him nor them any good to denounce reality and demand a New International Economic Order in which stubborn failure will be rewarded. Still, some means of assuring poor nations of a minimum return on their exported produce are surely worth attempting, and can be made to work if the producers understand that what they have is a bridge over the fast-running waters of necessary change, not a ladder to the stars.

Agricultural trade among developed nations is a bedeviling subject. Growing worldwide dependence on American food exports and growing U.S. farm dependence on foreign sales (by 1980, a quarter of U.S. cropland raised food for export) make the problem particularly upsetting for the United States. American farmers and their congressmen expect their government to knock down barriers that deter the export of American foodstuffs, and to force elimination of foreign government subsidy to exports that cut Americans out of markets. American consumers and their congressmen expect their government to see to it that food prices do not go up at home because foreigners are bidding edible commodities away from the normal channels of trade. U.S. politicians are always tempted to regard access to American food exports as a privilege that should be denied the truly naughty. Dealing with food aid and commodity price agreements, the State and Agriculture departments are likely to be on the same side, with the Treasury fussing in the corner about expenses and Congress looming as a budgetary process in the wings. Given a serious shortfall in the soybean crop or a Soviet invasion of Afghanistan, however, the executive departments begin to pull in different directions; the White House takes over, and acts in haste to repent at leisure.

Washington is not alone in short-sighted reactions to unexpected agricultural developments. Moscow must now view the Soviet grain purchases of 1972 as a case of short-term cleverness that had dumb long-term consequences. Prior to 1972, shortfalls in the Russian grain harvest had led to the premature slaughter of herds and a reduction in Russian meat consumption. This had done Khrushchev no good, and Brezhnev's Politburo decided that it could avoid similar consequences by exploiting the susceptibility of a free market to monopsonistic purchasing. Instead of advertising its total demand for grain imports, which might have led to negotiations giving substance to the empty term "détente," the Soviet Union sent purchasing agents to the five large American grain dealers with offers to each to buy a large but not destabilizing quantity from U.S. stores (which were then quite large). The dealers all sharpened their pencils to win so large an order—and then the Russians hit all the bids.

It became necessary (and it really was necessary) for Washington to subsidize these exports to keep the grain trade from collapsing in bankruptcy as market prices rose far above the price in the Russian contracts. The prosperity of the farmers was a great help to Nixon in the 1972 campaign, and the subsequent negotiations with the Soviets to see that nothing of this sort ever happened again helped the American merchant marine (the United States was able to secure an agreement that half the grain exports to the Soviets in future years would be carried in American bottoms), but otherwise the results were not such as to make anybody very happy.

Seven years later, when the Russians invaded Afghanistan, the apparent dependence of the Soviet Union on American grain exports tempted the Carter administration to embargo all shipments over and above the minimum specified in the treaty that followed the 1972 fiasco. This was done over dead bodies in the Department of Agriculture (especially the FAS), and done in what must be described as the typical half-assed manner of that administration. As late as four o'clock in the afternoon of the day the embargo was announced, the Department was authoritatively informed from the White House that no such step would be taken. Then the President got on national television in prime time to tell the world that he was striking at the breadbasket to punish the Russians for picking on their poor, weak neighbors.

The Russians were in truth disturbed by Carter's actions. I was in the Soviet embassy in Washington not long after, being informed by the deputy chief of mission, Vladilen Vasev, that I would not be welcome in the Russian Foreign Ministry and indeed would not be given a visa to enter the Soviet Union, because reporting—like diplomacy—is a political act, and the Soviet Union had just received such striking evidence that it could not trust American diplomacy or reporting. Learning that my next appointment of the day was with Dale Hathaway, Under Secretary of Agriculture for International Affairs, Vasev praised Hathaway as "a *great* diplomat. When you meet him," he added, "look at his trousers and see how they are worn away at the knees by the time he spent begging us to buy the grain. . . ."

But the instinct for the breadbasket is not the instinct for the jugular. The practical effect of Carter's decision was less to punish the Russians than to reward the Argentinians, who made up much of the shortfall in planned Russian grain purchases, at premium prices. In the end, the Russians became *less* dependent on U.S. grain, and thus marginally less sensitive to U.S. views of their international behavior—but only at the price of wide publicity for the failures of their agricultural policies.

Long-lasting and perverse effects were produced also by the Nixon administration's embargo on all American soybean exports in the wake of a weak crop in 1974. Here the proximate cause was the Japanese proclivity to panic at the smell of trouble. Foreseeing a possible shortage of soybeans, an essential in the Japanese diet and the foundation of Japan's beef industry, the Japanese came into the American market to stockpile, further escalating what would have been in any event a major increase in prices. But prices continued to rise despite the embargo, because U.S. speculators stocked up in anticipation of foreign sales when the embargo was lifted, and the long-term effect was to put Brazil in the soybean business with a Japanese bankroll, creating competition for U.S. producers in the Common Market as well as the Far East.

In all these matters—food aid, commodity stabilization agreements, tariff negotiations, quotas, embargoes—the State Department is theoretically the "lead agency" with the "action responsibility." Practically, the Department of Agriculture must sign off on food aid, the Treasury must be placated in commodity stabilization, the office of the U.S. Trade Representative in the White House supersedes State in the decision phase of tariff negotiations, Congress establishes quotas, and the President himself takes the dramatic action of embargoes.

Clearly, some division of labor is necessary: the State Department could not possibly staff the agricultural posts as strongly as FAS does. "After serving ten years overseas," says Larry Thomasson, "I look at an embassy as a small U.S. government, with the usual ratio of stars and incompetents. I don't buy the idea that you send only highly capable people abroad. I don't buy the idea that an FSO is going to acquire agricultural capabilities. You don't get to be DCM or ambassador that way. Most of us are farm boys. We bring a dedication and a motivation they just don't have." By the same token, authority to take decisions in international commodity policy cannot be left with the farmers. "We strongly defend the interests of American agriculture," Thomasson continued—but those are not the only interests the U.S. Government must defend.

To say that the State Department has been unhappy with this situation would understate the facts, and for years the Department, controlling the titles at the embassies, refused to give FAS employees a rank higher than "attaché." This not only denied the FAS people invitations to the best diplomatic parties, it impeded their access to high-ranking officials of the host government, a situation particularly galling in countries where other nations' embassies were staffed with agricultural "counselors" or even (at the British embassy) "ministers." In 1978, the Department of Agriculture stopped negotiating this dispute with the State Department, and went to the Congress. The Carter administration, seeking jobs for deserving reformers, had politicized the top level of FAS, appointing as administrator Thomas Hughes (Orville Freeman's former political aide and Walter Mondale's college roommate), as assistant administrator Thomas Saylor (from Hubert Humphrey's Senate staff). Between them, they had more than enough clout to get the Congress to include in the Agricultural Trade Act of 1978 a requirement that at least ten of the attachés in the more important posts be given the rank and title of "counselor."

Unable to lick 'em, the State Department now decided to join 'em. The Foreign Service Act of 1980, mostly written at State, considerably improved the pay and retirement benefits of FSOs—and instructed other departments of government to give their employees at the embassies the opportunity to take FSO status while remaining on their home department's payroll and subject to their home department's instructions. Most of the agricultural attachés and counselors made the move. What this peculiar bureaucratic anomaly will mean in the future, nobody knows; it may be fair to say nobody has thought much about the question. But in the manure of this personnel procedure we may be nurturing the seeds of an intelligent coordination, something better than either the "secondment" system of the Europeans or the rigidly divided U.S. embassy of the past.

III

People

6

PASSPORTS TO DIPLOMACY

An ambassador should be a trained theologian, should be well-versed in Aristotle and Plato, and should be able at a moment's notice to solve the most abstruse problems in correct dialectical form: he should also be expert in mathematics, architecture, music, physics and civil and canon law. He should speak and write Latin fluently and must also be proficient in Greek, Spanish, French, German and Turkish. While being a trained classical scholar, a historian, a geographer and an expert in military science, he must also have a cultured taste for poetry. And above all he must be of excellent family, rich, and endowed with a fine physical presence.

—Ottaviano Maggi (1596)

Let me control personnel, and I will ultimately control policy. For the part of the machine that recruits and hires and fires and promotes people can soon control the entire shape of the institution, and of our foreign policy.

—George F. Kennan (1970)

1

They are neither a motley nor a class, the world's diplomats. Some are the children of the rich, drawn by the graces of the life—but Career Ambassador Philip Habib is a dese-dem-an'-dose Brooklynite from a Lebanese immigrant community, whose college degree was from the University of Idaho and who rose from private to captain in the U.S. Army in World War II. Some were brought up as embassy brats, moving around the world

127

and attending exotic schools. More than one would expect have a military background: at the U.S. embassy in Singapore, for example, the ambassador was the West Pointer John Holdridge, later Assistant Secretary for East Asian Affairs and ambassador to Indonesia, who had quit the Army in 1947 when his unit was put to work reconstructing a golf course at a Virginia military base; his commercial attaché was John Hoog, who had spent two years in North Dakota as a missileman ("my finger hovering over the red button; after you spend all that time sixty feet underground, you want to get out for a while"). Most have origins in the upper-middle-class cross-section, the managerial-professional cohort, that is disproportionately dominant in American four-year colleges.

African diplomats usually have a chief somewhere in their backgrounds, and this can be misleading—Chief Adebo, the Nigerian who was for years the de facto leader of the African bloc at the United Nations, had originally come to prominence as a leader of the railway workers' union. Brahim Ghafa, Algerian ambassador to Tokyo, was rector of the University of Algiers; but many more from the Third World were high-school headmasters. The older Russians tend to be the children of industrial workers; the younger Russians are more likely to be children of the intelligentsia or the apparat—the Soviet ambassador to the United Nations is the son of the former chief interpreter in the Washington embassy. Latins and Europeans mostly are (and if they aren't, try to appear to be) from the highest social classes.

With the exception of the occasional potty aristocrat from a Latin country, however, the diplomatic cadre shares a common origin: they are the survivors of a highly competitive selection process. The circumstances of their selection, coupled with the rather tight boundary conditions of their work, give them a personal security—some call it arrogance—they will need both professionally and in their private lives, increasingly as the years pass and the options narrow.

"I knew I wanted to be in the Foreign Service," said Mme. Anne Vidal de la Blache, a young, blond, cardiganed, bespectacled, perfectly bilingual brisk administrative officer in the French Foreign Ministry bureau dealing with international organizations. "Therefore, I did not go to ENA [the reference is to the École Nationale d'Administration, successor to the famous École Centrale as the training ground for French Government leaders]. People come to the Foreign Ministry from ENA only from a narrow range of the students. The very top of the class, the best five or six, become inspecteurs des finances. The next best, ten or eleven, are assigned to the Quai d'Orsay [headquarters of the Foreign Ministry]. Below these notes [grades], you are assigned to other departments. When you enter

ENA you are already on the government payroll, and you promise to go at the end to whatever job you are sent. While I was in my last year at college, another student told me you could join the Foreign Service direct from university by passing an exam, and then you could be sure that you would work in the Foreign Ministry. What he did not tell me was that if you come here from any formation other than ENA, you are always in a second class." This is not just a matter of perception from below: in the formal structure of the personnel system in the French Foreign Ministry, graduates of ENA in the professional stream are Cadre A; those who arrive through other routes are Cadre A'.

"The top-level French negotiators are a real elite," said Ernest Koenig while the agricultural haggling was under way in the Multilateral Trade Negotiations in Geneva. "The next level is a pseudo-elite."

"Entry to the Administrative grades of the Diplomatic Service is by Open Competition," wrote a former head of recruitment for the Personnel Policy Department of the Foreign and Commonwealth Office in Britain, replying to questions asked by a parliamentary committee in 1977. "There are no back doors." Candidates must be under twenty-eight and "must hold a degree with honours from a British university or an equivalent academic qualification from abroad."

The examination is in three stages. First there is a "qualifying test," a series of written papers "lasting 1½ days and comprising a précis, a test of constructive thinking, a statistical inferences paper and a series of objectively marked tests. . . . Papers are marked by outside examiners, mainly from provincial universities. . . ."

Then a "Civil Service Selection Board," written tests plus two days of interviews during which the candidates are taken together in groups of five.

Lastly, a "Final Selection Board," an individual interview with a five-man panel chaired by the First Civil Service Commissioner and including two senior people from the Diplomatic Service and two outsiders, such as "a university Vice Chancellor, a trade unionist or a representative of management. . . ."

"Candidates declared successful may only be appointed to the Diplomatic Service when they have passed a full medical examination, been checked against the requirements of the Diplomatic Service Nationality Regulation, where necessary taken a language aptitude test and received a positive vetting certificate. Their appointments are for a probationary term of three years in the first instance. . . ."

About a thousand recent honors graduates start this examination process in England every year, and about twenty of them are eventually taken into the "A-stream" at the Foreign Office. Ninety-eight percent fall by the wayside. "We're looking for the best," said P. W. Unwin, director of personnel policy. "A depressingly large proportion of those who succeed is still Oxbridge [Oxford and Cambridge: the proportion in the 1970s ran about two thirds]. Of course, many of those are from humble origins. We try not to get into the class origins thing. In a sense, we've been almost too successful in getting people to apply from the redbricks [the provincial universities, everything not Oxford or Cambridge]. When the University of Aston near Birmingham puts in its tenth man and he doesn't make it, they say, We've been conned. But the redbrick candidates tend to fail more in the qualifying test, which is the same as the test for the Civil Service."

The total A-stream cohort in the Foreign Office runs about eight hundred (to man 220 missions overseas, plus many desks in Whitehall). There are about four times as many in an "executive stream," recruited by less difficult examinations, for which "school leavers" (people who never went to university) may present themselves. About thirty newcomers a year are taken into the "E-stream," twenty of them college graduates, the other ten not. People in the E-stream can rise as high as counselor in an embassy, and every so often they make the jump to A-stream. A more common jump is from the clerical staff to E-stream. Virtually all consuls, except those with major trade promotion responsibilities, come from the E-stream.

"They come to us from law, political science and economics," said Ludovico Ortona, director of the press office of the Italian Foreign Ministry and son of a former ambassador to the United States. He was walking about on the marble floor of his architecturally and literally cold office, under a ceiling three normal stories high, in the inconvenient Foro Italico that Mussolini built out along the Tiber for the Olympic Games he never got to stage. "Then there is a specific Foreign Ministry exam, the very difficult examination, though in the last few years it has become a little easier because school is a little easier in general. We are making efforts to draw from a wider sector, because the people we used to get were going to private industry. English and French are required, and there are exams in economics, diplomatic history and international law. Then orals in these five subjects, plus other orals. Of course, for the last two years," he added, speaking in 1978, "we haven't had examinations."

Elucidation was sought from Massimo Castaldo, vice-director-general in charge of personnel. "It was not a budget question. We do not find it convenient to give the examination because there were not enough people applying to take it. And there is resistance from the unions—the nonprofessionals are demanding an opportunity to move up through a special exam just for them. The women who take our examination for clerical careers come from good families, have made good studies in the university—often better studies than those who apply for the professional career. The working conditions are so agreeable in this administration—and it has good prestige—that they have no desire to move abroad. The law permits us to dismiss anyone who refuses to go, but the law is not applied because there would be a revolution."

The Foreign Ministry of the Ivory Coast is in part of a two-story stucco structure that frames the large dirt square of a littered cloister a few blocks from commercial Abidjan. Trees are planted all along the outside of the structure to shade the offices, but Konan N'da, director of personnel, qualifies for a window air conditioner. The office is dark and small, barely enough to hold two bookcases, a filing cabinet, a chair for a visitor, the small metal desk and N'da himself, a man too large for his desk, rather military with a brisk French manner. He wears a khaki shirt open at the neck. On the wall beside his desk hangs a large portrait of President Félix Houphouët-Boigny, resplendent in uniform, with the confident expression of a man who began his rule over an independent country with about two thirds the per capita income of its neighbor Ghana (the Gold Coast), and now governs a country with nearly triple the per capita income of Ghana.

"At the start of our diplomacy," N'da said in French, "the President named the heads of mission himself. He could not *form* the diplomats, and began to think about formation. We built an École Nationale d'Administration, which has a diplomatic section, forms twenty to thirty *secrétaires* a year. Now we have here eight secretaries of foreign affairs, three to five secretaries *adjoints* and another twelve or so directors of divisions, all trained by us. Students after earning their *license* used to get their title in the Foreign Ministry immediately, but now must pass a *concours* [competitive examination]. Then they have two years of study, one here, then a year at the Carnegie Endowment in Brussels [since closed], or at the Centre in Geneva—and *then* to London or the United States—or some to Germany or Madrid—for language."

We are interrupted by the arrival of the Ivory Coast ambassador to London, home for consultations, an elegant, rather grave man in a suit and tie, author of a book on Ghanaian foreign policy. The problems of the Less Developed Countries are different from those of industrial nations in personnel, too; the ambassador is being followed by and cannot shake a young lady in a sarong, baby on her hip, the wife, she claims, of the chauffeur at the London embassy. He signed on as a bachelor—and has definitely, the ambassador tells N'da after the young lady has been persuaded to come back tomorrow, been living as a bachelor. But there's not much doubt that this is his wife. . . .

All candidates for the Hungarian diplomatic service must first win admission to Karl Marx University, a beat-up urban college a few blocks down the river from Budapest's shopping center: marble floors, plaster walls covered with posters for entertainments, discos, jazz concerts, film clubs. Nothing is taught here but political economics and international affairs. About five hundred students enter every year, and two thirds of them take the first-year courses that permit entry in the second year to the diplomats' training program. Only thirty are chosen, to compete at the end for only ten jobs at the Foreign Ministry.

Like the rest of the university, the international studies faculty works for the Ministry of Education rather than the Foreign Ministry. "We are a little corner of Hungarian higher education," said Ferenc Kreskai, the director of the program, "poor but proud." Kreskai himself comes from the faculty of law rather than the diplomatic service (and speaks with Western visitors in French rather than in English), but ex officio he holds the rank of a department chief at the Foreign Ministry. "I must go to meetings at the university *and* at the Foreign Ministry," he sighed. "All the useless meetings." The disciplines are world economy, international law and diplomatic history—all, of course, from the Marxist perspective. Still, Kreskai values his students' freedom when they do research for their theses: "At the Foreign Ministry's Institute for Research, if the minister calls for a special study on the Near East, the results must stay within the boundaries of the opinion of the *direction*. Our opinion here is scientific, independent of the Foreign Ministry, and that is *très agréable*."

Career counseling is part of the program. "From the beginning," Kreskai said, "we give advice on the merits and demerits of foreign service. The general public knows little about it, and our first-year students are part of the general public. All thirty students in our program go to the Soviet Union for language studies, for a month or so. One of them returned after two weeks, because he was married and his wife didn't like his being away. We suggested he look for another career. . . ."

"There are three main divisions here," said Amos Ganor, director of personnel for the Israeli Foreign Ministry. "One—the administrative services here in Israel, people not part of the Foreign Service—includes chauffeurs, cleaning people, maintenance . . . but also communications, some of whom serve abroad, archives, and the legal staff. Legal is included because of the union contract. The legal branch of government service in Israel is somewhat privileged, don't ask me why.

"Two, the administrative and consular service abroad. In theory, there are two ways we get personnel here. We announce through the Civil Service Commissioners once a year, and they draw up an exam. But no one enters this way. By our agreement with the union, employees who have been with the Ministry in Israel for seven years and have passable English, French or Spanish can apply to transfer from category One to category Two. We employ many university students in archives and communications—communications works in shifts, which is useful for students—and some people stay. The Ministry has a dynamic of its own, people want to become part of this continuously moving stream. Enough people transfer every year so we don't need recruitment from outside. After three years in overseas administrative branch, with a minimum age of thirty-five, the employee can transfer to the diplomatic service. With a university degree it's a possibility. Not many people do it.

"Three, direct entry into the diplomatic service. This is only through a trainee system. The Civil Service Commission once a year will announce an exam. We have four, five hundred applicants. They must be under thirty—there are so many frustrations in the Foreign Service as it is, we don't want people to have supervisors younger than they are. Remember, an Israeli high-school graduate must do three years' military service, which takes him to age twenty-one. And to take the exam for the Foreign Ministry, he must be a university graduate or a senior. So he must move soon."

From the five hundred or so applicants, the Foreign Ministry chooses about twenty to take a three-and-a-half-month course with ten hours of classes a day. "We insist," Ganor said, "on a general education in literature, art and music and—very important—in Jewish tradition. We don't want somebody who at the synagogue won't know what he's supposed to do." The candidate then enters an apprenticeship mode, with a year divided into four months in each of three departments. Next, a second basic course in consular work, finance and administration. A committee then sits in judgment—"the assistant director general for administration, yours truly, a section head, and an ambassador." They review the comments by the candidate's various bosses and the examination results and decide, in Ganor's words, "whether to take them for the Foreign Service or thank them for their patience." About two thirds of the entering group usually jump all the hurdles and sign on.

In Israel, any university degree, whatever the subject, qualifies an applicant to take the tests for the Foreign Service. Yosef Gal, a young second secretary in the Israeli embassy in Washington, a compact, earnest, confident young man in thick, large, almost rimless glasses, was working toward a master's degree in mathematics and statistics at Hebrew University when he signed up for the exam. "Math has nothing to do with this job," he said, "except that it gives you a different perspective on the so-called science of diplomacy." Gal remembered a year of tests—"psychological tests, history tests, Hebrew tests, other languages." (Among the languages Gal could offer was Arabic: his parents were refugees from Morocco, who still spoke Maghreb Arabic at home.) Then he had three months in the European division, three months in the economics division, and three months in the "official guest" division, squiring visitors from other governments around the country. In his Washington post he was "what the French call *chef du bureau*" for the ambassador, deciding what and whom his boss should see, drafting replies to letters and cables, working out schedules, etc. This is a big job—"My predecessor," Gal said, "was on his fourth overseas assignment." He thought it might make a problem for him when his five-year tour (!) of duty ended, because he would be too young to qualify for any other job of similar importance.

"In Israel as elsewhere," Gal said, "people look upon diplomacy as glamorous—cocktail parties, receptions, black tie and white tie. But if you asked me today, which do I prefer—going back to mathematics and statistics or this—if I were honest, I would have to say, going back to mathematics and the university. But most educated Israelis feel they should make a contribution, and going back to mathematics would be for me a luxury.

"I wouldn't advise my best friends to join the Foreign Service—it's tough. And our wives are not allowed to work except here in the embassy and as Hebrew teachers. In 1975 there was this story about our ambassador to Denmark, his wife wanted to open a beauty shop, and the Ministry objected. Because it would not be a dignified job. . . ."

"We always have more vacancies than people," said Geoffrey Yu, first secretary in the Singapore embassy in Tokyo. He is a young man with a startlingly high forehead, wearing thick glasses and a serious expression. "I was a graduate in sociology, with minors in history and economics, and they were short of people. Instead of inviting applications, they were approaching people: 'We have studied your background. . . .' We have an *awful* selection system. You apply for the civil service, and list preferences. Then you are interviewed by a committee of seven or eight, who interview twenty other people also, in two hours, and who know nothing of what it means to be in the Foreign Service. And they decide. Until two years ago the tendency was to take the brightest graduates and put them in the home ministries, mostly Treasury. There's a lack of understanding in our country of what Foreign Service work involves. There's no snob appeal, no feeling of the grandeur of foreign representation, as there is in Western Europe."

The view from the top was different. "No Singaporean was in the Malaysian Foreign Service," said Foreign Minister S. Rajaratnam, thinking back to the days of his city-state's sudden severance from the mainland in 1965. "And we had never conceived of an independent Singapore. The first week of our independence, I was a Foreign Minister with one secretary, and that's all. I started to build an infrastructure of clerks, and then I began to pinch people from other ministries. We sent ambassadors to Kuala Lumpur, London and the UN, also accredited to Washington, and that was the sum total.

"We had the British to help us out; they did our consular work. For training, we sent people to Britain or Canberra. We still move people among the departments of government; it began as a necessity, but I have come to believe one should have a Foreign Service not confined to career officers; that gives you a bureaucracy. Crossbreeding is better than an in-group, who can become ossified. Our first ambassador to Kuala Lumpur was a businessman—no knowledge of diplomacy or international law. But as a businessman he knows how to get along with people."*

Singapore's small Foreign Service is notable for the proportion of women in the professional cadre. At one point its UN mission in New York was entirely female except for the ambassador. "As soon as Singapore became independent," Rajaratnam explained, "we introduced national service. The young men were taken into the Army, and I couldn't recruit them. The available university graduates were women, so we recruited heavily among the women. And we don't want to waste our trained women."

Elsewhere, women have had a much more difficult time breaking in. (Even in Singapore, things are far from hunky-dory, the Ministry having decided that it already has enough women serving abroad.) "As a fact of life," said Ferenc Kreskai at Karl Marx University in Budapest, "women are not ideal for the Foreign Service. In the Arab world women are practically useless. They are not barred here, but one must discourage."

Barbara Angus, who was second-in-command at the New Zealand embassy in Washington, remembered that she had been the first woman sent

---

* Rajaratnam's ambassador to Tokyo for some years was a professor of inorganic chemistry. I sat next to this aging, delicate, amused Chinese scientist at a dinner in Singapore, and looking to make small talk mentioned that my younger son was a metals chemist, and apparently quite a good one. Several universities were aggressively competing to persuade him to use his National Science Foundation fellowship to take his Ph.D. in their academic groves, and a letter from him had been waiting for me in Singapore, relating his experiences on a visit to Texas A. & M., where the street traffic seemed to consist entirely of pickup trucks with shotguns in the cab. My interlocutor, who had never been in the United States, nodded at the mention of Texas A. & M. "Cotton," he said. "Best man in the field. If your son has a chance to study with Cotton, he should grab it." There is more than one kind of international conspiracy.

abroad by her country in a diplomatic capacity; someone commented unkindly on her arrival *en poste* that at age thirty-eight she was the oldest second secretary in the world. When the Japanese learned that the only person in the Papua New Guinea Foreign Ministry who could speak Japanese was female, they offered the PNG Government four scholarships for diplomats to study at Japanese universities. Putting together the Israeli Foreign Ministry, Walter Eytan flatly refused to take women for diplomatic posts (though he could not keep Ben-Gurion from sending Golda Meir to Moscow). "A woman serving away from home," he wrote smugly, "tends to be afflicted by loneliness to a degree almost impossible to bear." Still, all was not lost: "Women do, however," Eytan continued, "play an important part in the Foreign Service—as their husbands' wives."

In 1909, in the United States, an Assistant Secretary of State warned that the introduction of civil service principles in the selection of future American diplomats should not become a back-door means of the admission of women. "The greatest obstacle to the employment of women as diplomatic agents," he wrote, "is their well known inability to keep a secret." Joseph Grew, as first chairman of the unified Foreign Service Personnel Board in 1924, "feared that women would interfere with the convivial atmosphere of the Foreign Service, that they would ruin morale by demanding special treatment, and that they would not be competent for South American duty, since the sexual attitudes of Latin Americans would make it impossible for them to do their work. He could see the reputation of a woman diplomat being shattered one night in South America were she called upon to deliver an official note to a bachelor colleague. . . . If the State Department was not free to send women to Latin America, 'it would be manifestly unfair and inconsistent to send women to our more desirable posts in Europe, leaving the men to fill the undesirable ones.'" Grew went so far as to make personal appeals to mothers of female applicants to keep their daughters from taking the written tests, and women who passed the written tests were purposely failed in their oral examinations "on the grounds that they do not possess the necessary qualifications for the Service."

Even in an age of feminist outrage and "affirmative action," the world is full of unthought discriminations against women who choose careers in their nation's Foreign Service. Mme. Vidal de la Blache in Paris, for example, noted that the French Foreign Ministry had been active around the world seeking treaties or reciprocal exemptions from local laws that would permit the wives of Foreign Service Officers to continue their careers in the countries to which their husbands might be sent—but that no such efforts were made for the husbands of female Foreign Service Officers. Her own husband was a lawyer specializing in the legal consequences of nuclear energy, a subject of no small interest in a number of countries—but it was considered bizarre that she should ask for assignment abroad to a post where he, too, could continue his work. Since Mme. de Staël drove Napoleon crazy with her demands for the legal rights of women *qua* women in the early nineteenth century, masculine France in its French way has been more conscious of the subtleties of these problems than the leadership of any other country—but the needs of the woman in the Foreign Service are still too special even for the French.

2

Almost by definition, a Foreign Service must be an elite. (In the United States, the Foreign Service Act of 1980 calls for a Service "representative of the American people," but also "operated on the basis of merit principles.") These are the people who symbolize the nation beyond its borders: the impression they convey must be as positive as talent and training can make it. They should know, appreciate and to some degree embody their nation's cultural heritage, its accomplishments in the sciences and in political institution-building. They must of course be citizens (and except in the United States, where recent legislation changed the rules, their spouses must be citizens too). And diplomats cannot marry foreigners without their government's permission if they wish to remain diplomats). And there is always a political litmus test, sometimes formally enunciated: "The Government have decided," says the formal announcement of *Appointments in Administration* of the British Civil Service Commission, "that no one may be employed in the Civil Service in connection with work the nature of which is vital to the security of the State if he is or has recently been a member of the British Communist Party or of a fascist organization; or if, in such a way as to raise legitimate doubts about his reliability, he is, or has recently been, sympathetic to communism or fascism, or associated with communists or fascists or their sympathisers. . . . All members of the Diplomatic Service must undergo positive vetting."†

† "Positive vetting" (in American English, "security clearance") came to the Foreign Office only in the wake of the discovery that the Soviet Union had penetrated—indeed, had all but taken over—the Ministry's Secret Intelligence Service. It was a reform, Andrew Boyle writes, "calculated to outrage the sensibilities of many senior colleagues reared in the [Whitehall] 'Club' tradition of unquestioning trust and mutual respect." Oddly enough, the State Department would seem to lack such powers under the Foreign Service Act of 1980, which requires "equal opportunity and fair and equitable treatment for all without regard to political affiliations. . . ." But perhaps the matter is covered under the general "Saving Provisions" at the end of the Act, which continue in effect all "determinations, authorizations, regulations, orders, agreements . . . or other actions made, issued, undertaken, entered into or taken under the authority of the Foreign Service Act of 1946 or any other law." Don'tcha wish you could write like that?

When there were royal courts, it was imperative that diplomats reveal a suitable savoir faire, eat their peas on the back of the fork, dance the approved dances, sit a horse well, hold their liquor, make small talk. There are still posts where the ability to hunt and shoot counts for something (it was particularly valuable in Yugoslavia under Tito, a great destroyer of wildlife). Charles Thayer noted, however, that "today standards are lower and a diplomatic shoot is often regarded by experienced hunters as one of the more dangerous pastimes. I have spent the better part of several diplomatic shoots flat on my face in a ditch while bullets whistled above me."

Hence the striped-pants cookie-pushers; this was, and to a degree still is, part of the job. Table manners is among the subjects taught in the Foreign Service training programs wherever they exist. These days, the children of the rich often need such training, too. In the Egyptian Foreign Service school, the class in social behavior meets at Cairo's elegant Tahrir Club, where new FSOs "learn to arrange the table and seat people." It is considered so important that several of the classes are taught by Boutrous Boutros-Ghali, Secretary of State for Foreign Affairs, the number-two man in the Ministry.

Service abroad is expensive, and the idea that this expense is like other costs of government, to be borne by the taxpayers, was a long time gaining acceptance in the legislatures. Until 1918, the British Foreign Office required candidates to produce documentary proof that in their first two years of service they would have a private income of at least $2,000 a year to supplement their official salary. The men who made the professional cadre of the American Foreign Service in the 1920s mostly started as unpaid secretaries to ministers and ambassadors abroad. As late as the 1920s, applicants to the State Department were told that "the remuneration of secretaries in the diplomatic service is unfortunately not such as to enable the department to assure them that they will be able to live on their salaries at all the posts to which they may be sent." A bachelor might just squeak through on the $4,000 a year of the best-paid "secretary" (the equivalent of today's "counselor") in a major embassy, the National Civil Service Reform League pointed out in 1919, but unless he had private funds, he could get married only if he found an heiress—or left the Service. Ambassadors and ministers were better paid (up to $17,500 a year in London and Paris, a figure set in 1856 and maintained until 1946), but they were worse off, because they could not escape official entertainment expenses for which they were not reimbursed. Until the Lowden Act of 1911 authorized the State Department to acquire residences, American ambassadors had to make their own housing arrangements at every post; not until after World War II did the U.S. Government undertake to make an official residence part of an ambassador's perks.

Mark Twain, for one, thought it was nonsense. Writing from Vienna in 1899, he compared a poorly paid American ambassador to "a billionaire in a paper collar, a king in a breech clout, an archangel in a tin halo." In her world role, he wrote, the United States had become like a girl reaching eighteen, who "adds six inches to her skirt, . . . has a room to herself, and becomes in many ways a thundering expense. But she is in society now and papa has to stand it; there is no avoiding it." Populists were torn between embarrassment that their country should be represented by people whose first qualification was their money and a feeling that tax revenues should not be wasted on such ceremonial nonsense.

The result was that the State Department developed a professional cadre not in the field but in Washington, among, as the French call them, the *sédentaires*. The first man to make a lifelong career in American diplomacy (and what a career!—fifty-five years long) was Alvey A. Adee, whose only foreign post was his first, in 1869, as protégé and private secretary to the American minister in Madrid, initially the preposterous Daniel Sickles, a Civil War general who had lost a leg at Gettysburg but never let it slow him down. Adee spent most of his time handling Sickles' private pursuits (wine, women and song—as a congressman, Sickles had enlivened the Washington scene by shooting his wife's lover in Lafayette Square and winning acquittal on the subsequent murder charge in one of the more dramatic examples of the unwritten law). But he also observed Sickles' interesting professional activities, which included a plan to buy Cuban independence from Spain as a prelude to American annexation of the island, and an effort to foment a revolution against the King of Spain after he proved uncooperative. Sickles resigned in 1874 in the aftermath of the *Virginius* affair, when Spanish forces intercepted an American ship running guns to Cuban revolutionaries and executed its captain and much of its crew. The United States demanded compensation, and when the Spanish Government chose to negotiate a settlement in Washington rather than in Madrid, Sickles, insulted, quit in a huff and went off to Paris, where he was conducting an affair with the deposed nymphomaniac Spanish queen. Adee was retained at the embassy to help Sickles' successor, who was inheriting a rather sticky situation.

When Hayes succeeded Garfield in 1877, Adee was offered a "temporary" clerkship in Washington. By 1878, he was chief of the Diplomatic Bureau, and in 1882 he became Third Assistant Secretary of State. For more than forty years thereafter, all significant diplomatic correspondence and intradepartmental memos passed over his desk. He annotated the incoming materials and policy memos for the guidance of his political superiors (and not infrequently for his own amusement, exercising an odd and individual wit: he once examined U.S. relations with Mexico as a question of whether the revolutionary government should be "recognized or wreck-ognized").

When the U.S. minister to Peru urged Elihu Root to consider that country's offer of Ferrol and Somanca bays as a fueling station and dry-dock for the U.S. fleet, Adee gave the dispatch a headnote before sending it to the Secretary: "Peru offers us Chimbote for our vessels. *Timeo Danaos.*" When in 1907 William Fox as minister to Ecuador was warning that France was about to acquire the Galápagos islands by purchase and the United States should immediately move to buy them itself, Adee sent on the dispatch with a covering note: "The Galápagos question has cropped up from time to time ever since I came into the Department. We have answered again and again that we don't want them ourselves and will not let Ecuador sell them to any non-American power. But—Ecuador needs twenty million dollars." All outgoing instructions to the field and official communications to foreign governments also passed over Adee's desk, and he either wrote or edited *everything*, in a formal, passive style entirely different from that of his memos.

Competent in most European languages when he wished to be (and in-competent in all languages including English when he did not: he was hard of hearing and used an ear trumpet), Adee was also a Shakespearean scholar of some repute. A bachelor and a recluse, he was in the office from early in the morning until late at night, and kept a cot in the room so he could stay overnight, perched at the center of the spider web. A bureau-cratic master (Philander Knox as Secretary of State complained that once you gave Adee a notion of where you stood on any subject, it was impossi-ble to get a view from him other than your own), Adee was the protocol-and-procedures expert of the Department and also its institutional mem-ory, with personal recollections of American policies and the reasons for them in every corner of the globe. Until the vast dimensions of American world involvement overwhelmed any individual's capacity to keep track, Adee stood athwart all efforts to reorganize the State Department and es-tablish bureaus with known tasks and responsibilities.

Adee's influence was doubtless greatest during the time when John Hay was Secretary, for he and Hay had been personal friends since the 1860s in Washington, and corresponded throughout the last third of the century. (Adee did not always win: when the Colombian Senate voted unani-mously against the treaty that would permit construction of a canal through the Panamanian isthmus, he advised strongly against American involvement in a Panamanian revolution: "Such a scheme could, of course, have no countenance from us," he wrote Hay. "Our policy before the world should stand, like Mrs. Caesar, beyond suspicion." And the next day he added the suggestion that negotiations should be begun again with

Nicaragua: "We are very sorry, but really we can't help it if Colombia doesn't want the Canal on our terms.")

Adee's amusing and sometimes sardonic memos were very different from the formal and flowery style of the State Department correspondence he supervised, and he got on Theodore Roosevelt's nerves. In March 1908, Roosevelt complained in a letter to his son Kermit about an episode that had begun with a telegram from the President of Peru inviting a visit from the U.S. Navy. "I never saw it," Roosevelt wrote. "Adee, in the State Department, prepared one of the usual fatuous answers, into which he unwarily put the statement that I extended to him all good wishes from 'me and my people.' Jaded, overworked Root did not have his attention attracted by the phrase, and as it was a routine telegram signed my name and sent it off. Thereupon all the New York papers had hysteria over this, as showing marked imperialistic and megalomaniac tendencies. . . . Of course I could not possibly explain because to do so meant that poor President Pardo would have had his feelings deeply hurt by learning that I had never seen his telegram or my answer."

That December, Roosevelt as a lame duck finally exploded with a written message to the State Department about a speech prepared for his use at a reception in the White House for the new Chinese ambassador: "I did not deliver it as handed to me because it was fatuous and absurd. . . . There should be some kind of effort to write a speech that shall be simple and that shall say something, or, if that is deemed inexpedient, that shall not at least be of a fatuity so great that it is humiliating to read it. In the draft of the letter handed to me, for instance, I am made to say of the letter I receive: 'I accept it with quite exceptional sentiments as a message of especial friendship.' Of course, any boy in school who wrote a sentence like that would be severely and properly disciplined. The next sentence goes on: 'I receive it with the more profound sentiments in that you bring it now no less than from the Emperor.' What in Heaven's name did the composer of this epistle mean by 'more profound sentiments'? . . . Can he not write English? Continuing: at the end of the same sentence, he speaks of the New Government and what he anticipates from it, in terms that would not be out of place in a prophecy about Alexander the Great on the occasion of his accession to the throne of Macedon. Politeness is necessary, but gushing and obviously insincere and untruthful compliments merely make both sides ridiculous, and are underbred in addition."

Adee, of course, survived, because he was necessary. The tradition of such speeches on diplomatic occasions survived, too, though whether that has been necessary is not so clear. Roosevelt and the attitudes he embodied, alas!—mostly, alas!—we lost.

After 1909, when the regional bureaus were formed and began to squirrel away expertise, Adee's uniqueness as the institutional memory was breached, though in both Latin American and Asian affairs his recollection was probably better than the bureau's files. With his muttonchop whiskers and billowing tie, his willingness to talk at length about almost any country or international issue (he briefed diplomats on their way to their posts), Adee was to some degree a figure of fun to the young men in the Department. But he sat astride the communications channels, and to write that he "was a quaint reminder of the old days, more concerned with form than with system," as one of the best historians of the State Department does, is to forget all we know about the importance of communications in a bureaucracy. If Adee was unconcerned with the State Department system, it was because he controlled it.

Adee hung on into his eighties; he was given the honor of being made First Assistant Secretary in 1924, shortly before his death and before the Rogers Act made all Assistant Secretaries equal. According to Dana Munro, who served under him, Adee grew "very deaf and unable to speak intelligibly. He no longer wrote the witty policy memoranda which had once instructed and delighted his colleagues, but nearly all outgoing instructions and letters still had to pass through his office before being presented to other officials for signature. His two very efficient secretaries, Miss Margaret Hanna and Mrs. Ruth Shipley, exercised an autocratic authority in matters relating to the form and style of the Department's correspondence and compelled several generations of young officers to learn to write State Department English. Not infrequently, they influenced decisions on policy, especially where precedents were involved." It is a measure of Adee's legacy to the Department that his secretary Ruth Shipley became the tyrant of the passport office, administering "her law" as she saw fit, though presidents themselves complained, into the Kennedy administration.

The other *sédentaire* in Washington was Wilbur J. Carr, whose career at the State Department lasted almost as long as Adee's—from 1892 to 1939—and put him in a foreign post only at the very end, in 1937, when Roosevelt sent him as minister to Czechoslovakia. George Kennan, who served under him in Prague, thought the appointment "a well-deserved tribute to a long life of unassuming service." Carr himself, bitter at the extent to which he had been supplanted in his administrative duties by Roosevelt's rich friend Sumner Welles, thought he had been packed off to Czechoslovakia because the President thought the Germans would get there first.

Writing about *The Making of the Diplomatic Mind*, Robert Schulzinger described Carr as "a small, neat man with the colorless moonshaped face of a copy clerk." He had indeed started as a copy clerk, an

Ohio farm boy who had attended a "commercial college," learned short-hand, and arrived in the State Department in 1892 via the civil service examination route. By 1902 he had made himself chief of the Consular Bureau. The consular service was considerably larger than the diplomatic service (318 posts against 41 in 1900), and considerably better paid (in 1915, the consul general in London was paid four times as much as the highest-ranking diplomatic officer other than the ambassador himself). A consulate also offered splendid opportunities for graft—and, indeed, still does: every so often the administrative bureaus have to scurry around to cover over a scandal in passports or visas or export licenses.

One can easily exaggerate the contrast between the consuls and the dip-lomats. Townsend Harris moved easily enough from consul general to minister to Japan, and the first black American diplomat, Ebenezer Don Carlos Bassett, coupled the jobs of consul general and minister in Haiti in 1869–77. Political reports from consuls as from ambassadors passed across Adee's desk. Political pull being necessary for both types of appoint-ment, consuls became ambassadors. Consular clerks, like diplomatic secre-taries, were drawn of necessity from the ranks of the well-to-do because both had to pay their own transportation expenses to their posts. Most consuls had been to college—a quarter of them, indeed (as against three quarters of the diplomats), had been to Ivy League universities. Still, on the average the consuls were men of much lower social standing than the diplomats, at home and abroad.

To the supercilious Bostonian Joseph Grew, another of Roosevelt's rich friends, Carr was "the Little Father of the Consuls." His achievement was to become, as the State Department centennial history labels him, "the Father of the Foreign Service." From early on, he made it his life's work to apply principles of "scientific management" to State Department offices abroad, to create a personnel system of entrance by competitive examina-tion and promotion by merit, and to merge the consular service and the diplomatic service into a single Foreign Service. With the Rogers Act of 1924, mostly drafted in his office, he succeeded.

Carr was, Waldo Heinrichs writes, "an intensely ambitious person, eager for prominence in the political and diplomatic worlds of Washing-ton." He was from the great American tradition of self-improvement and self-education. In his diary he wrote that he was "conscious always of an inferiority of preparation and of mind, lacking in information but by de-termination and endless hours of labor doing what better educated and more highly placed men had failed to do." He studied violin, read Pliny, Aristophanes, Thucydides and Dante's *Inferno*, while solidifying both his political position within the Department and his external relations with the congressmen's constituents who did business with the consuls. He and

Adee were virtually the sole survivors when William Jennings Bryan became Secretary of State for Woodrow Wilson and shook out the job slots to make room for deserving Democrats.

The State Department centennial history suggests as the first U.S. career diplomat William Lindsay Scruggs, a Southern lawyer and newspaper publisher who turned Republican after the Civil War and at the age of thirty-six was appointed minister to Colombia.‡ He spent most of the next twenty years working for the State Department in that post, as consul general in Canton, and as minister to Venezuela. He was fired from his Caracas post (as the centennial history does not mention) when the Secretary of State learned that he had bribed the President of Venezuela (possibly keeping some of the money for himself) to secure partial payment of a dubious claim against Venezuela by an American citizen.

Shortly thereafter, Scruggs signed on as an agent of the Venezuelan Government to raise support in the United States for the Venezuelan boundary claim against British Guiana. Concealing his *parti pris,* he wrote a pamphlet entitled *British Aggression in Venezuela, the Monroe Doctrine on Trial,* which precipitated a nasty if in retrospect faintly farcical imbroglio between the United States and Britain. Adee was sufficiently annoyed by Scruggs' distortions to have a true copy of Monroe's Doctrine printed up and distributed to the press, provoking Scruggs to describe him to the Venezuelan Foreign Minister as "a foreigner [!] who scarcely speaks the English language, who crept into the service as a sort of clerk many years ago; just how nobody seems to know. He is now Second Assistant Secretary of State! He is a person of limited intelligence, narrow mind, and hypocritical and false in character."

Echoes of this episode, incidentally, reverberate in our time, because the most recent extension of the treaty between Venezuela and England that resulted from the ensuing arbitration is about to lapse, and Venezuela is preparing to reassert its claim to the lands on the other side of the Orinoco River, now part of independent Guyana (home of, among other horrors, the Jonestown massacre). Plans for conquering this territory and

‡ Political oddities like Southern Republicans were and still are prime candidates for the reward of an embassy. Having lost his chance to be President by rousing the urban Irish against him when he denounced the Democrats as the party of "Rum, Romanism and Rebellion," James G. Blaine as Secretary of State to President Benjamin Harrison in 1889 appointed as minister to Chile Patrick Egan, an Irish Fenian refugee with a price on his head in Britain, who had become a Republican power in Nebraska. William Jennings Bryan, the great enemy of the money trusts, appointed as ambassador to Constantinople the financier Henry Morgenthau, who had been the largest single contributor to Woodrow Wilson's 1912 campaign. Egan presently backed the wrong horse in a Chilean revolution, involving the U.S. Navy along the way; Morgenthau got the political and military situation all wrong in his dispatches from Turkey through the early years of World War I.

hopes for American support in the venture—even beyond the F-16s unwisely sold to the Venezuelan air force—motivated Caracas' unlimited support for Argentina and outrage at American attitudes in the Falklands war. Guyana being a Soviet client and Venezuela a highly significant U.S. ally in the Western hemisphere, the old boundary dispute in which William Lindsay Scruggs fanned the flames has become again a possible source of Great-Power conflict. In his work for Venezuela, as John Grenville and George Berkeley Young have claimed, "Scruggs secured for himself a sure place in the history of American foreign relations"—but not, perhaps, the place that the State Department historian has chosen to assert for him.

The most plausible candidate for founding father of a professional American diplomacy is Robert Schulzinger's choice, Henry White. Born in 1850 to a wealthy Baltimore family and educated mostly in France and England, White sought out the job of second secretary at the U.S. legation in London in the late 1870s mostly because his bride "complained that it was improper for an intelligent man of twenty-nine to have no vocation." In 1883, "disturbed at the difference in quality between the American and European diplomats," White resolved "to become the nucleus, if possible, of a permanent . . . non-partisan . . . service, to which appointments should be made on the basis of fitness only."

The drive to remove diplomatic and consular appointments from the spoils system meshed well with the progressive movement. The spirit of the industrial revolution had done its work in diplomatic services, too. As late as the 1830s, Lord Melbourne could accept the Order of the Garter with special pleasure because "there's no damned merit to it," but by 1856 Britain was committed to the idea that the sovereign should be represented abroad only by those who had come through the fire of an examination. Civil service reform took root in the United States, too, but the 1883 legislation that began the removal of government employment from the political spoils had exempted the State Department.

In 1895 by executive order Grover Cleveland (who had permitted White to continue in London despite his disability as a Republican appointee) put entrance to the Washington end of the State Department on a merit basis, either by transfer from existing jobs or by examination, and Congress confirmed the order by legislation the next year. Nine years later Theodore Roosevelt issued the orders to make the examination process more or less systematic, and included entrants to the consular corps.

William Howard Taft then dropped the other shoe, requiring examinations for entry to the lower grades of the diplomatic service, and even directing the Secretary of State "to call to the attention of the President from time to time those professionals who showed such skill and maturity in their work as to be worthy of promotion to the rank of chief of mission. This was," Henry Wriston writes, "an extraordinary step: it removed the ceiling over promotion and set up a systematic basis for a corps of professional diplomats." Eighteen of Taft's chiefs of mission were "professionals" appointed from the lower ranks. (But Taft dropped Henry White, and enforced a geographic state-of-origin quota on consular appointments to placate the senators.) Taft's order too was later confirmed by statute, though not until 1915, after Taft had left the White House— and by then Bryan had restored the spoils system with a heavy hand: nearly all of Taft's career ministers and ambassadors had been fired and replaced by political appointees. But—there is no black-and-white in this business—Bryan brought the Republican Wendell Phillips back to the State Department as Third Assistant Secretary because he admired the skills Phillips had shown in negotiating with Mexico on a quasi-official appointment direct from Woodrow Wilson. Legislation does not seem to be binding in State Department personnel matters. The Foreign Service Act of 1980 provides that "contributions to political campaigns should not be a factor in the appointment of an individual as a chief of mission," but several of the Reagan appointments of 1981 cannot be explained on any other basis.

The drive toward professionalism in the State Department had stumbled—and still does stumble—over the inability of either Foreign Service Officers or academics to formulate a usable job description for the title "diplomat." There was little operational value in Ernest Satow's great definition of diplomacy itself—"the application of intelligence and tact to the conduct of official relations between governments of independent states." For the consular service, Carr initially thought that the best bet would be commercial training of the kind that would also fit graduates for employment abroad by American businesses, but even the consular jobs seemed broader than that—and everybody felt the diplomatic jobs would require something more complicated.

During the 1900s, the National Business League floated some trial balloons for the establishment of a consular academy along the lines of West Point and Annapolis, to train Americans for foreign service. In 1907 the College of Political Science of George Washington University ("modelled," wrote Dean Richard D. Harlan, "after the famed École des Sciences Politiques in Paris and the London School of Economics and Political Science") opened its doors with the thought that the State Department might make it at least a semi-official training center. By then a number of universities around the country—not only Harvard, Yale, Columbia and Chicago but also state universities in Illinois, Iowa, Kentucky, California and Wisconsin—were offering international relations courses in part to prepare students for careers abroad. Later there would be the Fletcher School at Tufts and the School of Advanced International Studies at Johns Hopkins; and Georgetown would make a major investment in Washington itself. Despite some gestures of support from Secretary of State Elihu Root the George Washington school never acquired any special standing.

Carr himself finally came down to the position that the Foreign Service should recruit from among the best graduates of the best universities, without worrying too much about what they had studied. He wanted men who were "hearty, personable, manly, shrewd, business-like, observant, and well-informed, with a good knowledge of human nature" plus, of course, "the instincts of a gentleman in the finer sense."

For the rich young men who came into the diplomatic service in the high tide of progressivism, the requirements for a career in diplomacy seemed more closely related to birth and status. Waldo Heinrichs compiled an astonishing list of men who entered as secretaries in 1893–1917 and "went on to become ministers and ambassadors. The wealth of Joseph C. Grew, later ambassador to Japan, derived from the wool business, the China trade, and western mining, and his wife, a Boston Perry and Cabot, had her own resources. As a secretary at Berlin, he spent $15,000 a year on a salary of less than $3,000. . . . Peter Jay was a descendant of John Jay, and pre-Civil War fortunes stood behind John W. Garrett and Leland Harrison.* Chicago meat-packing and soap manufacturing underwrote the careers of Norman Armour and Alexander Kirk. Lloyd Griscom's family, descended from original Philadelphia Quakers, flourished anew in rails, oil, and shipping, and boasted liveried coachmen. One grandfather of John Van Antwerp MacMurray, later minister to China, had founded an iron works in St. Louis, and the other, a descendant of original Dutch settlers, was a prosperous Albany banker. One grandfather of Arthur Bliss Lane had built a $2,500,000 business, and the other was a successful cotton broker. Corporation law and castor oil ('Castoria—Children Cry For It') set up Robert Woods Bliss in diplomacy, the Knickerbocker Club, and Dumbarton Oaks. Irwin Laughlin was treasurer of Jones and Laughlin Steel Company at thirty-three when he entered diplomacy. William Phillips, whose great-uncle was Wendell Phillips, became financially independent at twenty-one."

These men mostly knew each other. A number of them shared bachelor quarters in a house they bought together at 1718 H Street for use while in Washington. They called themselves "the Family"; at the least they were what Hugh Wilson, later Roosevelt's catastrophic ambassador to Hitler,

* Jay and Harrison took their pre-university schooling at Eton.

called (in conversation with Wilbur Carr, yet!) "a pretty good club." (Wilson himself was a little on the edges of the club; in Heinrichs' delicious comment, "he knew where his money came from," having worked in his father's shirt manufacturing business; but he was a graduate of the Hill School and Yale.) They agreed that examinations before entry were desirable, but they wanted the passing level low, so that other factors could play a larger role. They were willing to see a unified Foreign Service (though not a unified promotion list) because they felt that wealth alone should not be the requisite of entrance to diplomacy and they disliked the idea of being paid less than the consuls. In the end, however, their major goal was to cut political appointees out of the ambassadors' jobs in confident expectation that they would inherit. "The professional diplomatic service they sought," Schulzinger writes, "was not a true profession but a job with a secure tenure."

Neither the consular service nor the diplomatic service, then, could come up with a program of educational requirements. In the end, Schulzinger writes savagely, "diplomats, academics and businessmen decided it was more important that Foreign Service officers go to school than that they learn anything while there."

The examination, however, grew increasingly long and elaborate. Responding to a query by Harold Nicolson in 1939, the State Department described it as comprising "a wide variety of subjects, including the following: elements of international maritime and commercial law, arithmetic as used in common statistics, tariff calculations, exchange, and simple accounting; modern languages (French, German or Spanish is required, and in the subsequent oral test, a candidate may offer, in addition to one of these, any language in which he may be familiar); elementary economics, including the natural, industrial and commercial resources of the United States; political and commercial geography; American history, government and institutions since 1776; and the history of Europe, Latin America and the Far East since 1776. Candidates will also be examined in political economy, and will be rated in English, composition, grammar, punctuation, spelling and penmanship as shown by their examination papers. This written examination usually occupies four days. . . ." An oral exam followed, and candidates were then placed on an "eligible list" in order of their examination marks. It is perhaps a measure of how these tests were graded that Daniel P. Moynihan, who had prepared for them at Fletcher, flunked the composition section.

The merely qualifying exams of the early days, and the willingness to accept social class status as a major argument for acceptance into the Service, permitted the entry of some very queer fish indeed. Charles Thayer, whose grandfather had been the first U.S. ambassador to France in 1894, recalled that he himself entered the Foreign Service in 1929 concerned about the crowd he was joining: "That summer, a Foreign Service officer whom I had known, but not well, was arrested on a streetcar in Washington for indecent exposure. Then a consul general in Australia was thrown off a boat in Sydney harbor for molesting two boys. Finally a consul general in Prague suffered a mental breakdown and shut himself in his hotel room, where he lived on beer and raw beef. When he got word that the consul was coming to take him into custody, he jumped into a taxicab and headed for Carlsbad, scattering hunks of beef on the way, presumably to divert his pursuers."

Sir Ernest Satow wrote with mixed emotions of the British Foreign Service Officers with whom he served in Japan as a young man in the 1860s, before anybody had to pass exams. He remembered, for example, "a First Assistant, sociable and accomplished, musical, artistic and speaking many languages beside his own, but no lover of hard work. In his hands the accounts fell eighteen months in arrear, and the registers of correspondence were a couple of years behind hand. It was his function to preside over the chancery, and he left it to his successor in a condition which the latter aptly compared to that of an 'Aegean [sic] stable.' He was the sort of man who is always known among his friends by his Christian name, and no higher tribute to personal qualities is possible. In the course of time he became a consul, and retired from the service at an early age, carrying with him the regrets and good wishes of everybody who knew him."

Yet Satow was skeptical about the British examination system, on the grounds that "it takes no account of moral qualities." Harold Nicolson was particularly unhappy about the results of competitive examinations, partly because the emphasis on high levels of language competence restricted success to those who could take the time to live some years abroad ("It was found that these young men might be extremely proficient in languages, but that they knew little else"), but more importantly because the service became in a sense committed to the candidate who conquered this one challenge: "It had been easy enough to weed out the probationers under the old system since their nomination as attachés had been merely an act of favour; it was far more difficult to reject a young man at the end of his probationary period if he had spent some years of his youth in studying for a difficult competitive examination."

George Kennan paid affectionate tribute to one of the last of the rich dilettantes who formed the first American career foreign service. Alexander Kirk, U.S. ambassador to Berlin in the late 1930s, was, Kennan wrote, "a carryover from an older day when to be rich entitled you to be eccentric. . . . Deliberately, I think, as a gesture of defiance and self-protection, and in the indulgence of a fine sense of the theatrical, Kirk worked at giving himself the aspect of exactly that sort of American career diplomat of which the American philistine has always been most suspicious: elegant, overrefined, haughty and remote. It was a manner of enlivening life by playing the buffoon. He was anything but an intellectual. He never wrote anything if he could help it. He was even suspicious of many of our efforts at interpretative reporting, discouraged them, and preferred that we make our points obliquely by a shrewdly selective coverage of the Nazi press. His understanding was intuitive rather than analytical. His conversation consisted largely of weary, allusive quips. His posing sometimes went so far as to raise doubts whether he was serious.

"But behind his facade of urbane and even exaggerated sophistication there lay great intuitive shrewdness and a devastatingly critical sense of humor, directed to himself as well as others. No one impressed him. . . . He despised the Nazis and held them at arm's length with a barbed irony. . . .

"I have realized, in subsequent years, that I learned much from Kirk— more, perhaps, than from any other chief. Unintellectual as he was, his instincts were very sound, and when one learned enough to see through the poses and to look for the deeper meaning of the quips, he was a good teacher. I am particularly indebted to him for the impressive lesson he gave me, by example even more than by precept, of the importance of the means as compared with the ends. . . . 'Never, never do anything abrupt,' he advised me. 'It never pays.' He disclaimed all further interest in the Foreign Service, since his mother's death. He had entered it, he solemnly maintained, only to spare her having her bags inspected at frontiers. But he could not just resign, especially in wartime; that would have been abrupt. 'When the war is over,' he said, 'I shall leave it so gradually and quietly that no one will know I am gone.'

"He did. . . ."

3

Though the Rogers Act was drafted by Carr and passed by a Congress that wished to see the diplomatic service become more like the business-oriented consular service, its initial workings favored the diplomats, who gained control of the appointments mechanism. The promotion list of 1927 that outraged the Congress by favoring the diplomats over the consuls was in fact the work of Secretary of State Frank Kellogg (who favored the people he knew) rather than that of the Personnel Board, but the resulting uproar moved the Department (and eventually produced legislation) to make the written examination more one of aptitude than of achievement, to reduce drastically (from about 20 percent to about 5 percent) the fraction of candidates who passed it, and to place the appointments-promotion process in the hands of Carr's bureaucrats and *sédentaires* rather than Grew's diplomats and voyagers.

American diplomacy began to lose its eccentrics. Examination systems that select only a small fraction of the candidates tend to produce winners whose habits of mind are like those of the authors of the exam. The cadre that scores best on the Graduate Record Examination is the psychology students; and three generations of detailed written examinations, with appointment only to those scoring the very best grades, have produced in New York City a cohort of school principals who are virtually clones. Eccentrics do not gravitate to the tasks of examination construction, and as time passes a grayness descends upon those professions where entry is offered only by the examination route and only to a small fraction of those who start out on the journey.

In the late 1920s, with business riding high and Wall Street offering high prestige as well as endless opportunity, the diplomatic service lost many of those who resented the grubbiness of consular work. In the 1930s, with the economy in shambles, the diplomatic cohort cherished its civil service immunities, accepted assignments to consul-generalships and even to Latin America (Roosevelt with some glee assigned the elegant Leland Harrison, with his English accent, Eton education and Rolls Royce, to be minister in Uruguay, and he went), and agreed to Wilbur Carr's demand that everyone making a career in the unified Foreign Service had to spend at least some of his time in a consulate.

Having lost its social exclusiveness, the State Department won from Roosevelt in 1939 complete control of American civilian representation abroad, as the 105 commercial attachés and nine agricultural attachés were detached from their domestic departments and folded into the Foreign Service. (Interestingly, most FSOs resented the "lateral entry" of these 124 attachés, who had not gone through the Foreign Service exams and risen through the ranks; the fact that the Department now had control of future commercial and agricultural attachés was less significant to them than the dilution of the existing cohort.) And immediately after the war, Congress passed a bill written at the State Department that marked high water for the Foreign Service as a self-governing profession—and as a power in American governance.

The Foreign Service Act of 1946 assumed that all the international functions the government had acquired during the war would come under control of the State Department. The law assumed also that a relatively small cohort of FSOs (there were fewer than 825 of them in 1946, mostly working abroad) would be capable of supervising all these activities, aided by clerical and technical assistants (in a separate Foreign Service Staff) and by specialists on temporary appointment (Foreign Service Reserve Officers, who would have the rank and salary of FSOs, but could not serve more than four years). Control of personnel, both on entry and for promotion, was vested in boards composed of FSOs, and their decisions were to be carried into effect by a Director General who by law had to be a Foreign Service Officer. The Secretary of State himself could not overrule these decisions, though in a pinch he could change the personnel of the boards. Some lateral entry to the higher grades of the Foreign Service was permitted, but only through a route which required both passage of an examination and four years' experience with the Department.

As rulers of the State Department, this self-contained Foreign Service would have an astonishing variety of responsibilities. Much of the wartime OSS intelligence operation had been assigned to State at war's end; also the propaganda activities of the Office of War Information; also what remained of the Foreign Economic Administration. Some ten thousand new civil servants had joined the Department, many of them doing work FSOs knew little about. The opportunity was there for the Foreign Service to enlarge its scope, function, and importance by enlarging itself. Instead, the Service reacted in horror, apparently concerned only to distinguish its own dignified "policy" role from the grubby "operations" roles taken by others, and to retain its purity by fighting off anyone and everyone who sought entry to its middle grades without having paid the proper dues. (Allowing such persons to assume FSO status, George Kennan wrote indignantly, would be "violating the entire principle of fair competition in entry and advancement.") In Dean Acheson's words, "either the Department was not imaginative enough to see its opportunity or administratively competent enough to seize it."

By 1949, the Hoover Commission on the organization of the government recommended that the Department staff up for expertise in geographical regions, accept much more frequent lateral entry to the Foreign Service to acquire the use of more specialized talents and knowledge, and return control over personnel decisions from the Director General to the Secretary of State. Following the first rule of a large bureaucracy attacked by a small commission (roughly, "If you can't lick 'em, ape 'em"), the State Department late in 1949 set up its own committee of three headed by James Rowe, to recommend changes in personnel procedures. Recommendations like those of the Hoover Commission emerged, with even more stress on "the need to attract and retain topflight specialized talent in such fields as economics, agriculture, public affairs, administration, and political affairs."

The most obvious way of acquiring such talent was to hire it, bringing in new people at levels consonant with their accomplishments. This was too much for the Rowe Committee, which accepted only the proposition that lateral entry should be permitted to civil servants already employed by the State Department in jobs that Foreign Service Officers might hold if they were working in Washington. Even under those terms, few newcomers were allowed through the heavenly gates: the Wriston Commission in 1954 found that two thousand State Department civil service employees had applied to the Foreign Service for transfer under the Rowe conditions, and only twenty-five had been accepted.

In retrospect, the Rowe Committee was a last stand. State had been unable to perform the functions allocated to it by executive order and the 1946 legislation. Intelligence had been removed early. In 1953, Eisenhower took away the information service and foreign aid (then directed by a Foreign Operations Administration), and Congress authorized the Agriculture Department to build its own Foreign Agricultural Service once again. Joe McCarthy was gnawing at the vitals of the Foreign Service, with no small help from his friends. (Vice-President Richard Nixon boasted that the Eisenhower administration was "kicking the Communists and fellow travelers and security risks out of the government . . . by the thousands." It would be funny if it were not so sad a comment on the state of American historiography that our "revisionist" historians busily blame for the sabotage of Roosevelt's friendly partnership with the Soviet Union and the ensuing Cold War the same people the McCarthyites and Nixonians called traitors subservient to Moscow.) Recruitment into the Foreign Service simply stopped; at home and abroad, everyone who worked for the State Department was subjected to the indignity of new security clearance, usually by people who thought the burden of proof lay upon the Foreign Service Officer being cleared, not on his faceless accuser.

In this atmosphere, John Foster Dulles in March 1954 appointed yet another committee to examine State Department personnel policies. It was headed by Henry M. Wriston, president of Brown University (and father of Walter Wriston, an FSO for one year, who moved on to become *lider massimo* of Citicorp); and it was given all of two months to review all previous studies and the present situation, and present its recommendations. First among these was a vast expansion of the Foreign Service, to be accomplished initially by conferring FSO status on a huge cadre of State Department administrative officers and other civil service employees who worked directly on international problems of any sort, then by increasing to 500 a year the annual intake of new officers. The second recommendation was not carried out—recruitment did get as high as 250 in one of the Lyndon Johnson years, when all government was flowering like a rose, but the norm ran between 100 and 150. The first recommendation

brought results: within three years, the wonders of lateral entry had bal-
looned the Foreign Service from twelve hundred officers to thirty-six hundred, most of them, obviously, people who had not performed the professional rites of passage. "Wristonization" is still a bitter memory in the
State Department, kept green by the new FSOs who learn about it in
school, and for whom it is often enough a code word signifying opposition
to more recent affirmative actions. By the late 1960s, two thirds of all deputy chiefs of mission abroad—the key posts in a Foreign Service where
many ambassadors were political appointees—were Foreign Service
Officers who had achieved that status through lateral entry.

This dramatic change raised a number of questions about the future
effectiveness and efficiency of the State Department, three of them being
most important:

1. Could one enforce in so large a group the Foreign Service oath of
availability to serve anywhere in the world? Most of the civil service,
Reserve and administrative people now to be placed in the Foreign Service
were distinctly Washington-based, and had not expected to move around
the world. A survey done for the Rowe Committee by the National Opinion Research Center had shown that three fifths of the departmental
(non-FSO) employees "place some kind of restriction on their availability for overseas assignment." Still, this difficulty proved manageable:
given the real benefits and status gain offered by incorporation in the Foreign Service (and in some cases their confidence that they could manipulate the personnel system cleverly enough to stay in Washington, anyway),
the departmental employees signed on.

John Franklin Campbell noted scornfully that "civil-service employees
were importuned to 'integrate' and take foreign posts lest they lose the
better salaries, ranks and pension rights that could be obtained only in the
Foreign Service," and approvingly cited Dean Acheson's remark that the
Wriston reforms were "contemptible." He also complained that Wristonization "destroyed one of State's most useful assets—a permanent,
Washington-based staff of civil servants." Harr, on the other hand, stressed
the benefits to the Department from the great increase in the number of
FSOs holding jobs at the center in Washington (119 in 1954, more than
800 in the 1960s and thereafter).

2. Would "integration" reduce the average quality of the Foreign Service and damage the morale of the FSOs? The belief that it would was
most strongly held, of course, among the FSOs themselves, and was
greatly strengthened in 1956 when the Department under continuing pressure to "democratize" dropped its previous requirement that candidates
for the Service know a foreign language. (Wriston himself bitterly opposed
this change, and was right. Virtually all candidates are college gradu-

ates, and every college teaches foreign languages. It was not unreasonable to demand that people considering careers in diplomacy make the small prior commitment of studying a language in college. Moreover—and to save some time I will speak here *ex cathedra*, cashing in ten awful years of pulling at oars in the galleys of educational research—foreign languages are the subject for which social class and ethnic background seem to matter *least* when one correlates students' backgrounds and achievements in various areas of study. Of course, few people in the State Department would know that; few people in education know it.)

The short answer to the question about quality is the success of many of those who entered the Foreign Service in the mid-1950s at mid-career level. Though selection boards were dominated by veterans of the pre-Wriston Foreign Service, by 1970 two thirds of those in the top career ranks (FSO-2 and FSO-1, presumably the equivalent of brigadier general and major general in the Army) were people who had become FSOs by lateral entry. On the lower levels, where administrative personnel had been made FSO-6s and FSO-5s (lieutenant and captain), Wristonized civil servants were less successful; in the mid-1960s the Department enlarged the Foreign Service Staff category to keep useful people out of a competition they were certain to lose. But on the levels that the critics of Wristonization care about, the newcomers seem to have done fine.

Morale questions are more difficult to answer. In the three years immediately following the adoption of the Wriston recommendations, about two hundred FSOs from the old cadre resigned from the Service. Obviously, a tripling of the size of the Service reduced the promotion possibilities for those who had been in the original, smaller group (though the onset of nationhood for scores of former colonies probably opened enough new good jobs to prevent serious loss of opportunity). Samuel Lewis, ambassador to Israel and an FSO through the examination route, warns that morale is *always* bad in the State Department because everybody thinks he should be influencing policy and only about fifty to a hundred ever have any reason to believe that they do. There can be no question that the typical young FSO still feels himself superior to others in government service. "The guys assigned to international affairs at other agencies," said Richard Dols, political counselor in the U.S. embassy in New Zealand, "will often say, 'I wanted to be an FSO, but I failed the damned exam.' It gives the FSO the feeling he's among the chosen; gives the man at the other agency a chip on his shoulder."

3. Were the specialists who would be incorporated in the new, expanded Foreign Service really the specialists the State Department needed? This question was raised more or less delicately in 1962 by the

Herter Commission, a privately funded study group brought into being at the informal request of President Kennedy, headed by the man who had succeeded John Foster Dulles as Secretary of State for Eisenhower. Members of the Commission included former members of the Hoover, Rowe and Wriston committees, and scholars of the quality of Milton Katz, who had been Averell Harriman's number two and successor in the Marshall Plan operation in Paris and was teaching at the Harvard Law School though not himself a lawyer. These were the heady days of the New Frontier, and the Herter Commission proclaimed the existence of a "New Diplomacy."

The goal of this New Diplomacy was to speed the development of the developing countries, to help the good guys win "the conflict between the free countries, struggling to build a world of free, independent, peaceful and progressive peoples, and the Communist world."† To carry out his duties, the New Diplomat would need skills in "intelligence; political action; technical assistance and various forms of foreign economic aid; military aid programs; information and psychological programs . . . measures to counter insurgency movements." The specialists who had been folded into the Foreign Service by Wriston were not such a much for that.

Mostly, indeed, they were not such a much for anything. The Foreign Service Reserve jobs had been limited-appointment positions with no chance of continuation, and no chance of promotion. FSRs had been second-class citizens, and it is not easy to recruit first-class people to the status of second-class citizen. And for those who were or could develop into first-class specialists, there would be the problem that the best jobs in the Foreign Service were defined as "generalist" positions.

In 1977, Carol Laise as Director General was still awkwardly wrestling with the problem (the reader cannot here be protected from the cold blast of the reality of State Department language): "A specialist," she wrote, "is one who normally expects—and is expected to—remain in his or her chosen field of expertise throughout an entire career. Specialist career ladders rise to different heights. . . . It must be presumed that those who choose a specialist career are aware of the career ceilings before them. When either a generalist or a specialist serves as an office director or deputy assistant secretary, he or she remains in a primary-skill code category. To shift into the 'program direction' skill code requires evidence that such an individual possesses managerial skills that are transferable. . . . 'Program direction' is by definition a generalist skill. . . . Service in program direction

† It is interesting to note how much of the thrust of the Reagan administration, the tax cut in domestic affairs and the Manichaean view of international relations, derives from the Kennedy days. The neo-conservatives, who were once Kennedy liberals, are right to feel at home.

skill code assignments is a precondition for acquiring that skill code." FSO or not, the specialist remained a second-class citizen.

But all such questions merely dance around the issue that confronts not only the State Department but Foreign Ministries all over the world. There are disputes about how able Foreign Service personnel really has to be (the Berrill Report in England argued that *the work is being done to an unjustifiably high standard,*" and that "the Service should recruit a smaller proportion of the ablest candidates"), about the kind and degree of training required for diplomatic work, about the usefulness of people from substantive departments of government in Foreign Service work, about the mix of specialists and generalists within the Service, about the criteria for entry and promotion, about the proper placement of both people and posts on the continuum between pure bureaucracy and pure professionalism.

People arrive in an organization with ceilings on their performance set by their capacities, but nobody in the world works all the way up to his capacity. Systems of organization may limit the quality of work that can be got from even the best people, or may multiply the usefulness of the work done by drones. Policies are never better than their execution, but execution (thank God) can be better than policy.

In a field like diplomacy, where there are no objective measures for people's work, neither the system nor its servants' adaptation to it can be taken for granted. There is never a full substitute for having an end in view, but the training, acculturation, assignment and promotion of foreign service personnel will certainly influence the effectiveness of diplomatic efforts—and will probably, in most parts of the world, influence the policies that are adopted.

7

TRAINING, ASSIGNMENT AND PROMOTION

In diplomacy, whatever you do, you come into a thing that has already started and you leave it before it is finished. It's usually not so important that you know the details.

—Heinrich Pfusterschmid-Hardenstein,
Director, Diplomatic Academy, Vienna

On 31 October [1968] . . . the General Assembly in its 1709th meeting elected Finland into the [Security] Council on a mandate belonging to Western European and other countries. . . . The problems considered by the Security Council during the years 1969 and 1970 can be divided into five categories: 1) the crisis concerning Africa (52 per cent), 2) the problems relating to the Middle East (21 per cent), 3) the continuation of the mandate of UN troops on Cyprus (12 per cent), 4) organizational and procedural questions (9 per cent), 5) other matters (7 per cent). There were 33 motions, of which 29 were adopted. . . .

—précis of a master's thesis written
by a young Finnish diplomat at the
Diplomatic Academy, Vienna

The grayness of the people is reflected in the grayness of the reports.
—Sol Linowitz

1

Of all the schools that train people for diplomatic careers, the most surprising is the International Relations Institute of Cameroon, a collection of half a dozen one-story concrete buildings on a partly grassy, partly dusty hilltop some distance from the center of that country's capital city Yaoundé. About sixty resident students, drawn from a dozen or so African countries, take courses here in two languages—English and French—under the guidance of an academic faculty drawn from universities around the world—from Poland, Scotland, France, and Switzerland as well as Cameroon itself, Sierra Leone and Zimbabwe.

IRIC was probably the brainchild of Adamou Ndam Njoya, a Cameroonian education specialist working at UNESCO in Paris in the 1960s. (Njoya later became Minister of Education in the Cameroon Government, and thus unavailable to visitors: he makes appointments but doesn't keep them. This is a little hard on the visitor, who stands in the tiny hot anteroom because soldiers are sitting in the only two chairs, while the luxuriously leather-covered doors to the Minister's office swing open and shut behind urgent bureaucrats and the Minister's secretary assures, "He knows you're here.") The theory behind the school was that the newly independent African nations would need highly skilled diplomatic representation, if only because colonialism had meant outwardly directed economies. Whether they chose to develop along lines of expanded exports or of import substitution (creating their own manufacturing industries protected by tariff walls), all the African countries would need foreign aid to pay the costs of capital investment. And to the extent that African unity was to be meaningful—it is a term of immense emotional resonance throughout the continent—African diplomats would have to be able to work together in the world capitals and in the international organizations.

Cameroon was a logical place for an all-Africa diplomatic academy. The country could be a paradigm of the European influence on tropical Africa. Located at the hinge just below the bulge in the continent, central Cameroon is hilly enough to have a mostly pleasant climate, hot in midday but refreshing at night. Coastal Cameroon is abominably sticky, mountain Cameroon is unbearably wet—the foothills of Mount Cameroon, the highest peak in West Africa, are the wettest place on earth, with more than 350 inches of rain a year—and the northern stretches are perilously dry. But political Cameroon and its capital Yaoundé are in the mild green hills.

The reasonable fraction of Cameroon land that can be cultivated produces the southern cash crops—coffee, cocoa, rubber, bananas, palm oil, etc., on a smallholder basis in the hills and on oversized state farms (a colonial legacy) nearer the ocean. The mountains and the rainfall combine to create major hydroelectric resources, neatly matched with bauxite deposits for the production of aluminum. The slave trade was extensive here in the eighteenth century, Americans buying people on the coastal plains, which became variously Christian, Arabs on the savannah, which became nominally Moslem. For the future, there is oil, probably a fair amount of it, and substantial mineral wealth.

In the late nineteenth century the area came under formal European control—in this case, German control—as Kamerun. The northern and western borders were formed by, respectively, the German drive to get a military toehold on Lake Chad and a series of deals between Berlin and Paris, swapping German claims in North Africa for pieces of the French Congo. During World War I, the British coming down from Nigeria and the French cutting west from Chad and French Equatorial Africa ousted the German colonial administration and its forces, and the League of Nations later confirmed the division the armies had made, recognizing separate mandates for French and British Cameroon. The two pieces of British Cameroon were separately carved out of the French mandate, and did not have a common border.

There had been no such country, of course, before the European invasion. At least two hundred separately governed tribes lived on this land, speaking at least twenty-four different languages. (One scholar estimates "136 identifiable linguistic groupings" in the former French Cameroun and "about 100 vernaculars" in the formerly English Cameroon.) Throughout West Africa, there could never have been "nations" without the European takeover, because communications among the tribes were at best sporadic and always hampered by linguistic incompatibilities. Though local kings might extend the areas that paid them tribute, meaningful large-scale political integration could occur only after the European schools (mission schools, mostly) gave the inhabitants a tongue they shared.*

* This does not mean, of course, that these areas have no history. Willard Johnson, for example, notes that some of the Cameroon tribal kingdoms "claim particularly close ties, such as the Bamoun and the Nsaw. The Sultan of the Bamoun claims to be a 'brother' of the fon of Nsaw, and also that the Nsaw are derived from the Bankim, one of the three branches of the Bamoun. The latter allegation appears heavily influenced by the ethnocentricity of the Bamoun. Anthropologists consider the ties between the two groups more distant since they place the Bankim within the Tikar group, from which both the Bamoun and the Nsaw are derived. In any case, the cultures of the two groups have diverged as the Bamoun have embraced Islam, exemplified by the transformation of the traditional designation for chief, 'Fon,' to the Moslem title, 'Sultan.' Moreover,

German governance—which lasted only thirty years—demonstrably did produce the idea of a national identity. When liberation movements began to stir in West Africa after World War II, residents of British and French Cameroons came together under the German name to lay claim to the entire territory. They were not able to revive the use of German, but they were able to persuade the southern half of English Cameroon to throw in its lot with the French-speaking Cameroun rather than with the English-speakers of Nigeria. Thus Cameroon became the only bilingual African country, with both French and English as official languages.

At the beginning, the arrangement was a "Federal Republic," with separate legislatures in the linguistically different regions and separate English and French Prime Ministers running separate administrations under the general authority of a national President. But the secession of the northern half of the English-speaking territory, which voted to join Nigeria rather than a Cameroon nation in a UN-sponsored plebiscite in 1961, left the French predominant in the new nation, which presently became a "Unified" rather than a "Federal" Republic. A true national consciousness was forged in the shared experience of fighting off a persistent left-wing guerrilla movement sponsored by Nkrumah, Touré and Nasser, given refuge and arms in the Congo (Brazzaville), and supported at the United Nations by the Soviet bloc. The tribe most prominent in the guerrilla movement spanned the linguistic border, and suppressing the rebellion required cooperation that might not otherwise have come about.

French Cameroun was always larger, more populous and (like French colonies generally) more Europeanized than British Cameroon. Nevertheless, the commitment to the English-speakers was sincere. Ahmadou Ahidjo, Prime Minister of the French colony who became and until 1982 remained President of Cameroon, ostentatiously studied English and learned some. Education was proclaimed bilingual from the beginning, and while the proclamation far exceeded the achievement (most students had enough trouble learning one European language), the University of Yaoundé made a gallant effort to offer all programs in both languages. An imaginative proposal to pair each professor with an assistant who spoke the other language failed only because the English were certain they would get all the assistantships.

Bernard Fonlon, an English-speaking Cameroonian who was fluent in French and wrote about both cultures, founded a bilingual magazine and

the two chiefdoms have been hostile in the past. The Nsaw once routed the armies of the Fon of Bamoun, Nsagguf (the grandfather of the current sultan), and beheaded him in battle." Africans can and should study this stuff, while Europeans learn about Gustavus Adolphus and Americans pore over Daniel Webster's fights with John C. Calhoun in the Senate. This proposition has a corollary the reader can develop for himself.

gave his country a grand mission: "When President Ahidjo says that this country is a pilot state," Fonlon wrote, "he is not bragging, nor is he using a phrase void of meaning. It is precisely the historic opportunity to effect an integration of these three cultures [African, English, French] that has invested Cameroun with the singular, enviable mission to pilot the rest of Africa into continental unity." IRIC was an expression of that mission.

From its intellectually modest beginnings in 1972, with a four-month training program for consuls, IRIC has expanded to a full-fledged graduate school and research center, and the directors have ambitions to offer a doctorate in the mid-1980s. In 1980, the school's sixty students were equally divided into three cohorts—first- and second-year students in the master's program, and young diplomats already in Service sent by their governments for a one-year training program. In 1979–80, about half the master's degree candidates were Cameroonian (representing about 5 percent of the Cameroonian applicants), and the rest were scattered among six other countries (five each from Chad and Ghana, three from Congo, two each from Burundi and Zaire, one from Mauritania). The eighteen students making the one-year *stage diplomatique* were drawn from nine countries: Congo, Togo, Upper Volta, Angola, Gabon, Zaire, Burundi, Mali and Niger. One or two in each group were female. Of the five-thousand-dollar annual cost per student, about three thousand was paid to the students in lieu of salary, about eight hundred went to the school as tuition, and the remaining twelve hundred covered room and board at IRIC. Financial aid has been available from Swiss, German, French and Belgian sources—and, since 1980, from Libya.

All students must be university graduates. Joseph Owona, who became director of IRIC in 1976, when he was all of thirty-one years old, said he preferred candidates whose degree was in economics, because "African diplomacy is development diplomacy." But many of his students came from the law faculties, as Owona did himself—his great accomplishment is an *agrégation* (the highest French academic honor) in public law, won in Paris in 1977. Others were from literature and even, Owona said with a gesture of contempt, journalism.

In principle, everyone is bilingual on arrival, and classes are taught in both languages. Colin Ngwa, a young professor from English-speaking Cameroon who studied and taught at the University of Massachusetts en route to IRIC, reported that when students got in trouble in English he found it best to switch to French. (Some Ghanaians, Tanzanians and West Cameroonians get in trouble in French and switch to English.) "But they *admire* bilingualism," Ngwa said approvingly. The announcement to candidates informs them that the program "requires not only a considerable and sustained personal effort through the course of the year, but equally a certain level of knowledge in the areas of economics, international relations, political science and international law." Asked if he personally, after his American experience, considered the IRIC program tough, Ngwa said, "I would call it excruciating. They take eight courses, and have to attend seminars and write seminar projects." Grades are given on both written and oral examinations, on the French scale of 20. An average of 12 is required for graduation, and the quality of the master's thesis (and its oral defense) counts for 40 percent of the total grade.

These theses have been quite ambitious. Some deal with more or less popular subjects ("The United States and the Problem of Human Rights in South Africa" [French]; "Some Legal Aspects of the Refugee Problem in Africa" [English]; "International Efforts to Stabilize the Prices of Primary Products" [French]; "The Soviet Military Presence in Africa" [French]). Others are highly specialized ("Policy Coordination and Institutional Development Within the East African Community" [English]; "Regional Political Integration: the Accord for the Development of the River Senegal" [French]; "The African Organization for the Protection of Intellectual Property and the Promotion of Technology in Africa" [French]). Each topic is proposed not only to a faculty adviser but to a seminar before the student begins work, discussed with the seminar as the work proceeds, and defended before the seminar at its conclusion. The seminars are a culture shock for many Africans. "We have to make students understand," said Colin Ngwa, "that the purpose is to help, not to criticize. In any case, most of them are supposed to be diplomats; they should be able to express themselves, diplomatically."

Ludwik Dembinski, the Polish-born director of studies at IRIC, defended the academic approach: "First, mastery of the techniques of research and intellectual rigor are the qualities that will be essential in the future professional life of IRIC graduates. Second, it is only through the quality of the written work of its students that one can establish the academic level of IRIC. Finally, the field of international relations in Africa has been relatively little explored, so that each piece of original research, however modest it may be, constitutes a real contribution to knowledge in this area." A quick browse through manuscripts in the IRIC library and a morning's listen to seminar discussions of three thesis projects did not leave this visitor overwhelmed by the quality of the results—but student work at the Fletcher School or Johns Hopkins or Georgetown is not all that good, either—and aficionados of these subjects will have noted the standard set by the banalities of the average article in *Foreign Affairs*.

Dembinski's third point was certainly true. In the seminar discussion I overheard, two Cameroonian students revealed almost embarrassing gaps in their backgrounds in discussing their projects—an English-speaking

young man who was investigating the World Bank's policies and procedures in reorganizing the state operation of the great plantations of West
Cameroon; a French-speaking young lady (very elegantly turned out from
Paris shops, gold earrings and open-toed shoes worn to class) who was ex-
ploring the history of the negotiations by which Pechiney-Ugine-Kuhlman
of France got the land to build an aluminum plant in Cameroon, with
power from a hydroelectric dam guaranteed them cheap in perpetuity. But
if these young people in IRIC did not conduct such investigations, nobody ever would. And the young lady's costume was a souvenir of her
working journey to Paris to get data at corporate headquarters.

The Germans have maintained a faintly wistful interest in Cameroon
(encountered at a party in Yaoundé, the German ambassador commented
that you still find old people in Douala, the port, largest city and seat of
the old German administration, who can speak the language). IRIC students get a three-week visit to Germany paid for by the German Government, as part of their program; the emphasis there was on commercial
work. The students liked it, of course; the faculty was of two minds. "We
had to interrupt our program for three weeks to prepare for it," said Abdul
Aziz Jollah, dean of students, a lean, lightly bearded Sierra Leonian with a
Ph.D. from the University of California, whose leisure suit and open shirt
contrasted entirely with director Owona's barrel chest, deeply formal countenance and three-piece suit. Before 1980, moreover, the students simply
went and returned, to Jollah's distress; thereafter, each degree candidate
had to write a formal "minute" on what he had learned, and was marked
on it.

Jollah was the administrator and educational planner. "We try to give
them conceptual baggage," he said, "to enable them to comprehend whatever environment they find themselves in. The response is not so much a
function of the content itself as of the enthusiasm of the students—and
their feeling of how much their personal advancement will be affected by
how well they do at IRIC. Those who feel they will be promoted or
blocked because of other considerations, personal contacts, etcetera, are
less likely to work hard. And there is always, of course, their response to individual teachers—they may come wanting to do international law, and
get turned on by a professor of economics."

Students live at the school in a group of hut-like round concrete dormi-
tories divided into six individual cells, offering the standard collegiate cot,
desk, bookshelves, desk chair and reading chair; concrete floor, usually
with a woven rug beside the bed; private toilet and shower, private door to
the outside world. Classrooms, distressingly unornamented and filled with
those old wooden chairs with pancake right arms, occupied a square building around a paved central cloister. With their tile floors, bare walls and

open windows, they were noisy: my notes contain complaints about a racket being made outside the seminar by students not in class, including one who seemed to be crowing like a cock. But it was a real cock, and twice there was also a real jet plane overhead.

Sharing a somewhat larger structure down the hillside were a place to eat and an air-conditioned, quiet library with a high ceiling, still less than ten thousand books but growing (mostly, of course, through gifts, which inevitably produces things like the collected works of Kim Il Sung and the speeches of Ferdinand Marcos). There was what looked like complete sets of the works of George Kennan and Raymond Aron; Churchill in French; Lenin in English. However limited, it was serious, not a polemical collection. For most students, said one of them, Francis Ngantcha, a slight, matter-of-fact young English-speaking Cameroonian, "this is the best library they have ever seen." It was particularly heavy on periodicals—130 of them, drawn from all over the globe.

Ngantcha came to my hotel to sing the praises of his school. Any Cameroonian who did well, he said, was pretty much assured a job in the Foreign Service. His own French was only fair, but he could read *Le Monde* and *Express*. Anyway, "English is a very useful language in international relations." He knew precisely what he wanted to do: he hoped to become part of the Seabed Authority to be formed by the Law of the Sea treaty. The Cameroon ambassador to the UN was titular chairman of the committee that developed the concept for this Authority. He had come to IRIC as a visiting lecturer and had performed Jollah's function of turning a student on. Now he was promising to be helpful in finding young Ngantcha a job.

Alumni of IRIC have done well. "One is a director of a United Nations branch in Geneva," director Owona said proudly (in French). "One is the *recteur* of the university. One is a *chef de cabinet*. One is director of civil aviation. All the others are in foreign ministries and international organizations. We are trying to form an alumni association." Whether the school would be successful as the eighties wore on, however, was problematic. IRIC gets lip service at many African Foreign Ministries. "We will be sending our people there rather than to Europe, for training in African affairs," said a senior man in the Ivory Coast diplomatic service, who then pointed out that he himself had of course attended the School of Advanced International Studies in Geneva; and the fact is that at this writing Ivory Coast has never sent anyone. "The Organization of African Unity is still very interested in IRIC," Owona said. "But the governments want their own national schools. We think that is not good for Africa. African diplomacy lacks a cadre of middle-level diplomats." At the request of the governments, IRIC was reluctantly planning to revive its short-term consular program, abandoned as part of the academic assertiveness of the late 1970s. In other fora, Jollah was suggesting that the governments support the proposed doctoral program as a source of university instructors: "Africa also needs African-trained teachers."

At the U.S. embassy in the Ivory Coast, DCM Gerald Friedman recalled approvingly from his time in Yaoundé that the school had been a benefit to the United States in its global competition: "When they came to us, they had a Q and A session, but when they went to the Russian embassy the Russians wouldn't allow questions." (It wouldn't have done the IRIC students much good to ask questions of the Soviet ambassador in 1980: he was one of those squared-off apparatchiks the Russians cannot keep from sending abroad, speaking neither English nor French.) But in 1980, despite the cordial relations between Ahidjo (one of few Moslem heads of state to go down the line for the United States when the Iranians took hostages in Tehran) and U.S. Ambassador Mabel Smythe (formerly head of the National Council of Negro Women, a person of great warmth, charm and political sense), the embassy tended to regard IRIC as a nest of what used to be called comsymps.

This was wrong. Obviously, students from Angola, Benin and Congo brought their own intellectual baggage, but the reading suggested to all students in the summer before matriculation was almost entirely Western-oriented, and Marxism was presented in the comparative systems course syllabus as merely one of many possible approaches. The problem, probably, was Owona, a man to stimulate the novelistic juices in almost anyone, with chips all over his shoulder and his heart hopelessly exposed on his sleeve. Neither a diplomat by training nor a teacher by temperament, he clearly felt that his authentic distinction of intelligence and academic achievement was undervalued by a Cameroon bureaucracy that did not understand what it meant to be a *professeur agrégé*, by a French academic community that patronized Africans, by students who were slaves to journalistic simplifications—and especially, perhaps, by Americans *tout court*. Unfortunately, the one place where he had been taken as seriously as he thought proper was Brazzaville, which had made him more sympathetic than most to tyrannical roads to "socialism." At the seminar presentations of thesis topics at IRIC, he laughed loudly at students' mistakes, and dealt with them sarcastically. Such attitudes, of course, reflect a teacher's insecurity and concern rather than malevolence, but they do produce students who hate teacher's guts. One seeks then to regain their loyalty by making violent statements in public on the popular side. A number of American university presidents come to mind from the sixties. So Owona tweaked Uncle Sam's beard (and also—this was considered very sinister—failed to denounce Soviet intervention in Afghanistan), and what little benefit U.S. support of IRIC might have conveyed to the institution was denied it. Pity.

2

IRIC represents one model for training Foreign Service Officers. Though its founding was to a degree coordinated from Geneva, where the Carnegie Endowment and the School of Advanced International Studies of the University of Geneva worked closely together, its closest analog in Europe was probably the Diplomatic Academy in Vienna. Founded in 1967, the Diplomatic Academy had replaced a long-standing Consular Academy which counted among its graduates the men who were in 1981 Secretary-General of the United Nations, President of the International Court of Justice at The Hague, and Foreign Minister of Austria, among others. They had formed a little alumni association that met in New York for the UN General Assembly session each year.

Located in one of those long, low, early nineteenth-century bourgeois palaces that line the relatively narrow streets radiating out from what had been the city walls and is now the Ringstrasse, the Academy has a tiny door to the outside world and a park-like garden on the inside. Like IRIC, it is a small school (forty to fifty students), serving both the local Foreign Ministry (which gets three fifths of its young diplomats from the graduates) and a range of outsiders. It reports to both the Foreign Ministry and the Education Ministry. The program is eighteen months, by statute, with some sentiment that it should be extended to two years. Everybody is required to produce a research paper, shorter and somewhat less scholarly than what IRIC hopes to elicit.

The locals are not yet members of the Austrian Foreign Service—"You have no guarantee," said director Heinrich Pfusterschmid-Hardenstein, formerly Austrian ambassador to Finland (a larger job than one might think, because the SALT talks oscillated between Helsinki and Vienna, and the ambassadors had considerable administrative coordination to accomplish). "You have to pass exams, it's a good challenge for the Academy." Foreigners, however, are usually young diplomats sent by their Ministries. In 1978, when I visited, the foreigners were drawn from the Soviet Union, Bulgaria, the United States, Italy, the Philippines, Belgium, Ivory Coast, Tunisia, Finland, Poland and Yugoslavia.

The Diplomatic Academy boasted a faculty of forty-two, mostly moon-lighters from the universities of Vienna or Salzburg, plus people from the Foreign Ministry. They offered thirty-five separate courses, one taught in

English (Public Relations) and one in French (*Histoire contemporaine depuis 1945*). The school also offered language courses in German (for the foreigners), French and Business French, English and Business English, Russian, Spanish and Arabic. In the mid-1970s, the Austrian Parliament passed a law requiring the Academy to make its language courses available to the MPs. Business English turned out to be the most popular with politicians; only one (Conservative) deputy enrolled for Russian.

Austrian graduates of the Academy wind up working for the Bundeskammer, the Chamber of Commerce, doing the work that Americans assign to government–employed commercial attachés; some go to the Finance Ministry and the Agriculture Ministry, some to the international organizations—and the banks. A tall, grave man, Pfusterschmid-Hardenstein urged his students to take an additional year's study at an English, French or American university, "because you are going to live in an international community. At a university, you make friends of foreigners. Once you are in the Service, you also get your friends among foreigners, but it isn't the same thing at all, because then your friend is already on the other side, in a sense."

Though the only nuts-and-bolts courses were on Protocol, Public Relations and Data Processing, Pfusterschmid-Hardenstein tried to infuse the program with a practical sense. "People need an intermediate training between university and practice. The greatest shock is that you leave university thinking you know everything and you find you know nothing. Our entrants all think they are going to be ministers, but at the embassy you get a very small job. Consular questions in an embassy are the most important ones—someone comes in and says he has lost his passport, he's been robbed, and you have to decide. You can't refer it to Washington or Vienna; they will say, 'You decide.' "

In France and Britain all these things are handled on an apprenticeship basis. "We have never managed to introduce as a general policy the 18-month period of specialised overseas study of languages, economics and history recommended for new entrants to the Administrative stream in the 1943 White Paper," the Chief Clerk of the British Foreign Office wrote as part of the formal reply to the Prime Minister's Berrill Report. ". . . . At present, after a 1-week introductory course, the new recruit is given his first assignment in the Foreign and Commonwealth Office as a desk officer, perhaps dealing with relations with one or two foreign countries, working under close supervision, but learning by practical experience. This stage may last up to 2 years, during which the training on the job, with guidance and support from a more experienced superior, is backed up with some more formal training courses in subjects such as economics, the European Communities, international law and Communist affairs. Most new recruits, after a long period of academic study, relish the opportunity to get down to a job, and we find this practice generally satisfactory."

Paddy de Courcy-Ireland, head of the Training Department in the Foreign Office, a confident young man with jet black hair and thick-rimmed glasses to match, remembered that when he joined the Service, "I had a six-week course in policy issues, and it bored the pants off me. Most people had learned all that in preparation for the examinations and interviews. It was hard for them, or the lecturer, to pay attention. So now we post them straight into a job. For the first year their primary task is to demonstrate that they can get on top of their job. Some get used as supernumeraries— the jargon term is 'sitting with Nelly.' You watch how Nelly does her job. We don't like that, we try to give people some specific responsibilities. Of course, they have to refer. Most jobs are not covered by the rule book—it's a question of judgment. My own feeling is that you learn judgment by practising it. The problems arise because the people doing the training don't have the time; we keep urging people to sit down and explain. Everyone is on probation for his first three years. There's a six-month report, then a twelve-month report, and thereafter an annual report and an annual career interview. . . ."

The third model, a training school within the Foreign Ministry itself, for those already selected to be diplomats, prevails in the United States, Germany, Egypt and the Eastern bloc (except, as noted, in Hungary). The Institute of Diplomatic Studies in Cairo, founded in 1966, is perhaps the most interesting of these. It occupies a villa on the grounds of the old palace beside Tahrir Square in the center of Cairo, where the Foreign Ministry has its headquarters. Every six months about fifteen university graduates are selected from about five hundred applicants, on the basis of an examination in international law and relations, economics and foreign trade, and Egyptian-Arab-African affairs. Candidates must write papers in both English and French. They are appointed for a two-year probationary term at the Foreign Ministry, and spend the first year at the Institute.

"We start with administrative affairs and consular matters," said Ambassador Gamal Barakat, Director General of the Institute since 1978. "When they come here, they all think they are going to sign treaties. But we have signed only two treaties in all my forty years here—one with Britain, and one with Israel. So first we have to bring them down to earth. We give them courses in espionage and counterespionage, terrorism, all that. We teach diplomatic expressions and terminology, protocol and practical protocol. We send them to our club so they learn how to arrange the table and seat people.

"We try to give them some idea of what happens at an embassy, instead of letting them learn it the hard way. Some idea of economics—not the subject, but actual world problems. After that we give them the idea of the UN, how it functions, its conferences and actions. We arrange practical exercises, simulation games where they divide themselves into groups. And we always avoid the duplication of what they have already studied at the universities.

"We try to give them the idea of *Kultur*, in the German sense. *Beaux-arts*—art, sculpture, painting, music. If they are posted in Paris, at least they should have some idea of fine art by the big painters and big writers. We take them to the Cairo Museum—they haven't been there since they went to school. We teach them about journalists and media of information, the press and diplomacy, how they can be useful to our press. We introduce them to the contemporary problems of our country. They visit the Suez Canal, Alexandria, come to know their country a little more. Everyone improves in English and French—the French embassy sends instructors, and we have British nationals to teach English. They make two trips —one to Paris, one to Berlin, the EEC in Brussels, and Geneva for the UN. Now I have succeeded in having the British take them for ten days. I am trying with the United States; I haven't succeeded yet.

"We don't have a permanent staff," Barakat continued as we sipped sweet Turkish coffee. "Most people are part-timers. Some are from the universities—we want to keep our connection to the academics—but we depend more heavily on senior diplomats past and present. Heads of departments and even the Minister himself come occasionally to discuss current diplomatic problems. We may invite the desk officer over to talk about the Iran-Iraq war, and then set up a conference—some students take the Iranian position, some the Iraqi position. This week we had two people—a professor from Latin America, who lectured on the Law of the Sea, and the day before yesterday, a German who talked about the EC, and stayed for a Q and A that lasted a good half hour. We have good connections with the embassies, of course. [Barakat's connection with the U.S. embassy was especially good, because he and U.S. Ambassador Roy Atherton had served together as consuls in Aleppo, Syria, in the late 1950s.] Last year we had a number of U.S. professors, and the French come in big numbers.

"At the end of the course they have to write a paper on a subject suggested by the Ministry. Everybody succeeds. We give only a certificate of attendance, to avoid the academic reference, but they like to have something for their year's work, so we give them a piece of paper. Then we try to help personnel assign them intelligently; we don't always succeed."

The Institute also offers special "mid-career" programs tailored to special purposes—for example, a three-week cram course on Arab-Israeli relations for eighteen people the personnel department was sending to Tel Aviv to open the Eygptian embassy there. And there have been occasional programs for foreign students—one for forty-three (count 'em, forty-three) Sudanese information officers to help them handle the press at the African summit in Khartoum in 1978. Two groups have come from Oman for special six-month programs, and by authority of the Sultan the Institute on their graduation awarded them the title of Palace Chamberlain. . . .

3

In the United States, a Foreign Service School was created within the State Department by the Rogers Act of 1924, which unified the consular and diplomatic services. At the beginning, it was a supplementary part of the recruit's training in the Department, a nine-month program taking two hours of a day otherwise spent in an apprenticeship mode, clerking in a bureau. Its first purpose, according to Schulzinger, was the creation of an *esprit de corps*: "From his very first days there, a new recruit was persuaded of the need to acquire a professional diplomatic outlook. Reformers hoped that the close association of the recruits in their year at the School would continue throughout their careers, in much the same way as the members of the same class at the military academies thought of themselves as a distinct group within their services. By encouraging each entering group to think of itself collectively, the reformers hoped to create strong bonds of friendship and shared association among the new men." Inevitably, the shared attitude was that of the higher-status diplomats: their "idea of world politics and the career of diplomacy," Schulzinger writes, "became the code of the Foreign Service."

Most of the time in the School was given to lectures by leaders in the Department (Allen Dulles as chief of the Near Eastern Bureau was especially active at the School) and by university professors imported for a lecture or two. From the descriptions, the lectures were highly philosophical, not to say windy, a tradition that has endured. Languages were not taught. People scheduled for assignment to countries where the language was Japanese or Chinese could be sent to study at universities at Department expense, but other languages were the FSO's private responsibility. In 1925 Secretary of State Kellogg, noting that French was no longer enough in Eastern Europe and that acquaintance with various "exotic" languages might be useful to young diplomats, got a budget out of Congress to send some recruits abroad for language training. Thus, George Kennan studied Russian at the University of Berlin, and Charles Bohlen attended the

École Nationale des Langues Vivantes Orientales in Paris. But none of this was the responsibility of the Foreign Service School.

The great moments of the Training School, as it came to be called in the 1930s, were during the period toward the end of that decade when G. Howland Shaw became chief of Foreign Service Personnel. The most aristocratic (Boston's Somerset Club), intellectual (Phi Beta Kappa from Harvard) and socially involved administrator the Department has known (on the side, he was an active promoter of prison reform and melioration of the treatment of juvenile offenders), Shaw moved the lecture program away from the comfortable generalities dear to policy-makers and self-important professors, and toward the real complexities of the outside world. While counselor in Turkey, Shaw had pushed the younger officers at the embassy into scholarly studies of Anatolian life and times. Now he invited young FSOs just back from their first tours abroad to lecture on what they had found. Heinrichs offers a list: "the position of the Quichus Indian in the social structure of Ecuador, the labor movement in Mexico, minorities and irredentism in Hungary, and Sanskrit as a cultural force in the Near East and Indo-China."

Shaw built the Department's first cadre of trained economists, finding funds to send young FSOs to Harvard, Chicago, Princeton and NYU, and he was among the earliest protégés of the protean Harold Lasswell, who introduced the use of tools from modern psychology to forge explanations of political behavior. But Shaw believed in specialization that, in Heinrichs' words, "would require some adjustment of the needs of the organization to those of the individual," and in "advancement . . . based on further specialization rather than capacity to direct the activities of others." No bureaucratic system could long tolerate these attitudes in a leadership post, and Shaw, having risen to the title of Assistant Secretary for Administration in 1941, was pushed into retirement in 1944. His successor Selden Chapin was the principal author of the Foreign Service Act of 1946, which enshrined the generalist approach and created a Foreign Service Institute with a permanent faculty that could assert specialized expertise (if any) only in geographical regions.

In 1980, FSI was an $18-million-a-year operation, with about $10 million of that in instructional costs (the rest went to salaries and allowances for students). Home base was an office building in that clump of mid-rise boxes across Key Bridge from Washington in Rosslyn, Virginia. The staff of 237 gave about a quarter of the classes, with the rest divided between people from State and other governmental agencies and about a thousand lecturers from outside the government (half paid, half volunteer). About a fifth of the budget was spent overseas, for language training at embassies and consulates; about 3 percent was spent to send FSOs for sabbatical years at universities, and another 3 percent went for extension service courses by mail.

Intellectually, the offerings of FSI were something less than impressive. Apart from language training, the only program that occupied any substantial chunk of time was Foreign Service Economic/Commercial Studies, which ran twenty-six weeks and was "designed to give participants the equivalent of a strong undergraduate major in economics with additional professional instruction in commercial subjects. . . ." That was a lot to ask for twenty-six weeks, starting from scratch ("No prior economic knowledge or training is required"), especially when passage of the course would "qualify the participants to fill a broad range of positions in the field and in Washington." Still, serious work *can* be done in twenty-six weeks.

More typical, unfortunately, was the Human Rights course, "an intensive exploration of the impact of recent human rights legislation on the conduct of American foreign relations"—in three days. Or Negotiations— "a course designed to make the participant more efficient in the techniques of negotiation"—in one week. Or Theories of International Relations: "A survey of the principal theoretical approaches, particularly the new scientific approaches, now prevailing in the academic disciplines of international relations and to show their present and potential relevance to government analysis and practice of foreign affairs"—also one week.

These courses were offered by the School of Professional Studies. There was also a School of Area Studies, which "administers a series of two-week Area Seminars, designed for persons assigned to a particular geographical area for the first time. . . . The seminars cover the historical background and geography of a region and its principal countries, significant cultural factors, political and economic institutions, an analysis of some of the major contemporary problems in the area, and discussion of the U.S. posture toward them." You may wonder, who "them"?—but in two weeks it can scarcely matter.

In November 1977, the Area Studies course on South Asia included eleven films in ten working days (for example, one entitled *Phantom India: Dream and Reality*, described in the syllabus as "Kerala: the temptation of the exotic, pale-fringed beaches, superb women, tea plantations, game reserves, primitive fishermen, a kind of lost paradise. Yet Kerala is the only state where a local government has a Communist majority, and where the problem of India's political future is most forcefully posed"). Meanwhile, the students of Latin America were getting seven films, then two hours on the history and role of the Catholic Church, an hour and fifteen minutes on Foreign Investment Policy in Latin America (seventy-five minutes to cover "a review of the historical trends of invest-

173

ment in Latin America, an analysis of their costs and benefits to the recipient countries themselves, and an assessment of current U.S. policy regarding foreign investment, etc."). On three of the ten mornings, all the Area Studies students met for general sessions—one on Human Rights, one on Communication Across Cultures, one on The Changing Role of Women in the World, this one taught by a female Assistant Secretary-General of the United Nations.†

Those who remain longer at FSI, studying languages, have the opportunity to take Advanced Area Studies for four hours every week. The sheet given to the student at the start begins, "Welcome to the Advanced Area Studies (AAS) program, which you will be taking in conjunction with language training at FSI. The program derives from a conviction that knowledge of the country/region of your assignment is highly important to your future success. Such knowledge is, in fact, what often separates the foreign affairs professional from the amateur. . . . The formal group lectures and films will normally not take more than two hours per week. . . . You will be expected to spend the balance of the time (or its equivalent) in carrying out your personal study program. This will require some discipline but the program will enhance your professional status and future performance and is well worth the effort."

Add one more piece of evidence—that the young FSOs are taught how to behave on formal occasions not by weary diplomats at a club but through literature from the Mormon Church—and the defense of the U.S. Foreign Service against the charge of elitism can rest. We seem to have other problems.

4

What FSI tried to do more or less seriously was general orientation to working for the State Department (five weeks), language training, and

---

† The choice of a person from the United Nations to lecture on women's role is almost as amusing as the idea that young American FSOs need consciousness-raising before they can go abroad. The UN is a sexist organization almost beyond the imaginings of the ordinary American. Harassment of the female office staff is routine there to a degree that would be inconceivable in any American business or even in government. And the FSO is not likely in any but a handful of posts to find women's issues taken seriously by the local society. My late wife, Ellen Moers, went with me to Europe in 1978, lecturing mostly on the subject of her last book, *Literary Women*. That lecture was unacceptable in Hungary, where she was asked instead to speak on Theodore Dreiser, the subject of her previous book. I had a little fun with this when speaking to the head of the American desk at the Hungarian Foreign Ministry, who shook his head patronizingly and said, "You must understand, there is no 'women's issue' in Hungary. Hungarian women are *very* satisfied."

preparation for working in a consulate. "This is not an educational institution in an academic sense," said Director George Springsteen, an FSO who had never served abroad. "It is a vocational training institute." Most of the basic orientation course is an introduction to State Department forms and procedures, with some small exposure to what United States Government policy *is* (where known) and to the tasks and situations that the FSO will encounter when he goes to work in an embassy. Modernity having struck the Foreign Service Institute some years ago, there is a certain amount of role-playing in this section of the program, in which "Victor Junioroff," briefed by a long narrative of a mythical country and its appurtenances, must handle himself in meetings where fellow students play the characters the briefing papers describe.

Young Junioroff, for example, studies a diagram of an ambassador's office, to learn "the note-taking position," goes to the front of the class with the mock ambassador and "his local interlocutor," and takes his notes. A member of the class says, "How large a role does nonverbal communication play in reporting a conversation?" Instructor Richard Kilpatrick, the model of an FSO, long nose and neat prematurely white hair, nods sagely and says, "Considerable. Considerable." He offers useful sophistication for the students: "The French won't share information,‡ the Germans rarely share. It's the Brits, the Canadians, the Australians, the New Zealanders, sometimes the Japanese—they'll be helpful."

Once these introductions are completed, the students are taken around to other departments of government—Defense, Treasury, Commerce, Labor, the Supreme Court, etc.—to find out something about how their work is to mesh with that of others in Washington. Where young Egyptian diplomats are given a basic grip on the culture behind their society, with visits to the museum, Luxor, Alexandria, the Suez Canal and the like, FSO trainees are taken to Congress to study the workings of the committee system. The unspoken and probably unconscious lesson is that in moving from private status to government service one has become a spokesman not for the society (certainly, of course, not for oneself), but for the government.

"They're insecure when they arrive," said Executive Director Kenneth Hartung, a precise man in steel-rimmed glasses, who picked up his own higher education in the Army and passed the Foreign Service test without academic preparation. "They quickly realize they're a very bright group. We have some EEO [Equal Employment Opportunity] people, too, who are even more insecure. They're in competition with each other. We want to encourage an old-boy/old-girl feeling of measuring your achievement

‡ The French really *don't* share. They knew the Shah had cancer, and never told anybody.

175

against the others in your class." Part of the effort to build the class as a unit is a jaunt away from Washington, when the thirty or so in each orientation group spend a week living together in a conference center at Harpers Ferry.

Philosophizing about the job is encouraged, not always with the hoped-for results. "When I was teaching political science," said one of the older members of a recent entering class, "we had these interminable meetings about what political science *was* and what it was supposed to be. I thought I'd escaped that, but all these briefings keep asking what the State Department *is* and what it's supposed to be—and nobody has an answer."

Language instruction takes half the budget of the FSI. Having eliminated language requirements for entrants to the Foreign Service (in 1956), Congress turned around and demanded that "Foreign Service posts abroad will be staffed by individuals having a useful knowledge of the language or dialect common to the country in which the post is located." FSI is supposed to make these essentially contradictory rules come out right, and labors mightily.

No fewer than forty languages are taught, mostly by a total-immersion direct method in classes that average fewer than four students per teacher. There are six hours of classwork a day, and a language lab for those who find it useful (most don't). Students are graded separately for Reading and Speaking, on a scale from 1 (useless except maybe in restaurants) to 5 (bilingual). In Western European languages, the expectation is that a student will reach an R-3/S-3 level in five or six months; in other languages, the expected floor is R-2/S-2, and it may take people as much as three years to get there in the hardest of the hard languages, Chinese, Japanese and Arabic. About a fifth of the annual FSO intake already knows a language well enough to go off on their first assignment without FSI language training.

Getting paid to learn a language is no small perk of being an FSO, with the bonus that wives are eligible to take the course themselves, free of charge. Most people seem happy with the program. How efficient it is would be hard to say. Assistant Dean Lloyd Swift in the School of Language Studies estimated that about twenty of the language teachers are trained "instructional linguists," which leaves sixty or more who are not, whose sole real qualification is that they are native speakers of the language. (A fair number are the wives of foreign diplomats stationed in Washington.) I and my late wife, who was a professor of comparative literature, spent a couple of days wandering around language classes at FSI in 1978, and came to the not surprising conclusion that a great deal depended on the individual teacher and individual student. "I don't think we *care* if they're trained teachers or not," said Executive Director Kenneth Hartung, rather aggressively. "We have our own system, and insist that it must be followed."

Language competence, of course, is a universal problem in diplomacy. Different countries require different language skills from diplomats. Indonesian, for example, is very important for the Australians. And different Foreign Ministries have different views of what constitutes language competence. In Italy, candidates for the Foreign Service must demonstrate their ability to handle both French and English before they are accepted, but this visitor found a trip to the Foro Italico a very useful refresher for his Italian, and if I had not known Italian there were several interviews for which I would have needed an interpreter. In Austria, however, the thing is real, and everyone must offer a paper on an economic subject written in English, and one on a political subject written in French.

For the "hard languages," residence in a country where the language is spoken is usually considered obligatory, and there has been a tradition of collaboration between the American and British Commonwealth foreign services, with British diplomats attending an American-sponsored language school in Japan, Americans studying their Arabic in a British institution formerly in Beirut, then in Tunis. The Russians simulate a foreign experience at the language schools in Moscow University, where students not only do all their work in the language they are studying, but are expected to eat together and speak that language at meals. Diplomats from the other Eastern-bloc countries are always included in the group.

The Japanese, who find all other languages "hard," send virtually all new FSOs for a year or more to a university in the country where the language they are studying is spoken. This has been a problem when the language is Chinese (also "hard" for Japanese speakers), and Japanese FSOs destined for specialization in Chinese affairs have mostly gone to Harvard to perfect their language skills and study East Asian affairs. It will be noted that this procedure gives the Foreign Ministry two—English and Chinese—for the price of one. At any one time, the Japanese have about twenty FSOs studying in the United States.

Outsiders tend to overestimate the weight diplomatic services place on language skills when evaluating their officers. Decisions on people's careers, after all, are made at the center, where the native language is what counts. "A good linguist is not necessarily a good diplomat," said Paddy de Courcy-Ireland, head of the Training Department at the British Foreign Office, "and a good man can be trained to be a good linguist." The decision-makers are either themselves fluent in foreign languages (in which case they consider it easy, and regard language disabilities in others as rather odd), or they are not fluent (in which case they can't take the problem very seriously). When he was Undersecretary of the Australian Foreign Ministry, Allan Renouf, later ambassador to Washington, refused to allocate funds for people to study French, on the grounds that (as a subordinate put it), "everybody can speak French if he has to." Alois Reitbauer, Secretary-General of the Austrian Foreign Ministry, remembered a party in Norway at which a member of the Norwegian Foreign Service noted with pride that he had just mastered his sixth foreign language—and one of his colleagues, when he had moved out of earshot, commented, "Now this man will express his idiocies in a sixth language. . . ."

A career based on a language skill obviously promotes clientitis and a highly bilateral view of the nature of foreign policy. Most nations therefore have something like Kissinger's GLOP (Global Orientation Program), to make sure that Foreign Service Officers remember that they represent their own country. Egypt, for example, divides the world into five zones, and requires that people serve in a zone other than that of their first assignment (and presumed linguistic capability) before they can return. No doubt, people who have learned Hungarian or Amharic or Burmese will during the course of their careers serve more tours in Hungary, Ethiopia and Burma than they would otherwise. An exotic language is a particularly good stepping stone to a DCM post, because an ambassador always wants as his deputy somebody who can talk with the natives. (Indeed, even greater things may be expected. Lars Hydle, president of the Foreign Service Association, the house union at the State Department, complained bitterly in the Carter days that "the President has made a lot of appointments to Eastern Europe of Foreign Service people, but not East Europe specialists. It's made for dissatisfaction: people have learned Bulgarian and they see the plum taken away.") But when serious business is to be done, when treaties are to be negotiated or heads of state are to exchange views, the authorities call in an R-5/S-5, an interpreter with skills far beyond what can be acquired in school, regardless of how experienced the FSO may be.

Language skills are probably most important as assurances to the FSO himself that he knows his trade and can handle his job. ("When I went to Burma, I wanted to learn Burmese," said Michael Elizur, Israeli ambassador to Australia, "not only to be more useful but to make the job more *interesting*.") Even politically appointed ambassadors tend to be apologetic about their inability to speak the language of the country to which they are posted—and rather vain of their accomplishment if they can make speeches and respond to interviewers in the local tongue. Americans rather expect, of course, that ambassadors sent to the United States will be entirely at home in English. . . .

What is remarkable is the size of the investment the State Department and other Foreign Ministries are prepared to make for this purpose, paying the salaries not only of beginners but of mid-career officers moving to a new post, while they attend language school. On the surface, it would seem that this investment is wasted if the scoundrel, having lived off his government and studied a language at the taxpayers' expense, then quits the Service and sells what can be a highly salable skill to some company that does business in that language. And in fact the Department does not take kindly to such behavior, which discourages private employers from raiding the ranks (an employee whose name evokes scowls at his embassy may not be too useful to a company in its foreign dealings). But in the larger view, the United States probably benefits at least as much from someone who takes a job with a private firm and uses his skills in generating trade and investment as it does from the linguist's continuance in diplomacy.

The other task FSI takes really seriously is training beginners in the intricacies of consular work. This course is required of everyone whose next post will be in a consulate, and who has never served in one before. The program takes precisely twenty-three days, and includes films, lectures and reading—especially in a thick loose-leaf book of laws and regulations, which the new consul will take with him when the course is finished. Essentially, there are three areas of study: passports, visas and welfare cases.

"Welcome," said a taped lecture, "to the stimulating world of death. In most posts local employees may know what to do, but in a post where the death of an American is a rare occurrence you will have to handle it yourself. It presents an emotional situation that may affect the rationality of the individual involved.

"The first stage is the responsibility of the duty officer. You get as much information as you can from the person who notifies the consulate. It may be a hotel clerk, the police, a tour operator. You determine first that the person is an American citizen, which is usually not difficult. You find out where the body is and where in town the body will be sent. In tropical countries, there may be a twenty-four-hour burial rule, and you don't want that to happen.

"You must, without committing money—and we're not advocating that you tote or even accompany the body—find a freezer facility. You have to control the property of the individual for his next of kin. You contact the next of kin, send a cable, provide a fair amount of information—how the death occurred, any local laws, how much shipping the body back will cost. *Do not expend funds.* Do not *promise* money. Do not authorize any major action, like embalming.

"You're treading water till you get authorization from the family and the funds. If there are no instructions and/or no funds, the body is buried at local expense—*not* our expense. When they accept an entrant they take that responsibility. There's a story about a consular official who kept a body with ice chunks in his bathtub—it was quite a shock for the children. Remember that after you've told someone, 'Your son has died,' he may not hear anything else you say, even if he keeps saying, 'Yes.'"

Consular training is conducted at "ConGen Rosslyn," a model consulate general located on the eighth floor of the FSI building. Simulation is even more extensive here than in the orientation course. Students are implanted in small rooms behind desks, an American flag on a pole behind them. Faculty, friends, the milkman, a visiting reporter, anybody who sets foot in the door can expect to be pressed into service playing the role of somebody who wants something from the consulate. This observer was assigned to be a doctor born in Argentina to American parents and educated there, who voted in Argentine elections, and in general behaved as an Argentinian until he got an offer to practice his medicine in the oil fields of Saudi Arabia. Here someone told him that as the child of American parents he was entitled to an American passport, in itself a better thing than an Argentinian passport, and he has come into this mock consulate to procure one. And in fact, having supplied his birth certificate suitably registered at the U.S. embassy in Buenos Aires, he was entitled to a passport.

This entitlement is of fairly recent origin, the result of a Supreme Court decision and not of any change in the law. Just as Secretary of State Haig had been told at school by the nuns that if something God forbid happened to the President and the Vice-President the Secretary of State would be in charge in the White House, the three apprentice FSOs to whom I told the doctor's tale were still prisoners of the folk wisdom that you lost American citizenship by voting in a foreign election. Still, they didn't turn me down; they said they would have to check with Washington. And in real life, they probably would have checked with Washington.

No small part of the psychological training FSI attempts in dealing with new recruits to the consular jobs grows out of an effort to persuade FSOs that they are paid to make decisions, not refer questions higher up. (One should not, of course, rest decisions so important to other people simply on one's own recollection; the approved form is to say, "I have to do some research" rather than "I have to look it up"; but then one is supposed to act.) Risk aversion has become endemic in American society, even (perhaps especially) among the young, but these young FSOs' refusal to make decisions seemed extreme. Former Secretary of State Cyrus Vance reported that his early efforts to push decision-making down in the bureaucracy, protecting his time and that of his senior assistants, were frustrated by a general reluctance ("human nature") to take responsibility. But it is at least possible that the image of the diplomatic career is such—and the personality traits rewarded by the selection exams are such—that the Foreign Service draws more than its share of mice. From which, *something* follows, though exactly *what* is a reasonable subject for argument.

5

First assignments tend to be accidental, determined by the location of the vacancies. In the United States, the openings are posted, and the new FSOs are given a list of the possibilities while they are in their orientation program. They apply, listing their preferences in rank order, and Personnel pretty much draws straws to determine the winners of the most coveted posts, the losers who must go where nobody wants to go. Languages do count—people who speak Portuguese will have an edge over their fellows for that opening in Rio—but they don't control.

In countries with fewer posts, language may count for even less. Gunnar Blaehr, head of personnel in the Danish Foreign Ministry, said that "in principle an applicant who can speak the language does *not* have priority. When they go, they are given money for language lessons." Istvan Fazekas, second secretary and press officer in the Hungarian embassy in Washington, spent four years in Moscow studying Swahili—but fifteen years into his career had never served in East Africa. The British are probably the most language-conscious: young FSOs are lured to undertake the hard languages by salary supplements that may run more than a thousand pounds a year (for Chinese and Japanese); out of twenty new entrants in 1979, eighteen applied for training in Chinese. "The investment in a hard language," said the Chief Clerk in a statement to Parliament, "can have a major effect on the shape of the individual's future career. A sinologist can expect to spend perhaps half his career, either in the Far East—on postings in Peking, Hong Kong or Singapore—or dealing with it in London or, perhaps, in Washington."

"All early jobs are training jobs," said Paddy de Courcy-Ireland. In practice at most Foreign Ministries, this means beginning with several very short first tours of four to six months in different sections of the Ministry, but in the United States first tours are normally for at least a year (in consulates, for two years), and many of them involve postings abroad. Philip Habib said that "the most important thing is the assignment process— what kind of experience does the man have? If you go out as a visa officer you do nothing but stamp passports eight hours a day, and you get weekends off. A political officer works all day and all night."

But the fact is that for the beginner consular work grants the experience of authority; quite apart from the increasing interest in immigration among legislators, the work may have surprising political importance. Lars Hydle recalled that his first post was in the Belfast consulate. "There were people who wanted visas who we had reason to believe were members of the IRA, an organization which believes in the assassination of public officials. But the Department was subject to pressures from the Irish bloc in Congress to let these people in." On the other hand, becoming a gofer (an "administrative aide") to an ambassador may look like an interesting introduction to the Service but turn out to be dull and demeaning clerical work.

Promotion to FSO-7 is routine (older officers may start at that level), and carries no change of status. Meanwhile, the dossier of "efficiency reports," a phrase left over from Wilbur Carr's belief in scientific management, has been accumulating in the files of the personnel department (in State Department parlance, the Office of the Director General). Three to four years after entry to the Service, the young FSO confronts the "junior threshold," the first opportunity for entry to true career status, with appointment by the President rather than the Secretary of State and a panoply of job protections. A Selection Board reviews the papers, and unless somebody made a profound miscalculation of numbers when the entering class was chosen, the great majority move ahead to become FSO-6s and "mid-career Foreign Service Officers."

Assignment at this point is not merely to a job, but to a "cone"—political, economic, consular or administrative. Hereafter, a promotion presumably will result from the officer's progress in a "skill" associated with his "cone"—and also, because salary goes with rank, on the size of the promotion list authorized by the Congress and the Office of Management and Budget. The normal tour of duty is two years, though an effort has been made recently to leave people in place for three. People change jobs in the summer in every Foreign Service, to minimize the disruption of children's schooling. The State Department in the fall sends around by cable to all posts a list of the jobs that will be vacated the following summer, and the lists are updated every two weeks through the winter as more positions are filled and others thereby opened.

Every FSO is assigned to a "personnel counselor" in Washington who advises him on his prospects for various posts and what would make sense for him to take as part of a career path. (At last report there were seventeen such counselors—four each for junior and senior officers, three for those in the political cone and two each for the other cones—to help about thirty-four hundred FSOs.) In general, people are expected to take one job outside their own "cone" during the twelve to fifteen years they spend in the four ranks of the mid-career band (FSO-6 through FSO-3); and officers can and do switch cones, if they believe the grass is greener elsewhere. Some detours can get a man to his goal more quickly than the main route: an assignment as a political adviser to one of the Chiefs of Staff in the Pentagon, for example, or even (a great oddity, the particular pet of Senator James Pearson of Nebraska) as a personal aide to a mayor of a city or a county commissioner, to learn how things are going back home and widen the horizons of the provincials.

The attitudes behind the "Pearson program" are leftovers from the days before Wristonization, when FSOs might take virtually all their career abroad. Since the time of Thomas Jefferson, who urged that everyone in the diplomatic service should be called home for a period of domestic work after no more than six years outside the country, the worry has been that diplomats would become deracinated, unable to represent the nation abroad because they did not know what they were representing. Since the former civil service group in Washington was merged into the Foreign Service, however, there have been as many jobs for FSOs in Washington as there are in all the missions put together, and most FSOs will take something like half their career working inside the United States. Indeed, it has become possible to rise to the top in the Foreign Service without ever serving in a post abroad—Joseph Sisco, who became Under Secretary of State for Political Affairs, the highest career post in the State Department, never held an overseas appointment.

In general, of course, people join a Foreign Service because they wish to serve abroad, and as part of their oath they pledge "worldwide availability." In the past, there was no great problem getting FSOs out of Washington, for life was far more attractive out in the missions, where the government provided housing and PX privileges, the dollar was strong, wives could have servants and the conditions of diplomacy provided regular boosts to one's self-esteem. Moreover, the Service was structured so that promotions came more slowly in the State Department than in the civil service outside, leaving the FSO a second-class citizen at home. This essential second-classness was emphasized in the Carter administration, when State became just about the only Department to enforce rigidly the limits on air conditioning in Washington's African summer—in a building where (for security reasons) the windows cannot be opened. After six o'clock (and everybody works late), the air conditioning was shut off entirely. Finally, a post abroad offered escape from the State Department's food, otherwise almost inescapable, the nearest plausible restaurant being half a mile away and the Assistant Secretaries' dining room offering the same garbage from the same abominable kitchen that stocks the cafeteria.

Nevertheless, the balance tipped toward Washington work. PX privileges were cut back abroad, the dollar weakened, wives decided they would rather keep their jobs in the United States than run households in countries where they would not be allowed to work, and terrorists changed the frame of reference for life abroad. The huge lateral entry of the Wristonization year caught up with the personnel system and the "cone" image became a graphic statement of the problem: there were too few jobs for the too many FSO-1s, 2s, even 3s. Taken together with Carter's zero-based budgeting, the severe inversion of the normal job pyramid began choking off promotion possibilities. The last straw was laid on the camel by the courts, which in 1977 forbade the Department to continue its practice of compulsory retirement at age sixty.

Meanwhile, partly for affirmative action reasons, control of personnel was being more and more centralized in the Director General's office. Prior to 1975 or so, ambassadors had been able to choose their own section chiefs and counselors. Ellsworth Bunker recalled that when Lyndon Johnson asked him to go to Vietnam, "he said, 'You can have anybody you want out there—and if there's anyone you don't want, he'll be back here in forty-eight hours.' " Who you know has always been an important question in assignments, in all foreign services. Asked how he came to be in Washington, Zbigniew Bako, Polish minister for press, disarmament and religious affairs, the man who set up Billy Graham's first Eastern European tour, noted that "the ambassador was my teacher at university, and later his daughter was my student. . . ." But since 1975, U.S. ambassadors have retained the right to choose only from a list of approved possible deputy chiefs of mission; otherwise (in theory) they have had to take whatever Washington sends.

Justly or otherwise, FSOs began to feel that the high road to better rank and better jobs lay through assignment to Washington. "I made a mistake," said George Anderson, labor attaché in Vienna, an Iowan who started toward the Foreign Service with a Fulbright scholarship at the University of Copenhagen in the early 1950s, a man with a splendidly curled and waxed Gay Nineties mustache who was taking early retirement at the age of fifty and going off to tend agricultural enterprises with his brother. "I could have had a job holding the horses for an Assistant Secretary of State, but I thought I should get in the field in an embassy. Those who stayed and held horses are now ambassadors."

Being around at the right time unquestionably can be helpful. Mary Olmsted, an FSO-2 in the economic cone, a rather schoolmistressy toughminded lady with tied-back gray hair, was on assignment to personnel work in Washington when the decision was made to open a consulate general in Port Moresby, capital of what was the Australian colony of Papua and would soon become independent Papua New Guinea. She put in for the job of consul general, and won it—and became, as the person on the spot, the logical first U.S. ambassador to the new state.

Among the problems of the State Department in the 1980s, then, is the desire of mid-career FSOs to work in Washington rather than abroad. The French, with a similar problem, have handled it with the usual Gallic logic, arranging the compensation schedule so that people *en poste* get paid about twice as much as people in Paris, but that sort of thing goes against the American grain. The new Foreign Service Act restates the requirement of "worldwide availability" and eliminates the FSD ("Foreign Service Domestic") category that had appeared in the 1960s as part of the effort to manage the side effects of Wristonization. But the problem remains.

6

"The personnel system of the Israeli Foreign Ministry," said Amos Ganor, who ran it, "is complicated beyond the human mind to conceive." Other Foreign Ministries and the State Department could make a similar claim. Like the military, a Foreign Service places the rank in the man, and in theory people can hold jobs normally occupied by officers at a considerably higher or lower grade. Zvi Brosh, minister of information and press at the Israeli embassy in Washington, had served as ambassador in Third World countries, and remembered that when he was consul general in New York he'd had two former ambassadors serving under him as consuls. In the French and Italian foreign services, people with the rank of counselor are eligible for ambassadorial posts, and may be transferred from that dignity back to counselor positions in larger countries. The most highly paid person in the Cameroon embassy in Washington in 1980, other than the ambassador himself, was a second secretary, a woman who was a full professor at the University of Yaoundé and had been sent to Washington to supervise the embassy's efforts with Cameroonian students in America, a post that held the title "cultural attaché."

In the United States, five or six personnel selection boards of five members each meet annually, entirely for the purpose of examining candidates for higher rank. FSOs in the mid-career grades are in theory and in law subject to a rule of up-or-out: after five years in the same grade, a man is supposed to be severed from the Service, which happens every year to about 2 percent of those who are at the limit. Supposedly, these decisions to promote or pass over are determined entirely by the "efficiency reports" that supervisors—DCMs in the missions, deputy assistant secretaries of state in Washington—must file every year about everyone in their group. These are narrative descriptions, for which supervisors make up their own adjectives, which may carry private meanings.

By contrast, the personnel department in the British Foreign Office distributes a form that presents a number of skills and traits considered important for a diplomat, and asks each supervisor to rank his juniors somewhere on a continuum between two given descriptions. Reading the form reminds one how much rougher English rugby football is than American football (the English don't permit substitutions for injured players).

Judging the junior diplomat's "Powers of analysis," for example, the supervisor is to rank him somewhere between "Goes straight to the heart of a subject and picks out the essentials" and "Seldom sees below the surface of a problem."

Analyzing his judgment, the supervisor can check off that his "Proposals or decisions are consistently sound" or that he "Lacks judgment."

Estimating his reliability, the supervisor places him between "Unflustered, competent and dependable even under pressure" and "Easily thrown off balance; not reliable even under normal pressure."

Moving on to "Proficiency" questions, the supervisor can rank the candidate's "Accuracy" between "Always gets the facts right" and "Slipshod or careless"—and his "Information" between "Has an exceptional knack of picking up useful information" and "Unobservant."

On "Personal relationships," the supervisor can evaluate his "Interest in welfare of staff" on a continuum between "Makes a valuable contribution to welfare and morale" and "Could not care less."*

The poor devil thus rated, moreover, will never have the chance to see what his smiling supervisor had to say: the document is entirely confidential. By contrast, the American FSO has the right to read—and challenge—all "efficiency reports." M. O'D. B. Alexander, head of personnel operations for the British Foreign Office, disapproved of the State Department's rule: "It leads to assessment by corridor gossip and private letter, which is the worst situation."

Not until 1978 did the Department hire its first outsider with personnel experience. Most members of selection boards are FSOs serving in posts abroad and have to be brought to Washington for their meetings. Not everyone is happy with this amateur orientation. "It's very clear to me," said Carol Laise shortly before her retirement, "that you need people with

* The Israelis do the same sort of thing, and add a trick question—where the positive response would involve a tick on the right-hand rather than the left-hand column—to make sure that the supervisor isn't just expressing general fondness for the individual. But in the Israeli diplomatic service people sign the cables they have written, which is not true in the U.S. or British foreign services, where everyone steps blushingly into the shadow of the ambassador's signature when communications go home. So the files also contain much direct evidence. "The circulation of the cables," says Hanan Bar-On, "makes people *automatically* known."

training, with skills you don't get from people who come into personnel for two years and then move out again."

But this amateur orientation does of course match the sociologists' definition of a profession, which includes the assumption that only peers are capable of making judgments on an individual's performance. ("All professions," Bernard Shaw observed, "are conspiracies against the laity.") And there can be no doubt it contributes to the rather surprising degree of satisfaction with the boards and confidence in their "fairness" that an inquirer finds among the overwhelming majority of FSOs. The man who beats the game tends to be admired rather than resented. Thomas O. Enders, for example, has become a kind of folk hero in the Foreign Service, because he rose from FSO-8 to FSO-1 in eleven years. He was clearly a special case—spectacularly tall (six foot eight) and handsome, very smart and tough (he was Kissinger's proconsul in Cambodia, and William Shawcross in *Sideshow* says he personally controlled the B-52 bombings there from a command post in the embassy), well-connected in Connecticut, and extraordinarily well trained (he wrote a thesis at Yale on the economy of medieval Morocco, earned a doctorate at the Sorbonne and did graduate work in economics at Harvard). Moreover, he had been forced to start late in the Service, because the Department had held his appointment until his foreign-born wife acquired American citizenship.

Much less confidence is expressed in the assignment procedure, which still pits the Director General's office against an ambassador or an Assistant Secretary (or a National Security Adviser in the White House) who knows what he wants and demands it. "You're promoted on the files," says the cant line of the Department, "but you're assigned on your corridor reputation."

An FSO who ultimately became an ambassador and an Assistant Secretary remembered that he had tried to use the personnel counselor system only once: "I was sitting in Brasília. I have five kids and my stated tour was coming up. I wrote my counselor, said: 'Tell me what I'm going to be doing six months from now.' I got a nice letter back, three, four pages long. Morale is bad in Washington. People are walking the corridors, there are no assignments. While I was reading it, the phone rang, it was ARA [Bureau of American Republic Affairs]. 'How would you like to be DCM in Caracas?' I said, 'I'm reading this letter, it says there are no jobs.' He said, 'Who's it from? Personnel counselor? Why did you write *him*? He doesn't know anything.'

"I suppose," the Assistant Secretary said, "there's not quite so much of that today. But if you read the efficiency reports, every report on a desk officer is the same. He may do important work—but the guy who's carrying Brzezinski's bag [this was during the Carter days], everybody knows him."

To some extent, people earn the more desirable assignments. "They used to send to Europe," said Joshua Livnat of the Israeli embassy in Washington, "only people who had had their first heart attacks, served in Africa and got their malaria." Some posts are inevitably rewards for long and meritorious service, and tend to be stocked with burnt-out cases, London being the most notorious. This is hard on the incoming ambassador—Kingman Brewster was the most enthusiastically cooperative ambassador in the Service when the State Department in 1977 ordered reductions in force in the hated MODE (Monitoring Overseas Department Employment) program that sent amateur efficiency experts out from Washington to "nibble" (as a disgruntled DCM put it) at the embassy staffs. But there is no very good reason why London should *not* be an easy post, and a reward for the diligent at the end of their careers.

The length of a tour is in part a function of the hardship of living at this post. France sends people to Upper Volta for ten months; Australia sends them to Hanoi for one year. Most U.S. tours are for two years, and there is some feeling in the Service that shorter tours open chances for more rapid promotions—but the rest of the world is unanimously of the opinion that as a normal matter two years is too short. "You become more useful after three years," said Mognes Warberg, Danish ambassador to Australia. "You can begin to explain things to people." Ghana's Kojo Debrah in Australia argues that "everyone should stay four years. The first year you meet people, the second year you begin to talk with them, the third year you begin to know them, the fourth year you begin to exchange ideas, the fifth year you get cynical and should go home."

7

The American FSO advances through four levels in his mid-career, and then encounters the "senior threshold." Those who cross this threshold will become not only FSO-2s but DCMs and deputy assistant secretaries of State, very possibly ambassadors and assistant secretaries. A very few will reach the supergrades of Career Minister and Career Ambassador. (In France, only the six "Ambassades de France" are allowed to claim the title when at home; the others are ambassadors only when *en poste*.) They become, in effect, part of the State Department chapter of the government-wide "Senior Executive Service." The State Department's dilemma is that the emphasis here must be on the word "executive"—on the FSO-2 level and above, people are going to have managerial responsibilities. Which creates the significant defense for the "generalist" principle: if specialists are good at management, it's an accident.

Barriers like that between FSO-3 and FSO-2 exist in the world's other foreign services. In Denmark, the importance of this senior threshold is expressed very formally. Up to "Level 36," an employee of the Foreign Ministry, regardless of where he serves, is part of the civil service, represented by the professional employees' union, with wages and perquisites established under the master contract. Out of 325 professional positions in the Foreign Ministry and the embassies, about 110 are at or above that level. Though the rank is very much in the man—people who make it to Level 36 are summoned across the courtyard in the palace and formally invested with their rank by the monarch in a ceremony that has been around a long time—in general, it is associated with promotion to a post that has been held by people of that rank. The personnel department fights the tendency of the system to produce acting heads of division and interim ambassadors who get their promotion because they are holding the job.

Danish FSOs begin applying for Level 36 positions and status when they are in their late thirties, and some of the older ambassadors are itchy about a "youth movement" that has moved some people up before the rest of their entry class has even been seriously considered. These "spring appointments," as the Service calls them, are seen by some of the veterans as "creating an enormous competition—people get more interested in their elbows, they don't dare take responsibility because they are afraid they will make mistakes." One Danish ambassador observed darkly that the result of this policy has been that "we used to have a very good Foreign Service, and we don't any more." Copenhagen does not agree.

The opposite principle, of course, is that of the Japanese, who advance each entering class pretty much in lockstep until the group is in its mid-forties. "Everyone gets to be Grade One the same year." Because the Ministry is divided into nine bureaus, each of which has seven or eight divisions, there are a large number of "division chief" positions available to people who have not yet crossed the senior service bar, whose work in highly responsible posts can be studied by the powers that be. People can be appointed to these posts while still in their thirties, which gives a tip-off on prospects. "And even at division head level," said personnel chief Kuriyama, "there is an implicit break among jobs, and those judged highly qualified will get more important divisions."

Job assignments are made by the Deputy Vice-Minister for Administration after consultation with the head of the personnel division, who will check out the acceptability of the man to his supervisor at the post he is to be given. There are no committees. No one is eligible to be made an ambassador or a bureau chief until his class has been in the Ministry twenty-five years. Until 1978, thanks to the very small entering cadres of the MacArthur years, everyone in a class eventually did get some kind of ambassadorship, but no longer.

This observer inquired of one of the most savvy members of this most impressive troupe what the *first* consideration was in determining promotion prospects in the Japanese Foreign Ministry. "Do you," my interlocutor inquired, "want an honest answer?"

"Wouldn't," I said, "have asked the question otherwise"—the Japanese, I note in passing, like to tease and be teased; if you can get across the first bars, they are fun to spend time with.

"Handwriting."

"*Handwriting?*"

"Yes. If your supervisor can read your handwriting, he is well disposed toward you."

Interestingly, this was true in the nineteenth century in the Western countries, too: all the lists of desirable attributes for Foreign Service candidates in the early years include a reference to handwriting. Alvey Adee was particularly exigent in handwriting. But the typewriter took over, and the secretary with her dictation pad. There is no Japanese typewriter except for the preparation of formal documents (IBM has invented one, probably in hopes of sabotaging its rivals' culture), and communications within the Ministry are by notes jotted with what seems to a visitor from another culture incredible speed.

This also opens a window of understanding to the famous code-breaking episode of the pre-Pearl Harbor period: the Japanese could use the telegraph only by first performing a transliteration of their words into Roman alphabet, which limited the vocabulary that could be used because the language has so many sound-alike words. The situation changed in the 1960s, when the development of communication satellites and facsimile systems enabled people abroad to put their handwritten notes into a machine and have them roll out the machines at the other end, nine thousand miles away.

Because so much Japanese communication is on the telephone (one does not circulate handwritten memos), the Japanese Foreign Ministry is probably more dependent than others on personal impressions rather than file material when promotion and assignment decisions are to be made. On the other hand, the Japanese are more persistent and (given that culture's astonishing absorptive power) more successful in giving everyone both geographic and functional specialties plus extended experience outside the specialty, which means that candidates for the highest posts are likely to have met the decision-makers during their peregrinations. This is not unique to Japan ("Whenever there is a man coming into promotion range," said Chief Clerk Sir Edward Youde in Britain, "particularly if he's a possible chief of mission, I take out his file and see to it that the next time he's around, I see him"), but the Japanese are as always more efficient at it.

Coupled with the elaborate secondment system that puts people at division chief level into Ministries other than their own ("Very difficult," says a Japanese FSO with unintended irony, "because you have to work on foreign territory, and get the cooperation of colleagues who are not similar in experience"), this personnel procedure seems to leave the Japanese uniquely serene about the generalist/specialist dichotomy that troubles everyone else. "We are more flexible than the State Department," says Kuriyama placidly. "We try to train officers in various fields. Most people move from regional bureau to functional bureau to overseas assignment and back. . . ."

The British, not surprisingly, are committed to the code of the generalist. "There *is* room for area expertise and language expertise," says P. W. Unwin. "But excessive specialization is extremely wasteful. You wind up with lots of pundits advising and nobody getting the job out of the door—and you have nobody at the end to be ambassador."

In the United States, the pendulum swings. "We're generally reactive to things rather than able to think ahead," Carol Laise said despairingly a few weeks before her retirement as Director General. "We've never done manpower planning, we've just grown. There was the whole period of the Ugly American. Our mistakes in Vietnam were because we didn't understand the Vietnamese. So area specialization became the great drive. Then Kissinger came in and found everybody so parochial, and said, 'We've got to move people around.' Once you've done that, you set certain things in train that sort of carry on. The complaint now in the bureau is that we're losing our area expertise. I worry about our people who deal with the Soviet Union and the Chinese. At one time, they were a group, there was an *esprit*. Now . . .

"Everybody agrees we need both generalists and specialists," Ms. Laise (in private life, Mrs. Ellsworth Bunker) continued. "We can have a single system, recruit the skills we need, and develop generalists in the system through assignment, training and promotion. Or we can say that diplomacy is itself a profession, a generalist's profession, and you recruit specialists when you need them. The FSO system is a generalist system. Cones were introduced for the specialist element. There is a strong feeling in this building and abroad that the specialist category does not lead to the top. The view around town is that the prestigious escalator to the top is the generalist cone. So everybody tries to stretch his specialty *into* the generalist cone.

"So we have a lot of compromise on the structure. One of the things I have tried to do—unsuccessfully, I may add—is rationalize the system so people can have a better sense of what they can expect. They don't have much sense of it now."

The difficulty is that the number of jobs for which one needs a grand overview of the world is very small, even in the U.S. Foreign Service. Modern, bureaucratized diplomats are most useful not in negotiation—which lawyers like Sol Linowitz or Gerard Smith or Elliot Richardson, businessmen like Ellsworth Bunker and Averell Harriman and David Bruce are likely to do better—but in formulating positions for the negotiators. That, like effective representation, requires an understanding of the realities not only beneath the rhetoric but beneath the briefing, which only the most extraordinary generalist is likely to have. And no system on earth will prevent the extraordinary generalist from acquiring specialties.

"Mankind is naturally specialist," wrote Alfred North Whitehead. ". . . . Whenever you exclude specialism you destroy life."

IV

Systems

ORGANIZING A GOVERNMENT FOR THE CONDUCT OF INTERNATIONAL RELATIONS

The Department Timothy Pickering inherited from Edmund Randolph was an administrator's nightmare. . . . Consider, for example, what may have been the most embarrassing moment of 1795, as far as Pickering was concerned. Thomas Pinckney, the American Minister to Spain, had just negotiated a very favorable treaty with that power. He was located in what was a very hot corner of Europe at a moment when Spanish diplomacy was undergoing a change that was to have a dramatic effect on Spanish-American relations. Early in October one of Pinckney's coded dispatches was received in Philadelphia. Search for the code key was fruitless and an embarrassed Secretary sent Pinckney's undecoded message to a puzzled Chief Executive [George Washington] with a note explaining that the State Department had lost the key to Pinckney's cipher.

—Gerard H. Clarfield

The Secretary was astounded when he came to find everybody reporting to him.

—Kenneth W. Dam, Deputy Secretary
to George Shultz

Research undertaken for the Commission highlights many instances in the past where policymakers have failed to understand why foreign governments were taking certain actions, or to anticipate the impact of a U.S. action, and thus have designed actions aimed at one objective which in fact triggered contrary reactions by foreign governments. . . . The State Department and the Foreign Service must be equipped to fulfill [their] role of foreign assessment. . . . Other departments will have superior competence in specialized tasks; other departments will be able to participate in direct negotiations; other departments will have close and continuing contact with their counterparts in other governments and international organizations. But no other department can provide the government with detailed understanding and judgment of the dynamics of foreign societies and governments and multilateral groupings and agencies.

> —Commission on the Organization
> of the Government
> for the Conduct of Foreign Policy, 1975

If a bureau differs with H on a substantive response, whether positive or negative, the matter should be promptly referred by the action office within the established deadline, with the views of the bureau, H, and L clearly indicated, to the Deputy Under Secretary for Management for decision by M or, on reference from M, by another Seventh Floor principal as appropriate.

> —memo to All Department Personnel
> on Responding to Congressional
> Requests for Information, from
> Secretary of State Cyrus Vance,
> April 5, 1978

1

The beginnings of the bureau organization of the State Department seem to lie in the ambitions of one man, William Phillips, a wealthy and aristocratic Bostonian, one of a whole generation of Harvard students galvanized by Theodore Roosevelt and sent off in search of a "strenuous life" in the public service. He started on that quest as the unpaid private secretary to Joseph Choate, Roosevelt's ambassador to London, where Phillips found himself mostly copying in a fine hand—we are still before the age of the typewriter—Choate's dispatches to the State Department. But his time in London also gave him a chance to meet William Rockhill, the U.S. ambassador to China, who invited him to Peking as second secretary. He returned to Washington on his own motion in 1907, and the State Department found him a job in the "colored messenger service."

This was a time when the Far East seemed the most important area for American foreign policy. The Russo-Japanese War had ended only two years before in a peace negotiated at a conference in the United States (for which Roosevelt had won one of the early Nobel peace prizes). The Japanese had taken over Korea, with the implied consent of the United States. Secretary of War William Howard Taft and Japanese Prime Minister Taro Katsura had initialed a secret agreement on the subject, by which, in effect, the Japanese agreed to support American proprietorship of the Philippines while the United States gave Japan a free hand in Korea, where the Emperor had thought himself protected by American policy.

There were problems of the "open door" in China, especially access by American railroads and banks to what looked like profitable business there. E. H. Harriman, Averell's father, had negotiated with the Japanese a deal that gave him and the Japanese Government equal ownership of the Chinese Eastern Railway in Manchuria. (The Japanese eventually backed out, and kept control for themselves, though the Russians got a piece of the action; a bombing on this railway in 1931 became the apparent excuse for the Japanese seizure of Manchuria.)

Young Phillips could claim expertise in several of these matters, and he noted that the volume of communications from Asia had become greater than Second Assistant Secretary Alvey Adee could comfortably read, given all the other demands on his time. Using his social access to Secretary of State Elihu Root, Phillips succeeded in establishing himself as a one-man Division of Far Eastern Affairs,* to process, digest and pass on communications from American representatives there. Roosevelt was tickled by the story of an elegant Bostonian who pushed, and invited Phillips to the White House, where he became part of the informal "tennis cabinet," and studied diplomacy at the feet of French Ambassador Jules Jusserand (who also played tennis and rode and climbed rocks with the President). Jusserand introduced him to Henry Adams, who introduced him to everybody else, and presently young Phillips was Third Assistant Secretary of State.

He replaced in that post an odd fish named Francis M. Huntington-Wilson, a rich Chicagoan who had served seven years as second secretary in Tokyo. He had been called to Washington, Walter and Marie Scholes write, because Root was smitten with his wife Lucy, described by the military attaché in Tokyo as "one of the most beautiful and intelligent women the United States had ever produced." Sent to Turkey on a special mission in 1910, Huntington-Wilson first pasted blue paper over the glass panel on the door to his office to make sure nobody could look in. Joseph Grew, after a week at the State Department under Huntington-Wilson, "declared that he would have greeted the Sphinx with shouts of joy at finding something really human again." Root, who was a hearty fellow, was sure to get sick of that fairly quickly; and Huntington-Wilson was

---

* The official order read: "Mr. William Phillips, a clerk of the $900 class, is hereby designated Chief of the Division of Far Eastern Affairs (correspondence, diplomatic and consular, on matters other than those of an administrative character. . . .)"

solaced for the loss of his Washington job by appointment as minister to Argentina.

Before Huntington-Wilson could leave, however, Taft replaced Roosevelt in the White House, Root went to the Senate, and Philander Knox became Secretary of State. A rather distant and irritable man, Knox liked only the people he liked (whose rewards then included superb dinners and wines: traveling in the Caribbean while Secretary of State, Knox took with him "three dozen quarts of Pol Roger Brut 1900 and the same number of Roeder Carte Blanche, three dozen quarts of Chambertin, three dozen quarts of Château Margaux and six dozen quarts of Château Latour Blanche"). One of those he liked turned out to be Huntington-Wilson, who was summoned to be First Assistant Secretary of State—and immediately shipped Phillips out of the country as counselor to Ambassador Whitelaw Reid in London.

Knox badly needed someone to run his Department. The Scholeses describe his working habits when in Washington (he spent as much time as he could at a summer place in New England, a home in Valley Forge and a winter colony in Florida): "His three-story home on K Street was his headquarters. Knox did some of his work in the first-floor library, which was lined with shelves of handsome volumes and furnished with pieces that included a huge French desk with brass trimmings, a bust of Napoleon [Knox was only five foot five] and a portrait of himself. He did a great deal of work early in the morning in a small library next to his bedroom. He liked to get up around five, when his butler would bring him a thermos flask of coffee, and then, with the morning paper, State Department material, and other pertinent information at hand, he considered the problems of his department. He arrived at his office in the old State Department building at about ten or ten-thirty and seldom returned there after luncheon except on Thursdays, the regular calling day for foreign representatives who had business with him. . . .

"About three times a week Knox took . . . Huntington-Wilson to lunch either at the Metropolitan Club or the Shoreham Hotel. After a cocktail or two, they would settle down to either terrapin and a bottle of champagne or canvasback duck, done very rare, with a bottle of red wine. The ritual luncheons were a combination of business and pleasure. Huntington-Wilson always briefed himself carefully and during the meal would draw from his pocket a list of the matters in the department that were too important to go forward without the approval of the Secretary. He would explain each item and make recommendations, which Knox usually approved. Luncheon over, Knox strolled home for a little nap, and later, if the weather permitted, he would motor out to Chevy Chase for golf."

Huntington-Wilson got Knox to request a one-hundred-thousand-dollar appropriation from Congress for the reorganization of the Department, and launched four new divisions—for Latin American Affairs, European Affairs and Near Eastern Affairs, plus a Division of Information. (In his memoirs, he claimed it had been he who had put the idea of a Far Eastern Division into Phillips' head two years before.) Some of this, no doubt, was to get around Adee, who turned seventy in 1910 and whom Huntington-Wilson described in a rather mixed compliment as "the Nestor of the Department." A high-level "counselor" was added to the Secretary's staff to help with legal matters, and a post was created for a "resident diplomat," a career officer with service abroad. The job of the Third Assistant Secretary was redefined to give him control over the diplomatic service abroad, and the consular service was given a "director" presumably on an equivalent footing. There remains in the State Department, incidentally, this essentially meaningless distinction between assistant secretaries (who must be confirmed by the Senate) and directors (who are appointed by the Secretary). "You can tell who has the really important jobs," one of the assistant secretaries confided, "by looking to see whether they have a private bathroom." I did that, and noted bathrooms beside the offices of several directors.

Unquestionably the most important of Huntington-Wilson's reforms was the creation of the Division of Information, not then a press office but a coordinating center for the efficient collection, storage, retrieval and transmission of information within the Department. Huntington-Wilson gave the Department its first usable filing system. (Prior to Root, who introduced his own idiosyncratic method, files had been kept according to bureaucratic category—instructions, dispatches, agreements, etc.) For the first time, it became possible to do serious analysis of reports from the field, correlating them with press reports in foreign publications, official statements by foreign governments and—after World War I—the astonishing output of the Black Chamber, located in New York, where Herbert Yardley and his small crew successfully cracked the codes of Argentina, Brazil, Chile, China, Costa Rica, Cuba, the Dominican Republic, El Salvador, England, France, Germany, Japan, Liberia, Mexico, Nicaragua, Panama, Peru, the Soviet Union and Spain.

Then Henry Stimson became Secretary of State, saw some of the output, and closed down the operation in 1929 with the comment that "gentlemen do not read each other's mail." But the State Department's successful use of this material in the 1920s, especially in the negotiations for the naval disarmament conference, contrasted so effectively with the military's bungling both before and after Pearl Harbor (when Stimson, oddly enough, had returned to government as Roosevelt's Secretary of War), that the initial postwar planning for American espionage efforts gave control to State. Then State blew it, partly because Assistant Secretary for Information William Benton was uncomfortable with the notion that he should supervise both propaganda and espionage.

Huntington-Wilson's new Division of Information also tied the posts abroad to Washington, supplying a weekly summary of decisions taken and opinions held inside the Department, congressional developments, etc. This *What's-On* still survives (now monthly), much criticized in the embassies because it concentrates so heavily on the texts of speeches by big shots (in the Kissinger days, there were issues that contained nothing but the Secretary's pronunciamentos). But when the Carter administration tried to cut it out as an economy measure, the field rebelled: at the worst, it was better than being entirely dependent on the international edition of *Time*. Essentially, after all, what a Foreign Ministry does is collect, evaluate and communicate information. Its output is recommendations, not actions. And the force of these recommendations is a function of the quality of the information behind them.

Keeping the world surprise-free for the political leaders of the United States was easier when Huntington-Wilson introduced his reorganization. Looking across the Pacific, the State Department saw only two local independent actors—China and Japan. Indochina was French, Indonesia was Dutch, India and Burma were part of the British Empire, and Australia and New Zealand, as part of the British Commonwealth, maintained no foreign relations of their own. (Until 1948, indeed, New Zealand had no Foreign Ministry. "We got copies of all dispatches home from British embassies," said Permanent Undersecretary Frank Corner. "And we had one man here in Wellington, the Imperial Affairs Officer. Every few years there was a conference of Prime Ministers in London, a stately kind of thing, and the Imperial Affairs Officer spent his time preparing for that. He prepared packing cases of briefs, to inform the Prime Minister where Abyssinia was, that sort of thing. Then every morning on the ship to London there was a class based on these briefs, and the Prime Minister got to London quite prepared to participate.")

Coaling stations in the Pacific were important, but Hawaii had been annexed by President McKinley after Grover Cleveland refused to countenance the conspiracy by which the American residents, led by the U.S. consul, had overthrown the Hawaiian queen. ("As I look back upon the first steps in this miserable business," Cleveland wrote a friend after McKinley's action, "and as I contemplate the means used to complete the outrage, I am ashamed of the whole affair.") Pago Pago had been taken over by the same administration following considerable *Sturm und Drang* (especially *Sturm*, the six confronting U.S. and German gunboats having all been sunk by a hurricane). Among the changes in the international scene wrought by the jet plane and the ballistics missile has been the disappearance of the Pacific Islands from the mental maps of Western Foreign Ministries, where they had been bright dots. This saddens the New Zealanders, who feel they safeguard the atolls in the interests of the Western alliance, and should get some credit for it, ideally in the form of cheese quotas. "You used to have people in the State Department who cared about the Pacific Islands," said George Laking, former New Zealand ambassador to the United States, "because they'd been involved in planning what to do with them after the war. All those people retired, and nobody took their place."

In Europe in Huntington-Wilson's time there was no Poland, Czechoslovakia or Hungary, and the battles of the Balkans were not something America cared about particularly. Our interests in Scandinavia were largely restricted to free passage of the straits to the Baltic; and our interests in the Near East were mostly navigational (the Turkish straits and the Suez Canal) and religious-humanitarian (the starving Armenians, the pilgrims to Jerusalem). Oil was beginning to become a factor on the international scene, but the United States had more of that than it knew what to do with. And the United States, of course, had no "alliances": the warnings of Washington and Jefferson still lived. Huntington-Wilson, as a good Chicagoan, was highly Anglophobic and would have resented personally any suggestion that the United States had some "special relationship" with England.

Thus the State Department's worst problems in keeping track were concentrated in Latin America, where there was a large number of corrupt and incompetent governments, which were somehow the responsibility of the United States. Under the Monroe Doctrine, the United States had announced that it would not permit any European power to acquire colonies or dominance in the Western hemisphere, and Theodore Roosevelt had propounded a "corollary" that because the United States would not permit the Europeans to protect their citizens or collect money owed them in Latin America, it had an obligation to police this world itself. This "right" of the United States to intervene in the affairs of the republics to the south—indistinguishable in form and substance from the modern "Brezhnev doctrine" that claims suzerainty for the Soviet Union over the states of Eastern Europe—had been in the case of Cuba written into that nation's constitution by the Platt Amendment. Then Woodrow Wilson went a step further, proclaiming a doctrine of "constitutional legitimacy," which meant that the United States would recognize changes of government in Latin America only if they were accomplished by free elections.

So American Marines went to Haiti and San Domingo, to Nicaragua and Cuba. American accountants collected the customs duties at their ports, and made sure that European and American creditors were paid before the local politicos got their hands on the cash. Woodrow Wilson sent Marines to Vera Cruz and ordered search-and-destroy missions for bandits (often indistinguishable from leftist revolutionaries) in northern Mexico; and his successors maintained a war of nerves against that country in response to the nationalization of "subsoil rights" previously granted to American mining and oil companies. Gunboats cruised near capital cities to remind local authorities of their responsibility for the health and safety of foreign visitors, no small fraction of whom were businessmen and plantation owners squeezing profits out of a downtrodden populace.

Under Woodrow Wilson, these had been essentially military operations: the State Department's attention through the European war had been necessarily focused on Europe—in the end, most unsuccessfully so, for Wilson in Paris ignored his Secretary of State and the Foreign Service Officers in his entourage, as he ignored the Senate that would eventually have to ratify his treaty. Then Harding came to the presidency with a collection of nonentities and crooks for a Cabinet, except for Hoover at Commerce, Mellon at Treasury, and Charles Evans Hughes at State. A formidable figure, later to be Chief Justice, previously his party's candidate for President against Wilson, Hughes took command of the Latin American operations and much else.

With help from Republican Senator Henry Cabot Lodge and Democratic Senator Oscar W. Underwood, Hughes bullied the Navy Department into accepting a naval disarmament proposal that would have scrapped eight hundred and fifty thousand tons of American warships (almost two thirds of the fleet) and completely stopped the procurement of larger ships for ten years. Security in Washington in those days was sufficiently tight, by the way, that he was able to launch this proposal as a bombshell at the ceremonial opening of the disarmament conference.

In foreign economic policy, Hughes insisted on maintaining the requirement first put into effect under Wilson that American banks lending to foreigners—or selling foreign bonds on the American market—had to clear their activities with the State Department. The State Department did not seek to judge the economic soundness of a loan—something Hoover very much wanted the government to attempt—but rather its consonance with American policy, especially with relation to the running sore of European debt repayments and German reparations. Loans were also denied to foreign cartels because they violated American antitrust laws and the general rule of the open door; one was denied to a Czech brewery on the grounds that the "administration could not consistently approve a loan for the manufacture of a beverage abroad considered illegal at home." According to Dana Munro, who worked on such questions, the State Department also tried to be sure that the bankers were not beating up on the Caribbean nations by exacting unconscionable terms. Given the recklessness with which U.S. banks made foreign loans in the late 1920s, and the dishonesty with which they peddled foreign bonds to U.S. citizens, everybody might have been better off if Hughes had listened to Hoover. Indeed, there was a pretty strong case to be made in 1983 that the United States and Mexico and Brazil and Argentina and Chile and the international financial system would all have been better off if our greedy and not very talented bankers had been forced to listen when the Federal Reserve examiners looking at their loans said (as some did), "You guys gotta be kidding."

In the Latin American situations, Hughes insisted that State Department policy—and thus the ambassadors, linked closely now to Washington through the miracle of wireless telegraphy and telephony—had to control the activities of the military. Though the Latin American division was strongly led by FSOs on Washington assignment (first Sumner Welles, then Francis White, then Dana Munro), the ambassadors in Central America were *all* political appointees, with painfully little staff support. White noted sourly that the U.S. embassy to Belgium had a counselor and three "diplomatic secretaries," while the five Central American embassies made do with one shared FSO—although, White thought, a Central American embassy had more work to do each week than the Belgian embassy turned out in a year.

The combination of heavy responsibilities and light staffing put more strain on the Latin American division than it could bear, especially after Frank Kellogg became Secretary of State for Coolidge and insisted on keeping all decisions in his own hands. (Kellogg boasted that he read every page of every dispatch from every ambassador, and all memos from assistant secretaries; this kept him chained to his desk for long hours all year long, and did him little good with Coolidge, who not only was sleeping or hunting when Kellogg called, but often refrained from returning the calls.) When serious business was to be done in Latin America, the Republican Presidents often turned to outsiders from the legal or business world—Henry Stimson, Dwight Morrow, Cameron Forbes—to organize and implement American policy, often without much reference back to Washington.

Under Hughes and Hoover's Secretary of State Henry Stimson, the State Department kept searching for ways to pull back from the military interventions in Latin America. In 1924, Hughes got the Marines out of San Domingo. In 1928, Under Secretary Reuben Clark wrote a "Memorandum" on the Monroe Doctrine that found no warrant for Roosevelt's corollary (which was then explicitly dropped by the Congress in a resolution in 1929). Reporting on his first year as President, Hoover listed the activities of the Marines in Haiti and Nicaragua, then added, "In the large sense we do not wish to be represented abroad in such manner."

Stimson abandoned Wilson's "constitutional legitimacy." In a speech before the Council on Foreign Relations in 1931, he cited a Thomas Jefferson letter of 1792: "We certainly cannot deny to other nations that principle whereon our own Government is founded, that every nation has a right to govern itself internally under what forms it pleases, and to change these forms at its own will; and externally to transact business with other nations through whatever organ it chooses, whether that be a king, convention, assembly, committee, president, or whatever it be." He added that the Hoover administration was following Jeffersonian precepts: "As soon as it was reported to us, through our diplomatic representatives, that the new governments in Bolivia, Peru, Argentina, Brazil and Panama were in control of the administrative machinery of the state, with the apparent general acquiescence of their peoples . . . they were recognized by our government." Asked in 1932 whether he would land American forces to protect American life and property in Chile and Colombia, both wracked by guerrilla warfare, Stimson replied, "Not on your life."

Much of this represented a growing assertion of State Department authority over the conduct of foreign relations. Though it was waggishly maintained that Kellogg decided American foreign policy by ringing Senator William Borah's doorbell, the climate of isolationism, by denying attention to foreign policy decisions, gave the Department much greater freedom of motion than it had previously enjoyed or would later experience. There is a sense, indeed, in which the 1920s mark the heyday of the State Department. Because the United States was not a member of the League of Nations and did not vote there, the Department was unencumbered in its instructions to the "observers" who after 1922 increasingly sat in on all the League's business. (They were official representatives of the U.S. Government, but not officially accredited to the League; in effect, the United States got most of the benefits of influence that membership in the League might bring without paying anything for them.) Congress gave the Department the Rogers Act, enlarging the Foreign Service and amalgamating the diplomatic and consular branches essentially under diplomatic tutelage.

The price for all this, of course, was complete elimination of the Department as a factor in the making of domestic decisions with foreign implications. Noting that American tariffs were up for revision with the arrival of the Hoover administration in 1929, Bundy and Stimson wrote that "to Stimson's great relief this subject did not fall within the jurisdiction of the State Department."

As part of an effort to bring the diplomatic service down to earth, William Jennings Bryan had added a "trade adviser" to the staff of the Secretary of State, and during the war the Department had sought to increase its influence on the conduct of nonmilitary hostilities and Allied relations by creating within that office a bureau of economic intelligence. Hughes could see Hoover's objection that such an office would tread on the toes of the Commerce Department, and its members were scattered among the geographical divisions. The trade adviser was restricted, Munro reports, to "economic matters which involved more than one part of the world." When Hoover became President, he automatically won his old argument with Hughes, and moved the trade functions out of the State Department entirely. Stimson thereupon appointed a very different sort of person to the new post of "economic adviser": Herbert Feis, not only an economist but also a brilliant chronicler, who would later invent and successfully practice the genre of instant diplomatic history; our knowledge of what the government did before, during and just after World War II is far greater than would have been possible without Feis' work. He was the only member of Stimson's staff retained by Cordell Hull.

But through the 1920s the work of the State Department could be conducted almost exclusively through the geographical divisions, where the Department had a clear comparative advantage. The divisions were genuinely specialist. The high-powered types in the diplomatic service concentrated their attention on Europe; the Near Eastern people were chosen from a cadre interested in intrigue (Allen Dulles was director of the division); the Far Eastern division was dominated by careerists who had learned the languages; and the Latin American division, the largest, was a world in itself, where at the cost of learning a single easy language a man could serve in literally dozens of different posts.†

"The geographical divisions," Munro writes, "formulated policy and drafted instructions. Questions relating to more than one division were discussed informally by the officers concerned and there were few committees. There was also much informal contact with other departments of the government. The relatively small number of persons involved made the transaction of business easier than it is today." In fact, the geographical bureaus still do draft the instructions, though they can't honestly claim to "formulate" policy. "Even if we don't make the decision," Harold

† Though they have lost some of their expertise through the "generalist" orientation of the Department, the geographical divisions retain temperamental distinctiveness. "They always reflect their clients," said a man who has worked with all of them. "AF [Africa] is full of missionaries. NEA [Near East] is devious, throws sand in your eyes. EA [East Asia] is mandarin, and then . . ." He made a gesture of pulling a knife out of his belly. "EUR is suave and sophisticated. And ARA [Latin America] . . ." His head dropped on his chest. "*Mañana.*"

Saunders said when he headed the Near East Bureau, "we *shape* it by writing the draft." Maybe.

What happened to the State Department organizationally was that ever increasing numbers of actors from elsewhere in the government—indeed, elsewhere in the society—acquired strong interests in the foreign policies of the United States. The process began in the Roosevelt years. Stimson had been grateful that tariffs were not part of the subject matter of the State Department; Hull was interested in reciprocal trade agreements beyond anything else, and relations between him and Roosevelt never entirely recovered from the President's decision to wreck the London monetary conference by means of a "fireside chat" in 1933. Hull had hoped to achieve substantial reduction of tariffs and removal of trade barriers, but Roosevelt opted for a nationalist policy of raising prices to help the bankrupt American farmer.

Domestic politics became the controlling force. Richard Kottman has described the development of the American position in the trilateral negotiations of 1938, among the United States, Canada and Britain: "Officials in all three countries . . . were sensitive to the political influence that protected industries could wield. In the United States textile and lumber organizations carried on the expected campaign against greater foreign competition. The attitudes of the American farmer were more nebulous. . . . The first important poll came into [Agriculture Secretary Henry A.] Wallace's possession in December, 1937, or early January, 1938. The Gallup organization . . . filed with the Department of Agriculture an unpublished report of the opinions of farmers. . . . In the Far West and New England, where Democrats had to work for votes, support [for trade reciprocity] was almost nonexistent. . . . This information, regularly collected, gave substance to remarks about political realities made by State Department officials to the British. . . . The congressional election scheduled for November 1938 made the administration even more aware of the political framework within which they were operating."

Within the executive branch, however, such discussions in those days not only were informal, they occurred on the Cabinet Secretary level. Though there was a Foreign Agricultural Service in the 1930s, it was charged with monitoring and reporting duties, not policy formulation. Secretary of the Treasury Henry Morgenthau, learning that the Canadian ambassador had called on one of his people to inquire about expectations on lumber duties, immediately notified Hull of the impropriety: no section of the Treasury in those days had the right, let alone the job, of dealing with foreigners. (This was, of course, the same Canadian ambassador Acheson memorialized for the quality of his lunches and the shrewdness of his inquiries.)

Relations with the military were always more complicated. Control of the armed services was divided between two agencies—a War Department and a Navy Department—and coordination of military and civilian affairs was and is through the person of the President, as commander-in-chief. When President Kennedy made his ambassadors boss over all American government employees in their countries, he specifically exempted military units serving in the chain of command. (Later, General Maxwell Taylor, who had stressed the importance of this exemption as a Kennedy adviser in Washington, became ambassador in Saigon and got himself made chief of the military operation there, too.) The War Department had virtually no contact with the Department of State prior to the Spanish-American War, which left units of the Army emplaced all over the Far East; even after imperialism had taken root, Stimson as Secretary of War successfully resisted the use of Army as distinct from Marine units in expeditionary forces to Latin America and China. But the Navy Department, with ships on the seven seas (en masse in 1907, when Theodore Roosevelt sent his "Great White Fleet" on a spectacular circumnavigation of the globe), was necessarily involved in the nation's foreign relations—and its Marines were the spearpoint of any military intervention the United States might choose to make abroad. When the United States chose to pick up the white man's burden, it "sent the Marines."

Commanders of naval warships were in fact significant sources of information for the State Department through the days when consuls were living off their fees and might have business connections where they were stationed. The importance of this information was heightened in the period of "gunboat diplomacy," when Americans (and American consuls) often felt they were entitled to help from Uncle Sam against the enforcement of local laws governing their persons or their businesses.

That feeling was, in fact, pretty much the policy of the U.S. Government in the period 1895–1915. "Some American gentlemen engaged in railway building and other large affairs in Ecuador," John Hay wrote the Secretary of the Navy, "say that it would be a very great advantage to American interests generally in that Republic if a United States national vessel should occasionally, in passing by, stop at Guayaquil for a day or so. They say the effect on the public mind and, incidentally, the effect on business interests, would be advantageous." Philander Knox urged the visit of a flotilla to Nicaraguan waters with the words, "This Department regards the presence of these ships as important at this juncture for purely political reasons, quite apart from actual military considerations. . . ." Huntington-Wilson suggested that the right way to gain a concession from the Dominican authorities was to "synchronize the presentation of diplomatic notes with the arrival in Dominican waters of a first-class warship with landing forces." When the United States grew serious about John Hay's open door in China, one of the first steps taken was the construction of a fleet of gunboats to ply the Chinese rivers.

Naval officers off on a frolic of their own occasionally presented a problem in diplomatic relations, both in Central America and with Turkey, where the captain of a force sent to protect American lives and property during the Young Turks' revolution took it upon himself to visit ports without prior clearance from the embassy and to threaten Turkish officials with reprisals. By and large, however, the Navy was less bellicose than the American consuls on the spot, who itched for the protection of gunboats and the Marines—and thus less aggressive than the State Department, which relied on reports from the consuls.

Alvey Adee read the dispatches from the naval commanders as well as the State Department traffic, and had no reluctance to see the Navy used for political purposes. (Discussing developments in Haiti in 1908, he noted, "More than two years' continuous smoke suggests *some* fire dangerously near the historical explosive called Haiti. The only hope of better things is . . . a comparatively pacific revolution with the installation of a decently civilized [ruler]. . . . Tyranny, however, may precipitate a revolutionary movement at any time, and if it comes, the story of Toussaint l'Ouverture and Soulonque may be repeated. Moral, keep ships there!")

Adee supported the outrageous American actions in Nicaragua in the Taft administration, when the United States in effect evicted a cruel and corrupt but independent President who had kicked out the U.S. bankers, made his loans and arranged his railroad construction help in Europe, solicited a treaty with Japan, and garnered diplomatic support from Mexico. But eventually Adee learned to have sympathy with the views expressed by Admiral William Kimball, who believed most of the trouble in Nicaragua arose "from the fact that aid and protection is apt to be given to any American interest that is financially powerful enough to secure good counsel, no matter whether it be a legitimate interest or, as has so often been the case, a claim for spoils resulting from a fraudulent concession or monopoly worked through by the aid of corrupt and heavily bribed officials."

Writing about a dispute on Honduras which had drawn Navy vessels to its side, Adee noted wearily that "the banana question is merely one of rivalry between American interests. First one side and then the other makes it worthwhile for the local authorities to side with it. . . . The *Marietta* is not in Honduran waters, however, on banana police duty, but to exert a moral influence toward political tranquillity at this juncture when we are after bigger game than bananas."

That bigger game was the expansion of American commercial influence and activity in general. The notion that this policy was driven from Wall Street, while long promoted by academics, appears not to be true. Like much of what the Reagan administration attempted, the Taft administration's dollar diplomacy was ideologically motivated. At one point, indeed, the Morgan bank found it necessary to remind Knox that "while it was all right to be making history, their business was to make money." Nor was personal greed a factor: Philander Knox had represented an American company heavily involved in Nicaragua, but he probably sold his stock in that company before taking office.

In any event, there was never any question of the pervasiveness as well as the finality of civilian control. Every so often, a military man would make a flap—Army Chief of Staff Arthur MacArthur, father of Douglas, roused Theodore Roosevelt's wrath by a public speech proclaiming the "inevitability" of war with Germany. But in general, the problems ran the other way. Having achieved a measure of coordination (if not cooperation or cohesion) through the Joint Board, the Navy and War departments sought to set up a Council of National Defense that would include the State Department. State demurred, leading one of the military advocates to write that "if the State Department is not represented then the Department will do as it has done in the past—establish policies without regard to the military preparedness of the country to carry through these policies. . . . If trouble ensues, then the onus falls on the military branches and the State Department steps out." When the Navy Department sought a conference with State to coordinate positions in the London naval conference of 1909, the Solicitor of the State Department replied that his agency "is charged with the administration of foreign affairs, and . . . this conference . . . falls within the jurisdiction of this Department. . . ."

The nadir of military influence on American foreign policy was the New Deal, when the only relations between nations that were perceived to count were economic relations, the arms manufacturers had become the "merchants of death," the colleges grew pacifist groups like the Veterans of Future Wars who swore never to serve in the military, and the Congress passed a Neutrality Act prohibiting the export of war materiel to either side of any foreign dispute. The officer corps of the services was seen as right-wing politically, skeptical of the Administration's Good Neighbor Policy in Latin America, and prone to exaggerate the threat from Japan to the Philippines (which were in any event to become independent) and the danger that Germany's resurgence and Mussolini's ambitions would start a war that the United States could not escape. America First was an entirely respectable movement intellectually—Robert Hutchins was its co-chairman—and the view that the United States was essentially invulnerable was all but universal.

With the conclusion of the war, there was a return to prewar emotions, with exclusive possession of the atom bomb substituting for the oceans as the insurance of invulnerability. There could not, of course, be a return to isolationism: the United States was committed to a number of international organizations, to various relief and rehabilitation efforts abroad, to the military governance of defeated Germany and Japan, to the military occupation of "liberated" Austria. Treasury was in the international loans business, Commerce was trying to pick up the pieces of international trade. But the feeling was that with the return of peace, management of the nation's foreign relations should be returned to the State Department, which had been largely frozen out of decision-making during the war. (Harriman in Moscow, Winant in London, Stilwell in China, Murphy with Eisenhower had reported directly to the White House rather than through the State Department.) A State-War-Navy Coordinating Committee was established in 1944 to look ahead, and began churning out recommendations before V-E Day.

"I opposed the efforts of the War Department to transfer to the State Department control of our occupation organizations in Europe and in the Pacific," wrote Secretary of State James F. Byrnes. "The State Department is not adapted for such work. It cannot recruit an efficient organization because the appointees could, at best, be promised only temporary employment far removed from their homes. If the burden of carrying on shipping, maintenance of transportation, policing, inspection and all the myriad duties of occupation forces were transferred to the State Department, its capacity to define wisely important foreign policies would be seriously hampered. . . . The proponents of the transfer system argue that there is a division of authority between the War Department and the State Department, but I do not believe the argument is sound. There is such a division in all matters affecting foreign policy. The President determines our foreign policy. He makes his decisions upon the recommendations of the Secretary of State. The policy as determined must be executed by the War and Navy departments. . . . There must, of course, always be close coordination between the State, War and Navy departments. . . ."

In lieu of control, the State Department set up a liaison office called the Assistant Secretary for Occupied Areas. But here—as in the fields of intelligence, propaganda, aid and the organization of the specialized agencies of the United Nations—State found that like an opponent of Joe Louis it could run but it couldn't hide. All these areas of work were turned over to State with a high degree of exclusivity in the period immediately after the war. The Department was still divided along geographic lines, and Byrnes enforced the preeminence of the geographic divisions by "demanding that the formulation of statements of policy be given top priority in the work of the Department. Country committees for every nation in the world were created. These committees sought to draw up a rounded program that tied our political, economic, intelligence and information activities into a commonly conceived program. . . . As they were approved, these became our operating guides."

These statements gave the assistant secretaries something to talk about with the Secretary when he was in town, which was not often in 1946 (Byrnes estimated that of his 562 days in office, 350 were spent "at international conferences"). They did not, really, tell anybody what to do. The "office directors," as Byrnes called them, met with Under Secretary of State Dean Acheson every morning at nine-thirty (the "Prayer Meeting," they affectionately called it), and Acheson met periodically (as chairman) with the State-War-Navy Coordinating Committee. But at all such meetings, Acheson had to put the pieces of the puzzle together all by himself—even the intelligence function had been, over his violent objections, scattered among the geographical bureaus.

At the end of the day, moreover, coordination among the departments of government was still ad hoc, and on the level of the Secretaries themselves. Byrnes considered himself an independent actor rather than a spokesman for his Department. He refused to report back to the State Department on what was happening at the London Conference of Foreign Ministers: "I may tell the President sometime what happened," he told the secretary of the American delegation, "but I'm never going to tell the State Department about it." Not informed, let alone consulted, the Department staff grew surly: "The State Department fiddles," one FSO punned splendidly, "while Byrnes roams." The tasks assigned to the Department were not performed; in general, as the Hoover Commission bitingly pointed out, the Department malfunctioned.

2

The modern State Department is essentially the creation of George C. Marshall, who arrived from the Army and diplomatic experience in China to be Secretary of State in 1947, and immediately saw what was wrong. No staff. *Grosso modo*, no planning: no real sense of who the other actors were, domestically. For the failures of the State Department did not and do not fall most often in its area of assigned responsibility, the conduct of foreign relations. They were and are failures in the establishment, coordination—even understanding—of *American* policy. Thus the geographical divisions, which give the Department its comparative advantage in the debates within the government, are necessarily insufficient as sources of information and guidance to the Secretary. There must be a system that draws information from outside the Department, from people who know what is on the minds of the other departments of government, the Executive Office and the Congress, for the purpose of focusing the information the Department itself provides. The Secretary can successfully advise the President only if he speaks in terms useful to the President, and he cannot do that if he is buried in the problems of whatever country is causing the present crisis or creating the present opportunity.

Marshall of course came out of a military tradition, with its clear separation between line authority and staff decision. Line authority was to be concentrated in the office of the Under Secretary, who would "run the Department": there would be no access to the Secretary until after the Under Secretary had considered the question and the means of its answer. Marshall had used Acheson as his liaison back to the State Department while trying to sort out the China mess as Truman's special emissary; he was happy to retain Acheson as his Under Secretary for as long as Acheson would stay (about six months). And Acheson used his nine-thirty Prayer Meeting as the device to communicate to the assistant secretaries what they'd bloody better well do today while gathering from them what they thought General Marshall should know tomorrow.

The basic information stream came through Marshall's "Central Secretariat" (later, more grandly, Executive Secretariat), a creation for which Marshall brought with him an ex-Army man: Colonel Carlisle Humelsine, who knew what the general wanted. All paper for the Secretary's consideration and all orders to the troops funneled through this new Secretariat —with two exceptions: memos from the Under Secretary, and memos from the new Policy Planning Staff. This office was created in a hurry in May 1947 to handle the construction of what came to be called the Marshall Plan, but it had been projected by Marshall some months earlier: George Kennan had learned in February, while he was teaching at the new National War College, that he was to be director of such a group. Policy Planning had no line responsibilities whatever, and thus was permitted direct access to the Secretary.

In July 1947 the National Security Act was passed, creating a National Military Establishment headed by a Secretary of Defense (though the Army, Navy and Air Force secretaries continued for a while to hold cabinet rank), setting up a National Security Council and establishing a Central Intelligence Agency, which would coordinate the work of the intelligence services in the State Department, the military branches, the FBI and the Treasury (which contains the Secret Service). In its early days, the NSC had virtually no staff of its own, and the cabinet-level personages who were its members met without assistants present. Thus the decision papers on which the NSC worked had to be drawn up by the subordinates of one of the members—and Marshall had his Policy Planning Staff in place to accept just that challenge.

George Kennan, moreover, was the perfect man for the job. A Russian expert, he had helped open the first U.S. embassy to Moscow (the Czars had been headquartered in St. Petersburg), had been counselor to Ambassador John G. Winant in London during the war, and had returned to Russia as minister-counselor to Averell Harriman late in the war. He was immensely self-confident, a Midwesterner from Princeton who considered himself a unique combination of common sense and savvy; he was also a hard worker, and he wrote very clearly. His famous eight-thousand-word telegram in February 1946 had laid out the first systematic analysis of why relations between the United States and the Soviet Union were souring, and had proposed for the first time the policy he would later (in the famous "X" article in *Foreign Affairs*) call "containment." But he also had a sense of the limits on what America could do, set by the rapid demobilization of U.S. forces very soon after the war. And he had Marshall to reinforce that sense: "I remember when I was Secretary of State," Marshall said some years later, "I was being pressed constantly . . . to give the Russians hell. . . . At this time, my facilities for giving them hell—and I am a soldier and know something about the ability to give hell—was 1½ divisions over the entire United States. That is quite a proposition when you deal with somebody with over 260 and you have 1½."

Crucial to the status of State's Policy Planning Staff in the early years was the fact that it had virtually no competition. Despite the perceived Russian threat in the eastern Mediterranean and the confrontation that had developed along the line Churchill called the Iron Curtain, Defense Department budgets were still declining, and the real war that obsessed the generals and admirals was the defense of their revenues and bureaucratic turf. Though the Joint Chiefs of Staff could occasionally put together a policy paper with specific recommendations, its members were so deeply engaged in jockeying for allies elsewhere in the executive branch and in the Congress that they could rarely maintain a common front. Thus it was Kennan as policy planning chief in State who wrote the basic *military* policy for the United States in the Mediterranean:

"1. The use of U.S. regular armed force to oppose the efforts of indigenous communist elements within foreign countries must generally be considered as a risky and profitless undertaking, apt to do more harm than good.

"2. If, however, it can be shown that the continuation of communist activities has a tendency to attract U.S. armed power to the vicinity of the affected areas, and if these areas are ones from which the Kremlin would definitely wish U.S. power excluded, there is a possibility that this may bring into play the defensive security interests of the Soviet Union and cause the Russians to exert a restraining influence on local communist forces."

Thanks to Marshall's reorganization and the personal capabilities of Kennan and his successor Paul Nitze (who drafted National Security Council Memorandum No. 68, the foundation stone of American policy through the Cold War, today a tedious blast at a foreign power said to seek "the complete subversion or forcible destruction of the machinery of government and structure of society in the countries of the non-Soviet world"), the planning staff at State became the leading force in formulating all American foreign policy and defense policy in the period before the Korean War. As Thomas Etzold puts it, the years right after the war "were years of soaring prestige for the Secretaries of State and, for a time, the Policy Planning Staff. George C. Marshall and Dean G. Acheson both proved influential not only with the President but within the NSC system. Both used extensively the more than sixty papers of the Policy Planning Staff from 1947 to 1949. Many of these papers, by virtue of their political vision, logic, and felicity of expression, became the bases for drafts of NSC study memoranda and recommendations." But at the same time, Etzold notes, these were "years of drastic decline in the State Department as an institution."

The system as Marshall designed it and Acheson perfected it was rooted in a brief period when the long-range problems were also the immediate problems, so that policy did arise naturally out of planning. The Bureau of Congressional Relations, which Marshall created in 1949, had a simple product to sell, and it had few competitors. Internationally, too, the State Department benefited by the exhaustion of its allies: "It was," Henry Kissinger said much later, "a period when you did everything by cooperation and consensus—which meant, American hegemony."

As the East-West dichotomy became background to a complicated game, with many more players, the State Department often had to react rather than plan, and Policy Planning lowered its time horizons. Lincoln Bloomfield argues that the National Security Council took over, and that Policy Planning "became essentially a staff operation for the secretary of state in his capacity as a leading NSC member." Robert Bowie as Dulles' planner and Gerard Smith as Christian Herter's were strong occupants of the office; Bowie traveled with Dulles around the world and spent weekends with him at his home. What is in doubt is whether they actually made *plans*, or simply helped the Secretary chase around putting out fires.

"A Secretary of State or National Security Adviser or whatever," said

Anthony Lake, a former FSO and (briefly) Kissinger protégé who became Vance's director of Policy Planning, "seldom has time to read long papers not related to some decision or action that person has to take. So we always have an action hook." He flashed what has to be described as a boyish grin from under his graduate student's horn-rimmed glasses. "The temptation," he added, "is to become a busybody and have fun, to get involved because it's inherently interesting." Gerard Smith told Bloomfield that he personally "had no use for the ivory tower."

Bloomfield draws general conclusions, arguing that Marshall in setting up the Policy Planning Staff was "misled by the relatively successful history of military planning. It is universally accepted that war plans require definition of potential adversaries, identification of contingencies to be prepared for, and logistical wherewithal. The plans may be disastrously wrong-headed, the strategies left over from previous wars, the anticipated contingencies irrelevant to the future. Nevertheless, the military cannot land on a beach without extensive advance planning. But a political leader can land on the front pages—or in a war—with no preparation, leadtime, or plan.

"It is the inherent nature of foreign policy-making institutions that makes it so difficult to isolate a planning function in a way that would be natural and obvious in, say, an army or a post office department. In fact each desirable quality of planning is contravened by a distinctive institutional feature of the foreign office system, which is hierarchical, politically loyal, careerist, traditionalist, and incrementalist. More simply put in the form of Bloomfield's law, 'nothing happens until it has to.'"

Late in 1982, George Shultz, whose hope was that the Department could find ways to educate him in the areas where he felt poorly informed, reorganized the Policy Planning Staff into a Policy Planning Council that would serve first as a kind of think tank. It would organize, for example, the Saturday seminars the Secretary requested (and attended) to bring him up to speed on China, the Middle East, etc., before he had to participate in meetings at which significant American decisions affecting these regions would be on the table. (Vance had requested similar meetings of instruction for himself, on economic matters, but when the time came he never—not once—came to the meeting.) And like the French policy council, Shultz's planners would draw heavily on university expertise, retirees, and people with direct corporate hands-on experience in the area. Papers prepared for such occasions could, in truth, hold this Secretary's attention—provided the President, the Congress and the press left him time to think. As an institution, the Policy Planning Council would seem unlikely to survive Shultz's tenure.

On the practical level, the Marshall-Acheson system carried the seeds of three destructive growths:

1. The military would eventually seek to increase the weight of its influence on foreign policy. The process began under Secretary of Defense Louis Johnson, who developed a staff to compete with Kennan's in writing option papers for the NSC, and pushed for much more aid to the Nationalist Chinese than the State Department thought sensible. This development was masked in the Korean War years by the very close relations between Acheson and Marshall, who had returned to government as Secretary of Defense. "It may seem extraordinary, but it is nevertheless true," Acheson wrote some years later, "that not until General Marshall's tenure as Secretary of Defense had the Secretary of State and his senior officers met with the Secretary of Defense and Joint Chiefs of Staff for continuous discussion and development of policy."

There is some evidence that this did not work so well as Acheson thought. "In our regular periodic meetings with representatives of the State Department," wrote General Lawton Collins, Army Chief of Staff during the Korean War, "the Chiefs constantly tried to pin down at any particular time after the Chinese intervention, just what our remaining political objectives were in Korea, but our diplomatic colleagues would always counter with the query 'What are your military capabilities?' . . . The Chiefs could only deduce that our State Department co-workers . . . wanted us to attain the maximal military results within our military capabilities. But the military would have to assume all the responsibility if things went wrong."

The military tends to approve the use of force—heavy force—when it is sure of winning: the Pentagon wanted to take out the Soviet missiles in Cuba with bombing raids, and urged Johnson to intervene in the Dominican Republic. When there is a risk of more extensive conflict and the outcome is uncertain, the military pulls back: the Joint Chiefs vetoed the suggestion of sending an armed convoy up the Autobahn at the time of the Berlin blockade, and were prepared to sacrifice Quemoy and Matsu. In general, of course, the Defense Department has a stake in saying the armed forces are not ready: they need more men, more weapons, more facilities. Operationally, this attitude makes the military more likely to be a restraining than a driving force in times of crisis. "You should never trust the experts," Lord Salisbury once said. "If you believe the doctors, nothing is wholesome; if you believe the soldiers, nothing is safe."

Eventually, then, for good reasons or bad, the Defense Department would develop its own mini-State Department, the Office of International Security Affairs (ISA), later headed by no less than Paul Nitze, an alumnus of State's Policy Planning Staff. This forced the State Department to create a Bureau of Politico-Military Affairs, now more than a hundred strong, to fight for the Department's role in security policy—and this in turn would lead to the implantation of politico-military analysts at the geographical bureaus, seeking to defend their prerogatives.

A further dimension was added by the growth of American arms sales abroad, managed by the Defense Department, necessarily on the basis of its own interests. Most often, Defense seeks the largest orders it can get from foreigners, because expanded production runs produce lower costs for the services' own procurement. But one of the great failures of postwar American diplomacy happened in 1962 when Defense decided that Skybolt, an early air-to-ground nuclear-tipped missile, could not be made cost-effective as a weapon, and canceled the program without consulting the British, who had built their strategic planning around projections for its possible use. The resulting furor in London left not only the State Department but the White House with egg on their faces. Kennedy had to face an outraged Harold Macmillan at a summit meeting in Nassau—"Kennedy seemed somewhat taken aback," Macmillan noted some years later—and the State Department took the blame for its failure to hoist the warning flags. At State, the appetite for a program of surveillance over the Pentagon became compelling.

2. The CIA would grow tired of depending upon the State Department for information, and would sprout a network of its own agents, who would provide information different from that arriving through State Department channels and probably more persuasive to the White House, where its minions would be permanently implanted. Acheson in a famous passage about the CIA warned Truman that "as set up neither he, the National Security Council, nor anyone else would be in a position to know what it was doing or to control it." This happened fast—and the situation took a grave turn for the worse in 1948, when the National Security Council approved "covert" operations by the Agency. Kennan had supported this proposal, and later regretted his support: "It did not work out at all the way I had conceived it."

What Kennan should have realized but did not was that once covert operations began, the Director of Central Intelligence would have not merely different information, but different *policies* from those of the State Department—and there would be no way to resolve the differences below the level of the President himself. It is inconceivable, for example, that the State Department could have consented to measures like the CIA attempts to assassinate Lumumba and Castro: regardless of moral considerations, assassination is a wrongheaded tool for a great power, because small powers can use it equally (if not more) effectively.

Again, the State Department responded to the growth of a competing bureaucratic entity by enlarging its own bureaucracy, to the point where the Bureau of Intelligence and Research as a purely analytical, counter-punching office acquired three hundred employees, more than it had needed during its period as an intelligence gatherer. These people "are broken down on a geographical basis, and a functional basis," said William Bowdler, director of I&R under Vance. "Much like the Department itself—ARA, Europe, Near East, South-East, Africa, and economics, political, military. . . ."

3. In a world where foreign relations were increasingly commercial and economic, the Department lacked depth of personnel and understanding in economic matters. Kennan himself, though he liked to write occasionally about economics, knew little of the subject and sympathized less. One of the prime actors in the famous "fifteen weeks" of the development of the Truman Doctrine and the Marshall Plan had been Will Clayton, who had worked on economic warfare matters at the Commerce Department during the war and transferred to State as Assistant Secretary for Economic Affairs. (He was later given the title of Under Secretary, Acheson reports, because his wife resented his being ranked below Acheson, whose superior he had once been; the title of Under Secretary for Economic Affairs was eliminated when Clayton left, to be resurrected by Eisenhower in 1958.) But Clayton's staff was small and isolated—and in any event the rest of the government was unwilling to leave economic policy in the hands of the State Department.

As the Marshall Plan moved toward reality, Truman appointed no fewer than three committees—one headed by the Secretary of the Interior, one by the Secretary of Commerce, one by the Chairman of the Council of Economic Advisers—to examine the impact of the European Recovery Program on the American economy. What they had to say would clearly be more important than anything coming out of the State Department. Control of the program was ultimately vested in a separate administrator, Paul Hoffman, who did not report to the Secretary of State; and it was run from Paris, very independently, by Averell Harriman.

Given the monetary and budgetary implications of the Marshall Plan, Treasury's role was more central than that of State, and inside the Treasury there grew up a large international division that reported to the Under Secretary for Monetary Affairs, an office that was to grow mightily in influence under Kennedy (when Robert Roosa held it) and again under Nixon (when the occupant was Paul Volcker). American nominees to the "executive boards" of the International Monetary Fund and the World Bank reported to Treasury, not to State. Treasury attachés were implanted in the embassies of the financial centers, and reported home via the Navy Department cable system rather than via State. Post-OPEC, Treasury even acquired a separate Office of Saudi Arabian Affairs, headed by an Assistant to the Secretary. Thus Treasury, too, had a source of information separate from the State Department; and as time passed, a greater say in policy.

In the long tale of humiliations suffered by the State Department in the years since Roosevelt (who took positive delight in hiding what he was doing from the diplomats), perhaps the most irritating was the Nixon Camp David meeting in August 1971, when the United States slammed closed the gold window, demanded that other nations accept a devaluation of the dollar that would harm their trade balances, and slapped a 10 percent tariff on imports, by executive order. Nobody from the State Department was present at the meeting, and it was cold comfort that Henry Kissinger as National Security Adviser wasn't there, either. Secretary of the Treasury John Connally was; and so was his Under Secretary, Paul Volcker; and Arthur Burns of the Federal Reserve Board; and Pete Peterson of Commerce. But nobody from State.

Meanwhile, an older war had begun again: the Commerce Department, low in the pecking order of American government, improved its self-importance by attacking the performance of State in trade promotion. Businessmen, not always happy with their reception by the pretty boys in the embassies (or even the consulates), joined in the onslaught, with special emphasis on the Department's reluctance to pick fights with foreigners over their barriers to imports from the United States. After the collapse of the negotiations for an International Trade Organization (which was to be a companion piece to the IMF and the World Bank), the State Department became increasingly a reluctant servant of purely domestic interests as round followed round in the permanent floating crap game of the General Agreement on Tariffs and Trade.

Dissatisfaction with the performance of both Commerce and State in the management of trade policy in the 1960s led to the creation of a new office in the White House, that of the Special Trade Representative, who would beat on the Japanese to open their markets to American goods in ways that the State Department might not and toothless Commerce could not. The financial institutions formed to help American companies sell abroad—the Export-Import Bank, the DISC (Domestic International Sales Corporation) tax-reduction machine, the OPIC (Overseas Protective Insurance Corporation) insurance scheme to reduce the political risks of foreign investment—were insulated against State Department influence.

The budget for services to support American exporters in foreign countries was controlled by Commerce, not State—and eventually, in 1979, pursuant to an act of Congress that could have been interpreted differently,

President Carter transferred supervision of the commercial attachés themselves from the State Department to Commerce. ("I was a witness at the House Commerce Committee hearings," Under Secretary for Management Ben Read said glumly. "Not a soul had a good word to say for the Department of State, and not a soul had a good word to say for the Department of Commerce.") When the Tripartite Commission on Trade —Europe, United States and Japan—met for the first time in January 1982, the U.S. delegation was headed by the Trade Representative and an Under Secretary of Commerce, with State merely represented on the team. George Shultz magnified the State Department's clout in economic policy—but he did it as an individual, leaving the bureaucratic structures in place (Treasury, for example, continued to chair the Senior Interagency Group on international economic policy), because it was a fight he knew he couldn't win. When that cat departs, the mice will be at liberty again.

Even the aid program, clearly an element (not to say a weapon) in the conduct of foreign policy, lodged only shakily at State. Though the members of the aid cadre were Foreign Service Reserve Officers with a status permitting their appointments to be renewed ad infinitum, and there was some transfer of people back and forth between State and AID, (Agency for International Development), the administration of foreign assistance was lodged in an essentially separate bureaucracy. In 1979, indeed, Congress established a largely independent International Development Cooperation Administration with a director who would not be part of the State Department and would report separately and directly to the President. This law was a parting gift to the dying Hubert Humphrey, who had always hoped to see American aid distributed on the basis of need and merit, free of political interference, and Congress regretted its action almost immediately: nobody objected when the incoming Reagan administration announced that this office would be left unfilled, and that State would make IDCA's case before the Office of Management and Budget.

"Aid has political as well as developmental goals," said Michael Samuels, former ambassador to Sierra Leone, which had lost its U.S. aid program by incompetence and corruption. "If you don't care about their problems, why should they care about yours?" The de facto restoration of State Department control over the assistance program may be why a foreign aid appropriations bill actually passed Congress for the 1982 fiscal year, after three years when aid had been funded by continuing resolution and ad hoc supplement. But the separate foreign aid organization remains, divided like the State Department into a series of regional and functional bureaus which report up the line to their own administrators rather than to the assistant secretaries.

Again, the Department sought to hold its own by forming new "offices" within the "divisions" of the Bureau of Economic and Business Affairs (EB), which became second only to the Bureau of Administration in the number of its employees in Washington. And, again, in response to this growth in a specialized bureau, the geographical bureaus added economic analysts (rarely economists) to their staffs—so that, for example, people supposedly knowledgeable in the economics of energy could be found in every one of the geographical bureaus as well as EB, and I&R, and Politico-Military, and Policy Planning. During the Ford and Carter administrations, the Bureau of Economic and Business Affairs was very strongly led—by Thomas Enders, Julius Katz and Deane Hinton—but except in the area of commodities agreements when Katz was Assistant Secretary (and recognizably expert in the subject), its effectiveness was slight. "The Seventh Floor view," Hinton said rather bitterly in the Carter days, "is that the United States has a broad political policy, and the economics bureau can if beaten into shape provide some chips. There's no sense at all that what we have is a broad economic policy to which the political side can make a contribution."

Under Eisenhower, the Department also acquired, probably permanently, an Under Secretary for Economic Affairs, a staff position with no line responsibility (the Assistant Secretary reports to the Secretary, not to the Under Secretary). This has been an important post when its occupant had access to the President, as the banker Douglas Dillon did under Eisenhower, the lawyer George Ball under Kennedy. It helped that Dillon was an immensely able man who liked to make decisions, and that Eisenhower had charged him with a detailed overview of the impact of both economic and military assistance programs. But that has little to do with the State Department. Carter's Under Secretary Richard Cooper and Reagan's Under Secretary Myer Rashish were essentially fifth wheels on the go-cart of governance. Rashish's successor W. Allen Wallis, who started with the advantage of having been the dean of the Chicago business school who appointed Shultz to his first professorship, disappeared into the building apparently without trace. "We see the briefing papers," said an Under Secretary's assistant, "when it's too late to change them."

By the time of Carter, several other fifth wheels had been added in a feeble effort to keep the bureaucratic juggernaut on some sort of track. The functions once performed by the Under Secretary as alter ego had been transferred to a Deputy Secretary, and no fewer than four Under Secretaries were in the Table of Organization. The Under Secretary for Political Affairs has usually been an FSO, and the post bears a certain resemblance in theory to the job of Permanent Undersecretary in the British Commonwealth structure or Secretary General in the European Ministries —but in fact people churn in and out of it, and the lines of both authority and responsibility run directly from the Secretary to the assistants. "I feel sometimes," said Walter Stoessel, a small, gray, bespectacled career ambassador who later moved up to Deputy Secretary, "as though I'm not really as well-informed as I would like to be. There's a lot that goes on that you never hear about up here."

The Under Secretary for Management presumably has the all-important budgetary responsibilities—but in fact, again, the assistant secretaries organize their own bureaus, and the walking delegates from the Inspector General's office who visit the embassies are personages of such dignity and significance (mostly former ambassadors) that they are not to be constrained in their recommendations by undersecretarial policy. The Under Secretary for Science and Technology is a Pooh-Bah Lord-High-Everything-Else, with responsibilities (but no authority) ranging from arms sales and military assistance to narcotics control to technology transfer, including controls on such transfers to Communist countries. The post was first created to give dignity of title to a Kissinger crony, and is almost necessarily political; Lucy Benson, former head of the League of Women Voters and friend of House Speaker Tip O'Neill, held it under Carter; former Senator James Buckley, brother of William and one of the great charmers of American conservatism, received it under Reagan, who extended the mandate still further to cover economic aid programs. "I don't see myself running these things," Buckley said amiably a few months after taking the office, "but as trying to think through which countries are important to us. . . ." In reality, he was used most heavily to carry Secretary Haig's bags at congressional hearings ("I go in a decorative capacity") and to lobby former colleagues on budgetary matters.

The burden of making this organization coherent had to be carried by Marshall's Executive Secretariat, which was thereby reduced from serving the Secretary of State to serving the departmental bureaucracies. Its information control procedures had to be divided three ways: a secure seventh-floor duty office manned day and night by a "watch team" of two young FSOs who sit on a raised platform overlooking an array of machines that print out the NoDis (No Distribution) and ExDis (Exclusive Distribution) cables and the news bulletins, a large map on the wall to facilitate everyone's understanding of where this moment's trouble is occurring; an "operations center" in cubicles to receive, distribute, edit and digest the incoming cables for the "Secretary's Morning Summary," and to prepare the daily National Intelligence Estimates that the Secretary finds on the seat of his limousine (together with a collection of press excerpts) when he leaves home every morning (a second edition is prepared for the late afternoon); and a separate staff to "task" the bureaus—to solicit, receive, schedule and edit (or rewrite) memoranda and other paper.

Two dozen FSOs, each responsible for liaison with "his" bureau, are assigned to the memo-processing function alone. Alvin Adams, Jr., who supervised this section in the early days of Haig's State Department, said there was no way *he* could read all the memos directed upstairs for the Secretary's attention. A computerized tickler file tracks what is happening to the Secretary's requests and to queries from congressmen (a category of paperwork that looms very large), and what is being done in preparation for committee meetings, the real calendar for the Department's work. "There's paper for the White House," a staff member said wearily. "How are the multibureau projects to be coordinated? The mechanical things—who duplicates the shit? who gets it up there? who's responsible for the interagency clearances? who does the speechwriting? who makes sure there are meetings to review the drafts?"

The general though not invariable rule is that nothing goes to the Secretary until it has circulated for comment and advice through the serried ranks of the assistant secretaries.‡ With the passage of time and the growth of competing bureaucracies, the number of actors who might have reason to complain if they were not included in the Secretariat's distribution grew mightily. Even on rather narrow questions—say, approval of the use of GE engines in Israeli Kfir fighter planes for sale to Bolivia—a great number of bureaus within the Department, plus the White House, Defense, Commerce and Treasury, would have to be kept informed and given the impression that their views had weight. ARA, NEA, the Office of Arab-Israeli Affairs, EB, Human Rights (Bolivia was *awful*), Politico-Military, I&R, Policy Planning would all be involved, and each of these would be relating to different departments and agencies elsewhere in the government through assorted IGs (Interagency Groups). It might even be a matter that an Under Secretary should take up with a SIG (Senior Interagency Group); and the White House would have to be kept informed.

Within each of the bureaus and agencies, there would be several individuals who would feel it part of their function to "sign off" on the memo describing the problem and making recommendations. "When I say we get too many cables," Policy Planning Director Anthony Lake explained, "my people say, 'Jesus—we've got to see that or we're at a competitive disadvantage.'" Disputes about who needed to know would be even more time-consuming than the job itself, and were thus to be avoided in the only way they could be avoided—by lengthening the routing slip. So the

‡ The exception was the NoDis Cherokee cable, named for Dean Rusk's home county of Cherokee, Georgia, which ambassadors could use in urgent situations to get their views directly before the Secretary. The category was abused, the Executive Secretary was given authority to decide which cables should go directly to the Secretary and which should be circulated, and finally in the last years of Vance this version of "Eyes Only" was abandoned.

memos would go out in increasing numbers; there would be meetings, revisions, more meetings, more circulation of documents. "The name of the game is 'clearing,'" said Polish desk officer Jack Seymour rather wearily. "You have to get people on board almost every piece of paper." At the center of the web, the Secretariat assumed the function of "maintaining," as a senior member put it, "bureaucratic fairness."

Charles Frankel in his book tells a story that may be apocryphal in detail but is surely true in spirit: "A memorandum came to me one day which I was asked to approve before it was transmitted to the Secretary. It was on a subject which seemed rather dimly related to anything I was doing, but it took less time to read the document than to explore the reasons it had come to me, so I dutifully read it and affixed my initials at the bottom of the page. A week or so later, the document came back to me. It had indeed been sent to me by mistake. Would I, therefore, erase my initials and initial the erasure?"

Each memo requires some sort of action in some time frame from each person receiving it. The result is an overburden of paper and meetings that keeps everyone at the State Department behind in his work, unable to take the time to think about which of his tasks requires thought, present in the building for intolerable hours. Rusk himself was the worst: he is believed to have taken off only three days in eight years. "His idea of a vacation," said a man who worked closely with him, "was when he wore a sweater to the office." An FSO who was duty officer in the Secretariat one New Year's Eve fondly remembers the Secretary of State coming in at midnight to share a bourbon-and-water.

Today Rusk professes to admire the Soviet system which requires everybody to take a month off every year—by law. His successors, while not quite so masochistic as Rusk, were in the office virtually every Saturday if they were in Washington, and they expected the assistant secretaries, sometimes their deputies, and always the members of the Executive Secretariat, to be present and ready for work. In 1981, a member of the Secretariat said his hours were "eight to nine—eight in the morning to nine at night—except that it's okay if you don't get to the office before nine on Saturday." It is all a variant of Parkinson's Law: work having expanded beyond the available time, an extension of time generates still more work. The Shultz team in its early months thought it could get a handle on the system. Kenneth Dam as Shultz's deputy claimed in late 1982 that he could push a decision through the Department in twelve hours. "I'm sure we've got the routings right because I'm hearing so many screams." Even if that pressure could be maintained—and the old-timers say that once Shultz began traveling the screws worked loose—it wouldn't solve the most serious problem. "I know what I think is important every day,"

Deane Hinton said while Assistant Secretary for EB, "and I know what I want to accomplish. But some days I can't even *start* on it. The Secretary says he wants views on something or other, and that becomes the most important thing I have to do."

Formally, control over the process is accomplished in a very hierarchical way, which occasions derision among observant visitors. "When I was back this time," J. K. Galbraith wrote savagely while ambassador to India, "one of my assistant secretary friends attended the Secretary's staff meeting from nine-fifteen till ten. Then he had a meeting with the Undersecretary on operations until ten-thirty. Then he took until eleven-thirty to inform his staff of what went on at the earlier meetings. Whereupon they adjourned to pass the news to their staffs. This is, I am told, communications."

There are too many meetings, and too many people at each of them. Galbraith again: "Everyone insists on, and by common consent everyone is accorded, a finger in every important pie. Every civilized group acts in some degree by unanimous consent. So one cannot get agreement on anything new. When a deadline approaches everyone repairs hurriedly to what was agreed on several years ago."

And all this is on top of the monstrous quantities of paper—the Xeroxed memos and the two-million-plus words of cable traffic a day, with the cables copied to posts, offices, bureaus, other departments of government, so that there is virtually no effective division of labor in the reading of them, except hierarchically. "I see a large volume of cables already digested," said I&R director Bowdler. "I try not to get involved in raw cables." What the Secretary gets from I&R, then, is a digest of a digest, by someone who has not applied his own judgment to the originals.

The weight of decision on the Department increases steadily as technology improves the connections between the embassies and the center. For all the obeisance to ambassadors, the State Department now believes that they can and thus should refer all matters affecting relations with the host country back to Washington for "policy guidance." But there is no way for the Department to produce replies to the queries in a useful time frame, which leaves the ambassadors with the feeling that they have been betrayed by the desk officer. To let Galbraith vent the steam yet again: "My desk officer . . . combines a great verbal felicity with a remarkable inability to accomplish the most minute task, a considerable reluctance to try, and a total unawareness of any inadequacy."

"Bill Crockett," said Carol Laise, referring to Kennedy's Deputy Under Secretary for Administration, a much-hated man among the FSOs because he had entered their ranks through Wristonization and took reorganization seriously, "Bill Crockett liked to say that if you didn't have the manpower to really centralize decisions, then you had to put greater authority in the field." But there was a third option: put everything through still more committees.

Graham Martin, en route to a difficult embassy in Rome and then an impossible one in Saigon, blamed much of this steady growth of "layering" on the recruitment of captains of industry to government service after World War II: "Sometimes," he wrote in 1968, "the techniques, which had proven of value to Procter & Gamble and Ford, were either totally irrelevant or downright mischievous when they were superimposed on fields where subjective professional judgment simply had to be the determining factor. The result was a reinforcement of the already latent tendency to emphasize that responsibility and loyalty should be given only to those in the direct hierarchical chain of superiors from whom alone came advancement. The competitive instincts thus loosed eroded, subtly yet progressively, the search for the national interest.

"The effect of these new lines of loyalty was quickly felt in the various mechanisms set up to 'co-ordinate' the varying interests in foreign affairs of the agencies and departments which had expanded in the postwar period. Rarely was the objective consideration of the national interest now the paramount concern. Rather, the highest accolade was reserved for those who successfully imposed their agency's point of view. Failing that supreme accomplishment, the 'name of the game' was to block all action by withholding 'concurrence.' Robert A. Lovett summarized this phenomenon:

" 'This device of inviting argument between conflicting interests . . . needs some careful examination because there is, I think, a discernible and constantly increasing tendency to try to expand the intent of the system to the point where mere curiosity on the part of some agency, and not a "need to know" can be used as a ticket of admission to the merry-go-round of "concurrences." This doctrine, unless carefully and boldly policed, can become so fertile a spawner of committees as to blanket the whole executive branch with an embalmed atmosphere.' "

That this system works at all (it cannot work well) is a tribute to the capacity and group cohesion of the middle-level FSOs who serve in the Secretariat, as personal assistants to the assistant secretaries (a kind of minisecretariat in each bureau), and as "country directors" maintaining liaison with the larger nations and groupings of the smaller nations in each of the geographical bureaus. Through this "back-channel," the Secretariat learns unofficially what seems to be most important to the people closest to the situation—and feeds the Secretary's desires into the bureaus through the people who actually control the flow by determining what their bosses see. (An Israeli Foreign Ministry bureaucrat says that the cable is the indispensable tool of internal communications in Jerusalem: "My boss would be too busy to read a memo from me. But if I put it in the form of a cable to one of our posts in Europe, with a copy to him, he reads it." This would not work in Washington: the personal assistant would cut the cable off at the pass.)

For a time while Kissinger was Secretary of State, the assistant secretaries themselves, in self-defense, kept each other informed. The Department was unusually cohesive under Kissinger, partly because the pressure from the top was so personal and so unceasing, partly because Kissinger had filled all but one of the assistant-secretary slots with FSOs, most of whom had known each other a long time.

Unfortunately, the fact that everybody is very busy does not necessarily mean that anybody is getting anything done. Much of the time required by the consultation and sign-off system, after all, goes to advocacy of the position that nothing should be done—at least, right now. Structures of interlocking committees necessarily generate delay, sometimes with serious consequences. "The right way to deal with the bureaucracy," McGeorge Bundy told the Murphy Commission in 1975, "is to get close to it, to use it, and to build persistently and sympathetically on its own almost instinctive desire to turn toward the sunlight of Presidential leadership." But presidential leadership is far removed from most of the questions that paralyze the committees—and when it looms over the horizon, exaggerated in apparent size like the rising sun, the system has no way to respond.

This problem is known generically in the State Department as "the Turkish missile syndrome," referring to the general belief that President Kennedy had ordered the withdrawal of the American Jupiter missiles from Turkey some months before the Cuban missile crisis broke, but found himself confronted in the fall of 1962 with a situation where the Russians could plausibly propose a politically impossible quid pro quo for the removal of the IRBMs they were installing in Cuba. Francis Rourke of the School of Advanced International Studies at Johns Hopkins explains that "the earlier indication by the president that he wished to have American missiles removed from Turkey had been a signal to the department to begin the lengthy process of diplomacy necessary to accomplish this objective, not an order to by-pass these standard operating procedures."

In fact, the matter was more complicated than that: the missiles were actually put in place by Kennedy himself, following through on an Eisenhower promise to the Turks. They were installed over the objections of the Defense Department, which found the Jupiters too provocative to the Russians and too vulnerable to be of any use. The committee that looked into the situation for Kennedy was chaired by the State Department rather than by Defense, an indication to Barton Bernstein of Stanford, who has analyzed papers not available to Rourke, that "the President probably cared more about not offending the Turks than about withholding the Jupiters. This message was probably clear to the chair and other representatives."

A reverse signal was given in August 1962, when the group formed to consider what would now be the removal of the missiles was chaired by Defense—but, Bernstein points out, the question put to that group was "What action can be taken?" and no answers were found. By then, doubtless, Kennedy (or Bundy) had come to feel that the missiles should go, but the later belief that the President's plans had been sabotaged at State, while widely accepted, is almost certainly wrong. Bernstein observes that "a chief executive may . . . express preferences (not orders) for policies, and . . . may sincerely reinterpret them as *orders* when his own inaction leaves him woefully unprepared in a crisis. In this way, a president can place blame on a subordinate. . . ." In terms of the attitudes that follow upon presidential blame, of course, inside or outside the State Department, the truth is not that important.

Getting a new policy out of the machine may be all but impossible. Pat Moynihan remembered from the days when he was head of Nixon's Domestic Policy Council a meeting on the problem of heroin flooding into the cities from Turkish opium. The State Department was terrified of taking steps that might irritate a NATO ally. "They said," Moynihan recalled, " 'The consequences might be very difficult.' I said, 'Well, what would they be?' They said, 'Impossible to say.' I said, 'If it's impossible to say, how can you know they would be very difficult?' I didn't get an answer."

"Once the decision-making apparatus has disgorged a policy," Henry Kissinger wrote shortly before he became Nixon's National Security Adviser, "it becomes very difficult to change it. The alternative to the status quo is the prospect of repeating the whole anguishing process of arriving at decisions. This explains to some extent the curious phenomenon that decisions taken with enormous doubt and perhaps with a close division become practically sacrosanct once adopted. The whole administrative machinery swings behind their implementation as if activity could still all doubts." And of course the policy that does emerge may have been constructed with very little input from the people on the scene or those in Washington closest to it. Walter Stoessel, then Under Secretary for Political Affairs for Haig, was proud of the fact that he had included the desk officer for Poland in one of the scores of meetings on what to do with that unlucky land. Thinking back on his time as ambassador to Czechoslovakia when the Russians moved, and reflecting that nothing changes,

Jacob Beam noted that "our desk people in Washington know the cast of characters, but of course that doesn't get up top."

On the few occasions when policy is decisively reversed, it will be because a new man who does not understand what happened in the previous negotiations arrives on the scene—and even then it may be necessary to conduct bloody purges in the agencies responsible for the previously approved proposals. Disconcertingly often, there is an element of accident in the situation. Thus, the delegates from the various bureaus to the standing committee on Law of the Sea issues met shortly after the Reagan inauguration to plan American participation in what was supposed to be the final staging of that long-running show, leading to an actual treaty-signing ceremony. The stumbling block had been the terms on which a United Nations entity to be called the Enterprise was to be funded and provided with know-how to enable it to share with private mining companies the bounty of mineral nodules on the floors of the oceans; and thanks to the persistence and ingenuity of Singapore's Tommy Koh, head of the UN working party on this issue, a deal had been struck. In conversation around the table, several people urged haste to get the instructions out to the U.S. delegates, before those wild men from California took over and queered the deal. But one of the participants in the meeting was a new Reagan appointee, who got up and said, "I am one of those wild men from California," and left. His report upstairs produced the dismissal of the U.S. delegation to the conference, and an announcement that the United States was not yet prepared to enter into a treaty on this subject.

This was mostly wrong, incidentally—the creation of the Enterprise had been in effect a trade-off against treaty rights for U.S. warships to pass through the significant straits. While the terms of Koh's compromise may have been unduly burdensome for the private investors ("We are struggling against the tendency of our delegation to give away to others the common heritage of mankind," Economics Bureau Chief Deane Hinton had said in the dying days of the Carter administration), the result of that would have been that the Enterprise would abort, producing further negotiations subsequent to the treaty. But the new blood at State knew the *Wall Street Journal* editorials rather than the history, and wasn't terribly interested in learning more.*

In many situations, the result of the committee system is not just delay, nor blind adherence to past policy, nor casual reversal; it is . . . nothing. During the Carter administration the United States conducted negotia-

---

* In fairness to the Reagan crowd, the renegotiations would then have been conducted under a clause in the treaty providing that decisions should be made UN-General-Assembly-style—one nation, one vote—and acceptance of such a clause would create a precedent the United States could not possibly concede.

tions with the Soviet Union aimed at limiting arms sales by both countries
to the Third World, one of the most important issues on the international
table. The negotiations collapsed, Andrew Pierre of the Council on Foreign Relations reports, "more because of internal feuding within the Administration and a lack of clarity as to aims than because of substantive
disagreement with the Soviet Union at the negotiating table."

Abram Chayes, Harvard law professor and former legal adviser to the
State Department in the Kennedy days, provides a circumstantial example
from the International Nuclear Fuel Cycle Evaluation Conference, a centerpiece of the Carter administration effort to control proliferation of nuclear weapons by limiting the uses of spent fuel from nuclear reactors.
Chayes was not part of the U.S. delegation; he was chairman of the conference, above it all. "The Americans," he said, "were the best prepared,
the best motivated and the most numerous delegation at the conference,
and they had the most community-oriented policies. But they were the
least effective.

"The problem was the generation of paper, the requirement that everybody in the government sign off on everything. All suggestions had to go
to the Seventh Floor. We were always behind the power curve, as my wife
learned to say in the Air Force. [Antonia Chayes was Assistant Secretary
for Air in Carter's Defense Department.] It hurt to see people who were
so good and worked so hard coming up with their hands empty because
the train had already gone.

"I remember there was a special problem at the end. The Germans had
proposed an amendment to the communiqué that I knew the United
States could not live with—not so much a matter of substance as a form
of words. I called a recess, and I thought the U.S. delegation would be out
in the corridors, lobbying the Germans. Everybody else left the hall, but
the Americans were all in the corner talking to each other, debating what
their position would be. Finally I went out and spoke with the Germans,
explained the difficulty, and one of them went in to talk with the U.S. delegation. 'How would it be,' he said, 'if we changed our proposal *this*
way. . . .' Everyone was very relieved."

3

Galbraith warned Charles Frankel when he took an Assistant Secretary's
post that the State Department "is the kind of organization which,
though it does big things badly, does small things badly, too." Interestingly, this turns out not to be true: the Department handles its small
things remarkably well. The standard of housekeeping is high in the

World-War-II-vintage eight-story building, a gaggle of color-coded corridors that run into dead ends and resume again beyond. (Veterans say better care used to be taken of the building, and complain about the cheeseparing that began under Carter, when the quality of the paper in the washrooms was reduced.) Security is tight: gumshoes come through offices late at night, making sure the locked files are really locked and nobody has left confidential papers on top of the desk or in unlocked drawers or files—there is no privacy at State.

Abroad, one hundred and fifty State Department security agents supplement the fifteen hundred Marines as embassy guards (and as destroyers of paper and code machines if it looks likely that a mob will seize the embassy). Two architects are employed full-time to design physical security structures for American property abroad. In the aftermath of the bombing of the Beirut embassy in 1983, several congressional committees declared that no expense would be spared to make the embassies safe, and may have meant it. At home, about three hundred fifty agents stand guard over foreign diplomats, a service begun, incidentally, by Nixon personally at the suggestion of George Bush, then ambassador to the UN, after the Jewish Defense League took pot shots at the Soviet Union's East Side residence complex in 1971. Ambassador Jacob Beam had cabled the State Department from Moscow requesting that something of that sort be done, but he never got a reply.

A travel office efficiently books trips all over the world, ever mindful of strike situations and of the congressional requirement that U.S. Government employees travel on U.S.–flag airlines whenever possible. The State Department's advice on bargain hotels abroad is worth having. An "Art in Embassies" staff borrows from American museums, ships the art and insures it. (When this program was begun, under Bill Benton, the Department bought the art, but Congress raised hell about the godless pornography for which tax moneys had been expended, and the paintings were auctioned off, at a profit.) There is a banking office in the building, and a post office, and a barber shop, and a large medical office with seventy-five employees in Washington and refrigerators full of shots for exotic diseases. Slots in the desperately overcrowded garage are carefully allocated by a process that compels the bureaus to make their own decisions on who needs what (a renegotiation of these terms in 1979, by Assistant Secretary for Administration Thomas Tracy, was described by one of his fellow assistant secretaries as "the outstanding feat of negotiation accomplished by an American diplomat in this decade").

The crown of glory (and anguish) in the Department is the communications center, which runs out of a fifth-floor block of space in the center of the building, the area enclosed by steel-and-concrete walls and entered through double steel doors that can be opened only by a signal from inside. The center operates twenty-four hours a day, and requires a staff of 170. The clocks read in "Zulu time" (Greenwich mean time—the origin of the name is unknown), and the days are numbered 1–365 without any month reference ("Julian date"). The heart of the operation is a dark room with ten CRT units onto which the stream of incoming cables pops line by line in green lettering. A "communications analyst" who has had at least eighteen months of apprenticeship training—the degree of skill required has been a source of conflict between the State Department and the Office of Management and Budget, which periodically tries to downgrade the job and its salary—sits at each CRT and directs each cable to its proper recipients in the bureaus and in the other agencies of government. About a hundred sixty-five bureaus and agencies are on the possible distribution list.

Distribution within the State Department is accomplished in a printing room where seven high-speed laser-beam Xerox machines designed especially for the Department take input from two Control Data mainframe computers and duplicate, collate and staple at a rate of a page a second per machine. The documents are then rolled into tubes and directed around the building through a pneumatic piping system, appearing in the little mail rooms attached to each bureau. Electronic links to the Defense Department, the Commerce Department and the White House assure that cables useful in those offices appear automatically on their teletypes, while cables for Treasury, Energy, Agriculture, etc. are moved out by courier.

Until 1976, NoDis and ExDis cables moved over facilities controlled by the National Security Agency, an arrangement worked out in the 1960s, "when," to quote the Murphy Commission, "improved equipment required a sizeable outlay of funds the State Department was unable or unwilling to seek." Even now, with the cryptographic machinery moved to State (still the same, now rather beat-up machinery, looking like the UPI ticker in a country newspaper), these cables are not read by State Department communications specialists. They pass through the fifth-floor area electronically, printing out in the Secretariat's operations room upstairs. NoDis cables go outside the building only to the White House.

Though the State Department is reputedly a sieve, FSOs believe cables are much more tightly held here than elsewhere. One of them recounts that while stationed in London, he kept up with ExDis cables from other embassies in Europe that were not copied to Britain by wandering over to CINCNAVEUR (sorry about that: means Commander in Chief, Navy, Europe), which received such material automatically from the Pentagon. When Harold Brown was Secretary of Defense in the Carter administration, he okayed a State Department request to keep ExDis material off the Pentagon's teletypes, and personally read the single copy of ExDis cables sent across the river by the Secretariat, and wrote the routing slip for each in his own hand. Within the State Department, NoDis cables are numbered and directed to the personal attention of the assistant secretaries, and may not be removed from their desks; if they feel others in their bureaus should read them, they call them in to read the material—in theory in the Assistant Secretary's presence, in fact in his anteroom under the baleful eye of his secretary.

Among the disasters of the late 1970s was a quantum leap in the capacity of the printing and duplicating system, which enabled the Department to quintuple the distribution of cables. People who had previously come to work to find three times as much stuff in the IN box as they could hope to read now found seven or eight times as much as they could manage, and grew even more dependent on the judgment of the young assistants who filtered the material. Inevitably, the Department's budget for paper went through the roof, and in one of its many displays of meanness (Carter really *was* tight) the Administration mandated the reduction of the type size in the distributed cables. Together with the reduction of lighting in the offices to save electricity, this economy further reduced the already low capacity of the Department to figure out (let alone respond to) what was on the minds of the people in the field.

But in terms of getting the little things done well, the State Department communications system must be considered a triumph, an astonishingly efficient mix of Defense Department wires, satellite channels, leased wires from commercial services, direct lines to Latin America, Moscow, Japan and South Africa, nodes at Bonn to serve Eastern Europe, London for Western Europe, Athens for East Africa, Lagos for West Africa, Manila for Asia. From the moment a cable leaves a post many thousands of miles away to the moment of its appearance at the receiving end of the pneumatic tubes in several dozen offices in Washington, the elapsed time is less than one hour. NoDis of course takes longer—several hours. Doubly encrypted at the source, it must be doubly decrypted before it prints out on the seventh floor. . . . The more urgent the message, the more slowly it moves—but those are the penalties of security.

Then there is the State Department's overseas operation, the management of embassy property and more than $3 billion worth of housing in 240 cities, the need to pay salaries and benefits to ten thousand foreign nationals who work for the Department in their own countries, doing everything from mopping the embassy floors and answering the phones to planning trade promotions to interpreting or translating or maintaining liaison with significant figures in the host government. The best example of the complications in this infrastructure—and the Department's brilliance in managing them—is the Regional Finance Center (recently grandly renamed a Regional Administrative Management Center) in Paris, which since the late 1950s has paid the bills for all State Department operations, and now many other overseas activities of the United States, in Europe, Africa and the Near East. Even the Defense Department now uses the services of this State Department bureau for an increasing fraction of its foreign needs. "The military with all their sputniks and airplanes," said Leon Lerchbaum, a former New York department store merchandiser who ran the RFC's foreign exchange operation for eighteen years, "they still don't know how to pay a bill in Djibouti."

At the center of the RFC lies what is probably the largest nonbank foreign-exchange spot-purchasing operation in the world—$2 billion a year. Its home is a pair of small offices overlooking an ivy-walled garden two courtyards in from a nondescript nineteenth-century facade on the Rue de la Boétie in the gray area where fashionable Paris becomes commercial Paris. It is carried on for the U.S. Government by two rather shy dark-haired Frenchwomen, Chantel Chantoiseaux and Danielle Friedlander, under the general supervision of Michael Jackson, a sandy-haired, gangling, earnest FSO who never in his life worked a day in the private sector.

This is not exactly a trading room, though there are moments when the women are on the phone simultaneously with several banks, calling back and forth to each other, when a visitor could easily make the mistake of thinking it is. But this office never sells foreign exchange, it only buys—and for immediate delivery, too. Congress has been willing to authorize a lot of peculiar activity by the CIA, the State Department and the Defense Department, but it draws the line on speculation in the forward exchange markets by an agency of the U.S. Government.

Everything about this operation is very odd. The U.S. Treasury checks for that $2 billion are made out by Michael Jackson to himself, and he endorses them to an account in his name at Morgan Guaranty in Paris, which honors them for same-day payment in New York, still the only place where large dollar transactions can be cleared. The currencies Jackson purchases turn up two days later as deposits credited to the State Department in local banks in some eighty-nine countries. The money is then quickly removed from those accounts by people cashing their salary checks and by local tradesmen, craftsmen and vendors. Their checks, in the local currency, are also signed by Michael Jackson, and also issued in Paris. Some seven hundred and fifty thousand checks in seventy-eight different currencies, drawn on 102 different banks, are issued from this office in Paris in a single year.

The Mlles. Chantoiseaux and Friedlander buy foreign exchange on the market because the prices are lower when they do it than when the government simply asks a bank to supply a foreign currency. Checks to employees and suppliers around the world are issued from Paris rather than from the embassies because that procedure enables the State Department to do without a hundred-odd disbursing officers in the embassies and other posts—and issued from Paris rather than from Washington because Paris demonstrably does the job much better.

One of the reasons inflation raises U.S. Government expenses faster than those in private industry is that the government is slow pay, a fact that vendors build into their bidding for government contracts. Processing a voucher in Washington takes anywhere from six weeks to three months. At the RFC in Paris, every voucher that arrives before ten-thirty in the morning is paid before the close of day unless the computer finds a reason to kick it out of the machine. A few years ago, some people in Washington started a half-serious petition to get the payrolls and expense vouchers of the home bureaucracy moved to Paris so people could get their money faster.

A computerized cash management program tells the RFC how much of each currency it has to buy each day to make sure the U.S. Government's checks in that currency will not bounce. The traders begin each day by calling at least three banks—one each in France, Britain and Switzerland—to get opening quotes and views of where the market seems to be going in about twenty-five currencies, and they check back with various sources as the day progresses. Every so often their order is indeed big enough to move the market (the largest ever was $70 million of British pounds), and has to be spread around. "Basically," Jackson says, "there are two moments of decision. The first is, do we go to lunch? The second is, do we wait for the opening of the New York market? There's still an hour of trading here after New York opens, and that can change the price."

RFC Paris has been an unusually stable shop, despite the vagaries of the dollar, periodic moments of tension when State Department job analysts come by and reclassify (often downward) positions that have no real civil-service equivalent back home, and a degree of exploitation of staff who are neither French nor American citizens and are captive to RFC as one of the few places in Paris where they can be employed without a work permit. Robert Gingles, director of the operation, says he was amazed when he returned in 1980 to find that virtually everyone he knew when he was a junior officer on the staff in 1970–72 was still at the RFC. Claude Dowling, chief of data processing, an aristocratic native Parisian whose father was American and who spent the war years as a teen-ager in the United States, has been at the RFC from its beginnings in October 1959—"pay period number ten, Paris. This is one of those rare jobs where you have to like it," he says cheerfully, "because you can't do it at all if you don't like it."

In addition to the personnel management and the data processing systems, which employ about a hundred people, a lot of contractual arrangements are necessary to make this thing work. Many corporations have zero-balance bank accounts at the big international banks, but these deals involve a payment of fees and a promise by the corporation to wire in the funds to cover an intraday overdraft before the bank has to settle accounts in the clearing house. The RFC arrangement in Paris involves a paper check that cannot be got to New York, let alone cleared, before Morgan must transfer the money to scores of banks in Europe, Africa and Asia.

The system works because the Treasury has authorized the Federal Reserve Bank of New York to credit Morgan with, say, $10 million on receipt of a telex from Paris that the Morgan branch there has received a paper check in that amount properly signed by Michael Jackson. Morgan then instantly transfers that money to the New York accounts or correspondents of the banks that sold the RFC the foreign currencies.

The banks in Amman and Yaoundé and Budapest in which RFC maintains accounts are now informed by Morgan as their correspondent that their own balances have been credited with a certain number of units of their own currency, for the account of the State Department. The RFC negotiates individual deals with the local banks, preference being given to branches of American banks. If a non-American bank can give outstanding service, however, the RFC can override the preference: Dresdner Bank handles the State Department business in Germany despite the presence of several U.S. banks, and the First National Bank of Boston, which is trying to get started in Cameroon, will have to make a hell of a case before the RFC is willing to displace the Banque Internationale d'Afrique Occidentale, which has flawlessly managed State Department payments in French-speaking Africa from the beginning. Morgan itself is compensated by an interest-free Treasury deposit maintained on its books year-round.

This system was originally developed with Morgan, and rests on that bank's unrivaled network of correspondents throughout the world. American Express won the contract away in competitive bidding in 1980 and had a little trouble with it, especially in remote lands where Amex had no direct relations with local banks and worked through other people's correspondents. "They didn't realize," said Gingles, "how hard it is to get money into Addis Ababa or Kampala." In October 1981, to the relief of a number of RFC people, American Express moved on and Morgan took back the job.

Though paying the vouchers takes most of the money, calculating the payrolls takes most of the time from both people and machines. "Foreign Service Nationals" are not only paid in their own currency, they are paid according to whatever insurance, pension, medical, COLA adjustment and tax deduction schemes have been voted by their own governments. In the Soviet Union and much of the Third World they must be paid in cash, because people don't have bank accounts. "We have more than eight hundred data elements in the payroll file," Dowling says with his best Alastair Sim smile; "it's a monster." Other monsters can surface, too: through the hostage crisis in Iran, RFC Paris churned out checks in Iranian rials, for the local employees of the embassy, many of whom later surfaced in assorted parts of the world, and claimed their money.

Input arrangements from the embassies to RFC are a function of available techniques. Between Rome and Paris, two Wang computers speak with each other, enabling Rome to put in its own T&A (Time and Attendance) records, new employees, changes in local requirements, etc. (Rome was the first to come on line with the Paris computers because something had to be done about the Italian post office.) Other embassies have equipment to make floppy discs, and mail out their information ready to go. Some are still on the old Flexiwriter system that produces a punched paper tape, while still others simply send machine-readable pencil-marked cards through the mails and diplomatic pouch. The RFC picks up directly at the airports, Saturday and Sunday, to get last week's payroll on the machines by Monday afternoon. A few embassies telex in their payroll information, like news of revolutions, on the State Department cable net.

Americans are paid in dollars, nearly all of them by direct deposit to their banks back home (usually in the District of Columbia), but that doesn't help much with the data processing. Each post carries its own cost-of-living allowance (which may be different for two cities in the same country), updated as often as every month by an "allowance staff" when exchange rates are in rapid motion; and each federal employee has a bewildering choice of contributory pension and insurance plans. "The Federal Government's life insurance program just went wild," Gingles said. "There are now twenty-six different options—which does let us assign a different alphabet letter to each, but it keeps blowing our systems."

Then there are some situations specific to the State Department. The instant an ambassador's airplane leaves the ground en route away from his post, for example, a cable to that effect goes to Washington with notification that the deputy chief of mission has become *chargé d'affaires*. A copy of that cable goes to RFC Paris, because the DCM as *chargé* is entitled to a salary which splits the difference between his normal pay and the ambassador's, and that, too, must be registered in the RFC computers.

RFC was a reform of the Eisenhower days, looking forward to a time when the British and French colonies would become independent and the number of U.S. embassies would multiply. Dennis Collins, a Foreign Service Officer, designed it and ran it until his death in 1977. During the Vietnam War, a parallel operation was set up in Bangkok for twenty-eight countries east of Pakistan, and in 1979 the decision was made to get the Latin American payments centralized at an RFC in Mexico City. The Mexican operation has served mostly as a demonstration of how hard it is to staff these things and get them going—after three years, RFC Mexico City served only the local embassy and consulates. The nationalization of the Mexican banks and the imposition of exchange controls then made expansion unthinkable.

The success of RFC Paris put some people's noses out of joint at Treasury, and over the years there were a couple of attempts in congressional committees to move control of the operation away from Foggy Bottom and over to Fifteenth Street. More recently, though, the trend has been in the other direction. Rechartering the Board for International Broadcasting, which runs Radio Free Europe, the Congress ordered it to take care of its foreign currency needs through RFC Paris—and the Treasury itself in 1980 ordered the Air Force to acquire the foreign currency it needs for the NATO AWACS planes through the State Department. Maybe RFC Paris could handle some of the substantive questions, too: computers may be stupid, as the people who work with them always say, but at least they're quicker than committees.

9

ORGANIZING A COUNTRY

I was deputy executive secretary in the late 1960s, and I constructed a theory that there was no necessary connection between the Seventh Floor and the rest of the Department. The demands on the Secretary and his immediate entourage from the President, the press and the Congress are so severe. The Seventh Floor *will* use the Department if it feels the need to do so, but it doesn't have to. It responds to its own imperatives. I was reading Rusk's telephone calls with the President and McNamara. When you get down to the guts of White House thinking and Hill thinking, all the veils removed, it's very different from the way the State Department and the rest of the world think about foreign policy.

—Francis J. Meehan (later U.S. ambassador to Poland)

Once Kennedy, exasperated over the difficulty of getting action out of State, said, "What's wrong with that goddamned Department of yours, Chip?" Bohlen answered candidly, "You are."

—Arthur Schlesinger

We do not want to tie ourselves as we have done in the past to the United States, because she is unreliable and does not know her own mind and her statesmen do not know the mind of their own country. Nothing that is said by the President or any of their statesmen can ever be accepted at more than its face value, as we all know.

—Admiral Sir Ernie Chatfield, First Lord of the Admiralty (1934)

1

Relations between Presidents and their Secretaries of State have run a wide gamut. There have been Secretaries who believed that they rather than the incumbent should have been in the White House—Seward with Lincoln, Blaine with Harrison, Bryan with Wilson, Hughes with Harding, Byrnes with Truman, Haig with Reagan. And there have been Presidents who considered themselves perfectly capable of conducting foreign policy themselves, and wanted obsequious order-takers as Secretary of State— Cleveland with Bayard, Wilson with Lansing, Franklin Roosevelt with Hull and then Stettinius, Kennedy with Rusk (though both would have denied it), Nixon with Rogers, Carter with Vance. There have been cases of strong Presidents and strong Secretaries who got on famously—Jefferson with Madison, Theodore Roosevelt with Hay and Root, Harry Truman with Marshall and Acheson, Eisenhower with Dulles. In other instances, strong Presidents increasingly quarreled with strong Secretaries, leaving legacies of bitterness: Adams with Pickering, Taft with Knox, Hoover with Stimson.

Before 1968, Presidents usually spent considerable time with their Secretaries of State—Dean Rusk estimated that he saw Kennedy more than two thousand times in the thousand days. Recently, and unfortunately, both President and Secretary have become too busy, and too tightly cosseted by their staffs. But the Secretary still sends the President a brief memo every evening to bring him up to date, a practice that was begun by Acheson and maintained by all his successors.

Legally and indeed politically, the situation is quite clear. "Everyone in government," Dean Rusk said, "should have on his wall, framed, Section 1 of Article 2 of the Constitution: 'The executive power shall be vested in a President of the United States.' Nobody elected the bureaucrat. George Marshall put this in the extreme once. Harry Truman had pulled the rug out from under him pretty badly, and some friends said he should resign. He said, 'No. You can't take a post of this kind and resign because the President of the United States makes a decision he is constitutionally empowered to make. You can resign at any other time for any other reason— but not at that time for that reason.'" Cyrus Vance, obviously, did not agree that a Secretary should never resign on a matter of principle; Alexander Haig never understood that even the vicar of foreign policy must kiss at least the bishop's ring.

Since 1947, the instrument through which presidential control is imposed has been the National Security Council, which prepares for the President the "decision memoranda" that are thereafter binding on all agencies of the federal government. As a statutory matter, the members of the NSC are the President, the Vice-President, and the Secretaries of State and Defense, but each President can and does co-opt people—the Joint Chiefs of Staff and the Director of Central Intelligence are always "observers," and individual cabinet members and subcabinet officers will be summoned when the matters involved are especially within their competence. Lyndon Johnson reported that in his time attendance at NSC meetings ranged from twelve to thirty. Within this system there has been room for some sort of "crisis management" group, variously named according to taste.

At no time has the National Security Council arrived at "decisions" by taking votes: what is under discussion is always what Alexander Haig quickly learned to call "the President's policies," and decision is a presidential prerogative. "I can recall few situations under either Presidents Kennedy or Johnson," George Ball wrote from his experience as Under Secretary of State, "where the President had not already made his decision before calling a meeting of the Council. Thus the meeting had only two objectives: to inform the other members of what the President had already decided so they would not deviate from the line, and to give them at least the illusion of participation. This," Ball added, "is as it should be. Foreign policy matters cannot be intelligently decided in a large general meeting."

In the beginning, as noted, NSC was dominated by the State Department, partly because the best papers that came to it were from State's Policy Planning Staff (and NSC did not have a large enough staff to generate its own papers: "You saw nothing," said Harold Saunders, who joined the NSC staff as a Near East expert in 1961, "that wasn't summarized first by State, CIA or Defense")—and mostly because Marshall, Acheson and Dulles were very strongly influential with Truman and Eisenhower.

There was from early on a Special Assistant to the President for National Security Affairs (later National Security Adviser), and the post was held by distinguished people—Averell Harriman for Truman, Gordon Gray and Robert Cutler for Eisenhower. General Vernon Walters tells of Harriman arranging a general's star for the man he wanted to have as his deputy when he was appointed to this post. But even for Harriman—this is why he wanted his general—the task was mostly one of coordinating the departments. By the later years of the Eisenhower administration, the numerous "coordinating committees" of the NSC were filling the time of the National Security Adviser and his assistants with multiple meetings that had to be scheduled, prepared for and tracked. That the post was not considered intrinsically important is interestingly demonstrated by Dean

Acheson's bitter comments in 1960 on various proposals to "Parkin-sonize," as Acheson put it, the operations of the executive branch in the field of foreign affairs. "The National Security Council," Acheson wrote, "already has a staff of its own. This staff must have some one to report to; but must not bother the President, whom it was supposed to help, since he cannot give the time. . . ."

Eisenhower's competence as President was not in 1960 the object of the admiration that came his way twenty years later. Senator Henry Jackson's Subcommittee on National Policy Machinery noted in Eisenhower's last year that the proliferating committees of his NSC had become "a highly formalized and complex 'policy paper production system' that 'is not a cre-ative instrument for developing and bringing forward imaginative and sharply defined choices, particularly in uncharted areas of policy.' " Ken-nedy on arrival, looking for creative instruments and imaginative and sharply defined choices, junked the Eisenhower committee structure and looked for a single aggressive National Security Adviser, who would be a member of the NSC (indeed, he would call the meetings) and would take responsibility for supervising the coordination of the departments.

The post went to the political scientist McGeorge Bundy, nominally a Republican, dean of the faculty of Arts and Sciences at Harvard. Tough-minded, contemptuous of fools (a large category), personally elegant and amusing, Bundy was ideally suited by temperament, training and capacity to the task of putting together for this President the views of the various departments and laying out for him the plausible options that had been suggested. The son of a diplomat, Bundy understood and sympathized in-tellectually with Franklin Roosevelt's insistence that a presidential assis-tant should have "a passion for anonymity." He had written one book, as amanuensis for Henry Stimson. He gave no press conferences, wrote no magazine articles, and regarded any advice he might give as entirely con-fidential. And his opposite number at State was not Dean Rusk but Ben Read, a Philadelphia lawyer who had become head of Rusk's Executive Secretariat—and "who knew as much about what I did, said and thought," Rusk recalled gratefully, "as I did myself."

What complicated Bundy's life (and Rusk's) was that Kennedy really did want to handle a lot of things himself. Charles Yost reports that he "had a habit of phoning bureau chiefs or their subordinates to spur them into action. During the Laotian crisis . . . it was said that the desk officer for Laos was the President of the United States." The assistant secretaries in the State Department had been Kennedy's choices, not Rusk's (some had been appointed before Rusk was chosen), and Kennedy wanted to consult them. Not only Under Secretaries Chester Bowles and George Ball, but Assistant Secretaries Averell Harriman, Thomas C. Mann and (this was hard on Kennedy) G. Mennen (Soapy) Williams had access to the White House. When Richard Goodwin left the White House staff to become Deputy Assistant Secretary for Latin America, he retained the President's ear. When Walter Rostow, Bundy's deputy, was assigned over to State to head the Policy Planning Staff, Kennedy asked him to keep in touch, and meant it. Under these circumstances, there was no purpose to a large staff for the National Security Adviser, and Bundy made do with thirteen people.

Bundy's successor Rostow was a considerably more public figure. He had come to government from a professorship at MIT, where he had written an interesting slim volume on the stages of economic growth, asserting a law of economic development that dictated a "take-off" once a previously primitive economy acquired its modern infrastructure. Moving to State as Director of the Policy Planning Staff for Rusk, Rostow had written a truly dreadful book, *The View from the Seventh Floor,* offering fulsome support for Kennedy's and Johnson's Southeast Asia policies: "In Vietnam, we are committed to maintain the political independence of South Vietnam in the face of the guerrilla war mounted, in its present phase, from Hanoi since 1958. . . . It is too soon to say whether or not it will be necessary for us to signal that we are prepared to apply more force in order to achieve our objective—and to mean it." Bundy having departed to head the Ford Foundation, Johnson wanted someone to get up front on the Vietnam issue and draw some of the lightning away from himself, and Rostow was only too willing to oblige.

Rostow retained the Bundy system, which rested, he recalls, on the principle that "nobody had anyone working for him. Every time you have somebody working for you, it takes something out of your time, out of your life. Johnson found," Rostow continues, "that I could keep him informed. He would take great pride in the fact that McNamara or Rusk would call and say they had a problem—and he'd already know about it, because his chain of command was shorter."

Bundy had already taken steps to improve the flow of information into the White House, and Rostow moved further, with special emphasis on the intelligence reports. "The President was getting this thin, constipated flow from the bureaucracy, and he was a voracious reader. And it was all gobbledygook. I called the Defense Department, said, 'Do you have a Rhodes Scholar over there to write these things?'" Much more cable traffic from both State and Defense was fed into the White House basement. "You have to get the full flow," Rostow says. "Unless you have the sense of the quality of the data, you never know."

Richard Betts illustrates from a different perspective the problem Bundy and Rostow faced: "In September 1963 President Kennedy asked for reports on progress in the war from Saigon. Ambassador Lodge's assessment was grim, but General Harkins's was optimistic. Harkins's report, however, sounded strange. It was phrased in a way that made it seem as if it was based on the debate in Washington more than on the situation in the field. Suspicious White House aides noticed a reference in the report to a cable from Taylor. They sent to the Pentagon for it and found that the cable had explained to Harkins the divisions in the government at home and coached him on which questions to address and how to answer them. The civilian aides decided to have cable machines installed in the White House in order to prevent this sort of maneuver. The military cheerfully complied, fourteen machines were installed, and reams of routine cables churned out every day; the civilians were hopelessly overwhelmed by sheer volume. Unable to monitor the flow, they gave up and had the machines taken out."

Like his voraciously reading bosses, however, Rostow relied most heavily on the handful of people he trusted. "When you live with a staff," he says, "you can go through the paper flip-flip-flip. I could go down to the sit [situation] room, and get all my guys around one table. And when there's really a problem, the whole team that really effects the policy can be gathered together at the Tuesday lunch. Really, the organization is an inverted pyramid—in each department there's one guy on whom all the others depend."

It was Henry Kissinger, of course, who seized the reins into the White House—where he was given a splendid office at the end of the West Wing, fourteen-foot ceilings—and who made the post of National Security Adviser continuously newsworthy. He was not new to the game. In the first six months of the Kennedy administration, he had spent two days a week at Kennedy's request "consulting" with Bundy—and had learned, he later said, that "no adviser is ever listened to just because he insists on being heard." Arthur Schlesinger remembered him, however, as joining Abram Chayes and himself in arguing Kennedy out of a forceful response to the Russian interference with road traffic to Berlin in 1961.

Battening on Richard Nixon's fears of the bureaucracy, he developed a control bureau—staffed very largely by FSOs assigned to him—that could match the substantive organization of the State Department, almost post for post. "There is a mistake often made in Washington," said John Freeman, British ambassador early in the Nixon days, "that because NSC does important work it supersedes State. That's not so. Of course, if you're dealing with things that concern the President, you might see Henry." Kissinger's personal liaison at State was Under Secretary Elliot Richardson, who chaired various Senior Interagency Groups under the NSC aegis. "I consider Elliot Richardson in every important respect as good a man as myself," Kissinger told an interviewer* while he was National Security Adviser. "And I don't say that with false humility."

From 13 people, the Adviser's staff rose to 165, virtually none of whom ever saw the President: Kissinger kept that privilege and pleasure for himself (which was also, of course, as Nixon wanted it). Unlike his predecessors, at NSA, Kissinger traveled, seeking to establish personal relations with foreign leaders. Often he would refuse to permit the U.S. ambassador on the scene to accompany him to these meetings, destroying the usefulness of the man on the spot. He personally undertook "back-channel" diplomacy to seek an end to the Vietnam War that would not be humiliating to the United States, an opening to the People's Republic of China, an arms limitation agreement with the Soviet Union. As these ventures bore fruit (some of it poisoned, but you had to eat it to learn that), credit flowed naturally to the Adviser—and the State Department could not even answer questions from foreign embassies about what the United States was doing, because nobody at the State Department knew. Kissinger was so intensely suspicious of leaks from his staff that he had their home telephones tapped. He himself had good relations with the press, he liked to say, "because I always tell them the truth."

When Secretary of State William Rogers returned to private law practice, having dutifully served the duration of President Nixon's first term, Kissinger coupled the two roles of National Security Adviser and Secretary of State. Then President Gerald Ford remembered Section 1 of Article 2 of the Constitution, and installed General Brent Scowcroft in the west wing of the White House to be his National Security Adviser. Scowcroft moved the office back toward its Bundy days—but by now the job had been institutionalized. The staff remained at the size Kissinger had demanded—and Scowcroft's opposite number was Henry Kissinger, not Executive Secretary Lawrence Eagleburger.

Zbigniew Brzezinski, Carter's choice for National Security Adviser, clearly felt himself the equal of Cyrus Vance in the process of government. Though he told Bundy (and promised Carter) that he would cut back on the National Security Council bureaucracy, he made the reality different from the numbers, counting as members of their original departments the stream of people from State, Treasury, Defense, Energy, etc. who filled and overflowed the job slots. And Brzezinski, waving bye-bye to the PLO or threatening the Soviet Afghans with his own hand-held machine gun, became to say the least a public spokesperson for his President. Looking back some months later, he said that the real problem in Carter's White House was the President's failure to say explicitly that Brzezinski

* (me)

245

was boss: "There was always practical bifurcation, ambiguity intensified by the emphasis placed publicly on the primacy of the Secretary of State."

"The function of the National Security Adviser," said Cyrus Vance, still chewing on the bitter root more than a year after his resignation as Secretary of State, "must be as the one individual who pulls all the documents together. Makes sure they are properly before the NSC as a deliberative body. Then makes sure the President's decision is properly registered, communicated and executed. Mac Bundy handled the job very well; where it really got out of hand was with Henry. The National Security Adviser cannot be a spokesman without creating confusion in the public, the Congress, our friends and our adversaries.

"It's appropriate," Vance continued, looking at notes and expounding on bureaucratic organization, a favorite subject, "that the chair at NSC meetings should rotate according to the subject matter of the meeting, with the vast bulk of the material to be handled by State. The National Security Adviser is primarily a staff person and ought not to chair meetings. The chairman should make up the agenda. The minutes of every meeting should be distributed to the Secretaries involved *before* they go to the President. This was not done in the Carter administration because he was afraid of leaks. . . ."

As a practical matter, however, a strong National Security Adviser is going to make a lot of policy whether the Secretary of State likes it or not. He works inside the White House, not a mile away. (A case can be made for the argument that what really cut State down was Marshall's decision to move the Department out of what is now the Executive Office Building adjacent to the White House and over to a remote corner of the Washington swamps.) The Adviser sees the President more often, and sees the other people who see the President much more often, than the Secretary of State possibly can. Preparing the option papers, he can subtly or not so subtly write them to nudge the President toward the answers he wants. Moreover, he can with some reason claim that he is expressing the national interest in a way that a cabinet Secretary, tied down to loyalties within his own department, simply cannot rival.

Conceivably, this tendency to glorify the National Security Adviser at the expense of the Secretary of State was arrested by the Reagan administration. Like Kennedy, Reagan invited assistant secretaries of State to the Oval Office. By appointing Richard Allen as Adviser, he took a post that had become a platform for influence seekers and turned it over to an influence peddler. *That* the State Department could handle, experienced as it was with years of congressional intervention to get favors done for constituents. William Clark, Jr., Allen's replacement, was a man without background in foreign affairs or known views, who presumably could influence the President only as a conduit. (This presumption turned out to be false: it was Clark who, by saying solemnly, "Your credibility is at stake," convinced Reagan to adopt the folly of the pipeline sanctions.)

Still, the large and supposedly expert staff remains, with its hands on the process by which decision memos pass to the President. Egged on by the press, moreover, the Department and the staff of the National Security Adviser maintain a competitive—even adversary—relationship. A peculiarly jejune piece in *The Wall Street Journal* in late 1981 provides a reductio ad absurdum: "The nature of the struggle [between State and the NSC] is the same as that which should and did exist between a corporation's marketing and sales departments." Beneath all lies the cussed *simultaneity* of what confronts the government. "When you look at things retrospectively," says Abram Chayes from his resting place at Harvard, "you think of a Vietnam problem, a Berlin problem, a Cuban problem, step by step. But when you're there, all these things are on your desk at the same time." A President really cannot decide for himself what he must pay attention to today.

What has really gone wrong here is something rather different. By contrast to Marshall's Executive Secretariat, which became less the servant of the Secretary than the tool of the bureaus (maintaining "bureaucratic fairness"), the National Security Adviser system became too exclusively a service agency for the President. "That office," Kingman Brewster observed shrewdly from London, "has no habit of or instruments for deciding whom we should inform." Under Carter, as Vance pointed out, the minutes of NSC meetings were not distributed even to the Secretaries who had participated. Under Reagan, the depth of the conflict between Weinberger and Haig propelled the White House into procedures to compel rather than achieve assent to presidential decisions. And then the ascension of Clark, whose mind-set barred him from the essential understanding that in international relations there are independent others whose view of American policy will determine its efficacy, made the State Department's information-gathering and persuasion capacities all but irrelevant.

Meanwhile, other offices have been put into the White House to fulfill functions once delegated to the State Department. The Trade Representative holds meetings not only with Ministers of Trade abroad, but with Prime Ministers, and the planning of the silly annual "summit" meetings of the heads of government of the United States, Britain, France, Germany, Italy, Canada and Japan has been concentrated at the White House. The worst problem of all, however, from the State Department's point of view, has been the expansion of the role of the Office of Management and Budget.

This institution is a strange excrescence of American government. Prior to 1921, there was no unified budget of the U.S. Government (cynics may argue that in effect there still isn't, given the extent of off-budget activities, but somebody's always being nasty). Control of the purse strings was vested operationally as well as constitutionally in the Congress, with the proviso that all money bills had to originate in the more popular House of Representatives. The custom of separate "authorizations" and "appropriations" for the departments grew out of a system where the ultimate budget-making steps were taken in an "appropriations committee" rather than by people concerned with substantive questions.

Though able people held the title of Director of what was then the Bureau of the Budget—not least, James Webb, who became Acheson's Under Secretary of State and later the administrator who shaped the space program—the job was not in fact very high on the government's totem pole until the Lyndon Johnson days, when Charles Schultze became part of the "quadriad"—the Treasury Secretary, the Chairman of the Federal Reserve, the Chairman of the Council of Economic Advisers, and the Director of the Bureau of the Budget—who hammered out the government's basic economic program for the President. Robert McNamara had sold the President on the wonders of PPBS—computer-based Program-Planning-Budgeting Systems that would somehow take the politics out of the budget process. Even then, while he might question individual programs, the Director of the Bureau essentially worked to balance the demands of competing departments and agencies, each of which did its own PPBS, leaving them to fight before the congressional committees for money on specific lines.

Insensibly, as the staff of Nixon's reorganized OMB grew and grew, the new Office began to assert authority over the specific requests of each department or agency. And under Carter a fad for "zero-based budgeting" poked OMB's nose into every tent. The budget process spread out abominably in time—the State Department's work toward the fiscal 1984 budget, not a penny of which could be spent before October 1983, had to begin in April 1982. Responding to demands from OMB, the State Department would list in order of priority the consulates it wished to have, the aid programs it wished to fund. And then OMB, staffed by a cast of hundreds (mostly very young recent MBAs) would reorder the priorities, making its own decisions about which consulates could be dropped and which aid programs abandoned. Admittedly, the departments (including State) did a lot of game-playing when they submitted their rank orders, leaving programs with politically potent constituencies toward the bottom of the list as a threat to budget-cutters. But however bad the bureaucrats' judgment might be, there was no case for the proposition that the judgment of a bunch of twenty-eight-year-old Budget Office employees was going to be better.

In the Gerald Ford days, Kissinger shielded the Department from the worst of this interference, but OMB became more assertive under Carter—and fighting for turf was something Vance did very reluctantly, and badly. By the end of the Carter administration, it had become established not only that OMB had a line veto over State Department requests, but that the Secretary himself would take the appeal before the Director of the Office, which meant there was nobody left to go over the head of the Director to the President. There might be back-channel ways to get the congressional committees to restore funds to programs OMB had cut, even while the totals were kept in line by cutting other programs OMB had let lie—but it was cumbersome (not to say illegal) for the State Department's lobbyists to fight for a budget different from that the President submitted.

No doubt Lewis Dexter exaggerated when he said that the federal budget was "the work plan of the nation"—but the State Department budget is certainly the work plan of the nation's foreign policy. It was bad enough when item after item had to pass the hostile scrutiny of Congressman John J. Rooney of Staten Island, New York, for years the chairman of the appropriations subcommittee that passed on the State Department and foreign aid budgets—but there, at least, one could fight in public (more or less). Now one can jump and scream and leak and get James Reston to write a column in the New York *Times* about gross cuts in total budgets, or the elimination of whole categories of grants. But when OMB alters the priorities laid out by the Department in petty ways —budgeting more money for the "hardening" of some consulates by closing others entirely, reducing pledged contributions to the development banks, commanding smaller staffs at this embassy but not that one—the decisions are made in secret, by fiat. The erosion of confidence that results from this steady drip of defeat can have devastating effects.

2

The nodes of contact between the State Department and the President are more various than one might think. Dean Rusk remembered as almost routine an explanation from an Assistant Secretary that something was being done because "the White House wants it." He would, he said, have none of that: "My policy was that when somebody called from the White House my man was to say, 'Who in the White House?' Unless he's quoting the President verbatim, he can't tell the State Department what to do. I represent the President. You know, Acheson was once asked what he considered the first requirement for a Secretary of State. He said, 'A killer instinct.' What he meant was, Never let anybody get between you and the President." Acheson okayed the insertion of Averell Harriman as special assistant because he knew that Harriman, for all his immense vanity, would be a stickler for proper form. But it is not in fact possible for State Department people to brush off requests for information or services from people at NSC or OMB, who are reading the cables that flow through the Executive Secretariat and receiving memos from other departments that State may not have seen.

And people at the White House are also, unfortunately, reading something else: the press. Perhaps the most important channel of communication between the President and his State Department is the one that runs somewhat tortuously through the media. Sometimes the message is encouraging, when the President or the Secretary states the agreed-upon policy in a way that the other side considers particularly apt or forceful, but more often it is poisonous. Disagreements within the government are in fact news, as are advance rumblings of changes in policy that are not yet decided upon or are not to be announced until allies or enemies have felt their weight. It is the business of the press to dig up such material. Moreover, because news is news, people may be asked to react to developments somewhere in the world before the government has any policy, and "No comment" is often not a plausible answer.

Eisenhower was a master of the answer that was apparently responsive to a question but quite impenetrable when studied. The feelings of superiority to Eisenhower that suffused the press and the academic-intellectual complex during his administration† were such that people do not seem to have considered the possibility that Eisenhower's syntax might be not the stumblings of the overmatched blunt soldier from Abilene, Kansas, but the artifice of a born politician. Fred Greenstein has noted that Eisenhower stood tenth in his class at West Point in English composition. In his memoirs Eisenhower makes reference to the planning for one conference where a question was sure to arise about what the United States might do if the Communist Chinese attacked one of the larger islands in the Formosa Strait. Press Secretary James Hagerty thought Eisenhower and Dulles and lots of other people had already talked too much on that subject, and suggested that the President simply refuse to answer. "Don't worry, Jim," Eisenhower said. "If that question comes up, I'll just confuse them." Others are not so sure they can swing that, especially under steady

† In his farewell address, Eisenhower coupled this "academic-intellectual" complex with the military-industrial complex as something of which the public should beware; it is the last and best revenge of the intellectuals that only half his warning survives in our political consciousness.

pressure from follow-up questions, which a President can prevent but lesser figures cannot. When he moved from Director of the Bureau of Intelligence and Research to Assistant Secretary for American Republic Affairs, William Bowdler commented that the pressures on him would be much greater in the new job. "A situation comes up in a foreign country," he said with evident concern. "What do we say to the press about it?"

Officially, what is said to the press by the State Department comes from the "Spokesman," who holds a daily conference at noon in a crowded windowless room on the second floor, standing on a podium behind a lectern before what must be—thanks to the television networks—one of the best-known Mercator-projection maps of the world. Up to eighty reporters attend these briefings, most of them seated at curving tables that create the impression of a small auditorium. On a platform along the rear wall, eight to a dozen television cameras keep the Spokesman in focus as he speaks. Their lights are bright, obtrusive and hot. Behind the podium, stage left, four to six members of the Spokesman's staff sit a little uncomfortably on folding chairs, the women smoothing their skirts over their knees, ready to be consulted in moments of need, keeping records of the "TQs," the "taken questions," which someone will answer by telephone later in the day.

These daily occasions are never impromptu, and never routine. The Spokesman spends most of his morning—all of the last hour of the morning—rehearsing for his appearance. He normally sits in on the Secretary's first meeting each morning so he knows what is being said to and by the assistant secretaries and bureau directors, but basically he takes his "guidance"—his answers to questions—from the bureaus. Each of the geographical bureaus has a press representative of its own, who is the real source of information for the reporters as well as, on most matters, for the Spokesman. "A George Sherman," said one of the deputy spokespeople, referring to the press representative for the Near East Bureau, "can do more to convey an American sense of where we are and what we hope to do and how we're going to get there than anyone in the Spokesman's office. They're specialists, we're generalists. But that's on background. The press in conference is not looking for information but for on-the-record quotes. They get their stories from sources."

Between eleven and twelve the bureau press representatives filter into the Spokesman's office with statements from their bosses, views on what questions are likely to be asked, and suggested answers to those questions. At one session early in the Reagan administration, Spokesman William Dyess prowled the large room with its government-issue mahogany desk and leather armchairs, a cigar firmly between his teeth, as an assistant maintained the large leather looseleaf book, organized by geographical bureau, in which the "press guidance" for this day would be kept. Someone from NE was speaking:

"On the Pakistan business, we'd like to have a review of the issue, following the statement of the Secretary at breakfast. I'll see to it that there's a question."

Dyess took the paper. "I want to read this." He nodded and handed it to the assistant for insertion in the book. "Do you have any reason to expect that they're going to increase their purchases?" he said in the half-reportorial, half-scornful manner of a newsman at a press conference. "Well, obviously," he replied to himself, raising the level of scorn, "if we didn't have reason to expect it we wouldn't have said it."

Dyess was a career FSO—specialty, the Soviet Union—a large, somewhat portentous Southerner with a round face and watery gray eyes, a graduate of the University of Alabama with newspaper experience as a boy and intelligence experience for the Army (under an assumed name) before joining the Foreign Service in 1958. He had moved into the Bureau of Public Affairs on his own motion in the Kissinger days, when Kissinger signaled his desire to improve the status of the domestic propaganda operation by making the much-admired Carol Laise his Spokesman and cleaning away the burnt-out cases that had previously populated the Bureau. When Vance coupled the jobs of Spokesman and Assistant Secretary for Public Affairs in the person of Hodding Carter, Dyess was retained as Carter's deputy to run the PA section, and he moved up for a difficult year —en route to an ambassador's post in the Netherlands—when Carter departed. A polished bureaucrat very conscious of the career implications of every action, he was never really happy as Spokesman, by definition a position that can get its occupant into hot water if he misplaces a comma— especially under Haig, "who would rather not," as a member of the inner circle put it, "have a whole lot of discussion of what United States policy should be and what the Secretary's options are."

The phone rang and Dyess picked it up. "Yes," he said, "we have the White House on board. The *Post* [which had run a story that morning about a supposed fight between the White House and State] is wrong. The White House will say he's wrong. Brady has agreed to say he's wrong."

One of the assistants grinned at Dyess. "You're very negative today."

"It's because I've been dealing with journalists."

Dyess ran over some canned Questions and Answers on Middle East problems, and looked around the room, where people were perched on chair arms and tables. "Who's missing?" he said.

"ARA."

"As usual. Warsaw Pact maneuvers," he muttered. "Are we cleared on this?"

The document was passed to the visitor. It had been drafted by EUR/SOV, initialed by RL, EE and I&R. Dyess was now looking at a statement from the African Bureau, criticizing the visit by some South African military in mufti. "I can't have just, 'He approves it,'" Dyess said disgustedly. "Does the Secretary approve it? I haven't heard the Secretary say this—and it takes a new tack from what I've been saying. I've been saying the policy is under review. Oh, shit. Where's Crocker? [Assistant Secretary for Africa]" He reached for the phone. "Is Crocker there? Bill Dyess. I've got to talk with him. . . . Hi. . . ." And Crocker okayed the condemnation of the visit.

Dyess relit his cigar and looked at a piece of Associated Press flimsy his secretary had just brought him. He said to an assistant, "I've just learned that [California Senator] Hayakawa says we've sold thirty-six F-16s to South Korea."

The assistant said, "That was on our guidance list."

"I'll say on the record that we asked for guidance and didn't get it," Dyess muttered.

NE returned. "Are you aware—I'm sure you're aware—" the young man said, "that we have recommended to Commerce the issuance of the licenses on the sale of Boeings to Iraq?"

Dyess picked up the phone again and inquired. He listened and exploded. "I can't take details from the press on this. Hell, that's the press down there asking me questions."

The press representative from East Asia had gone into the outer office to call his people. He returned to say that he couldn't confirm the Hayakawa statement, the man on that desk wasn't there. One of Dyess' assistants shook his head and said, "You mean Senator Hayakawa knows about it and the State Department does not. . . ."

In fact, at the press conference the reporters hit heavily on Pakistan and El Salvador; there was no question about the F-16s or the South African visit. The inquiries on Poland and Warsaw Pact maneuvers exceeded Dyess' guidance, and he took questions for later answer, as he did also on specific questions relating to Nicaragua and to the Law of the Sea Conference. He referred several times to David Passage, a very young and very smart FSO with a background in (of all things) electrical engineering, whom Hodding Carter had pulled into the Spokesman's office from a job as political counselor in Canberra. ("I was in Canberra because I'd worked a year and a half for Kissinger in the Secretariat, and needed R&R.") Passage, who had a precise manner and a Bob Newhart look, would crisply respond with names and dates from what seemed a bottomless memory of U.S. policy statements over the previous half-dozen years, and Dyess would nod with satisfaction.

When the half-hour press conference was over and the TV cameras dismantled, a dozen or so reporters clustered around the podium asking Dyess questions "on background" (not for attribution). Several of them were foreign reporters, passing on parochial queries from their home papers. Dyess relaxed slowly, admitted he didn't know, suggested other people who might be called, and shook himself free to go to his downstairs office in the second-floor press section for a second-guessing session with his staff and a discussion of how to handle the TQs. Passage reported that one piece of minor misinformation (on a date) had been given out, and said he would call to give the correction to the reporter. It was generally agreed that nothing from that day's conference would show up on the evening news shows (always the riskiest place in terms of White House complaint), that the most difficult questions had not been asked, that—in brief—no harm had been done.

Relations between the State Department and the press are always darkly clouded by the potential for harm. Many of the world's disputes have been papered over by formulae—by agreements on wording rather than on substance—and any alteration in the form of presenting American policy can trigger headlines all over the world. Presidential assistant Edward Meese made a blunder of that sort early in the Reagan administration, when he casually referred to Israeli settlements without explicitly labeling them as "illegal settlements." When the Spokesman on the record changes the form of words, he starts speculation going not only in the press but in Foreign Ministries all over the world. Even background comments by lesser folk can raise hell. "If the *Times* ran a piece about American policy toward Costa Rica," a State Department press officer once hypothesized, "and it was all cockeyed and came from a postal clerk, it would still take at least an assistant secretary to convince the Costa Ricans it wasn't true."

But signals often *are* given, by the United States as well as by the Soviet Union, in just such Delphic ways. This provides apparent legitimacy for the sort of aggressive snooping that turns telescopes on molehills to see if they can be presented as mountains. Ambassador William Sullivan noted with distaste that when the photographers were sent in for the standard "photo opportunity" as President Carter wished him bon voyage to Tehran in 1977, "each photographer also carried a tape recorder; some of them even had assistants with microphones on long booms, presumably so that they could pick up any indiscretions that might occur in the small talk between the president and the other officials being photographed." I am not the one to be critical of such procedures, having gone on record once with the comment (to an irritated group of Ford Foundation-sponsored young and solemn education editors) that "all reporting is police-court reporting." But the saving grace of the beat system is supposed to be that the man on the scene knows enough of the background to understand which anomalies are significant and which are accidental. And the danger is that at the State Department the press corps, undernourished and offended by what they are fed, can present as significant whatever they dig up that is unexpected or contrary to the party line, or simply anomalous.

Toward the end of his brief tenure as Secretary of State, Edmund Muskie found some kind words for the press corps ("the people permanently assigned to the State Department are foreign policy experts in their own right"), and even for the coverage ("the press tends to reflect what's important to the country"). The question is not so simple as that, because expertise can be placed at the service of a single-minded drive for inches in the paper or seconds on the air—and because in matters like foreign policy, which are remote from the concerns of the citizenry, the press determines at least as much as it reflects what is important to the country. "It may not be successful much of the time in telling people what to think," writes Bernard Cohen, "but it is stunningly successful in telling its readers what to think *about*." In recent years the problem has grown more severe: "The Freedom of Information Act and the growth of the Hill staffs," Ben Read fretted, "make the need to avoid mistakes much worse."

The possibilities of disaster are increased when the State Department press officers seek to enlighten the reporters on what's going on in foreign countries. "We should not be saying what the facts are," an FSO observes. "It gets in the way of the conduct of diplomacy. If Reuters calls and asks, 'What's happening in Bolivia?' the answer should be, 'Go find out.'"

Then there is also, of course, the deliberate use of the press corps as a channel of communications within the government. "The thing most appalling to me in my new experience," said James Buckley after a few months as Under Secretary for Everything Else, "is the leak. It takes an incredible amount of time in second-guessing." The one absolutely sure-fire way for a bureaucrat or a congressional staffer to get a fact or an opinion to the attention of his boss is to plant it in the newspapers. If the story appears in the Washington *Post* or the New York *Times*, there is a chance that the boss will not only note it personally but find himself in a position where he has to clear up the matter to the satisfaction of *his* boss, yea up unto the seats of the mighty on either end of Pennsylvania Avenue. There is a symbiosis between the bureaucrat's or staffer's desire to make policy and the reporter's desire to make noise.

In point of fact, this problem is probably less severe at the State Department than elsewhere in the government. Despite the need to justify before the accountants the expense of all those foreign bureaus, the foreign affairs news hole is relatively small even in the best papers (though both the *Times* and the greatly improved Washington *Post* gallantly give their readers more foreign news than any readership survey says they want); and actual developments abroad are stiff competition for the State Department leak seeking a receptacle. Moreover, FSOs are less likely to go outside their own structure than others in government. Years of relative isolation in distant posts have reinforced the *esprit de corps* sought in their training and heightened their suspicion of outsiders. And, of course, most FSOs believe the international relations of the United States should be conducted entirely on the basis of professional judgment. For them, tailoring foreign policy to fit the preferences of public opinion is prostitution; seeking to influence policy by reaching out to the public would be pimping.

These attitudes are one of the reasons State's Bureau of Public Affairs ("the American desk") has historically been so weak. The line between explaining American policy and selling it is necessarily very fine, and the use of presumably nonpolitical bureaucrats for selling purposes is generally frowned upon by Congress. The Voice of America beams outward only; the U.S. Information Agency, which was part of the State Department when William Benton as Assistant Secretary began calling his bureau "public affairs," was prohibited by law from publishing for the American markets, running libraries or arranging lectures in the United States. Recommending more money for "more comprehensive public affairs programs" in 1975, the Murphy Commission was careful to add that the press and Congress should be relied upon to reduce "the risk of providing one-sided views."

By 1980, the State Department had an intensive and extensive propaganda service running inside the United States, concentrated on about six "issues" at a time. "We have four criteria for choosing what we cover," Dyess explained. "One, the issue has to be of substantial importance to the nation. Two, an issue where we must have public support or acquiescence to be successful. Three, an issue where we must get off our duffs or we won't get the public support or acquiescence. Four, an issue where we *have* a policy." In support of this "public information" effort, PA briefs people in the Department on the state of public opinion and sends FSOs to conferences around the country, seeking "outreach" to groups—ethnics, labor, women, etc. "It's made an impact on the bureaus," Dyess added, "which used to regard us as a kind of travel service."

No fewer than five thousand speaking engagements were filled by State Department employees under PA aegis in 1980, up from around five hundred in 1975. "And on any speaking engagement," Dyess said, "we put people into six or eight events. They do editorial backgrounders for the local papers and university seminars as well as the speech to the Rotary Club, and they appear on the local talk shows. We're highly computerized on this." One is not, however, dealing with the canned exposition of a party line. PA rules call for no more than fifteen minutes of a one-hour appearance to be taken by a prepared address, with the rest to be in the form of question-and-answer. (The prepared opening, however, is supposed to be cleared with the bureau that employs the speaker.) And it should be noted that Congress monitors this activity very closely: during the Carter administration, the General Accounting Office made no fewer than six investigations of the Bureau of Public Affairs—twice on the presentation of the SALT negotiations, once on the efforts to sell the Panama Canal Treaty, once on the domestic use of State Department publications, once on the Bureau's travel expenditures, and once on the nature of its public opinion analysis.

In the years right after World War II, the State Department did its own public opinion polling in the United States, using confidential funds (appropriated for intelligence services) to pay the freight. Congress raised hell about this, and the diplomats got out of the domestic polling business. (The U.S. Information Agency—now called International Communications Agency—was permitted to continue public opinion polling abroad.) The Murphy Commission rather regretted this decision, and "considered carefully whether to recommend that the government resume polling, possibly under the joint auspices of the executive and legislative branches, with the results to be made public. We have concluded," the Commission noted rather sadly, "that such polling is properly a private sector activity. . . ."

Seeking to influence public opinion, of course, one must have some notion what it *is*, and what factors seem to have produced current attitudes. PA produces a weekly summary of editorials published in 150 newspapers around the country, and a monthly report on public opinion on some chosen issues, summarized from a number of services. The Department does have a budget to purchase reports from the polling companies, which means operationally the opportunity to have them add to their questionnaires items of special interest to PA. Some polling organizations give their privately syndicated reports to State *pro bono*, most sell services to the State Department as they sell them to private corporations. One—Yankelovich—has refused to deal with the Department on the grounds that it leaks. Dyess estimated that 90 percent of the material the Department processed was "unpublished." In the Carter days, Democratic pollsters like Hart and Cadell got a good share of the business; since January 1981, more of the work has gone to polling organizations on the conservative side.

How one handles public opinion data is more important than the data themselves, and Dyess was particularly proud of the Bureau's success in upgrading its analytical capacity. The small staff was headed by Bernard Rothko, who had been editor of *Public Opinion Quarterly*, the leading academic publication in the field. His two-page reports, one topic at a time, circulated fairly widely in the building—"We're up from about two dozen copies in the mid-seventies to more than two hundred today," Dyess reported proudly, "all to people who have a need to know *and* have requested the service." Data from the polls also appear in the monthly cable from home to overseas posts, and PA sends out to the same market a separate survey of public opinion poll data, digesting the recent two-page single-issue memos.

The White House looks at PA's polling analysis mostly as grist for its own polling mills, but the really voracious consumer of the product is the Bureau of Congressional Relations ("H," for Hill). The use of such material with the Congress must be delicate, of course, because congressmen who feel pushed around by State Department polling data may resist voting appropriations for the acquisition of such data the next time around. It's a small corner, but you've got to maneuver in it.

3

The role of the Congress in the conduct of foreign relations has been a difficulty in American governance from the beginning. The Constitution gives Congress the power to regulate foreign commerce, and gives the President the power to appoint representatives to foreign powers and to negotiate treaties subject to the "advice and consent" of the Senate. George Washington took the prescription literally, and attended upon the Senate to seek their advice and consent to the instructions he had given to commissioners who were to negotiate a treaty with the Creek Nation. To Washington's fury, he was stuck in the presiding officer's chair (to Adams' fury, it was Adams' chair) while the Senate discussed whether it had enough information to give advice, and finally laid the matter over to the following Monday, when Washington came again. "Although in the end he achieved his purpose—" James Flexner writes, "—only minor changes were made in the treaty instructions—Washington had to sit hour after hour, listening to an inconsequential and boring debate. As he finally departed from the Senate chamber, he was overheard to say he would 'be damned if he ever went there again!'" Like so many other decisions by

Washington, this became a binding precedent, and no President since has subjected himself to this experience.

As early as 1794, the Senate requested the complete file of correspondence between an American minister abroad and the Department of State. Washington sent along an expurgated version, withholding "those particulars which, in my judgment, ought not to be communicated." Until the Nixon days, this was never challenged: Senate resolutions of inquiry into foreign relations traditionally requested only information the release of which would be "not incompatible with the public interest." Such phrases disappeared from congressional resolutions in reaction to the chain of bamboozlements perpetrated by Kissinger and Nixon, and fights over "executive privilege" in the withholding of information are now a regular part of the political scene; but it is doubtful that any of the powers asserted by Washington really have been lost.

The question of the role of the House of Representatives in the making of foreign policy also came to a head under Washington, when the pro-French House sought in effect to set aside the Jay treaty with Great Britain already ratified by the Senate. The implementation of the treaty would require appropriations, and the Constitution said that money bills were to originate in the popularly elected House. Two days after Washington had declared the treaty in effect, a motion was introduced in the House "requesting the President to submit . . . every document in the executive archives—Jay's instructions, all relevant correspondence, etc.—which might 'throw light' on the treaty and how it had been negotiated." Washington flatly refused, to the great benefit of his own policy.

"The leaders of the House's effort," Flexner writes, "had made a colossal tactical error. Although securing the executive papers would have increased the prestige of the House and probably have given an advantage in attacking the treaty, the documents were by no means necessary to the House's basic contention. The appropriation could be denied by refusing rather than passing a bill. . . . If the President adhered to his so far invariable rule of not moving out of his province to comment on legislative action in which the executive was not involved, his convictions need never have been expressed. But now his prestige had been brought to bear against the claims of the House. How could he so grievously have let the Republican leaders down? Why, oh why, had they stirred the old man up with a sharp stick?"

In the end, Washington got his appropriation, and general agreement that once a treaty had been accepted by the Senate, the House was constitutionally obliged to provide the implementing legislation—as it did, very reluctantly, to validate the Panama Canal Treaty for Carter. On the refusal of papers, however, the precedent was to be broken, dramatically, by

259

John Adams, who was called upon by the House to submit all the papers relating to the mission undertaken by Elbridge Gerry, John Marshall and Charles C. Pinckney to negotiate an end to French raids on American shipping and in general patch up Franco-American relations, which had deteriorated into what is called a "quasi-war." In fact, the mission had failed, broken by the hostility of the revolutionary Directory to the Jay treaty and the personal hostility of Foreign Minister Talleyrand (who had been denied an audience with Washington when he had come to the United States a few years before). Through intermediaries, Talleyrand had demanded a loan to France and a bribe to himself before he would even consent to see the American commissioners. (It was on hearing this demand that Pinckney was supposed to have said, "Millions for defense but not one cent for tribute!") After making a show of resistance, Adams complied with the request from the House, concealing the names of Talleyrand's intermediaries under the initials W, X, Y and Z.

"The House," writes Alexander De Conde, "immediately locked and guarded its doors, went into secret session, and spent three days examining the correspondence. As the tale unfolded, Republican members were astounded. They recognized that a wider disclosure would probably arouse the public to such frenzy as to precipitate the very war they sought to avoid. Knowing now that the President had not exaggerated the crisis, they stilled the clamor of their own followers for publication. But . . . after considerable argument, the House voted to print 1200 copies for the use of the members and their constituents."

The end result was that Adams, who could not possibly have got a declaration of war out of the House prior to the submission of the documents, was placed in a position where war was his to command. Fortunately, he did not want a war (though his Secretary of State Timothy Pickering very much did); instead, he used the public's revulsion from the friends of France to pass the Alien and Sedition Acts and suppress criticism of his administration.

The special difficulties inherent in the relations of a Foreign Minister and a legislature also surfaced in the eighteenth century. Congress made the State Department the repository of all governmental functions not performed by Treasury, War and the Attorney General (it was the State Department, for example, that handled patent and copyright applications; and to this day the State Department keeps the Great Seal of the United States: when I was appointed a member of the President's Housing Commission, I got a large certificate signed by Ronald Reagan as President and by Walter Stoessel, then Under Secretary of State for Political Affairs, the senior officer present in Washington that day, as keeper of the Seal). But it did not require the Secretary of State to report his activities to the

Congress, as it did with the heads of the other departments—a requirement which, as Flexner shrewdly points out, enhanced the influence of these departments on the Congress far more than it increased legislative control of executive activity.

The result was that everything the State Department did that required congressional sanction went first to the President. "Of Washington's three major advisers," Flexner writes, "Jefferson walked the most difficult road. Not only did the State Department have no connection with Congress which did not pass through the President, but Washington had, during his retirement after the Revolution, made a study of international affairs that enabled him, on assuming the Presidency, to act as his own foreign minister." The more it changes, as the French say, the more it stays the same. . . .

One constitutional question did not arise until after Washington's time. The President is commander-in-chief of the armed forces of the United States, but under Washington there was nothing but a ceremonial army of less than three thousand men. The states were to maintain militias that would be available on call from the President, and naval activities were taken care of (and how) by "privateers." Washington in his last address to the Congress called for the establishment of a navy, but it did not come into existence until the Adams presidency. Even in the heat of the quasi-war, Congress refused to give the commander-in-chief a "standing army" to command; what Adams was given was a "provisional army" of ten thousand and a paper "additional army" of fifty thousand if the French actually attacked—and even these disappeared within a year. Not until the end of the War of 1812 did James Madison win approval for a "standing army," and his request for fifteen thousand men was cut by a third. What military force the United States had in the eighteenth century was concentrated in the "revenue cutters" of the Treasury Department, which carried armed men called Marines. In 1798, Congress formally created a Marine Corps as part of the fledgling Navy.

Nevertheless, the President had the power to accept help from private ships and private armies in the conduct of American foreign relations— and did so, without seeking congressional endorsement. The Republican panic that provoked the demand for the XYZ papers was caused in large part by the feeling that Adams could by the employment of semiofficial American forces create a state of war that the French would be compelled to recognize by formal declaration. From 1801 to 1815, armed merchantmen and a scattering of American naval vessels conducted a running war with the beys and sultans of the Barbary Coast, and in 1805 William Eaton under the direction of the anti-militarist Thomas Jefferson took a more or less American army of five hundred across the desert from Egypt to Tripoli as part of the U.S. Government's campaign against the Barbary pirates.

In later years, without specific congressional approval, U.S. forces would fight in Spanish Florida, against Mexico, Japan, China, Korea, Turkey, a host of Caribbean and Central American countries and even the Soviet Union (how many Americans remember, as all Russians do, that there were U.S. forces in Vladivostok in 1920?). Congress had been given the power to declare war—but not, it turned out, the power to control even the most warlike aspects of foreign policy.

Nor could Congress compel bellicosity from a President who did not feel it. During the time of the Oregon dispute with Britain, in the 1840s, Senator William Allen, "the Ohio fog horn," chairman of the Foreign Relations Committee, made a two-day speech on the subject. Frederick Merk describes it: "Sixty-three years had passed, he began, since Great Britain had acknowledged American independence. Yet the British still maintained their law, handed down judgments, carried out executions, in a vast American territory, 640,000 square miles in extent, in the Pacific Northwest. No question remained any longer as to American title to that country. Even discussion of it was out of order. British pretensions were baseless; they were 'absolute frivolity.' They were, however, in character with other British aggressions on the United States—inciting savages to hack women and children to pieces, impressing American seamen, seizure of half of Maine by chicanery. One question alone remained to be answered: whether the American government had the nerve to maintain its rights, or whether it would cringe, quail and cower before the British. If the government would stand firm, the British would not dare fight. Surrounded by embittered rivals, threatened by domestic convulsions, crippled by a parliamentary system of instability, exhausted by efforts to keep 128,000,000 colonists in subjection, they were helpless. The American people were strong. They needed only to be told that Oregon was theirs. Ask them if they are willing to surrender this large part of their country because of mere dread of invasion by a rabble of armed paupers. Ask them this 'and they will give you an answer which will make the British empire tremble through its whole frame and foundation.'"

A closer friend of Polk's than Allen observed that the President was not in fact wedded to the claim for all Oregon to 54°40' (though the Democratic Party platform on which he had run had "Resolved, That our title to the whole of the Territory of Oregon is clear and unquestionable, that no portion of the same ought to be ceded to England or any other power . . ."). Allen and friends thereupon called on the President and "propounded the big question: 'Do you go for the whole of Oregon to 54°40', or do you intend to settle for 49°?' The President bristled. He would answer that question, he said, to no man. The foreign relations of the country were his charge, and it was unheard of for a President to say outside his cabinet what his foreign policy of the future would be."

Historically, treaties were the vulnerable point in a President's dealings with the Congress. The Constitution makes treaties superior to legislation, changing existing law and barring future congresses from law-making as absolutely as a constitutional amendment, which heightens institutional sensitivity—and of course their ratification requires a two-thirds vote of the Senate, which gives opponents a far better chance to block by the assertion of hypothetical horribles.

From the beginning, the Senate has denied presidential envoys the plenipotentiary power normally exercised by the negotiators of treaties: the Senate amended the Jay treaty with England, and scandal was averted only because the British accepted the amendments. Over the years, a ponderable fraction of the treaties negotiated for the United States have been rejected, Versailles being only the most prominent. Seward lost the purchase of the Danish Virgin Islands in the 1860s, Cleveland a fisheries treaty with Canada in the 1880s, Taft an arbitration treaty with Britain in the 1910s.

The treaty route remains perilous for Presidents. Carter's one-vote victory in the Panama Canal matter and his inability to carry the SALT treaty to a vote received the editorial attention, but that Administration also lost two significant if less publicized treaty battles in the Senate—one of them a Canadian fisheries deal, blocked by Senator Kennedy of Massachusetts and then-Senator Muskie of Maine as their predecessors in the 1880s had blocked Cleveland's similar treaty; the other, a treaty with Britain restricting the degree to which each could tax the other's multinational corporations. This last was defeated, incidentally, mostly by the efforts of Frank Church, chairman of the Foreign Relations Committee, and Alan Cranston, majority whip, who came from states that either imposed or planned to impose taxes that would lie on a fraction of a corporation's total worldwide profits rather than its actual profits in the state. (So much for party discipline in foreign policy.) The kind of tax the treaty would have forbidden is the sort of thing Congress has told the Less Developed Countries they cannot impose if they wish to receive American investment—but the rights and wrongs of such situations change when it's Americans who do it.

But relatively little of foreign relations is conducted through the cumbersome treaty process. The life of diplomacy is the conclusion of "agreements," and the executive branch does that literally every day. John Bassett Moore explained the matter in 1905: "A question arises as to the rights of an individual, the treatment of a vessel, a matter of ceremonial, or any of the thousand and one things that daily occupy the attention of foreign offices without attracting public notice; the governments directly concerned exchange views and reach a conclusion by which the difference is disposed of. They have entered into an international 'agreement.'" These agreements normally involve lower-ranking officers in embassies and Foreign Ministries, but they can be approved formally by ambassadors, the Secretary of State—even the President himself. The overwhelming majority of these agreements, prior to 1972, never came to the attention of the Congress at all: they were negotiated as part of the executive power, fulfilling functions the Congress itself could not possibly handle.

Extraordinarily important matters have been handled in this way, including the recognition of nations and governments and the exchange of embassies and consulates; economic assistance and military base arrangements; Roosevelt's lend-lease program that gave Britain destroyers in the dark days of the struggle for the Atlantic in 1940; Nixon's opening to China and Carter's "normalization" of relations with Peking. Moreover, major "policy" decisions can be taken by the executive without any action by the Congress. James Monroe, after his dismissal as Minister to France, was bitterly critical of Washington for conducting foreign policy without consulting Congress; but when the time came for him to proclaim a Doctrine, he did so without advance notice to anyone in Congress. Jimmy Carter's Doctrine—that the United States would never let the Russians get their grubby paws on the Persian Gulf—was announced *ex cathedra* without congressional consultation, as was Ronald Reagan's Corollary, that the United States would guarantee the rule of Saudi Arabia by the Saudi princes, *saecula saeculorum*.

The most serious examples of unilateral presidential action, of course, have derived from the President's role as commander-in-chief. Committing the nation's armed forces—as half the nation's Presidents have done, from the halls of Montezuma to the shores of Tripoli—the President inescapably commits the Congress, too. Revulsion against the results of these procedures—and against the mounting evidence that Presidents in what reports they made had repeatedly lied to the country—produced a decade of effort by Congress to capture some degree of control over decision-making in foreign policy. The first and perhaps most ambitious effort was a self-serving resolution passed by the Senate 70–16 in 1969, declaring that "a national commitment, . . . the use of the armed forces on foreign territory, or a promise to assist a foreign government, or people by the use of armed forces or financial resources of the United States . . . results only from the affirmative action taken by the Legislative and Executive Branches . . . by means of a treaty, statute, or concurrent resolution of both Houses of Congress."

Later that year, getting down to cases, an amendment was attached to the defense appropriations bill prohibiting the President from sending American ground forces to Laos or Thailand. Following Nixon's "incursion" into Cambodia the next year, the Congress extended the ban to Cambodia, and in 1973 made the cheese more binding by restricting "the use of any past or present appropriation for financing directly or indirectly United States combat activities in or over or from off the shores of North Vietnam, South Vietnam, Laos or Cambodia." The next step was the War Powers Act, passed in 1973 over a presidential veto. Under its terms, the President is permitted to commit troops without specific legislative authorization only if American forces are attacked or are in danger of imminent attack.

Meanwhile, in 1972, the Case Act was passed (and signed by the President), requiring the Secretary of State to transmit to the Congress the texts of all executive agreements. In 1975, an effort was made to drop the other shoe and give Congress a "legislative veto" over all executive agreements; but this bill failed. What did succeed was a more narrowly targeted measure requiring the President to submit to the Congress every arms sales agreement involving more than $25 million worth of guns and bombs, and giving the Congress power to stop the sale by vote of both houses within thirty days of the submission.

On the opposite side of the spectrum of concern, Congress mandated the creation of an Office of Human Rights in the State Department (exalted by Carter to bureau status) and an annual report by the Office on human rights policies and practices in countries around the world. On the basis of that report, Congress reserved the right to cut off economic and military assistance to countries that violate the human rights of their citizens.

The congressional arm reached out into relations with individual countries. Military assistance and arms sales to Turkey were cut off after the invasion of Cyprus, aid to the Angolan rebels was specifically prohibited, the Soviet Union was denied most-favored-nation status on the tariff schedule unless it would agree to free emigration for its Jewish population. The collapse of Idi Amin was probably caused more by a congressionally inspired ban on coffee imports from Uganda than by Tanzania's invading army. These things could backfire—seeking to get even with the Arab oil producers who had banned sales to America, Congress rescinded most-favored-nation status for OPEC members, thereby punishing countries like Nigeria, Venezuela, Ecuador and Indonesia, which hadn't boycotted the United States at all. Still, the device of amending appropriations bills to restrict the use of the appropriated money unquestionably got the attention of the executive branch and made American foreign policy with reference to a number of countries different from what it otherwise would have been.

How *much* difference the new laws made is hard to determine. They are not discussed a great deal in the State Department. The reporting requirements under the Case Act, Edward Kolodziej notes, "have not prevented the president or the secretary of state from making agreements that are divulged only after considerable congressional probing. The agreements made by Secretary of State Henry A. Kissinger with Israel and Egypt to induce them to accept the Sinai accords were not reported to Congress. . . . It has also been discovered that thirty-four agreements reached between the United States and South Korean intelligence services were also not disclosed to Congress." More than a hundred arms deals have been reported to the Congress without a rejection: even the idiotic sale of AWACS planes to Saudi Arabia, touted by the White House as a way to establish an American military presence in that country when quite obviously the Saudi purpose was to get rid of an existing American presence required by the mere loan of similar aircraft, was finally pushed through by President Reagan. And in June 1983, the Supreme Court denied the Congress any right to require specific approval of actions undertaken by a President under a general legislative grant of powers; the impact of that decision on the conduct of foreign relations awaits revelation in the fullness of time.

More ominous has been the neglect of the provisions of the War Powers Act that call on the President to consult the Congress "in every possible instance" before committing American forces. Under Ford and Carter, Kolodziej points out, "Congress essentially learned about eight minor engagements after they had been undertaken. These included evacuations in Da Nang, Phnom Penh, Saigon, Cyprus, and Lebanon, the rescue of the *Mayaguez* crew, the transport of Belgian and French troops to Shaba, and the aborted rescue mission to free the American hostages in Iran." Reagan added another when the carrier task force aircraft shot down Libyan attackers over a section of the Mediterranean that Libya (but nobody else) regards as territorial waters, and then went whole hog when American Marines were sent to Lebanon, prior to congressional consultation, in fall 1982.

Simply to mention the Libyan case, however, lets a very large cat out of the bag. There *are* inherent powers—and inherent responsibilities—in the presidency, and no amount of congressional intervention can change them. The Congress cannot give orders to the troops, and it cannot actually conduct foreign relations—though a Congressman Murphy or Congressman Wilson can go down to Nicaragua to buck up the spirits of Antonio Somoza when the State Department is trying to get him to leave

266

quietly, or Congressman Solarz can visit the Polisario guerrillas and become very impressed, or Senator Helms can send his staffers to London to disrupt the negotiations over the end to the various rebellions in Rhodesia, or Congressman Dellums can find kindred spirits in Mozambique. When Senator Percy, incoming chairman of the Foreign Relations Committee, took it upon himself to assure Chairman Brezhnev that the United States wanted to involve the Soviet Union in the Mideast peace process, the question raised was not whether American policy would change but whether the senator's well-known inadequacy for the post he was about to assume should bar his assumption of it.

The State Department cannot keep up with all the elements that should go into the blender before a decision on international policy goes into the oven. Congressmen cannot hope to latch onto more than a piece of the problem, and even their recently expanded staffs are likely to perform best in situations where the real problem is deception by the Department. Especially on the House side, moreover, these staffs may have their own agendas. A report on the congressional reforms that created ten foreign relations subcommittees in the House noted that their staffs "tended to be selected for their policy predispositions, . . . and to have been 'disaffected' members of the foreign policy apparatus, . . . to have sought a policy-influencing position, and/or to have a stronger partisan orientation . . . than their counterparts on the full committee and on most other subcommittees."

Conceding the problems that arose when "staff members developed interests of their own, with the end result that members had less time to think for themselves and were trapped into doing the bidding of their staffs," Senator Frank Church argued soon after his departure from the Senate that the more important problem was systemic: "One thing has happened in the last ten or eleven years in Congress that I think has backfired badly. It became fashionable to say and believe that Congress could deal more effectively with the executive branch if the staffs of the committees and the Congressmen were enlarged. It sounded good, but it's worked just the opposite way. As the staffs grew larger, they established contacts with their counterparts in the executive department and became more alike in their interests, their attitudes and their viewpoints. Congressmen became more and more served by staffs representing the viewpoint of downtown, and the executive wielded more influence on Congress than before.

"The way Congress is organized in committees. . . ." Church paused. A round-faced, slightly pudgy, gracious lawyer who retained after twenty-four years as a senator much of the boyish look he had brought to the Senate as its youngest member, Church really does speak in these splendid, rounded periods, and will delay if the sentence is not entirely in his mind. "In the course of time, each committee is to a large degree co-opted by a department of government, as the regulatory agencies are co-opted by those they regulate. You get sold on the program in the process of time. The committee becomes an advocate of the program over which it has authority, and goes to the House or the Senate as an advocate."

Getting the committees into that condition is the work of a Bureau of Congressional Relations (H), which employs about fifteen FSOs on two-year tours of duty. (By comparison, the Defense Department at last report had 227 people on congressional liaison duty.) "H" must sign off ("concur") on all prepared testimony by State Department people before congressional committees, answer queries from Congress, present the Department's positions in informal ways to congressional staff (which now numbers twenty thousand), run an early-warning system about amendments that may get tacked on to legislation the Department wants, and (perhaps most important) try to see to it that congressmen and their wives have a good time when they go off on junkets.

The Assistant Secretary who heads the Bureau usually sits in on the morning meetings of the Secretary of State, seeking to make sure his people can alert congressmen to anything they should know before the news gets out, and sometimes (depending on the personalities on both sides) providing an insight for top management into what reactions to a proposal are likely to be at the far end of Pennsylvania Avenue. In theory, there is also some coordination with the lobbyists at the near end of Pennsylvania Avenue, in the White House, but in fact the President's congressional relations people tend to let the State Department know what they are doing only after they have done it.

This Bureau was begun as an "Office" by Cordell Hull, himself a former congressman, and among its early bosses was Dean Acheson, who benefited considerably as Secretary of State in the McCarthy days from the fact that most senators had known him personally as a lobbyist. Marshall on his way out made the Office a Bureau, urged in that direction by the Hoover Commission (of which Acheson was a member). Under Dean Rusk, the Bureau ran a weekly Wednesday breakfast at the Capitol, which the Secretary himself attended fairly often, and which might draw more than a hundred congressmen. (Rusk in general was the most assiduous of the Secretaries in cultivating the Congress; Henry Kissinger once had a study made of how many hours Secretaries had spent at the Capitol, and called Rusk to tell him he was by far the champion.) But the Bureau historically was not well regarded in the Foreign Service, where the job was seen as one of toadying up to people who know less than you do. Even under Lyndon Johnson, who was once heard to remark that he thought congressional liaison officers were the most important people in every government department, FSOs assigned to H were less likely to appear on promotion lists than those in almost any other bureau, which strongly affects perceptions.

Congressional pressure on foreign policy in the 1970s improved the standing of H among FSOs. A minicourse in the operations of Congress is now part of the basic training at the Foreign Service Institute, and a score or so of junior officers climb Capitol Hill every year to serve a tour as congressional interns. "One of the nice things about this office," said Douglas Bennet, who had come over from the staff of the Senate Budget Office to be Assistant Secretary for H under Vance, "is that it's no longer regarded as a dung heap. You get a lot of responsibility here at an earlier stage in your career than you can almost anywhere else in the Foreign Service." Legislative Management Officers (LMOs) have been winning more promotions, too, though the Bureau is handicapped in that sweepstakes by the fact that tours there are almost never longer than two years. "It's part of our job," Bennet said, "to cycle people back into the Foreign Service who know the Congress."

This sort of war being too important to leave to the generals, most other bureaus have acquired their own LMOs, and many other assistant secretaries work the Congress themselves, sometimes by arrangement with and sometimes independently of H. The Under Secretary for Management (M) and the Assistant Secretary for Administration (A) maintain their own congressional liaison staffs to push for the Department's budget lines. Under Haig, James Buckley, a former senator, became a kind of super-H all by himself, keeping on the reservation Republican senators who might otherwise stray.

Almost everyone on the outside agrees that the State Department does not do enough to sell American foreign policies and the Foreign Service to the Congress. "Too few people on the hill," David K. Willis of the *Christian Science Monitor* wrote admonishingly in 1968, "know the names of the deputy assistant secretaries and country directors." A 1981 report by the Congressional Research Service urged the exaltation of the Assistant Secretary for Congressional Relations to the status of Under Secretary, very early consultation with Congress on emerging problems, and "an expanded commitment of people and money." It would not be enough, the author thought, to keep the members of the foreign relations committees informed: "many Members outside this category have been offended because they were ignored in the policymaking process."

The fact remains that this is awkward work for an FSO. Foreign policy has always been an issue in partisan politics; it was never true to say, as so many did in the Cold War days, that "politics stops at the water's edge."

269

Woodrow Wilson went to Paris for the peace negotiations shortly after elections had turned control of the Senate over to the Republicans, and Theodore Roosevelt from his deathbed sent a bon voyage message: "Our allies and enemies, and Mr. Wilson himself, should all understand that Mr. Wilson has no authority whatever to speak for the American people at this time."

Entering into lobbying activities, the FSO enters partisan politics. Because he has signed on to execute the policies of elected officials, and may be called upon presently to act on instructions quite different from those he now receives, his situation is always ambiguous when he walks the halls of Congress. Reagan and Haig denied "forward posting"—good jobs as DCM or ambassador—to a number of deputy assistant secretaries of the Carter State Department who had reason to expect progress on their career paths. There was a kind of indefensible meanness about some of these rejections—but it is also true that they were invited by the increased use of FSOs with the Congress in the Carter days.

From the State Department's point of view, Congress is an unmitigated nuisance. Its members are elected from districts or states and are expected to represent these parochial interests—as indeed they do, the scuttling of the fisheries and tax treaties being two recent examples. They bring ethnic pressures on policy: Nathan Glazer and Daniel P. Moynihan have argued that American foreign policy "responds to other things as well, but probably first of all to the primal facts of ethnicity." Though the embassies, like the congressmen's constituents, are usually obsessed by commercial questions, some congressmen can be effectively lobbied by foreigners in opposition to American foreign policy. A former counselor in the British embassy in Washington remembered rather dreamily from the days when Britain had the major responsibility in Cyprus a study he had performed to determine how many congressmen came from districts where 5 percent or more of the population was of Greek extraction. "There weren't many," he said; "but there were enough."

Most seriously, the congressmen take huge quantities of time. Tens of thousands of queries must be answered—quickly—every year. There are the all but incessant hearings—on budgets, programs, appointments, problems —all of them duplicated in the House and the Senate. Subcommittee chairmen usually want the highest-ranking representative of the Department they can secure, because that gets them publicity, though everyone knows that someone much lower down in the hierarchy would give better answers to questions. Policy Planning wastes its time developing "Q's and A's" for the Secretary, who must in any event bring with him an entourage of subordinates to whom he can turn for assistance. "They're going to have to learn some discipline in the Congress," James Buckley said wearily, but he had no suggestions about who might teach them.

What keeps the State Department from taking its congressional problem entirely seriously is, of course, the junkets, which are, inelegantly, a pain in the butt. "The boys-will-be-boys stories are true," Bennet said, "no question about it. The insistence that the PX be kept open till four in the morning so they can buy a bottle of Scotch—that happens. They travel when Congress is out and they feel they're on vacation. And congressmen are secretive. They start late, they don't tell you what their schedules are, they make it hard for the embassies to plan and make appointments for them with the Prime Minister. And they all travel at the same time."

Ghanaian Ambassador Kojo Debrah once observed that the radio, television and jet plane had been the ruination of the developing countries: "Radio enables people to hear all evil, television enables them to see all evil, and the jet plane enables them to go off and do all evil." Foreign Service Officers who have had to pick up the pieces after congressional meetings with foreign leaders feel much that way about Congress. But this attitude is less justified than it used to be, for the new breed of congressman is more serious-minded than his ancestors, and the objection from the travelers today is more likely to be that they haven't learned what they came to learn. "There's a question of the quality of the briefings," Bennet admitted. "We had an experience last weekend in Spain with a group of nine congressmen breaking a trip back from Khartoum. They stopped at an air force base, arrived 4 P.M., were bused to Madrid, where the ambassador on short notice had set up a reception. But nobody talked to them about the new Constitution Spain was to vote on in a few days."

Moreover, congressmen's annoyance at State Department procedures and anger at executive policy are often correct. Phillip Jessup recalled a UN General Assembly to which Senator Theodore Green was a delegate, and thus the recipient of "a telegram from the State Department marked with the favorite most-restrictive classification, 'Eyes Only.' 'Eyes only!' he shouted at me. 'What did they think we would do with it?'" More seriously, the Congress can see—if the State Department cannot—that when Secretary Haig suggests that four murdered nuns in El Salvador were shot because they were trying to run a checkpoint, he grievously diminishes the force of any objections the United States may later care to make to the behavior of the Polish Government.

Senator John Tower, urging the repeal of many of the measures enacted in the 1970s, opened his essay with a quote from John Marshall before he became Chief Justice: "The President is the sole organ of the nation in its external relations, and its sole representative with foreign nations." Samuel Huntington in 1960 went only a small step further: "Congress has, like

Bagehot's queen, 'the right to be consulted, the right to encourage, the right to warn.'" But the most accurate formulation is probably that of Edward S. Corwin, that the Constitution gave Congress the right "to struggle for the privilege of directing American foreign policy."

It is a struggle that cannot and should not be won—especially not by congressional staffs as opposed to the Congress itself. But as international and domestic considerations interpenetrate an increasing range of decisions, the voice that represents the people surely cannot and should not be stilled. The State Department must successfully integrate a wider range of outside influence into its work if it is to claim, as Henry Kissinger claimed while Secretary, that U.S. foreign policy is "a coherent and purposeful whole." On the day that claim is believed, congressional relations, too, will become more manageable.

10

ORGANIZING A NUMBER OF COUNTRIES

When politicians intervene there is, almost necessarily, a noticeable lowering of ethical standards, because they do nothing for nothing and only act on condition that the devoured association becomes one of their customers. We are very far here from the path of sublimity, we are on that which leads to the practices of the political-criminal societies.

—Georges Sorel

Other important WIPO activities in 1976 included (1) the convening of an *Ad Hoc* Committee of Experts on the Revision of the Nice Agreement which recommended that some minor procedural changes be approved by a diplomatic conference of revision in 1977. . . .

—U.S. *Participation in the UN*, Report
by the President to the Congress
for the Year 1976

To give them all that money and then see what they do with it; that is not nice.

—Anne Vidal de la Blache, International
Organizations Bureau, French Foreign
Ministry

1

The most important and successful venture in international cooperation ever attempted by governments has its home in Brussels, in an S-shaped

273

skyscraper office complex dating to the free days of the 1960s when architects unhampered by cost constraints were trying to make sculptures of buildings. Something like twelve thousand bureaucrats and supporting staff work here—twelve hundred of them in interpretation and translation alone—to plan and administer the rules of the European Economic Community, or "Common Market," which now incorporates ten nations—an original core of six in 1958 (France, Germany, Italy and the Benelux trio), an addition of three in the 1970s (Britain, Denmark and Ireland), and since late 1981 a gamble in the southeast corner of the continent (Greece). In principle, Spain and Portugal are to join before this decade ends.

It is not farfetched to see the European Community as an expression of continental shame over the shambles wrought twice in this century by fratricidal hostilities. The preamble to the 1951 treaty that established the earliest Community (dealing only with coal and steel) proclaimed that the signatories were resolved "to substitute for age-old rivalries the merging of their essential interests; to create . . . the basis for a broader and deeper community among peoples long divided by bloody conflicts." But the driving force, of course, was economic, the need for a common market within which the different economies could produce efficiently for each other what they could make domestically only at much higher cost. When Nasser seized the Suez Canal, he greased the wheels of progress toward a second Community to pool national efforts in the area of atomic energy (Euratom) and helped push a number of skeptical European politicians over the fence of their own fears toward the fundamental economic unification decision enshrined in the Treaty of Rome, signed in 1957. The Economic Community formed by the Treaty eventually absorbed the other two.

The British were itchy. "Commonwealth preferences" provided protected markets in the former colonies for British manufacturers, meanwhile assuring agricultural and mineral sales in Britain for the farmers and miners of these newly or recently independent countries. In the negotiations leading to the Rome Treaty, the British played a spoiler's role, raising objections in the hopes that others would pick them up. The central problem was that Britain and France had drawn opposite conclusions from the Suez fiasco of 1956: the British had decided that Europe could accomplish nothing in the world without the direct help of the United States, and that therefore Britain's "special relationship" with big brother gave it unique bargaining chips at the European table; the French had concluded that the Americans were unreliable allies and that Europe had to cohere to create a countervailing force. Despite fears that the Germans would become preponderant in the new Community, the French pushed ahead without Britain, which responded by forming a European Free Trade Association (EFTA) of the nations surrounding the Community core. This was no great help to anybody, and by 1961 Britain was ready to resume negotiations on a more forthcoming basis.

From the beginning, negotiations about European economic cooperation had been coupled in one way or another to negotiations about military cooperation. Before the European Steel and Coal Community could be put into final shape, the Korean War had reduced American military commitments to Europe and produced pressure from the United States for a European Defense Community that would, despite the still bleeding wounds of war, accept a German contribution. Now British negotiations to enter the Common Market were complicated by the collapse of Skybolt, and Kennedy's offer of nuclear submarines and submarine-launched missile technology to Britain. De Gaulle, who had different strategic concepts and whose efforts to construct an independent *force de frappe* for France were being frustrated by the American refusal to share technology, blew up at this evidence of the British "special relationship" and in a dramatic press conference announced to the world his refusal to countenance British admission to the European Community.

Another thirteen years of British economic decline and French prosperity (interrupted by the riots of 1968) would have to pass before De Gaulle's successors accepted British participation. Denmark and Ireland came with Britain; the Norwegians rejected membership by referendum vote; the Austrians were ineligible by the terms of the treaty that had ended four-power occupation of that country; and the Mediterranean states that had been part of Britain's EFTA were put on hold, with associate status to minimize economic disruption.

What had been in the minds of the progenitors of the EC—especially Jean Monnet, whose Action Committee was for years the driving force behind it—was always a political federation that would produce European rather than merely national positions on the issues of international relations. A banker who had made much of his early career in the United States (he was briefly chairman of the holding company that controlled Bank of America, just before the Depression), Monnet always saw European integration as a process that would give his continent the political stability as well as the economies of scale that had been achieved on the other side of the Atlantic. Within each government, a mix had to be found between Foreign Ministry participation and international decision-making by ministers with primarily domestic responsibilities. In the end, all of them decided that their permanent representatives in Brussels should be diplomats, and that the Foreign Ministry should be the lead agency in dealing with the institutions of the Community.

As might be expected from its history, the Community has a complicated, cumbersome structure. Its revenues derive mostly from a 1 percent value-added tax, essentially a sales tax on all gross domestic product (except government services) in the member countries; this added up to about $15 billion in 1982. Its "directives," which in theory and almost always in fact have the force of law in every one of the member countries, are adopted by a Council composed of the Prime Ministers of all the members. The Prime Ministers meet only three times a year, but they can and do delegate their authority to other members of their cabinets. The agriculture ministers of the ten meet monthly, and the heads of other domestic ministries (energy, transportation, education, social security, etc.) meet less frequently. In all, the Council meets about seventy times a year. Presidency of the Council rotates among the member states, in (French) alphabetic order. The Minister representing the country that holds the presidency rises above the battle for its six-month tenure, chairing the meetings and presumably articulating the interests of Europe rather than those of his own country. His nation is represented in the meetings by an alternate.

Council meetings normally begin at around three in the afternoon and run until ten at night, and the proceedings are entirely confidential. With rare exceptions (in fall 1982 the French, bedeviled by bombings, used a Council meeting of justice ministers to propose a Europe-wide code on the extradition of terrorists), these are not sessions at which proposals are made. Normally, before the Council sees anything, the subject has been thoroughly—exhaustively and exhaustingly might be more accurate adverbs—explored by other elements of the Community, and has already been negotiated on the governmental level by the Council of Permanent Representatives, the "COREPER," which consists of the ambassadors to the Community from all the ten states.

COREPER meets formally twice a week—once on the ambassadorial level, once on the deputy level—to handle about fifty agenda items per meeting. Though each of the "permanent representatives" (the title the ambassadors bear) has a staff representing the various ministries of his home government—and the Council itself has about fifteen hundred staff members seconded by their own countries, not employees of the Community—aides usually come to Brussels from the nine other capital cities to sit in on COREPER meetings whenever anything of particular interest to their departments is on the table.

Items on which COREPER has reached agreement are placed on an "A-list" for the next meeting of the Council, regardless of the ministries that will be represented at the meeting, and are simply adopted as Community rules—agriculture ministers, for example, might vote to adopt a directive on the maximum permissible weight of trucks on European roads, if the governments assembled on the ambassadorial level in COREPER had agreed on the number. Items on which there is no agreement appear on a "B-list" restricted to subjects within the special competence of those at the meeting.

But "directives" do not begin in the COREPER, either. Mostly, they come to COREPER from the Commission, an essentially separate institution which administers its old rules while thinking up new ones—not unlike the departments of government in a nation-state. The fourteen Commissioners who are both the legislative and executive bosses are nominated by the member states—two each from Britain, France, Germany and Italy, one from each of the other six—but formally elected, to four-year terms, by the Council. One Commissioner is selected as President, also for a four-year term; each of the others, like a cabinet member in a government, has responsibility for a specific area of expertise and operations. ("The best Commissioners," says a French bureaucrat who has been in the system since day one, "are those with very deep technocratic background and some diplomatic experience.") Because there are no fewer than 21 "directorates-general," a Commissioner may have responsibility in more than one area.

Once in place, a Commissioner is supposed to speak for the Community, not for his own country; and most do. But service on the Commission does not necessarily remove people from future political life back home—French Foreign Minister Claude Cheysson was a Commissioner (with responsibility for Third World matters), and Roy Jenkins, who led the drive for a centrist third party in England, served as President.

The Commission works to a remarkable degree through consultation with outside experts. There are seventy multinational "consultative bodies," including no fewer than seventeen for different groups of agricultural products, one for consumers, one for nuclear matters, one for employment, one for social security of migrant workers, one for transport, one for central bank matters, etc. Proposals for Community policies percolate up through a hierarchy, always in the form of long, boring documents (in seven languages), which are supposed to be confidential but quickly leak to the national governments and to the eighty or so embassies from nonmember countries accredited to the Community. "Discussion" by outsiders commences early in the process. Though they speak for Europe, the Commissioners at this time do serve national functions, because representatives of member states, looking to make an early input in the Commission's deliberations, will normally tend to take their concerns to their own man in the big building—or rather, to be precise, to his personal staff, the members of his "cabinet," who are normally drawn from his nationality.

At the end, and it can be years down the pike, the Commission presents a "Proposal for a Council Directive." This is in effect a piece of Europe-wide legislation, and like national legislation it usually deals with some narrow rule. One that I picked up on my travels, for example, is "On the Approximation of the Laws of the Member States Relating to Methods of Testing the Biodegradability of Non-Ionic Surfactants"—i.e., common rules for decision-making about the acceptability of laundry detergents. Such proposals are the most likely subject matter when COREPER or the Council meets.

The Commission adopts its proposals on a basis of one Commissioner, one vote, and a simple majority rules. COREPER can make decisions only on a basis of unanimity—only complete agreement gets the proposal onto the A-list for a Council meeting. The Council works under more intricate rules, through a weighted voting procedure that in effect requires approval by 70 percent of the countries in the Community (i.e., four small countries can block an initiative by the big ones) representing 70 percent of the population (any two of the Big Four, or a combination of one big and two of the larger small countries, can produce stalemate). In addition, there was an "understanding," required by De Gaulle as a condition of French participation, that in matters affecting its "vital interests" each nation could cast a veto. This came unstuck in spring 1982, when a Britain that badly needed Community support in its troubles with Argentina sat still for a budget vote overriding Mrs. Thatcher's objections to the size of the British contribution: the few hundred million dollars at issue, the Council decided, were not a "vital interest." A representative of the Commission attends Council meetings, but does not have a vote. Any vote to amend a Commission recommendation, however, must be unanimous, which helps the bargaining power of both the Commission and the smaller member states.

The politico-idealistic end of the Community is the Parliament, a not-quite legislative body that has the second largest constituency of any freely elected assembly in the world (the Indian Parliament ranks first). More than 111 million Europeans voted in the first direct election of Euro-MPs, in 1979. Prior to that year, the Parliament, which traces its origins back to the "assembly" that advised the first Coal and Steel Community in 1952, had been made up of members of the parliaments of the Common Market countries, assigned to take a few days a year looking at EC matters.

The Parliament meets in Strasbourg for monthly plenary sessions that usually take about a week; the committees of the Parliament (and it is of course the expertise of the committees that makes a legislature effective over time) meet in Brussels; the secretariat is housed in Luxembourg. There are 434 members, who sit according to their political coloration rather than according to nationality. The cost of operating the European Parliament runs over $200 million a year, but at least half that total goes to translation services and the extra costs imposed when activities are spread among three cities.

In essence, the Parliament derives its powers from the Council, which has been grudging with them. The MPs can reject the Community's budget (by a two-thirds vote) but cannot write a new one. In the first year of the elected Parliament, the MPs did in fact reject the Community budget—only to bend six months later and approve a document very like the one originally submitted. If they become really enraged by the Commission, the MPs can (again by a two-thirds vote) dismiss the lot—not any one Commissioner, but the entire body.

Apart from these two "ultimate" sanctions, the Parliament plays only an advisory role: the Council and Commission must respond to members' queries (which run about three thousand formal submissions a year), and any major new directives or regulations must be presented to Parliament for comment before the Council acts on them. In fall 1982 the multinational corporations found it worth their while to lobby fiercely in the corridors of Strasbourg against a Commission proposal for a directive that would have required them to bare their books worldwide to the unions representing their employees in any Common Market country. Parliament thereupon gave approval only to a much watered-down version of the proposal, greatly strengthening the hand of its enemies in the Commission. Perhaps because of the date of its election, the EC Parliament has had a more conservative cast than the sum of the assemblies of the member nations; next time around, of course, especially if EC unemployment remains high, the results could be tilted in the other direction. Despite the very limited powers of the Parliament—and a poor turnout in Britain—61 percent of the eligible electorate voted in 1979.

Finally, the EC has a Court—necessarily, because governments cannot enforce their orders without courts. Proceedings against private companies and indeed member states that violate Community directives and regulations are normally taken within the Commission itself, which like an administrative agency in the United States issues a finding and an order.

When the Commission assesses a fine on a private enterprise—for violation of the anti-cartel rules, for example, or for polluting an international river—the company simply pays: even if the government of its headquarters disagrees with the finding, the company has assets elsewhere in the Community that can be made to pony up. When the Commission gives an order to a government, however, the situation is more delicate, for the governments have not renounced sovereigty to the Commission. The Court may then be summoned, either by the government appealing the Commission's ruling, or by the Commission, seeking an order to comply, if the government has refused to follow its dictate.

It sometimes takes a while for such orders to be followed—in fall 1982, for example, the British continued to refuse free entry to French turkeys processed in a plant in Brittany specifically for the English market, despite a direct order from the Court to let the birds enter. But it was recognized on all sides that this was a delaying action, and that the French fowl would eventually appear in British butcher shops, as Italian wines entered France after another such imbroglio, despite the fury of the domestic producers. Sovereignty *has* been renounced to the Court. If a country is to get satisfaction when the Court's ruling goes its way, after all, it must be willing to abide by the decision when a ruling favors its rival—or asserts a principle with distasteful applications. In 1982, Socialist France bowed to an EC ruling that its long-established state tobacco monopoly was an illegal price-fixing scheme, and agreed to permit private enterprise in imported cigarettes in France.

2

"For me," said Umberto Stefani of the Commission's Secretariat, "COREPER work is the most important of the activities of the Community, the alpha and omega. The Council wants to keep national powers, the Commission is supranational, COREPER is in the middle. This is a new diplomacy, neither multilateral nor bilateral. It's varilateral."

Gunnar Riberholt, permanent representative of Denmark at the EC, stressed that Commission work was always at least to a degree exploratory, while actions taken in the context of the Council, which includes COREPER, are definitive. "At Commission meetings," he said, "nobody engages anything. These are informal soundings, to determine the view of the member governments, as much or as little as they wish. The meetings always end with a thank-you-very-much, no decisions. In the Council framework the taxi meter is running all the time—there is no free ride. Every statement binds the government that makes it."

A tall, slender man of great tweedy charm and quiet authority, thinning hair over a domed forehead, Riberholt regarded the word "permanent" as meaningful in an EC context: representing Denmark in Brussels would, he thought, occupy him for the rest of his active career. The responsibilities of the Common Market job can spoil a man for a traditional embassy. "In a technical, logistical sense," Riberholt said, "a permanent representative is of course a diplomatic mission. But we are not abroad—we are in our home base. The American ambassador comes to me; I don't go to him. In real, functional terms this is more an extension of a national administration. Everybody in this house, including myself, is under the instruction of the *government*, not a Ministry. No Minister, including the Prime Minister, can instruct anyone in Brussels. Our instructions are always collaborative."

The French operate in a similar manner, essentially under instruction from the President's office; the Germans, by contrast, allow the individual ministries to tell the people in the COREPER working groups what their government's position shall be.

"That's very bad," Riberholt commented; "it gives constant difficulties. You can get frightening results if you don't respect the principle of collective instruction. For example, there's an environmental matter. The environmental Minister fails to consult the Minister of Labor. The measure affects working conditions, and you get into a frightful row with the trade unions.

"It's an extremely sobering process for a government. You can't dally. You have to decide, Can we accept this or not? Participation in this process has heightened the quality of speed and awareness in the government, it's a sort of consciousness-raising. You negotiate. You say to your government, 'The situation is now clarified. There are eight countries which can accept that, one is still out [this was before the entry of Greece]. That one will come along.' On another matter, you say, 'There's four on each side, with a compromise proposal from the chair. Can we accept that?' One of the true advantages of this method of work is the transparency—it's very difficult to cheat. Sooner or later everything has to come out in the open."

Back home in Denmark, Niels Ersbøll, an imposing gentleman with the manner of a large but not humorless banker, had returned from Riberholt's job to become State Secretary for Foreign Economic Affairs. He found that the need to instruct the Brussels representatives had slimmed down his government's decision-making process. "A question that comes up in the Community," he said, "is referred to the interministerial committee which meets every week. On Tuesday. Every Thursday, the government meets, so we have a maximum decision time of three days. Nothing from Brussels is ever laid over. One of the things we learned from the French is how to file the case. There is a separate file for *each* case, nothing in the general file. We work on the basis of the photocopy machine. People don't use the file, when they need documentation they request copies, which they throw away. The other thing we did away with was the hierarchical system. The lowest-paid official considers the question, ana-

281

lyzes it, and writes his own conclusion. He writes the instructions, and instead of memos we have meetings."

"Our young people are capable of carrying out responsibilities," said William Friis-Møller, chief of the Bureau of North American and European Affairs. "We have accepted that they make mistakes—there's an old Danish saying that when you trade, sometimes you lose. But surprisingly quickly they learn to make decisions; and with rapid action and great responsibility goes flexibility: the man on the spot *can* countermand his instructions."

"Being small has advantages," Ersbøll added. "The decisions are quick because the distances are small."

"And we know each other personally," said Erik Krog-Meyer, deputy undersecretary for commercial affairs.

"Yes," said Ersbøll. "That helps."

Virtually everything the EC does is domestically touchy somewhere in the ten nations. Its essence as an economic community was that it could make possible free movement of the factors of production across national borders. The first order of business, obviously, was the removal of tariff barriers, which was to be accomplished over a period of twelve years (in reality, the then Six eliminated all tariffs between themselves in ten years). This implied, of course, the construction of unified tariff barriers between all the states of the Community and the outside world: "If a market is unique," said Albert Maes of the External Relations directorate, "protection has to be common." Otherwise the importation of items into the Community would be controlled by the state with the lowest tariff on that item, in a kind of legal smuggling. In fact, the West Germans, to the mounting annoyance of their partners in a recessionary time, have been smuggling East German goods into the Community duty-free, in pursuit of a greater goal.

The second matter was the removal of restrictions on the movement of labor from one of the Common Market countries to another, to the point where citizens of any EC country need no work permits to compete for jobs in any other, the sole exception being government jobs. Everybody recognizes everybody else's educational credentials, a truly giant step. Jobs in nationalized companies are not government jobs; neither, incidentally, are appointments as doctors in state-run hospitals.

The third, and most difficult step was the union of the Community's capital markets, with the eventual creation of a single Community currency. Trade among the EC nations had been done mostly in dollars, and did not require a new currency, though a European unit of account was developed for bookkeeping purposes. But a European money for domestic circulation in the Common Market states was not and may never be possible, control of the national currency being a rock-bottom attribute of sovereignty. The European Monetary System which came into existence in 1978 was no more than a plan for minimizing exchange-rate fluctuations—and the British stayed out. But the European Currency Unit developed as its measuring rod could be the foundation for a greater structure.

One element of that foundation—perhaps the most remarkable—was slapped into place in 1980, when the nations of the Community adjusted their internal taxing policies to standardize definitions of tax categories across the national borders. Rates still vary from state to state, which affects relative prices for the same goods in different countries, but the possibility of equalizing burdens (eventually a precondition for success in all the other coordinating ventures) has been established.

Given the domestic sensitivity of much that the Community proposes and does, the Commission puts thought and effort into its press relations. There is a daily briefing at noon in a two-story-high auditorium large enough for ninety correspondents to sit in padded chairs at tables with earphones and consoles that switch among simultaneous translations. Another twenty or so journalists remain standing, mostly near the bar, which sells generous drinks at less than standard Brussels prices and remains discreetly open through the briefing. The day I attended, the opening announcements were made in English, and none of the correspondents used earphones; the detailed report by the "porte-parole" was in French, which sent several of the Oriental group (but no others) to the translations. This report was on labor conditions in the automobile industry, and once the spokesman used a German word—*Gastarbeiter,* for migratory laborers. He corrected himself with a grin—the ghost of De Gaulle might be listening—to *travailleurs en hôte.* Representatives of the Council or the missions of the member states are distinctly *not* welcome at the Commission's press conferences, and people from the Commission do not attend Council briefings or the meetings of the permanent representatives with the press corps of their own countries.

"Is this diplomacy?" Denmark's Riberholt asks philosophically. "It's a modern, highly sophisticated machinery for intelligent, operational, rational—sometimes rational—communications among social groups in the form of nation-states. The crucial element is that we are not making speeches to each other. This is not a speech-and-resolution process, it's a process for incurring obligations. The product that comes out of here is bland, never dazzling. But it's *rarely* spectacularly erroneous. I say, *rarely,* because there is the Common Agricultural Policy. The 'fool's CAP' doesn't function."

Among the factors of production, land is immobile; among the problems of governance, agricultural policy never goes away. Europe is a food importer (the EC takes more than 40 percent of all the world's food imports), and Europe had gone hungry in 1946–47. The conservative governments that held power in the late 1950s, when the Treaty of Rome was negotiated, were dependent on support from farming districts. In giving up tariff protection within Europe for its industrial product, France demanded preferential access for its agriculture throughout the Community, which meant setting prices high enough to guarantee a profit to French farmers and a "variable levy" on agricultural imports to make sure foreigners could not undersell the French.

Like much else the EC attempted in its early years, the Common Agricultural Policy aped what had been done in the United States. This was a mistake: the American price-support system had given farmers, consumers and governments—all three—the short end of the stick. Because prices had to be high enough to support the marginal farmer, all others had little incentive to improve their productivity; food prices were higher to the customer than they had to be; and the government wound up with huge surplus stocks of agricultural commodities, no small part of which had to be given away to poor countries (probably the real victims of the policy: because they could get American food cheap, they were encouraged in their brainless Peronist politics of holding down the prices they paid to farmers and pretending that their cancerously growing cities were supportable). But as the Americans backed away from the failed policies of the 1950s, the Europeans on French insistence (De Gaulle blocked progress toward all other goals until the CAP was in place) adopted them.

The result has been that European food prices are much higher than those elsewhere (Greenland as a semiautonomous and strictly nonagricultural part of Denmark voted early in 1982 to quit the Community to bring down food costs); that countless tons of the most heavily supported commodities have accumulated in warehouses (while shortages of less heavily supported foodstuffs have forced imports—of pork, for example—where there had once been self-sufficiency); that traditional patterns of agricultural trade within Europe have been radically altered (Germany no longer imports wheat from France because the support price is high enough to make it pay for German farmers to grow wheat on hillsides); and that two thirds of all the revenues allocated by the governments to the Community have had to be earmarked for farm price-support payments.

Setting the rise in support prices for the seventeen farm product groups takes more man-hours every year than anything else at the Commission. The "management groups" for cereals and for sugar meet once a week all year long. There is more voting here, too—more than fifteen hundred "procedures" a year to okay the Commission's recommendations (only one or two a year are rejected, partly because when a recommendation looks shaky the Commission withdraws, renegotiates, redrafts). The pressure in these groups, of course, is always to raise prices and give export subsidies to get rid of the surpluses. The North pushes up the prices of cereals and dairy products; the South, of wine and olive oil. "Everything is linked," said Danish agricultural attaché Poul Ottosen, a little wearily. "Nobody will give anything unless he's getting something for himself."

Community revenues were fixed from 1980 onward at the proceeds of a 1 percent value-added tax, or VAT, for all domestically consumed goods and services. (Prior to 1980, the nations had paid into the Community a fraction of their gross national product as estimated by experts; the move to a VAT reduced Italy's share by 10 percent, because so much of the Italian economy runs underground and pays no VAT.) The EC thus came into the new decade obsessed with the vision of a near future when the Common Agricultural Policy could no longer be financed. The potential entry of Spain emphasized the problem, for the cost of supporting Spanish olive oil at the prices set for Italian olive oil would be something more than $3 billion a year.

In summer 1983, Gaston Thorn, Jenkins' successor as president of the Commission, solemnly warned that unless the governments would agree to an increase in the EC VAT after 1984, to pay for the agricultural subsidies, the whole enterprise would go bust. "The facts make it quite clear," an official publication of the Community whined in 1978, "that Europe's agriculture cannot do without an economic and monetary union. By the same token, it cannot do without a social policy or a regional policy. Without these, decisions become more and more difficult, because each country tries to use the price system to protect its own marginal lines of production (cereal farming in one country, dairy farming in another)."

Meanwhile, CAP piles up immense surpluses in the products benefiting by the highest price supports—dairy, poultry, wheat. The United States has similar problems, though American support prices are much lower. In theory, this should make it possible for the United States to dispose of surpluses through foreign sales—but the Europeans specifically subsidize agricultural exports to bring their prices below those across the ocean. One of the two central objectives of the U.S. delegation to the "ministerial" meeting of GATT in November 1982—the first such since the "Tokyo Round" was launched in 1971—was an assurance from the EC that such dumping would stop. (The other objective was the start of the writing of "codes" to prohibit nations from interfering with the free flow of trade in services—banking, insurance, and especially data communications.) When such assurance was not given, the U.S. Department of Agriculture fired a shot across the EC bow, selling a million tons of wheat flour to Egypt (a

French customer) at fire-sale prices. Presently both sides were threatening a subsidy war in agricultural exports.

Most of the EC nations were agreed that export subsidies as structured in the 1970s could not be sustained, especially if the United States followed through on its threat to reply in kind. But France, which under Mitterrand had returned in many ways to the attitudes of De Gaulle, was unwilling to abandon any policy that propped up the CAP. Having faced down Ronald Reagan on his pipeline sanctions, the French thought the EC could successfully call another American bluff. But only political interests were involved on the American side of the pipeline dispute; agricultural trade rouses more fundamental and potent forces, and the conflict over export subsidies that intensified in spring 1983 could seriously damage the EC, the Atlantic Alliance, or both.

3

The secret of the Community's success in the 1960s and 1970s was not any will to unity among the political leaders (though regardless of their political leanings they all enjoyed the pageantry, the self-importance and the socializing of the thrice-yearly meetings of Prime Ministers), but the enthusiastic drive of European businessmen to standardize industrial processes and marketing across the continent. The most visible sign of the drive was the British move toward metric measurements and decimal money, but coordination in the machine tool industry—where French and German manufacturers had for generations used different screw threads and borings—was perhaps even more spectacular. These investments could be made profitable only by continued progress toward economic integration, and the governments were constantly pressured to advance by their industrial sector, including the nationalized industries. It was in large part to accommodate this drive that the Community developed standard rules on pollution, cartel arrangements, food and drug grading, etc.

What was done at Brussels in the 1960s and 1970s was the sort of thing normally accomplished (if at all) by domestic political decision, confirmed in democracies by the votes of legislatures. But the Community has remained the creature of diplomacy, and the role of the diplomats is if anything greater now than it was in earlier years. Under Article 113 of the Treaty of Rome, the Community speaks as a unit—through the mouthpiece of the nation then president of the Council—in international commercial matters. At meetings of the General Agreement on Tariffs and Trade in Geneva, for example, spokesmen for the member states are heard only in support of the Community's position (Britain speaks in GATT for

Hong Kong but not for Britain, which is represented by the president of the Community), and the EC always votes as a bloc. These are not basically Foreign Ministry questions, and only two countries (Belgium and Denmark) are represented on the "113 Committee" by diplomats; the rest are from ministries of trade. But the effectiveness of the consultation and resulting unity has been such that the Foreign Ministries have wanted in, and slowly through the 1970s the Community developed, quite outside the Treaty framework, a process of coordination on international policy issues.

Quarterly meetings of foreign ministers are now held, not in Brussels but in the capital of the then president of the Council; a representative of the Commission attends by invitation and not by right. These meetings increasingly result in Community positions on international disputes—Israel and the PLO, Afghanistan, Poland, Southern Africa, Falklands. Here the rule was unanimity until late 1981, when the arrival of a Greece headed by a violently anti-American American citizen required the institution of statements from which one state could abstain or even dissent.

In meetings of the United Nations, a tradition has grown up by which the president of the Council makes a statement for the Community (which is officially present at the UN only in "observer" status), and nobody contradicts him. If matters come to a vote, however, the member states are not bound by a Community position, and may appear on opposing sides of the tally.

All this requires an immense amount of work, mostly in the offices of the permanent representatives, who carry a complicated four-part responsibility. They are, of course, the agents of their own government, bound by umbilical cords to the belly of the state which nourishes them, and acting only under instructions—which means repeated visits back home to get the instructions changed. They are ambassadors to the Commission, and must forever nose around to learn what the Commission is up to. They spend even more than the usual amount of time with ambassadors from third parties—most notably, the United States, Japan and Canada—to make sure they have a good understanding of what these powers think of Community initiatives. Finally, they spend quite a lot of time checking with their own country's ambassadors in the other member states of the Community, to gather information that may help them predict how their colleagues in COREPER or their ministers' colleagues in Council meetings are going to conduct themselves on various issues.

For the ambassadors of nonmember states, life may be almost as strenuous. "The Commission is going to vote on the vegetable oil issue on March 5," said Thomas Enders when U.S. ambassador to the EC in early 1980. "Basically, two Frenchmen, two Italians and one Irishman are for it on a committee of thirteen. We needn't go after it too hard—if we do, we might get a solidarity reaction. I get hold of Washington, and we decide how to handle these things. Do I get hold of the Commission? Or of a few Commissioners? Do I work through a permanent rep? Or do I do a bilateral deal with a member state—you help us here, we'll help you there? We used to take a protective attitude toward the Commission, and defend it against the member states," he added ruminatively, "but now we're agnostic.

"When the President went for a grain embargo after Afghanistan, I went around—without instructions, but that didn't matter—the next day. I said to the Commission, Here's an opportunity for you. If you act, the ministers *can't* overturn you. The French bitched all over the place, but the Council of Ministers when it met had to ratify the Commission's actions. [The practical effect of all this activity, incidentally, seems not to have been very great: in March 1982, the European Parliament voted a rebuke to the Commission for having undercut the U.S. embargo by selling foodstuffs on concessionary terms to the Eastern bloc after formally agreeing not to increase food sales.] We have access to the Commission on every level; in an average week I'll see a Commissioner on one piece of business or another twenty times. Of course I pick up COREPER, because they ultimately are the only people who can handle the text. Another piece of the machinery is the European Parliament. It has very few powers, and therefore it doesn't have to broker interests and *therefore* tends to be more forward-looking and idealistic. I spend a lot of time lobbying the Parliament, because they can speak with an authentic European voice. I go to Strasbourg every month and I work the corridors, I hang around at the bar, I give dinner parties, grab people in their offices and off the floor.

"We've discovered that there are such things as relationships," Enders added. "Not just interests to be brokered—relationships. We found that out to our dismay in Argentina." A year later, Enders would be Assistant Secretary for American Republic Affairs, charged with buttering up the Argentine junta which had so profitably sabotaged the grain embargo he had sought to promote in Brussels; there is indeed some reason to believe that it was his intemperate sympathy while recruiting Argentines for the anti-Sandinist crusade that persuaded the generals the U.S. would be on their side in the South Atlantic. Such is the nature of a career in the Foreign Service.

Lots of countries have excellent reasons to keep a careful eye on the Community and seek to influence its actions. Since the early 1970s, there has been a continuing formal relationship between the Commission and the "ACP" nations (Atlantic, Caribbean, Pacific) that signed the Lomé Convention, a trade and development pact named for the capital city of

Togo, site of the conference that negotiated the treaty. Under the terms of the convention, certain goods manufactured within the ACP group are considered to have been produced within the Community and are thus exempted from tariffs, though they remain subject to import ceilings much lower than the ACP states would wish. Many of the countries involved were former colonies of EC members, and still have economies oriented toward the needs of the former mother country. The Commission has ambassadors in the form of "delegates" in 42 Lomé countries, all of which send their own ambassadors to Brussels.

Just about everybody has ambassadors in Brussels. Lots of countries have excellent reason to keep a careful eye on the Community and seek to influence its actions. At least until the Soviet decision to suppress incipient Polish democracy, Comecon (the Eastern-bloc economic union) made its plans on the basis of what the Community was going to do, and one of the bloc countries, Romania, even had a "Community Agreement" with the EC (like Yugoslavia, Austria, Finland, Iceland, Sweden and Norway). Then there are "association agreements," implying a degree of reciprocal obligation, with Algeria, Cyprus, Israel, Jordan, Lebanon, Malta, Morocco, Syria and Tunisia. The Brussels mission is important for the British Commonwealth nations whose trade patterns were considerably disrupted when Britain joined the Community—Canada, Australia and New Zealand, all beneficiaries of special exemptions from Common Market tariffs and quotas, but only within narrowing limits. The United States, thanks to feed grains and dividends from past investments, enjoys an immense positive balance on current account with the Community, competes fiercely around the world against Community exports, and has major financial (ca. $45 billion) and political stakes in the EC.

Making fun of the Community is a popular pastime for journalists and idealists. The annual arguments over the CAP and the relative shares of the Community's costs that should be borne by the different members have been unseemly, and the inability of the states to agree on a single location for the Parliament has been ludicrous. The bureaucracy is too large and overpaid, and its output is too small. Commissioners have been observed casually chartering jets at the Brussels airport, at Community expense, to fly them about Europe. There have been scandals associated with the two-tier Belgian exchange rate, which has enabled Eurocrats to increase their pay (in "international" francs, at a rate higher than the free-market rate) by fiddling in the currency markets. Among the periodicals prominently on display in the Commission *bibliothèque* is *High-Life Belgique*. Because the foundation of the enterprise is economic, there is an irreducible greedy grubbiness about what the governments say and do in their relations with the Community. "And with twelve different ministers coming into town eighty times a year," said Riberholt, "there's ample room for goofing."

"The EC is incredibly muscle-bound," said George Vest, a gentlemanly egghead of an FSO who was Assistant Secretary for Europe in the Carter State Department and became ambassador to the Community. "But a new habit of life has taken hold in European officialdom. When I was first in Europe in '58–59, ministers were in their own capitals shuffling paper and making decisions against their own national backgrounds. Now on major decisions—and less-than-major decisions—they think, I must pick up the phone and check up. They have the habit of thinking in group terms."

"In the larger perspective," Riberholt said, "I think that if the industrialized democratically governed countries are going to live up to the challenge of the next generation, either the ideological challenge from the Communist countries or the social-justice claim from developing countries, or the menace of blackmail by oil or other raw-material countries, cooperation more or less on the pattern you see here in Brussels *must* be developed. It will be a more painful process for countries like the United States and Japan than for the Europeans, who have already lived through the first infant steps."

4

Julian Walker is a compact Southerner with a neat dark mustache and a neat dark goatee, and he was smiling because he was finishing his two-year tour as the FSO responsible for the six-man staff in the State Department who put together the American delegations to some twelve hundred international meetings a year. Some of it, of course, had been fun:

"Larry Wales in ACDA [Arms Control and Disarmament Agency] has been special assistant for SSOD [the UN Special Session on Disarmament], and his secretary suggested we put Paul Newman on the delegation, because Newman has been very active in one of these disarmament groups. The idea was greeted with gales of laughter, but on looking into it . . . I thought, Well, Goddamn. We may be able to use him in the corridors up there. We fought hard to keep his name on. Every office that list went through, his name was taken off. But we kept him."

C. William Maynes, then Assistant Secretary for International Organizations, thought the 1978 SSOD was a big success from the beginning: "France," he said earnestly, "has joined the disarmament process for the first time. The French President addressed the Assembly. And this [Carter] Administration had real opportunities to build the constituency for disarmament—a constituency it will need in the SALT ratification process."

History has been unkind to these views. Paul Newman was indeed part of the U.S. delegation, and thus one of those assembled for briefing when Cyrus Vance came to announce that the President had decided he would *not* go to New York that afternoon to address the Session. This was something of a nuisance for Julian Walker, too, because he had to call the Waldorf-Astoria and cancel the two full floors of the hotel that had been reserved for the President and his entourage. French participation in the disarmament process turned out to be a smokescreen for a threefold expansion in French arms sales around the world (good for the balance of payments after the second oil shock of 1979). And the three years following SSOD saw the greatest expansion of arms budgets that the world has ever known, in the East-West blocs, in the poor Southern countries . . . everywhere. UN special sessions on disarmament seem unlucky: the second one, despite the boost of an immense nuclear freeze demonstration in its midst, was overshadowed to the point of invisibility by the Falklands and Lebanese wars. What happened to the SALT ratification process is well known.

American planning for an international meeting begins with the assignment of the problem to one of the six "program officers" in the International Conferences Office of the State Department's Bureau of International Organization Affairs. He gets the agenda and makes contact with the "substantive offices" at State that are concerned with its subject matter. They try to decide between them how large a delegation will be necessary, which involves clearing with a number of other substantive offices, much of the rest of the government, and indeed a chunk of "the private sector." For a shipping conference on standards of training for seamen and masters of ships, for example (nothing came of it), Walker found "we have to have a lot of union people. We have five groups from AFL-CIO. Then OES in the Department [Office of Oceans, Environment and Science] wanted in. So did the Environmental Protection Agency. But we felt they didn't have any business here. Before the delegation went, it had meetings with the Shipping Coordinating Committee, which is an intragovernmental agency, and they were briefed. And of course if the head of mission finds anything comes up that is beyond his authority, he gets in touch with the State Department and requests instructions."

The choice of individuals is complicated by the fact that the International Conferences Office is forbidden by law to keep personnel files. "The institutional memory," Walker said, finishing his two-year tour of duty, "is in my head. Of course, if people bomb, you call their sponsor." Conferences are also a way to make the Equal Employment Opportunities

Commission happy, beefing up the State Department's total roster of blacks and women and Hispanics and Amerindians or whatever.

When larger matters are afoot, the person chosen by the President to chair the delegation essentially decides how many people he needs and who they shall be. Arthur Goldberg accepted the job of representing the United States at the first Helsinki review meeting in Belgrade only after Carter gave him complete control of the delegation. On the other hand, some chiefs of mission are highly cooperative. "We've pared the Law of the Sea delegation considerably," Walker noted, "thanks to the savvy and muscle of Elliot Richardson. Last time it was more than a hundred people, and we've got it down to forty-odd—not counting the Hill. We never count the Hill. If they say they want to put a dozen people on a delegation, they put a dozen people on a delegation. They pay for it. But counting only Richardson and the *workers*, it's about forty people."

Logistically, of course, even forty people is a bunch, even in a conference center like Geneva, where this particular Law of the Sea meeting was held. "We had to rent office space in Geneva," Walker remembered. "And two minibuses to transport people. And hotel rooms." In general, the delegates tell the Department what they will need in terms of transportation and creature comforts. "Every once in a while a representative will write a letter to Santa Claus that we consider a bit long," Walker noted. "We may call and say, 'Are you *sure* you need that third pair of roller skates?' But usually they can have what they say they need."

Law of the Sea, the longest-running feature attraction in UN history, provided a special illustration of the process. The conference was called into existence by a resolution passed in December 1970 on the initiative of Malta. The high seas have always nurtured international discord, especially from the American point of view: if there is a single thread that runs through American diplomatic history, from the XYZ Affair through the *Alabama*, the *Maine*, the *Lusitania*, the destroyers-for-bases deal, the *Mayaguez*, it is the demand for freedom of the seas. The old three-mile limit, drawn to express the margin of safety from nautical bombardment by nineteenth-century guns, had become obsolete in an age of nuclear submarines and missilery, offshore oil drilling out to the edge of the continental shelf, factory ships that could deplete national fisheries for the benefit of foreigners. The conventions and declarations that guaranteed passage through the great canals and the narrow seas formed a crazy quilt.

Wrapping all of this into one compendious treaty—together with an international agreement on the conduct of mining the ocean floors, which are rich in certain relatively scarce minerals—presented a problem of quite spectacular difficulty. "Like four-dimensional chess," said Elliot Richardson, who served Carter as ambassador-at-large to this conference. A tall, elegant, slightly fleshy Bostonian, by no means so earnest as his manner, Richardson kept himself sane through the years of negotiation by drawing hundreds of thousands of beautiful owls with a blue felt-tip pen on yellow legal pads. In all, 158 nations were represented at the Geneva meeting of 1978, where the essential agreement was approached if not reached.

The first meeting on Law of the Sea, in Caracas in 1971, was perhaps the most disgraceful event in United Nations history. Venezuela had never been host to such an event before, and laid on too much in the line of booze, rich food, and women. Attendance at the meetings was sparse, because delegates had better things to do or were recovering from the better things they had done; no progress was made toward adjusting the dozens of texts of proposed treaty articles the different countries had brought with them; and the rules laid down for subsequent meetings were so poorly drawn that until 1981, when a formal meeting had to be assembled to award the site of the unfinished treaty's tribunal to West Germany and its secretariat to Jamaica, no plenary session of the conference was ever held.

Once Caracas was over, however, and the nations began looking seriously at their problems, common interests became visible across the usual bloc lines, and governments became interested in the idea of trading off political positions against possible economic or military gain. The Indonesians and Filipinos had special interests in archipelagic zones, the Americans and Russians (and to some extent the French and British) wanted to assure rights of passage for submarines and other warships, the United States on reconsideration could see merit in Ecuador's claim of a 200-mile "economic zone" in which nations could control fishing, drilling, etc.—provided that this zone continued to be "the high seas" on its surface. Austria, Hungary, Switzerland and Czechoslovakia found they had common interests with Afghanistan, Mongolia, Chad, Zambia, Uganda, Paraguay and Bolivia, among others, in the assertion of some benefits for the landlocked in the development of juridical rules for the use of the oceans. Canada, Zaire, Chile, Zambia, Cuba and Poland were concerned that certain minerals important to their economies might be so plentiful in the sea that their income from mining would be reduced. Clearly there was nothing to be gained by couching these interests in idealistic terms and making speeches in public forums.

Instead, the conference, meeting in annual six-week bursts (two of them in 1976), broke into "conference committees" in which informal discussions—all corridor and no meeting—were to produce "negotiating texts" certified by the committee chairmen as representing the preponderant opinion of the participants, leaving only highlighted sections for subsequent negotiation. The path to possible agreement was greatly smoothed when Henry Kissinger, speaking in the context of a separate "North-South" conference and representing the only nation that then had the technology fully developed for deep seabed mining, conceded that what lay on the ocean floors was "the common heritage of mankind," and that the United States was prepared to cooperate in the development of an entity that would split the proceeds of exploiting that heritage with the poor and landlocked nations.

These informal worldwide discussions became, rather surprisingly, a device for reconciling long-standing disputes between nations—among, for example, Indonesia, Singapore and Malaysia on the status of the Malacca Strait, between the Soviet Union and Turkey on the status of the Bosphorus and Dardanelles, the United States and Ecuador on the tuna fisheries. There was general agreement on the necessary rules for limiting pollution of the seas from vessels (especially oil tankers). What kept going off the rails completely was the seabed mining issue, which united the LDCs in an insistence that *all* the common heritage of mankind should be theirs under the terms of the fatuous New International Economic Order the UN General Assembly had proclaimed, King Canute *redivivus*, in 1974. The Cameroonian chairman of Conference Committee I foolishly took it upon himself to tamper with the agreed-upon composite negotiating text between the end of a session and the publication of its results, inserting language the United States had specifically rejected in the informal consultations. (Some participants believe he was mousetrapped by a member of the U.S. delegation who had a hidden agenda.)

This situation was quite brilliantly remedied by breaking out a "working group" under the direction of Tommy Koh, a youthful former dean of Singapore Law School. The most surprising success story among the LDCs (for the island has no resources other than the enterprise of its mostly Chinese polyglot population), Singapore was a member in almost good standing in the Group of 77, the omnium-gatherum of the LDCs, but economically oriented toward the West and capitalism. No nation had a greater stake in the conclusion of an enforceable Law of the Sea treaty, which would put behind Singapore forever the menace of conflict with Indonesia over the straits that are the city's reason for being. Singapore Prime Minister Lee Kuan Yew, a London School of Economics alumnus, needed no education in the significance of the treaty, and having co-opted Koh years before from the leadership of student dissenters at the University he was happy to give his representative all the running room he wanted.

A man of casual manners and obvious brilliance, Koh was able to get on with all the participants in the dispute, to understand that the Soviet Union would be happy to abandon socialist principle in return for some reserved territory for its own seabed mining ventures, and to play on the U.S. Defense Department desires for conclusion of a deal that had been built deeply into American strategic planning. In summer 1979, single-handedly, he hammered out a revised "negotiating text" that survived the next year's haggling and was about to be locked into treaty form in spring 1981 when the Reagan administration aborted the negotiations on ideological grounds.

The Law of the Sea negotiations under Carter were not simply a State Department responsibility. Richardson's office was at State, and his vice-chairmen were drawn from the State Department Legal Adviser's staff, but he also chaired an Interagency Group which was part of the National Security Council. Among the forty-five people he took with him to Geneva in 1978 were representatives from the Defense Department, the Joint Chiefs of Staff, the Transportation Department, Treasury, Commerce, Interior, the Environmental Protection Agency, the Council on Environmental Quality and the Geological Survey. It might well have been that if the treaty had been completed before Carter left office, the American delegation could not have got everybody in the government to sign off (the Economics Bureau of the State Department was deeply suspicious of several clauses). The issue on which Koh's efforts finally foundered, at a last meeting in spring 1982—when the LDC voting majority passed its treaty despite opposition from the United States and abstention from the Soviet Union—was one that would have doomed them in any administration: the insistence by the Third World that after twenty years the treaty could be amended without the consent of many of the contracting parties, by the one-state, one-vote procedures of the General Assembly.

But this may have been one of those rare situations where process really is more important than product. "Even if this document never comes into effect," said Elliot Richardson, "it will have an influence on the customary behavior of nations. There is no longer much debate about the two-hundred-mile economic zone, or the twelve miles of territorial waters, or the concept of archipelagic zones. One hundred and fifty-eight countries have to a remarkable degree succeeded in hammering out agreement on the majority of the issues presented in 1970." Expensively, unimpressively, on occasion discreditably, the UN process nevertheless worked.

Very few of the UN's special efforts show such results—or any results. Giant meetings on the environment, housing, the status of women, world hunger, etc., have produced bad papers, dishonest rhetoric, drunken delegates, overpaid secretariats, boredom beyond the capacity of any but veterans of these engagements to sustain. In solemn conclave, the Assembly votes Development Decades, Disarmament Decades, Decades for Action to Combat Racism, Decades for Women, Years of the Child, of the

Handicapped and so forth, and what follows are public-relations campaigns that serve no purpose other than the glorification of the participants.

The list of institutions created to meet demands for economic development drags on and on: the International Bank for Reconstruction and Development (World Bank), which preceded the organization of the United Nations and does important work; UNDP (United Nations Development Program); UNIDO (United Nations Industrial Development Organization); UNCTAD (United Nations Conference on Trade and Development); CIEC (Conference on International Economic Cooperation, locus of the famous "North-South dialogue"), IFAD (International Fund for Agricultural Development). Except for the World Bank, where voting is weighted according to each nation's contributions to the funds, all these institutions have become captives of the Less Developed Countries under the General Assembly's one-state, one-vote rule, and have placed politics far ahead of accomplishment.

Some of the specialized agencies associated with the United Nations go back well before its formation. The International Court of Justice, which hears a case roughly every five years but keeps a large staff ready for unlimited business in its grandiose Peace Palace in The Hague, was founded before World War I under a slightly different name. The Universal Postal Union, which makes it possible for people to send letters anywhere, using the stamps of their own country, dates to 1875; the International Telecommunication Union was launched by Napoleon III ten years before that. The International Labor Organization, which so effectively sees to it that workers everywhere are well treated in wholesome surroundings, their rights protected by unions of their choice, was a jewel in the diadem of the League of Nations.

What is probably the most effective and what is certainly the most wasteful of the major international organizations were both founded while World War II was still in progress: the International Monetary Fund and the Food and Agricultural Organization. IMF, based in Washington, was started as a bank to help maintain currency values and to ease the pains of transition when currencies had to be devalued (or revalued upward) to remedy fundamental economic imbalances. It occupies one of the earliest atrium buildings, three blocks from the White House; a rather pleasant restaurant for executives only (but most male employees qualify) overlooks the splendidly architected inner space. Six-figure salaries tax-free to those who are not Americans are paid to bankers and economists from the entire non-Communist world (plus Romania, which has been a member from the beginning; and Hungary, which joined in 1982; and Cuba, Vietnam, Afghanistan and China, which inherited membership from non-

Communist predecessors). Staff has the exclusive use of a private country club outside Washington.

Thanks partly to the absence of the Soviet Union and partly to a system of weighted country voting which maintains the veto power of the suppliers of the funds (a system which is the main target of the South in the North-South dialogue), the IMF has operated on predictable economic principles, with the result that it is the only world body that gives orders that are actually obeyed. In India, indeed, the left has been critical of Indira Gandhi's decision to seek financing for oil exploration from the IMF rather than from private banks, because private banks cannot order the government around, and IMF can. In recent years, with the adoption of floating-rate exchange systems, the original raison d'être of the IMF has pretty much disappeared, but it has become far more important in the real world, because its decision to give or deny a loan triggers or stops lending by private banks to the country involved. Only the IMF could have put together the package that in fall 1982 rescued the banks and the Latin American states (temporarily) from the horrifying consequences of their excessive lending and borrowing in overvalued dollars.

FAO came into existence at Hot Springs, Virginia, in spring 1943 because Franklin Roosevelt "regarded food and agriculture as perhaps man's most fundamental concern and a good place to begin postwar planning." Established without any clear purpose, the organization has never found one; its huge building in Rome and its continually rising budgets (just under $400 million in 1982) are a monument to the self-perpetuation and self-aggrandizement of international bureaucracy. Looking to say something to Ronald Reagan that he would enjoy hearing, the leaders of the Third World at the North-South Conference in Cancun, Mexico, in fall 1981 complained about how bloody useless FAO was.

When something of significance is to be done in the food area internationally—like the establishment of reserve stocks in the World Food Program, or the promotion of Third World agricultural production by IFAD —the contributors are careful to make sure that control of the funds is not lodged in FAO. A director resigned in 1976 with a blast at his own organization, where, he said, "Eighty per cent of [the] budget is destined to pay for a gigantic centralized bureaucracy in Rome, 11 per cent to put out publications that no one reads, and the remaining 9 per cent to holding meetings and for travel expenses that are largely unnecessary." An idealistic Carter administration Commission on World Hunger submitted a forty-thousand-word report on that subject without even mentioning FAO: nobody could find a good word to say for it, and under Carter it was bad form to say anything mean about any part of the UN.

We have still not scratched the surface of the organizations that throw out fat and sickly tendrils under the UN umbrella. There is WIPO, the World Intellectual Property Organization, owner of the biggest office building in Geneva, where people talk about copyrights and patents. UNITAR, the Institute for Training and Research, does some desultory seminars for people coming to work at UN organizations and publishes third-rate papers on The Future. The International Atomic Energy Agency from a base in the billion-dollar skyscrapers the Austrian Government built in suburban Vienna gives a modicum of assistance to countries acquiring nuclear generating facilities and ineffectively polices their agreement that radioactive materials will not be diverted to the construction of weapons. Alone among the UN agencies, IAEA in 1982 yielded to Arab pressure and expelled Israel, provoking the United States to "suspend its participation."

UNESCO, a very large organization with a luxurious base near the Invalides in Paris, has organized certain cultural manifestations like the rescue of Abu Simbel from the depths of Lake Nasser, and has played a marginal role in the sustenance of folklore; but as an instrument for the promotion or study of education, society or culture it has been an essentially negative force with a mission to validate bureaucratic control of intellectual and spiritual activities. Even when enlivened by the entertainment of stoning the Jews, whose excessive influence in matters of education, society and culture was well known even before Hitler, the biennial UNESCO conferences are notorious for their dullness: "There is no way," said Julian Walker, "that you can get a first-class person to agree to attend the whole thing."

Among the saddest sights of the postwar era was the presence of one of the great men of English social thought—Richard Hoggart, author of *The Uses of Literacy*—as Deputy Director General of this monstrous fraud. Doggedly, he stuck out a second term, apologizing for his colleagues who he was sure meant well, and went home defeated. Since the mid-1970s, the centerpiece of UNESCO meetings has been an effort by the Soviet bloc, supported by the petty tyrants of the Third World, to legitimize government control of information not only within a nation's own borders but internationally. In late 1982, in the opening address of a special conference to plan UNESCO's future, Director General Amadou-Mahtar M'Bow officially gave up its ghost, proclaiming that in a world "enmeshed in a tight and dense network of flows of all kinds" UNESCO would have to place political and economic issues at the head of its agenda.

The humanitarian agencies are more efficient, partly because their function is better defined, partly because they contract out much of their work rather than building permanent bureaucracies. Based in Geneva, the World Health Organization permits its field offices to solve their own problems. (A recent, neatly illustrative story tells of the WHO mission to Nepal, where goiter is endemic because of the very low iodine content of the mountain soils. Because iodine is absorbed through the skin and need not be swallowed, the WHO team was able to go to the witch doctors with supplies of iodine and encourage them to treat patients by swabbing the stuff directly onto the goiter, an activity for which no great training was required. The witch doctors were delighted to have a cure that worked, the patients were pleased to be cured and relieved that they did not have to do business with Western devils, and the WHO team accomplished its mission.)

As a result of work paid for and supervised by WHO, smallpox has virtually disappeared, the incidence of malaria is much reduced, some forms of schistosomiasis are curable, the geographic spread of sleeping sickness is down, bulk purchasing of standard drugs has reduced their cost to countries that could not otherwise afford medications, and almost every poor country can boast a considerable improvement in average longevity. Whether this increased longevity is really a boon to these countries is a more interesting question than most people will be prepared to admit (the Princeton geographer-sociologist Marion Levy has pointed out that if average life span in China reached that of the United States, "we shall see a day in which if senile Chinese are wheeled four abreast past a given point, their procession will never end"). This, not birth rates, is the source of the population explosion in the Third World: Everyone would have been much better off if the triumph of public health had followed rather than preceded a triumph of planned parenthood. Still, the increase in longevity was WHO's mission, and to a remarkable degree it has been accomplished.

Nobody is likely to find heavy fault with UNICEF (the Children's Emergency Fund), either, or with UNHCR (High Commissioner for Refugees, twice winner of the Nobel peace prize). This admiration may in fact be misplaced: an argument can be made for the proposition that UNHCR is one of the disastrous errors of our time. Europe after the war and again after the loss of the colonies was deluged with refugees; they were absorbed—not easily, but the thing was done—simply because there was no alternative. When the horrible population transfers between India and Pakistan had been completed after the greatest bloodletting of any six-month period in history, the survivors were set on the path of becoming citizens of the place where they found themselves. The North Korean POWs who refused to go home in 1954, the Hungarians who fled the Russian troops in 1956, the Cubans escaping Castro in 1960, the Asians chased from East Africa and the French fleeing Algeria—all these if they survived found homes, and jobs, and lives for themselves and their children. A million unwanted Indian migrants to Ceylon (now Sri Lanka), whom the Ceylonese Government wished to deport, were in part accepted and in part repatriated by agreement of the two governments after sixteen years of negotiations—largely because UNHCR was not involved. But the refugees who fell into the hands of HCR—the Palestinians, Cypriot Greeks, Rwandans, Vietnamese, Cambodians, Congolese, Ethiopians, Chadians, Afghans, Eritreans, Nicaraguan Indians—became separated and miserable societies with irredentist and revanchist ambitions, generation after generation being born and growing up buried in the misery of the UN camps.

5

In a sense, UNHCR is a paradigm for UN activities in general: the UN is a place where people and disputes are parked pending the discovery of something to be done with them. (Procedurally, there is no way to get an item off the agenda of the Security Council: even after a resolution has been passed, the item remains on the agenda.) This is not an ignoble or unnecessary mission; and it does diminish the incidence of violence in the world and the risk of war. When the heat is sufficiently high under the pot, the UN presents a way to concentrate it to some purpose.

Dean Rusk observes that "the UN earned its keep for the rest of this century in the Cuban missile crisis." He would agree with Hernane Tavares de Sá, the former UN public relations chief who wrote a highly negative book about the place, that the Russian ships en route to Cuba "were diverted because the Secretary-General of the United Nations [U Thant] had asked comrade Premier Khrushchev to consider the interests of world peace—not the threat of U.S. destroyers. Of course, the UN provided only a face-saving device, but this should not be lightly dismissed." At this writing, UN peace-keeping forces are stationed in Palestine, Lebanon, Cyprus and Kashmir. (The director of these operations, Under-Secretary-General Brian Urquhart, sends them forth with the injunction that they consider themselves not soldiers but supervisors in an insane asylum.) Though UN machinery has proved useful in only a small fraction of the world's bloody disputes, the availability of the Security Council as a body to which appeals can be taken has provided in important cases an opportunity for the warriors to reconsider.

At its foundation, the UN was to be the instrument by which a three-power consort of Britain, the Soviet Union and the United States would police the world. Together with France and China, the former as colonial power and the latter as future force, they would be "permanent members" of the Security Council, with power to veto any actions against the interests of any state. The Soviet Union initially demanded that permanent members have the right to veto the discussion of any matter in the Security Council, but Truman sent Harry Hopkins to Stalin to get the demand withdrawn; Secretary of State Edward Stettinius, perhaps unwisely, called Andrei Gromyko at his San Francisco hotel suite—both men were there for the final negotiating sessions on the composition of the UN Charter—to let him know his government's position had changed.

In addition, there would be a General Assembly of states to meet at least once a year, where all the member nations would have one vote regardless of their size. The Russians, in one of the most extraordinary moments of modern diplomatic history, demanded and got three votes—one for the Soviet Union itself, one for the Ukraine and one for Byelorussia, internal Soviet "republics"—on the grounds that Britain would control votes from the Commonwealth countries. Among the things the revisionist historians of the Cold War conveniently forget is that Stalin in the immediate postwar period considered that his most dangerous enemy was Britain under the leadership of Winston Churchill, a foe from the early days of Bolshevism, opponent of the Russians' then immediate ambitions in the Mediterranean, during the war the advocate of a second-front policy that would have sent Anglo-American forces crashing through the Balkans in the Russian sphere of influence rather than into France.

The General Assembly would elect a Secretary-General on nomination from the Security Council, and choose what are now ten nonpermanent (two-year term) members of the Security Council. It would approve a budget, and accept or reject membership applications previously approved by the Security Council—and, as the world turned, accept or reject the credentials of delegates claiming to represent member nations. Otherwise, it would have no significant functions. The foreign ministers of the member states arrive with pomp and pageantry each September for the opening "plenary," ostensibly to tell the Assembly what they said last year but really to socialize with their peers. (Half the top echelon of the State Department moves to New York for two weeks, marching behind the banner of the Secretary, to make sure every visiting panjandrum is properly feted.) Nothing is ever accomplished as the result of these speeches. Walter Lippmann noted a quarter of a century ago that "the General Assembly is a place where nobody can afford to stand up in public and be reasonable."

Nevertheless, as the annual sessions drone on, the representatives can talk, and thus vote, about anything. It quickly became convenient for the great powers to slough off to the Assembly certain issues relating to the old League of Nations "mandates" (now become UN "trusteeships") and eventually the fate of the colonies of the European powers. Thus it was the Assembly, not the Security Council, that voted the partition of Palestine, denied statehood to Eritrea, conducted the referendum that divided former British Cameroon between Nigeria and French Cameroun. And it is the Assembly that annually hears denunciations of the continuing American "occupation" of Puerto Rico and the Virgin Islands, and bars the participation of South Africa from its debates (the only sanction available to the Assembly) for its refusal to concede self-government to Namibia (the former mandate of South-West Africa).

The function of the Secretary-General was left unclear. Politically, he would have the right to participate without vote in the meetings of the Security Council (where the chair would rotate monthly among the members in alphabetical order), and under Article 99 to summon a meeting of the Council and lay matters before it if no member state had done so. He could also express his views of the state of the world and any part of it in an annual report to the General Assembly, and he could make his good offices available to disputants on their request. And he was, of course, the chief executive officer of the Secretariat.

In thirty-five years there have been only five secretaries-general: Trygve Lie of Norway, Dag Hammarskjöld of Sweden, U Thant of Burma, Kurt Waldheim of Austria and Javier Pérez de Cuéllar of Peru. All have been professional diplomats; it is not unfair to say that none was a man who had ever shown the slightest sign of administrative let alone managerial talent. When Pérez de Cuéllar was chosen in late 1981, a very senior member of the Secretariat, while celebrating the departure of the universally loathed Waldheim—an unprincipled trimmer who made his associates' lives a special hell late each fall when he was on pins and needles about his upcoming Nobel peace prize and early each winter when he was in a state of fury about not getting it—nevertheless observed that Pérez de Cuéllar had been an Under-Secretary-General for four years some time back, and nobody could remember anything he had done. It is perhaps not unfair to say that he lived up to this advertisement in 1982 in the Falklands and Lebanese crises.

Starting in 1948, the Secretariat was also charged with organizing programs to distribute money for "technical assistance" and development programs, with the fund actually to be spent, however, at the discretion of the recipient governments (the UN must never ever interfere in the internal affairs of its member states). This approach to the economic problems of the poor countries clearly implied greatly expanded staffs, with very poorly defined duties. In theory, all employees of the Secretariat were to be international civil servants owing a first obligation to the United Nations rather than to their home countries, traveling on UN passports, paying taxes to the UN itself rather than to their home governments, in no way subject to dictation from home. In fact, the UN hired from the start on the recommendations of member governments (U Thant once said proudly that he had *never* rejected a candidate recommended by a member state). Americans, of course, could walk in off the street; in 1949, Byron Price as administrative chief for Trygve Lie, at the suggestion of his boss, went to the FBI to request assistance in clearing Americans seeking jobs at the UN.

At best, the idea of an international civil service is probably a mistake: there being no cohort of people (as against states) to whom such a body is responsible, it quickly becomes self-serving with a purity outsiders cannot imagine. (I first ran into this phenomenon of multilateralism when I was involved with the International School of Geneva, where the teachers had a coffee break in midmorning. A fight broke out one morning on the grounds, and it proved impossible to get anyone out of the teachers' lounge to stop it: this was their coffee break, dammit, and that was more important than what might be happening to the children.) When jobs are filled entirely for political reasons, no measurable output is expected, and the management has no interest in managing—well, the results must be experienced to be believed.

"It may be said conclusively that there is no system whatsoever of reward for merit within the service of the United Nations," the novelist Shirley Hazzard, who had worked there, wrote in 1973. "Let a staff member demonstrate what abilities he will, these will receive no official recognition, and may even hinder his prospects by making him appear suspiciously singular." Ms. Hazzard remembered that "the section in which I worked for two years was visited only once or twice by its section chief, who had his office on another floor," and recalled, too, a farewell party for the retirement of an Under-Secretary "whose staff . . . were moved to murmur, 'So that's who he is. . . .' "

Moynihan points up the results from a historian's and political scientist's viewpoint. For him, the UN Secretariat inherits "the organizational spirit" of the League of Nations, a "spirit of a civil service as an elite class." But "the League Secretariat had two decisive characteristics. First, it was small—tiny, in fact . . . [and] it was loyal to the system, but otherwise neutral. But now, with respect to both size and neutrality, the United Nations had become profoundly corrupt. Envision the British Home Office of 1900 enlarged five hundredfold, teeming with the incompetent appointees of decadent peers and corrupt borough councillors, infiltrated and near to immobilized by agents of the Black Hand, Sinn Fein, and the Rosicrucians (some falsely representing themselves as devotees of Madame Blavatsky). That approximates the United Nations Secretariat three quarters of a century later."

303

With the budget in the hands of a General Assembly operated on a one-nation, one-vote principle, the Secretariat necessarily became the servant of the Third World bloc—the Group of 77, so-called, now expanded to more than 100. There was constant pressure from these countries for jobs for their nationals, and for reports that would buttress their positions. All but a handful of these countries are one-party states with a government-controlled press, where the leaders for whom the representatives speak at the UN are sustained in office by their power to jail or kill those who disagree with them. With rare exceptions, UN official reports became political documents, in which truth was a far less significant standard than compatibility with governmental professions.

In 1981 even the World Bank got caught out, publishing a ludicrously optimistic assessment of the Romanian economy just before Romania went bust, because the Romanian Government had insisted that only the figures it supplied could be published in an official international document. China, Chile, Tanzania, Cuba, Poland—all these have at one time or another been forced by circumstance to admit that the figures on their economies that the UN had published at their insistence were in fact false and known to be false. Garret Hardin's Environmental Fund has convincingly demonstrated that the population figures annually presented by the United Nations are in large part fabrications. U.S. Department of Agriculture figures on crop production are used worldwide in preference to FAO figures; UNESCO figures about the proportions of populations in school are notoriously overstated.

Concluding a UN-sponsored study on the future of the world economy, and seeking to develop "scenarios consistent with the spirit of the International Development Strategy and the aims of the Declaration on the Establishment of a New International Economic Order," the independent economist Wassily Leontief was finally constrained to warn that "some parts of the data base may prove to be relatively unreliable." You bet: absolutely unreliable, too. The fact is that except for WHO data, which are protected by the professionalism of a staff which is *not* permanently hired by the organization but serves limited tours, people doing serious nonpolitical work avoid UN data. And it was at WHO, of course, that the worst scandal of the UN information system erupted, when the plenary on the instruction of the governments angrily voted to reject a report from the staff that there was no scandal in the Israeli-administered health services on the West Bank. How *dare* the public health doctors who made that study place a UN institution in the position of supporting a nonpolitical truth?

Recalling the General Assembly session of 1975, Moynihan singled out from its concluding moments the annual report of the Decolonization

Committee, "wherein, *inter alia*, United States military forces on the Virgin Islands were described as a threat to the peace of the region. I went to the rostrum and explained that said forces consisted of fourteen Coast Guardsmen, one shotgun, one pistol, and an 82-foot vessel used for emergency rescue assistance. . . . The Committee's report was 'riddled with untruths' . . . [Salim Ahmed] Salim, chairman of the committee, seemed hurt that I felt his report was filled with lies. It was not clear whether he didn't believe they were lies, or whether he didn't believe that mere lies should come between friends."

Six years later, Salim, the delegate from Tanzania, put himself forward as a candidate for Secretary-General, and was vetoed by the United States. The press thought it was because he had once indulged in a somewhat unseemly dance on the floor of the General Assembly to celebrate the vote that shifted the proprietorship of the Chinese seat from Taiwan to China. Salim visited with USUN representative Jeane Kirkpatrick, who is reliably reported to have urged Washington to relent, such a charming young man and able, he understands that as Secretary-General he would have to be neutral on the great issues. Nobody appears to have considered it a disability that he was chairman of a committee that reported back dishonestly on the American role in the Virgin Islands.

The fact is that the UN lives in a politicized fairyland and limits its contacts with anything other than the unreal world of reified nation-states and their relations. At the height of the Vietnam War, I had occasion to ask an acquaintance, an Indian gentleman who also wrote novels, precisely what it was he *did* at the United Nations Development Program, of which he was an officer. He was planning, he said, the economic development of the Mekong Valley, dams and canal locks and highways and such. Wasn't there a lot of fighting going on in the Mekong Valley, I inquired. He was annoyed: that was not his concern; he was charged with economic development. We never talked of such matters again.

The issues that arise in the various committees of the whole are couched in the jargon of political dispute; the alliances on voting matters are formed without reference to the subject at issue. Everyone is a warrior for the working day, and except for the Arabs vis-à-vis the Israelis and some Eastern-bloc politicians who believe it redounds to their credit at home to maintain a dour disapproval of Western-bloc personalities at all times, after-school socialization is independent of the schoolhouse fights, however vitriolic the language the representative has been instructed to use. "It's an unreal world," said Frank Corner, Permanent Undersecretary of the New Zealand Foreign Ministry, who served six years in New York, "so you have to keep a moderately firm hand on it from headquarters. Whoever the ambassador is, he can be influenced by the forces there, which may not be the real forces in the world."

Hernane Tavares de Sá described the social aspect of General Assembly life: "New York waits outside, cold, impersonal, and throbbing with synthetic excitement. The newly arrived UN diplomat plunges thirstily into it at first, but after a few weeks he comes up for air, saturated with the dubious pleasures of the big city after dark. He then reaches out with relief and even a certain sense of anticipation for the conviviality of his colleagues, the clannish gatherings, the shoptalk of a working day stretching endlessly into the night. . . . He begins to feel secure and contented in this inner environment, somehow protected against the metropolis outside, which he has found to be aloof if not condescending. He begins to hanker for the tepid domesticity of his little UN world, and to think of most of his colleagues as his pals."

Within the UN complex on the East River, moreover, the UN representative is important, a grand seigneur with the fate of the world in his hand. The representatives read from press releases about what happened yesterday in the Third Committee, which are printed by no newspaper anywhere in the world; they admire the TV shows put together for the UN and hurled into a void by Visnews, a private, mostly English news agency which is paid for the service. Videotapes of Assembly meetings are available to the delegations for the cost of the raw tape, and informal dinner invitations to the home of Jamil Baroody, the Saudi permanent representative for thirty years, were among the most dreaded pieces of mail a UN delegate could receive, because Baroody's idea of entertainment for his guests was to show them the tapes of his speeches.

There is also a benefit to this insularity and clubbishness, which, Tavares de Sá writes, "carried with it some curious political overtones. . . . The best professionals among the delegates swiftly acquire a capacity for reading each other's minds, which cannot be developed by serving even in the world's key political capitals. The unique 'UN togetherness' develops a political sixth sense in gifted diplomats. Sometimes an impending shift in policy by an important country will be sniffed out at the UN while it is still under tight security restrictions." The UN, then, is a prime place for political information-gathering. For the Third World—indeed, for smaller countries not in the Third World—the UN becomes the place where diplomatic relations are conducted with all those others, avoiding the choice between costly representation in 150 national capitals and the feeling that one has no contact with other countries that may have similar problems. "We don't have an embassy in Africa," said Frank Corner. "Our contact with the Third World is through the UN. For a country of three million seeking to protect its interests in the world, the UN is very important."

Basically, of course, the small countries find the UN an attractive environment because by uniting they can control it. Lacking economic or military muscle even when united, they seek to politicize as many of the world's concerns as they can in order to use the instrument of the General Assembly. Everybody scratches everybody else's back in the standard logrolling procedure of legislatures—the Prime Minister of Grenada, for example, was a UFO freak, and to reward that infinitesimal country for its willingness to back the Arabs in the Middle East and the Africans in Namibia and the Chinese against Taiwan the Group of 77 pushed through a UN inquiry into flying objects. And in the end, of course, the economic, demographic, sociocultural forces that really make things happen simply steamroller all that political decision-making, leaving the UN General Assembly a comic spectacle, an empty shell within which reverberate the loud voices of beggars pretending to be horsemen.

6

The United Nations was essentially an invention of the United States, and American participation from the beginning has been wholehearted, expressing what was an all but universal American guilt at the nation's failure to join the League of Nations. Masochistically, most Americans saw World War II as a consequence of that failure. Thus Roosevelt insisted that even before there was a peace treaty there should be an international organization to enforce the peace, and the Charter of the United Nations was written and ratified while the war against Japan was in progress. Partly as an expression of the importance the United States would attach to the new organization—and partly because Harry Truman wanted to appoint James F. Byrnes as Secretary of State—the first U.S. representative at the United Nations was Edward R. Stettinius, Jr., who had to resign as Secretary to take the post, following Truman's assurance that it would be "the biggest job in the world today for an American outside the United States," a superbly ambiguous phrase. (It is amusing to note that the Soviet candidate for temporary Secretary-General to fill in between the signing of the Charter and the first meeting of the General Assembly was Alger Hiss; Andrei Gromyko said "he had a very high regard for Alger Hiss, particularly for his fairness and his impartiality.")

From the beginning, the UN was to be the center of American international relations. Control of atomic weaponry and peaceful uses of nuclear energy were laid on the table at the United Nations less than a year after the bomb was dropped on Hiroshima. The first wholly public expression of the Cold War (some weeks before Winston Churchill's "Iron Curtain" speech) was a visit by Secretary Byrnes to a meeting of the Security Council in New York, where he presented personally the U.S. complaint against the Soviet Union for its failure to remove its troops from northern Iran and its insistence on sustaining a Communist regional government in the area.

Reliance on the UN as an instrument of containment seemed justified when the Russians carelessly boycotted the Security Council in 1950 (in protest against Chiang Kai-shek's continued occupancy of the China seat), opening the way for a UN rather than merely U.S. military effort to beat back the North Korean attack on South Korea. Hoping to keep the armed forces in Korea under a UN flag after the Soviet Union had returned to the Council and begun exercising its veto, Secretary of State Acheson in fall 1950 proposed the "Uniting for Peace" resolution under which the General Assembly could take over from a Security Council paralyzed by a veto the power to authorize and maintain military units.

"Some time earlier," Acheson wrote in recollection, "we had asked the British Foreign Office its views on a proposal to turn to the General Assembly in case of aggression. . . . The response was a cool one. The Foreign Office wisely forecast the dangers of the idea in the future if the then majority in the United Nations should give way to one holding contrary views. But present difficulties outweighed future ones," Acheson added rather breezily, "and we pressed on."

Coupled with the power of the Secretary-General to bring issues to the Security Council (which was exercised almost exclusively, and heavily, by Dag Hammarskjöld), the Uniting for Peace procedure put UN forces into the Gaza Strip and the Sinai in 1957–67, and disastrously into the Congo. (In June 1964, U Thant reported to the Security Council on what the UN had learned in the Congo: "that the Congolese, in education, training and experience, and even in their understanding of the concept of nationhood, were unprepared to assume the responsibilities of independence." It is impossible to imagine a Secretary-General making such a statement today.) Though the Assembly, no longer dominated by the United States, has finally accepted the fact that "peace-keeping forces" can be effectively employed only if the Great Powers withhold their veto, the Uniting for Peace procedures survive as a way for the Third World to scream futile outrage at some action of a Great Power—at the United States for its support of Israel, at the Soviet Union for its invasion of Afghanistan.

Under Eisenhower, American insistence on the centrality of the United Nations achieved an extraordinary institutional expression. Needing a major post for Henry Cabot Lodge, who had been instrumental in winning him the nomination, Eisenhower made the job of U.S. representative a cabinet office, and put through an act that placed the representative under instruction *from* the President and only *through* the Secretary of State.

Robert Murphy remembered an episode from the Korean War days when Secretary of State John Foster Dulles instructed Lodge to cast a Yes vote on a resolution, and learned in the newspapers the next day that Lodge had voted No. "As soon as I could talk to him by long distance telephone," Murphy wrote, "I said, 'Apparently our instructions failed to reach you.' Lodge repeated, 'Instructions? I am not bound by instructions from the State Department. I am a member of the President's cabinet and accept instructions only from him.' . . . I protested, 'But you also are head of an embassy, and our ambassadors accept instructions from the Secretary of State.' After a moment's pause, Lodge replied, 'I take note of the Department's opinion.' "

Years later, Donald McHenry did something roughly equivalent, failing to highlight for the President some phrases in a resolution on Israel that would drive the Israelis straight up the wall, and—receiving no instructions to the contrary—voting for it. Secretary of State Vance gallantly stepped in and took the blame himself. "I couldn't let anybody *touch* McHenry," he said soon thereafter, "not even the President. Otherwise, they get your people."

This strange system for conducting U.S. representation at the UN reached apotheosis when Adlai Stevenson became Kennedy's representative—and blew up when Kennedy kept Stevenson in the dark about the Bay of Pigs, sending him to the Security Council table to lie for his country in the belief he was telling the truth. The personal affection felt for Stevenson at the UN made possible his continuance in the post ("Why do you send this man here?" asked Chief Adebo, the superbly impressive trade-union leader who then represented Nigeria at the UN. "He is too good for this job")—but the episode left him open to personal ridicule of the most painful kind eighteen months later when he had to present to the Security Council the evidence of Russian missile installations in Cuba.

Stevenson's presence had made the representative's post so prominent, however, that upon his death Lyndon Johnson was able to persuade Arthur Goldberg to leave the Supreme Court for it (which, contrary to Johnson's memoirs, he very much did not wish to do). Goldberg was not liked at the UN—there may never have been a social group that actually *liked* this amazingly vain man—but his unusual negotiating skills, coupled with the belief that he really had the ear of the President, made him probably the most effective representative the United States ever sent to the Security Council. It was Arthur Goldberg, serving by alphabetical accident as President of the Council in his first days on the job, who found the formula that brought a cease-fire to the warring Indian subcontinent—and Goldberg who preserved the institution itself by working out with the Soviets a deal to permit nations that did not wish to contribute to the cost of peace-keeping operations to retain their seat and their vote in the Assembly.

By then, however, American influence on the United Nations had been much diminished, and from the U.S. point of view the General Assembly had become what Moynihan would call "a dangerous place." Ever subtle, Moynihan did not blame the Soviet Union or Karl Marx; rather, he saw the source in the London School of Economics and Harold Laski. Colonialist guilt and a theory of socialism quite inapplicable to the real problems of underdevelopment created an atmosphere in which the new majority at the UN automatically blamed the West for their problems and expected as a matter of right an ever-increasing flow of charity from the industrial nations. Rattling doorknobs as always, the Soviet Union made their cause its own, producing in the voting patterns of the General Assembly an increasing (but by no means invariable) alignment of the nonaligned with the Russian position.

Into this cauldron in 1973 the OPEC nations poured the magic fire of the oil crisis. With a whoop of *Schadenfreude* as short-sighted as it was self-destructive, the Less Developed Countries imagined a world in which they as raw-materials sources would hold the whip hand, and invented the fantasy of the New International Economic Order. The lines hardened between the nonaligned and the United States—which still took the UN and its resolutions seriously, unlike the Europeans, who were prepared to play along with any game that remained a game.

7

What happened to the United States in the United Nations in the 1970s was foreordained. The American position in the institution had rested on a tripod of moral authority (the name "Roosevelt," the belief in self-determination), economic muscle and military predominance.

The moral authority began to erode almost instantly (the name "Truman," the need to placate the Latin Americans by pushing for the admission to the UN of Perón's Argentina). Then a choice had to be made between the self-confidence of a demoralized France and the desire of its colonies to assert an independent nationhood, and the French won the battle for American hearts-and-minds. Interventions to restore the Shah in Iran and to oust Arbenz from Guatemala, support for corrupt kings in

Morocco, Libya, Egypt, Ethiopia and Iraq, bungling interference by the CIA in Greece, Peru, Singapore, et al.—such positions showed the United States to be, as a moral force, a nation like any other. Not surprisingly. As early as 1958, the General Assembly's unwillingness to assume American benevolence led to an emergency session on the landing of U.S. Marines in Lebanon, at which even the personal appearance of President Eisenhower, flush with the continuing goodwill of his opposition to the Western powers' Suez adventure, was not enough to prevent the passage of a resolution quite different from what the United States had brought to New York.

Even in the Korean situation, where the United States having broken the North Korean attack was moving with UN authority to "reunify" the peninsula, the visible fact was that an industrial power was beating up on colored people. And then there came, of course, the disaster of the Vietnam War (triggered in part by the refusal of the American client to participate in the free elections agreed upon in the Geneva accords that got the French out of Indochina), where destructive weapons of great sophistication were used against barefoot pajama-clad guerrillas.

The economic muscle grew weaker as the United States ran a steady balance-of-payments deficit and the gold cover for the dollar leaked away, as Japan on one side and the EC countries on the other regained their prewar industrial strength. The key incident was Eisenhower's decision in 1960 to "tie" American aid to purchases of American goods, to reduce the balance-of-payments implications of foreign assistance. The dam broke in 1971, when Nixon cut the dollar loose from gold, slapped a 10 percent surtax on all imports, and destroyed the system of international trade and finance the United States had invented and owned since the end of the war.

Meanwhile, American power had been beaten back in Korea by the Chinese—and had been revealed as quite insufficient for the nation's asserted "liberation" policies when no finger was raised (except within the walls of the General Assembly itself) to help the Hungarian people in universal revolt against their Russian masters.

In any event, the United Nations was a place of states, not populations. Whatever the attractions of America to ordinary people—and the clamor for immigrants' visas to the United States has risen rather than diminished —to the heads of nation-states the United States offered only the model of an economic system in which the key decisions were *not* taken by the state (which meant that the head of state could not be all-important) and a political system in which they could lose their jobs. Democracy is not a highly attractive idea to an autocrat who sits at the top of an autocracy, and it was those autocrats who gave the orders to most nations' UN representatives.

Even if the language used by the United States in discussing human rights can be shown to be hypocritical, the very existence of the formal standard of political rights represents a threat to the legitimacy of most Third World governments, and it is deeply resented. For those sitting outside the UN context, of course, the response to this resentment can only be, *Tant pis*. For those inside, *which includes the U.S. delegation*, the felt need is to find reasons to sympathize with the majority. Thus the string of reports from U.S. missions to UN conferences, cited by Moynihan, claiming American "success" after the adoption of communiqués politically, economically and morally offensive to the United States, full of phrases, proposals and dishonesties they would not dream of defending in casual conversation with their friends. By participating in the formulation of this egregious junk, they felt they had fulfilled somehow an obligation to the little people of the world.

The United States was strongly represented in the UN through the period of the steepest decline in its influence—by the career diplomat Charles Yost, the future Vice-President George Bush, the able newsman John Scali (who had been for reasons never revealed the conduit of choice for the key message from Khrushchev to Kennedy in the Cuban crisis), the future senator Daniel Patrick Moynihan and the industrialist-politician William Scranton (whom the knowledgeable people at the UN Secretariat considered the most skilled U.S. representative ever sent to Turtle Bay).

Then Jimmy Carter made a bid to roll back the tide with the appointment of Andrew Young, a congressman from his native state and longtime political ally, who would carry to the UN the prestige of having been the right-hand man of Martin Luther King. The little states of Africa, fifty strong, fewer than half a dozen democracies (even sham democracies) among them, had become the dominant voting bloc in the General Assembly. Intelligent, ill-informed, reluctant to become confused by facts, African in remote heritage, veteran of a struggle not entirely unlike that of the national liberation movements, Young shared many of the attitudes of the more sophisticated African delegates. He could influence them, and through them—because the nonaligned movement worked through consensus, with fear and loathing of dissenting statements—the General Assembly majority.

At the State Department, leadership of the Bureau of International Organizations passed into the hands of C. William Maynes, a man with a firm belief that U.S. policy is a failure unless the Third World approves it. "The problem in this office," he said, "always is maintaining the UN perspective on policy issues which are important to the UN but where the UN perspective has not been solidly established." Maynes had come up from Princeton to take the job after Young in one of the most extraordinary misjudgments in the transitional planning for the Carter State Department decided that the incumbent Samuel Lewis was prejudiced against Israel. (Lewis thereupon became the U.S. ambassador in Tel Aviv and perhaps the only defender of Menachem Begin in the State Department.) But the closest communication between USUN and the Carter administration ran from the mission to the Bureau of African Affairs and Assistant Secretary Richard Moose, a former congressional staff assistant whom Young could count on for support at all times.

Seeking to influence the General Assembly majority by friendship, the mission in New York inevitably became trapped by the need to express the majority's attitudes. The difference between Young's often freehand statements and the votes the United States would cast when voting was required eventually left a sour taste in many mouths. "Andy Young's problem," said Dean Rusk from his lair at the University of Georgia, "is that he never had a boss before, never had to worry whether what he said represented somebody else's views." After Young departed, victim of his belief that because he meant well he could violate national policy against official contact with representatives of the Palestine Liberation Organization (something his friends in the General Assembly very badly wanted him to do), the post passed to Donald McHenry, his assistant for Third World matters.

An FSO, McHenry insisted on using his access to the President to fight for American assent to the so-called "global negotiations" in which the LDCs would get their hands in what they considered the real cookie jar, submitting the World Bank and the IMF to control by a General Assembly where the Seychelles or Nepal or Paraguay would have the same vote as the United States. The proposal shows total incomprehension of how the world works. The World Bank gets its resources by selling bonds in the world's financial markets, and the IMF can make loans because creditor countries are willing to accept Special Drawing Rights (SDR, the IMF's "currency") in payment of debts. Under the UN's New International Economic Order, nobody would buy the bonds and no industrial nation would hold SDRs, making the agencies useless. All the cabinet agencies consulted on the matter—State, Treasury, Commerce and Agriculture in the lead—told Carter to forget about it. McHenry tried to push the President a second time because he thought the issue was so important, and Carter gave rather firm and impatient orders that were much resented at the mission in New York. "The mixed role [of the UN representative]," Secretary of State Muskie said with some satisfaction when the episode was ended and a disgruntled UN conference had disbanded, "does lead to frustration. But being in the Cabinet gives the post prestige."

Ronald Reagan appointed to this amorphous post Jeane Kirkpatrick, a scholar of Latin American affairs, so far over on the right wing of the Democratic Party that she felt she had to apologize in print (a year before her appointment) for not becoming a Republican. Mrs. Kirkpatrick was the author of a magazine article distinguishing between "authoritarian" (on our side, okay if deplorable) and "totalitarian" (on the other side, very bad) governments. Her presence in the Cabinet was personally offensive to Alexander Haig, whose myrmidons chopped away at her as he believed the White House staff was chopping at him. Like Andrew Young, she had never had a boss before, and she felt no compunction about letting the world know—not just by leaking—about her disagreements with U.S. policy. She was widely believed to be the architect of the scheme by which Argentina would be America's Cuba, supplying instructors if not actual troops to the right-wing forces of Central America. (Forty Argentinians were in Honduras, training Nicaraguan exiles to organize guerrilla warfare against the Sandinista Government, when Britain's response to Argentina's invasion of the Falklands persuaded the military junta that Argentina was part of the Third World.) And yet, like all her precedessors except Moynihan, she soon found her *amour propre* bound up with people's respect for her job, and even began to blame her own country's policies for the lopsided defeats the United States suffered in the General Assembly.

USUN employs no fewer than five ambassadors: a permanent representative, a deputy permanent representative, and three deputy representatives. When the fall General Assembly session is in full cry, after all, there can be six separate committees of the whole to be covered. (To help the small countries participate fully, the UN budget includes funds for five round-trip passages for delegates from each nation.) There is also a U.S. ambassador to the UN in Geneva, one to UNESCO in Paris, one to the International Atomic Energy Agency in Austria, one to the Organization for Economic Cooperation and Development in Paris, one to the Organization of American States in Washington, one to the European Community in Brussels. Half a dozen other international agencies have permanent U.S. representatives of lesser title, and all these people have staffs.

Something like one hundred and seventy people work for the State Department's Bureau of International Organizations—and all the other bureaus at State (plus many bureaus in other departments) employ staffs to watch over UN matters. "For each major UN organ," said IO information officer Fred Blackly, "there is a little interagency committee." David Stottlemyer, planning officer for IO, said he had acquired "a Xerox phobia. In the old days you had the physical limitation of the typewriter and the carbons, and that limited your clearances. I get *tons* of paper here; there is *no* selection process."

Maynes described his Bureau as "like a mini-State Department. We have political affairs, economic affairs in the Second Committee and in ECOSOC [the Economic and Social Council], development through UNDP [United Nations Development Program], the administration of the UN, even personnel. That leads to all sorts of tensions with other bureaus." It is not entirely easy to grasp what all these people do—four months into the job (which he later quit for the more independent post of Assistant Secretary for Human Rights), Reagan's IO head Elliott Abrams admitted he still hadn't figured out the functions of most of the people in the Bureau. "All the time," Stottlemyer said disgustedly, "goes to a choice of words, punctuation, the use of an article. And preparing position papers. Most of these things are tactics, and a guy in an office in Washington can't decide on tactics."

IO does not control what a U.S. representative does in any international organization, but it must sign off on the instructions to all of them, which gives the Bureau an all but infinite power to delay. It is probably true, as Maynes said, that "the U.S. ambassador is always the most important person at the UN," but his effectiveness as distinguished from his importance is questionable. Since Arthur Goldberg, who really did have access to Johnson (and had the respect of Dean Rusk, with whom he had served, as Secretary of Labor, in the Kennedy Cabinet), no UN ambassador has had authority to participate in the give-and-take behind the scenes at Security Council meetings. Bernadette Lefort of the French Foreign Ministry planning office remembered from her tour at the UN that "you have to stay on the spot and wait for hours with nothing to do. The Americans can say nothing but, We are waiting for instructions from Washington. It's unbelievable, the hardihood of human beings."

There is a dirty secret here—that the United States, like the Soviet Union and the European Community and probably Japan—does not very much need the United Nations on a day-to-day basis. For the Great Powers, as former Indian Permanent Representative Arthur Lall put it, the UN is "a forum and not a force." Thus, concentration on multilateral diplomacy is not the way ahead for an FSO, and first-rate people tend to shun UN and UN-related assignments.

Wesley Kriebel, who ran the IO office that tried to get U.S. views on UN issues to other countries (mostly via the annual laundry list that goes out to all ambassadors), found it was "hard to get across to our desk officers, as well as to the countries involved, that bilateral relations would be affected by multilateral votes." The reason it was hard was that the desk officers and the other countries were right: votes in the UN are not considered important enough to affect bilateral relations. The Russians even allowed the Romanians to abstain on the vote condemning their invasion of Afghanistan. The real embarrassment for the United States in the Security Council vote on a resolution to tell the British to stop reconquering the Falklands was not Mrs. Kirkpatrick's meaningless change from negative to abstention after the voting had closed but the fact that Japan —which certainly would have deferred to American wishes in this area if leaned upon—provided the ninth vote that made a veto necessary.

Moreover, the IO data base is bad. Since 1972, the Bureau has been putting into a computer UN votes by all nations on matters of interest to the United States, but nobody ever calls for a printout. Ambassadors do dutifully carry the laundry lists to the Foreign Ministries of the countries in which they work, but few of them report back in any detail on the response. The best information available to the U.S. Government about how countries are going to behave in the General Assembly is of course gathered by the USUN ambassadors and staff in the delegates' lounge —and they rarely pass what they hear in the parties back to Washington. They don't *like* Washington: from the perspective of the UN, Washington is too much like the real world. "The problem of coordination is monstrous," said Kriebel. "But if I heard about all of that, I'd be swamped."

More than a quarter of the entire budget of the State Department goes for contributions to the United Nations, and the overwhelming bulk of that money—probably 90 percent—goes to the support of bureaucracies, conferences and studies rather than actual aid to anybody but bureaucrats, conferencers and studiers. The American contribution runs about a quarter of all UN income. There is no disagreement between the United States and the dozen other large providers, who among them give two thirds of the UN budget, that at $2-billion-plus a year the financing of the UN agencies is out of control. With the more than tacit agreement of the Russians, the annual budgeting meeting of the WEOs (West Europeans and Others) at the GGCL (Geneva Group Consultation Level) called for a 1982 rate of growth below the rate of world inflation. His acceptance of this target, noting East-West agreement on it, was among the factors that doomed Kurt Waldheim's bid for a third term as Secretary-General. Meanwhile, the specialized agencies continued a merry run of budget escalation, driven by the fact that three quarters of the vote on the budget is controlled by nations which among them put up about 5 percent of the costs. FAO, despite the private complaints to President Reagan by the South in the dialogue at Cancun, was awarded a one-third increase in expenditures—and the American delegate, while expressing bitterness, said the United States would pay it.

The first step toward achieving a more useful United Nations must come from the countries that pay for it, and can in concert cut down their contributions without fear of retribution. The Russians, strapped for hard currency, would probably cooperate—indeed, the Soviet UN ambassador in late 1982 joined the U.S. and British delegates in a formal remonstrance to the Secretary-General against the escalating costs of the agencies. Elliott Abrams, a Moynihan protégé, said while Assistant Secretary for IO that he had sought the job because he considered the UN essentially a theater for ideological warfare: "One of my specialties is ideological warfare, and I'm looking forward to it." But that attitude simply takes the reverse of a debased coin. What is important is to force a shrinkage, a concentration on purpose rather than on process.

In the course of sloughing functions, the UN organizations could return to first principles, to recognition of the limits on what can be achieved in economic and social matters by political means, to serious work on the difficult tasks of international institution-building. For there is a significant function to be performed by a UN in which the small nations predominate: even this reasonably proud citizen of a very large nation can see easily enough that leaving decisions to the Great Powers has been a lousy way to run the railroad throughout recorded history. The world does need a UN, but not the UN it has now. Looking toward the future, it might make sense to start with the model of the European Community.

11

SPECIAL CASE II:
THE ISRAELI FOREIGN MINISTRY

The solution of the Palestine problem based on a partition of Palestine into two separate states will be of profound historical significance, because this decision will meet the legitimate demands of the Jewish people.

> —Andrei Gromyko, Foreign Minister of
> the Soviet Union, November 26, 1947

Like virtually all other events of our century, the solution of the Jewish question merely produced a new category of refugees, the Arabs, thereby increasing the number of the stateless and rightless by another 700,000 to 800,000 people. And what happened in Palestine within the smallest territory and in terms of hundreds of thousands was then repeated in India on a large scale involving many millions of people. Since the Peace Treaties of 1919 and 1920 the refugees and the stateless have attached themselves like a curse to all the newly established states on earth which were created in the image of the nation-state.

> —Hannah Arendt

Moses made two mistakes: first, his choice of neighbors; second, his avoidance of the area where there is oil.

> —Yaacov Morris, Israeli ambassador
> to New Zealand

1

One enters an Israeli consulate or embassy through a steel door that leads into a steel-walled room the size of a walk-in closet. The door closes behind the visitor. The nozzle of a television camera protrudes from a corner at the ceiling. A man's voice, polite but tense, says "Shalom," and asks questions in English. Whom are you visiting? For what purpose? Do you have a weapon in your briefcase? The answers to these questions are known: the security officer has a list of all expected visitors and their missions, and a metal detector has invisibly scanned the briefcase on entry to the room. But the question period permits a trained examiner to study on his television screen the reactions of the interrogated visitor. When he is satisfied, the door on the other side of the closet swings open, and reveals a bustle of ordinary clerks and buttoned-down bureaucrats, little different from other consulates, other embassies.

It is a strange and unhappy outcome for a generation of effort by people whose pride and joy were uncontrollable when they first saw the raised blue-and-white flag with its Star of David, first sang their national anthem, first presented their credentials as the representatives of a nation-state, first opened their extraterritorial, diplomatically protected offices on a touch of soil really owned by Jews in lands where, by Zionist perception, Jews had previously lived only as tenants. Nor can the disappointment be masked by the fact that other nations—the Soviet Union, Algeria, Czechoslovakia, Turkey, India—also find it necessary to omit from the diplomatic list the home addresses of their ambassadors and attachés, to reduce the chance of terrorist attacks, and to increase the security of wives and children. For other countries, diplomacy is a peripheral activity. But for Israel, the practice of diplomacy has been central to the creation, travail and survival of the state.

"Israel," said Hanan Bar-On, Assistant Director General of the Foreign Ministry, "is the only country that came into being at the end of colonialism whose legitimacy was denied by its immediate neighbors. The borders and boundaries of the other newly independent countries were never in doubt, but Israel's were not recognized. Israel therefore had to establish this legitimacy on the widest possible basis, to compensate for the sworn enmity of the neighboring states."* There was a time, before the 1973 war

* Another such state, East Timor, was strangled by Indonesia before it could begin the process of establishing international legitimacy. And since Bar-On spoke, there has been yet another: Belize, formerly British Honduras, whose only neighbor, Guatemala, boycotted her admission ceremonies at the UN. It may be worth noting, sadly, that Israel is a major arms supplier to Guatemala.

and the full-court press on all the Third World by the Arab oil producers, when Israel had missions in more countries than any nation except the United States.

"Israeli diplomats are different from all other diplomats," said Efraim Haran, Director of the Common Market Division at the Foreign Ministry. "When I meet diplomats from other countries, I ask myself, 'What do these diplomats do but talk?' But there are always big questions of the day concerning Israel. When Israel is not mentioned in the international newspapers, something is wrong."

The origins of the nation trace back as a practical matter to the Balfour Declaration of 1917, which the chemist Chaim Weizmann, head of the British Navy's research laboratories, wheedled out of a British Prime Minister in wartime, promising the Jews a homeland in what was still at the time a parcel of the Turkish Empire. At roughly the same time, unfortunately, Sir Henry McMahon, to win the revolt of Sharif Husein of Mecca against the Turks, was offering British help with the creation of an independent Arab state to include Syria, Mesopotamia, Lebanon . . . and Palestine.† And in the Sykes-Picot agreement of 1916, the same British Government had divided the whole area between Arabia and Anatolia into French and British spheres.‡ By the terms of this agreement, the French were to control directly what is now southern Turkey plus Lebanon and to dominate exclusively whatever political unit held authority in Syria; the British, to control directly most of what is now Iraq and to dominate exclusively "Transjordania," the area between the Jordan River and the ill-defined borders of the desert wastes where dwelled Britain's client Abdul-Aziz ibn-Saud. Palestine was to be "internationalized," which left the door open for the Balfour Declaration.

Not surprisingly, the Arabs accepted only the McMahon-Husein deal. In March 1920, a council in Damascus pronounced the creation of a Greater Syria, with Faisal as King. France had invaded the western edge of this area once before, in 1860, to protect the Maronite Christian commu-

---

† According to Keynes, this idea persisted into the preliminaries of the Peace Conference in Paris, when "the Emir Faisal [Husein's son] . . . recited in M. Pichon's cabinet, unabashed by the naked charms of Rubens' Marie de Medici, a chapter of the Koran, whilst Colonel Lawrence, in his capacity of the Emir's interpreter, propounded an ingenious *politik* for the creation of an Arab hegemony from the Mediterranean to the Persian Gulf, over Damascus and Mosul and Bagdad."

‡ This same Sykes-Picot agreement, incidentally, negotiated in Moscow, awarded Czarist Russia Constantinople and the Straits, Turkish Armenia and Kurdistan, and the Black Sea littoral to Trebizond. No small part of our troubles with the Russians right after World War II traced to Soviet belief that, having been cheated of their "sphere of influence" after World War I, the Russians were entitled to claim these goodies from a neutral Turkey after World War II.

nity from persecution by the Druze Moslems (a persecution encouraged by the Turks), and in the wake of the army had come a large missionary and educational effort by French Jesuits, gleefully encouraged by the anticlerical governments of the Third Republic. Now the French moved not only to protect their interests and their Christian wards, but to assert what they regarded as their rights under the Sykes-Picot agreement. A French army conquered Damascus, Homs, Hama and Aleppo, and presently the League of Nations awarded the French and the British mandatory powers over the area, with borders not far off those envisaged in their secret wartime agreement. Faisal retreated to Iraq, where he and his heirs ruled until 1958.

Palestine was neither internationalized nor given to the Jews—it was just another British mandate. But the preamble to the mandate recited that Britain "should be responsible for putting into effect the declaration originally made on November 2, 1917 . . . in favor of the establishment in Palestine of a national home for the Jewish people, it being clearly understood that nothing should be done which might prejudice the civil and religious rights of existing non-Jewish communities in Palestine."

Two millennia had passed since the extinction of the last Jewish state on the eastern Mediterranean, and it was more than three millennia since Moses had discerned in Israel a land of milk and honey. Scattered around the world from Buenos Aires to Goa, with ponderable concentrations in central and eastern Europe, North Africa and the United States, the Jews had retained in their prayers a lamentation for the destruction of Solomon's temple in Jerusalem and a pledge to return there. A small, wretchedly poor colony of Jews was in Palestine already, living in medieval conditions, their energies consumed by the rituals of their faith. Few Jews anywhere saw much practicality in the "Zionist" dream of a return to this barren and bitter land. But in Britain, France, Germany, Austria-Hungary and the United States, an increasingly comfortable Jewish community was outraged at the Russian pogroms of the late nineteenth century and felt guilty about its inability to do anything to help. Palestine, as a place of refuge for persecuted Jewish communities, exerted a charitable attraction. Under the leadership of the French Rothschilds, who had been stimulated by the crusading spirit of the Hungarian journalist Theodor Herzl, European and American Jewish communities began to contribute funds for the purchase of land in Turkish-controlled Palestine, land that could be farmed by the predominantly rural Jews of Russia.

The Balfour Declaration, then, was the culmination of twenty years' argumentation and planning, all of which assumed that the benighted population on the spot would welcome and benefit by the growth of a more advanced European community in their midst. The British Army, oil prospectors, railroad builders and amateur Bedouin who knew the area warned from the beginning that the Arabs were not likely to take kindly to a Jewish homeland in their midst, and that the larger interests of Britain argued against helping the Jews. The Russian Revolution promised an end to pogroms (the large Jewish representation among the Bolsheviki, including Trotsky, gave the first Soviet Cabinet a reputation as a "Jewish government"), and thus to the pressure for Jewish resettlement. But the government of the new Polish state proved as viciously anti-Semitic as its Czarist predecessor, and the Wilsonian doctrine of self-determination within rather arbitrary geographical lines strengthened the intellectual drive for an area where Jews, too, could enjoy such blessings.

Then came the disaster of Nazism, the desperate need for a place where Jews could be safe, the rising incidence of Arab riots against the Jewish presence in Palestine (stimulated in part by the Germans)—and the effective repudiation of the Balfour Declaration by the British, who refused to accept Jewish refugees on the grounds that any change in the relative distribution of Jews and non-Jews in the mandate would "prejudice the civil and religious rights of existing non-Jewish communities." There grew up among the Jews of Palestine and Poland (Menachem Begin was a Polish Jew) a sure knowledge—belief would be too mild a term—that nobody but the Jews themselves would defend their right to a homeland.

Palestine, Syria, Lebanon and Transjordan had all been declared "Class A" mandates, territories on the edge of self-government from which the mandatory powers would recede in fairly short order. The United States, though refusing to participate in the League of Nations (partly because the Versailles Treaty carved up places like the Middle East for the benefit of the victorious European powers), took seriously the mandatory power's obligation to turn over these countries to governments of their own choosing. Under Roosevelt, indeed, the United States strongly advocated that the European powers liberate their colonies as well as their mandates. To placate local political forces during the war, the British and the French had promised nation status to their Middle East protectorates (to De Gaulle's fury, the British took the lead in promising nationhood to the French mandates), and the United States was determined to see the promises kept. But there was no government to which power could be transferred in Palestine. The British accepted the Jewish Agency and the Arab Higher Committee as communal spokesmen to be consulted, but nothing more.

Refugee camps in Europe were filled with terrified Jews snatched from the German death camps toward the end of the war. They did not wish to, and probably could not, return to their homes; they wanted to go to Palestine. The British were holding immigration to fifteen hundred Jews per month, a pitifully inadequate number. Boats were turned away from Haifa harbor, as they had been in the 1930s. President Truman urged Prime Minister Clement Attlee to approve the immediate entry of one hundred thousand refugees, and Attlee refused. An Anglo-American Commission was formed to make recommendations on the future of Palestine, and reported back that there were only three possibilities: a partition between Jews and Arabs, a federation in which Jewish and Arab communities would have their own communal institutions but would cooperate in a unitary state, or continuation of the mandate as a UN trusteeship. Desperate for governmental authority which would permit rapid immigration, the Jewish Agency accepted the idea of partition; the Arabs refused.

The British turned tail: they had other, more pressing problems; they had lived through the awful experience of communal strife in Ireland and India (a strife then regarded in the United States as *their fault*, with the full weight of the magisterial American liberalism that assesses blame for all episodes it dislikes); they thought Palestine an excellent area for the United States to begin exercising international responsibilities. Britain announced a departure date from Palestine: August 1, 1948; and then moved the date up to May 14.

As the United Nations developed, the General Assembly became a warped sounding board for the aggrieved, with little function in the lives of men, but decisions on trusteeships were in fact made by vote in that body. Palestine was the sort of problem for which the UN in the 1940s formed commissions; the Assembly asked Australia, Canada, Czechoslovakia, Guatemala, India, Iran, the Netherlands, Peru, Sweden, Uruguay and Yugoslavia to make an investigation and bring back recommendations.

Reporting in 1947, the Special Commission on Palestine recommended partition with economic union, and drew a peculiar map that showed a Jewish state to take about a quarter of habitable Palestine plus the Negev desert down to the head of the Gulf of Aqaba. But the two pieces of the Jewish state would meet only at the points of their respective diamonds, a crossroads that would also serve as a link for the two separated parts of the Arab state. Jerusalem would be in neither state; the holy city would be, somehow, internationalized as a *corpus separatum*. Again, the Jewish Agency accepted; the Arab Higher Committee refused.

It was in this context that the Jewish Agency (later to proclaim itself the government of the State of Israel) had to begin its ventures in diplomacy. There was no precedent for a mandatory power surrendering its mandate back to the League of (or United) Nations. The votes on the recommendations of the Special Commission on Palestine were likely to be crucial for the future of the new state. And Israel was highly disadvantaged in the bargaining. The Foreign Service of the mandatory power, influential around the world, was anti-Semitic and especially anti-Israel. The surrounding Arab states, saving only Lebanon (where the French had apparently—alas, it turned out only temporarily—resolved a not dissimilar problem of communal divisions in a small property), had vowed to use force to prevent the creation of a Jewish state in their midst. In the United States, Secretary of Defense James Forrestal believed American support for a Jewish state would over the long run imperil Western access to Arabian oil; Secretary of State George C. Marshall thought on the basis of his military experience that Arab forces would wipe the new state off the earth in short order, and knew that the United States would not intervene militarily to save it.

Only the Soviet Union, having lost its bid to replace Italy as the trustee power in Libya, frustrated in its efforts to dominate Turkey, looking to get a toehold in a region from which the British and French had excluded Russians since the days of the Crimean War, could be counted on to line up behind Israel, and the Eastern bloc was without much influence at the United Nations in the 1940s. Finally, by accepting the deal the Arabs had refused, the Jewish Agency had placed itself in a desperate negotiating position: obviously, any compromise would be less than what the Special Commission on Palestine had recommended.

Given that no nation but the Soviet Union (also, distastefully, the only one of the United Nations to have been in actual alliance with Hitler) would see its interests advanced by the creation of Israel, the representatives of the Jewish Agency had to work with what assets they could find. More important than people now realize was the attitude of the British Commonwealth countries (with the glaring exception of Nehru's new India, always hostile; Nehru in 1939 had described Zionism as "an accomplice of British imperialism"). They more than the United Kingdom had carried the fight in the Middle East, and their soldiers had taken rest-and-recreation in Palestine. (Or more: "The Minister of Justice here," said Yaacov Morris, the Irish-born Israeli ambassador to New Zealand, "was married in Jerusalem.") They knew and admired the achievements of the Zionist settlers, and disliked the Palestinian Arabs, who had been predominantly on Hitler's side in the war. Lester Pearson of Canada was among the most important leaders in the fledgling UN, and undertook the formation of a pro-partition bloc in the General Assembly. Though Australian Foreign Minister Herbert Evatt gave the Israelis fits with a paternalistic insistence that he knew better than they did how they should conduct themselves at the UN, the fact was that Australia sent an ambassador to Israel in 1950, before it established representation anywhere else in the Middle East.

Another advantage was the position of Zionist principle in the belief structure of many Christians. To this day, Israeli ambassadors work closely with evangelical Christian groups around the world (in the United States, the Israelis find that anti-Semites in the Moral Majority may be internationally sympathetic to Zionism in useful ways). In their theology, the Second Coming of Christ is to be preceded by the ingathering of the Jews to Israel; for those who hold that belief, the success of the Jewish state is a precondition of their own redemption. "They go on pilgrimages to Israel," Ambassador Zvi Kival said of the Japanese Christian sects. "Israel is part of their philosophy. They learn Hebrew songs and dance Israeli dances. . . ."

More generally, religious Protestants feel from all those years with the Old Testament in Sunday school a sense of familiarity with Jewish history and Jewish national ambition. Abba Eban remembered his lobbying visit to the Icelandic UN delegate, charged with the mission of reporting to the General Assembly on a last-chance investigation of possible reconciliation of Arab and Jewish demands. Eban was troubled that a significant role in the future of his people was to be played by a society so remote from all their history and concerns, but the Icelandic ambassador set him right: "He said that Iceland was far less remote from Jewish destiny than I presumed. In its culture it was deeply impregnated with Biblical memories."

The prospective Jewish state also rode the wave of socialist idealism that was carrying all before it in the West in the years right after the war. Zionism was predominantly a socialist doctrine. The desert had been made to bloom not by entrepreneurs but by the voluntary collective farmers of the kibbutz. "The Jewish state can come into being only if it is socialist," Nachman Syrkin had written in 1898. "Only by fusing with socialism can Zionism become the ideal of the whole Jewish people." For Europeans, and for the Latin American nations with their heartfelt if ludicrous "revolutionary" traditions, the kibbutz image was and is especially attractive. "A thousand Danes a year go through the Friends of the Kibbutz Movement in Denmark to work a year in Israel," said Ambassador Yitzhak ben-Ari in Copenhagen. "Many of them are very left-wing. And they are the best friends we have." Even the secular Japanese are not immune—among the regular contacts of Zvi Kival as ambassador in Tokyo was an organization called Shalom, "people who have visited Israel and lived in a kibbutz."

But the United States was necessarily the main target of Jewish effort. The facts of the Holocaust were well known in America, and public sympathy was overwhelmingly with the refugees in the camps in Europe who had no place to live and longed for Israel. Committed Zionists, from Jews like Albert Einstein to *goyim* like Eleanor Roosevelt and Republican congressional leader Joseph Martin, were prominent in American life. There was the useful—not controlling, but useful—oddity that President Truman's old partner in his failed haberdashery was an ardent Zionist. Chaim Weizmann himself had come to New York to be helpful, and was ensconced in a suite at the Waldorf-Astoria. Old, ill, already a figure of historic importance, he had access to the statesmen assembled at the United Nations—and to Truman, whom he dazzled.

Historically, American Jews had been of two minds about Zionism, but now they felt rage at what had happened to the Jews of Europe and guilt at their own inaction. They were as close to united as this community could be, and prepared to exert considerable leverage. Truman was necessarily conscious of the fact that the leading spokesman for American Zionism, Rabbi Abba Hillel Silver of Cleveland, was a Republican majordomo, and that Democratic victories in New York, Illinois and California might hinge on the Jewish vote. Moreover, as conflict with the Soviet Union became the principal concern of American foreign policy—the British evacuation of Palestine occurred almost exactly at the midpoint between the Communist coup in Czechoslovakia and the Berlin blockade—the Israelis could play subtly on American fears (their one asset at the State Department) that a Soviet-sponsored Israel would break the new cordon sanitaire against southern expansion by Russia.

Still, the United States in the United Nations was unwilling to impose partition on the Arabs, and its delegates were busy gathering support for a continuation of UN trusteeship over Palestine. The vote was delayed by parliamentary maneuvering by the Soviet bloc on behalf of Israel and by the Arabs, who felt that once the British had turned back the mandate they would be juridically free to complete the job Hitler had begun. The moment of British departure arrived and the Jewish Agency proclaimed itself the State of Israel within the boundaries of the partition resolution. And the political work paid off: Harry Truman personally (but as President) recognized the de facto existence of the State of Israel. Shortly thereafter, the Soviet Union extended *de jure* recognition. Gideon Rafael has written amusingly about the first night of the new state, when Foreign Minister Moshe Sharett labored over a cable to go out to every nation in the world, asking recognition—and the clerk in the telegraph office refused to accept the messages unless he was paid in cash. . . . But "the first signal of foreign recognition," Rafael noted grimly, came at dawn: "The Egyptian Air Force bombed Tel Aviv's airport and power station."

"We were not created by an international organization," said Hanan Bar-On, "but by an international crisis." Most Israelis outside the Foreign Ministry, while grudgingly admitting that the votes in the General Assembly had made a difference, would argue that their state was created by their own small but startlingly effective force of arms. Attacks came from Egypt (supported by the Royal Air Force under the terms of the Egyptian-British alliance), from Transjordan (where "Glubb Pasha" ran a British-officered Arab Legion considered the best fighting force in the Middle East), from Syria and from the Arab Higher Committee representing the Arab Palestinians outside and inside the frontiers. If these attacks had overrun the Jewish settlements, nothing that happened at the United Nations would have mattered. The miracle was that they did not, that despite the Syrian incursions in the Galilee and the Egyptian conquests in the Negev, the new state not only defended but expanded its borders. Even the lifeline to Jerusalem, a narrow corridor between Arab villages, through mountainous country that made for easy ambush, was kept at least partially open.

The Israelis at the United Nations asked for one thing: the internationalization of Jerusalem, site of the holy places presumably sacred equally to Christians, Moslems and Jews. In Jerusalem, the Jewish population was mostly elderly, unable to defend itself. Nothing was done: the Arab forces conquered and desecrated the Jewish holy sites, occupied the Jewish Quarter of the Old City and mistreated its inhabitants. The new state learned a lesson it has never seen any reason to forget.

At the General Assembly, the pending U.S. resolution for renewed trusteeship without Britain had clearly been mooted by Truman's action, and a substitute was carried to appoint a UN mediator, Sweden's Count Folke Bernadotte. At the Security Council, the United States and the Soviet Union jointly pushed through an order for a cease-fire (Britain abstaining), which the Arabs accepted only on June 11, after their attack had visibly failed and the Israelis had begun expanding their holdings. Even then, they agreed to hold fire only for a month, and in July they resumed their onslaught on the new state. In the second round, the Israelis were even more successful, recapturing much of the ground that had been lost to the first Arab attacks. But the second cease-fire was followed by a recommendation from Bernadotte to revive the idea of a union of only partly sovereign Arab and Jewish states in Palestine, with immigration restricted, Jerusalem in the Arab area, Haifa a free port, and the Negev part of Transjordania. It was Israel's great good luck that the Arabs rejected this proposal, Israel's great misfortune that Jewish terrorists thereupon killed Bernadotte, and further misfortune that these assassins, like the terrorists whose bombs crippled the Palestinian mayors of Hebron and Nablus in 1980, were never caught.

The second cease-fire had left Jewish settlements behind Egyptian lines in the Negev, and the Egyptians presently refused to permit their resupply. In October, the third phase of the 1948 wars was initiated by Israel to relieve its posts in the Negev. Within five days, all but one of the Egyptian positions had been cleared (the exception was an outpost commanded by a young major named Gamal Abdel Nasser), and Israeli forces had advanced down the Mediterranean shore of the Sinai past the town of El 'Arish. For once the territorial revisions attendant on a cease-fire were evenhanded: the Israelis abandoned their Sinai conquests, and the Egyptians turned over the rest of the Negev. Temporarily: in January 1949, Egypt struck again, with sizable air support from the Royal Air Force. But now the Israelis had Czech antiaircraft batteries, and six of the British planes were shot down as part of the rout inflicted on the Egyptians. England protested the destruction of its aircraft. . . .

By now, the Israelis had won their most important victory at the UN: a Security Council resolution calling on all the participants in the fighting to meet under the chairmanship of Ralph Bunche, the black American deputy to Secretary-General Trygve Lie, at armistice negotiations on the island of Rhodes. The Egyptians broke the first Arab rejectionist front and sent negotiators to sit in the same building with the Jews. Soon armistice lines had been accepted by all the Arab states contiguous to Israel (a category that does not include Iraq, which has maintained a state of war with Israel since 1948, a steadfastness that gave a color of legitimacy to the Israeli destruction of the Iraqi nuclear reactor in 1982). These armistice lines are the "boundaries" to which the State of Israel is to withdraw under the Arab interpretation of UN Resolution 242, passed after the Six-Day War of 1967. But because they are merely armistice lines, Israel can claim that the ultimate "boundaries" to which its forces should withdraw are still unknown, and must be negotiated by the parties.

The creation of a Jewish state in the teeth of Arab opposition set in train one of the great population migrations that have characterized the second half of the twentieth century. During the months before May 14, 1948, the Jews had established military control over hundreds of Arab villages in the area that was to become their state, while the Arabs maintained a drumfire of riot and attack on Jewish settlements on both sides of the partition lines. When the war began, hundreds of thousands of Arabs left their homes in Jewish-controlled areas. Whatever their reasons for leaving, they and their children and now their children's children are still in the refugee camps theoretically administered by the United Nations, actually governed until the Israeli invasion of Lebanon by the Palestine Liberation Organization. Many have fled four times: from Israel in 1948, from the West Bank in 1967, from Jordan in 1970, from Lebanon in 1982.

Meanwhile, the existence of an Israel produced as its creators had hoped a great ingathering of Jews—but not the Jews of the classic and sophisticated Diaspora of Europe and America. It was the African and Asian

Jews—the Sephardim—who found in the emergence of a Jewish state an epiphany mingling Messianic belief and escape from the persecution of their Moslem neighbors. They came from Morocco, Algeria, Tunisia, Egypt, Syria, Iraq, Iran and especially the remote fastnesses of Yemen at the edge of the Arabian peninsula, where no one had known there *were* Jews. Like the Arabs who fled Israel, they were driven by fear, a fear fanned by hostile neighbors and local politicos sharing the humiliation of the "Arab nation" after the defeat in battle and looking to gather the spoils of Jewish property after the Jews left. Their fear was encouraged, too, by Israeli emissaries, who believed (and still believe) that no Jew will ever be safe outside a Jewish state, and whose experience in the 1948 wars argued that Israel could be defended only by steadily expanding manpower.

The population shifts that followed the establishment of Israel were not by the standards of our time unusually large. Stalin evicted more Tatars from the Crimea and more Germans from Poland than the number of Palestinians who left Israel; twenty times as many Moslem Indians and Hindu Pakistanis were shifted across borders (with hundreds of times as much loss of life). In later years, refugees would flee Cuba, Vietnam and Cambodia, Chad, Ethiopia, Uganda and Afghanistan in similar or greater numbers. But the refugees from and to Israel have produced an apparently permanent agony with apparently permanent political effects. Quite apart from questions of oil and politics, the existence of so large a refugee colony of Palestinians for whom the United Nations accepted responsibility, for whose camps the General Assembly had to budget every year, would inevitably erode the Israeli moral position in the international community. And the rise in the non-European Jewish population of Israel to majority status, which happened in the 1970s, would bring to power the wing of Zionism that had never accepted partition, that had argued against seeking UN membership in 1949 because to do so would acknowledge partition, that took all of Biblical Israel as theirs by right rather than by any international agreement.

Indeed, the invasion of Lebanon in June 1982 argues that the Israelis have fully returned, body and soul, to the land that Joshua won them and to the enduring habits of life and death in the Middle East. This was not, after all, the first time the fields of Tyre were sown with salt. And the massive destruction worked on Sidon and West Beirut surely recalls what Jordan did to the Palestinian camps in 1970, what Syria did to them in 1975 (and then to its own overenthusiastic Moslems in Hama in 1982), what Iraq did to the Iranian cities across the Shatt-al-Arab. By accepting the mores of Middle Eastern behavior in war, the Israelis have in a sense completed the establishment of their legitimacy in their geographical location

—but only at the sacrifice of their own idealism, and their status as the Middle Eastern outpost of a higher hope.

2

At the beginning, the new Jewish state made two foreign policy decisions that would be central to its conduct of international relations for the next twenty years. First, that it was an Asian country. Israel was situated on that continent, and the fight for the Negev was a fight for an outlet to the sea east of Suez, on the Gulf of Aqaba. (It is interesting to note that except for Egypt itself, only Israel has a shoreline on branches of both the Atlantic and the Indian oceans.) Second, that Israel was an ex-colony, with special ties to others emerging from European tutelage. This would not be a perfunctory matter. "Israel," wrote Walter Eytan, the first Director General of the Foreign Ministry, "has cause to be grateful to the many small countries which did not hesitate to grant her recognition." It was, after all, the votes of the smaller countries (notably Latin American) that carried the day for partition in the General Assembly, and in May 1949 admitted the Jewish state to the United Nations.

Looking East, Israel launched an Asian Socialist Conference in partnership with Burma (then the only other avowedly socialist government on the continent), and sent to this fringe state as ambassador David Hacohen, perhaps the most important organizer of the Palmach, the fighting wing of the Jewish Agency. This conference was not quite a nonstarter, for a meeting was held with delegations in attendance from India and Indonesia, but after the Arab states excluded Israel from the Bandung Conference in 1955, there was little the Foreign Ministry could do. Like Japan, which recognized Israel in the first wave in 1948, the Jewish state was to be excluded from Sukarno's "New Emerging Forces." India had also recognized Israel, but had never (still has not) exchanged missions. Two Moslem countries accepted Israeli representation below the ambassadorial level—Turkey and Iran. Close relations with Burma (where Israel made a major effort of technical assistance) and with Thailand were the most the Israeli Foreign Ministry could achieve in Asia.

Africa was different. With a rush of enthusiasm, creating an Israeli myth that persists despite incessant rebuff at the United Nations, Jerusalem assumed and asserted an identity of interest with the Africans. An agricultural assistance team was sent to Ghana as early as 1956, two years before the formation of Mashav, the Division of International Cooperation in the Foreign Ministry.

"The real diplomacy for Israel," Rahamin Timor, Director of the Foreign Ministry's Division of International Cooperation, said in 1980, "is in developing countries. The art of diplomacy for Israel is there. From the 1950s, Israel has been a kind of mother country for the new nations. Its physical conditions and to some extent its social conditions were those of a developing country. Its people had been oppressed under the heel of a colonial power, had fought for their freedom and built their country.

"Israelis," Timor continued, explaining, "are nearer to God. Not 'a chosen people,' as the anti-Semites have it, but nearer to God. They come from Jerusalem. They are smarter than most people. You would be surprised at the extent that people in Africa especially believe that—they believe Israel is here to stay, and will succeed.

"I remember when a Minister from Ethiopia came. He said, 'I hear you are manufacturing cars. I would like to see the plant.' I said, 'We have only one, very small, near Haifa.' He said, 'It's important for me to see it.' So we took him—a plant that produced four cars a day. He said, 'I was forty days in the United States, they took me coast to coast. I saw a Ford plant where they produced a car every two minutes. I thought, "My God, we can never do this." But here we see something that in a few years we can do.'

"French experts told the Africans they couldn't produce cotton and corn, only peanuts and palm oil. Israeli experts came and showed them they could produce cotton and corn—it worked. Our embassies in Africa were manned by two people. In Togo, I would meet the President and talk with the President, and go to the post office and decode the cables. But our young people from the kibbutz would come and do a marvelous job working in the villages. The President of Togo came here to Israel and was very impressed. They put out an issue of stamps in 1964, honoring Israel.

"I was ambassador to Zaire in 1966–67. The community there asked me to help them establish a poultry farm. I cabled Israel, they sent me by air a shipment of day-old chickens. I couldn't find a truck; I drove the chickens to the community myself in a CD [Corps Diplomatique] car. An Israeli ambassador has to improvise. The Organization of African Unity was to have a meeting in Kinshasa in 1967, after the Six-Day War. The Arabs wouldn't come to a country where there was an Israeli embassy. Zaire asked us to take a week off. I said, 'No—if you insist, I will buy my people a one-way ticket.' Mobuto had been in Israel; we trained him as a paratrooper.* He accepted my decision, and we remained in Kinshasa. I did that on my own—didn't consult Israel. When you are an ambassador, you read your instructions the way you want. If what you do is successful, they

---

* Israel also gave paratroop training to the young Idi Amin.

will always say it's because of your wise instructions. If you fail, they can say it was because you misinterpreted or misunderstood your instructions."

In 1973, when the Egyptians struck across the Canal in the Yom Kippur War and the Gulf Arabs cut off the supply of oil to the United States and the Netherlands, the Arab states leaned on the Africans—and an Israeli effort of fifteen years was lost overnight. Within a week, twenty-eight Israeli ambassadors were back in Jerusalem, unemployed. In 1981, Israel had only four embassies on the African continent—in Malawi, Lesotho and Swaziland, and in South Africa. "There's not much use in our getting interested in the North-South dialogue," Efraim Haran said sadly. "We've been thrown out—not admitted to any group."

Still, a remnant survives, and Israel cares, deeply. When Zaire resumed diplomatic relations late in 1982, a delegation of more than eighty Israelis headed by the Foreign Minister trekked to Zaire to express their affection for Mobuto. Meanwhile, there are semi-official Israeli offices in the Ivory Coast, Ghana and Kenya (which cooperated in the Entebbe rescue), and students from half a dozen other African countries attend Israeli agricultural institutes, many of them on scholarships supplied by the Dutch and Swedish governments as part of their LDC aid program. "Their technologies are too sophisticated for these students," Timor commented, "and ours are right." (Not all the advice has been good. In a spectacular misjudgment, Ghana chose Israeli experts to design its income tax system, which promptly aborted, like Israel's own.) Other African states still come to Israel for feasibility studies on projects to be presented to the World Bank, where Israeli expertise is valued. Israeli trade with Africa in 1980 was double what it had been in 1972, but a high proportion of that was in weaponry.

The Latin American effort began earlier (for the Latin Americans were by far the largest bloc in the United Nations at the time Israel was admitted), and had a different focus, because there were Jews in Latin America. "Every Envoy Extraordinary and Minister Plenipotentiary of Israel," Walter Eytan wrote, "has a dual function. He is Minister Plenipotentiary to the country to which he is accredited—and Envoy Extraordinary to its Jews. . . . In each country, the foreign residents constitute what in their circles and in the diplomatic corps is known as a 'colony.' There is a French colony in Italy, a Swedish colony in Japan, a British colony in Peru. The Jewish community in many countries is seen by gentiles as the Israeli colony. . . . Israel does not claim their political allegiance. . . . But they are bound to Israel by sentiment, and to some extent by self-interest."

Joshua Livnat, counselor at the Israeli embassy in Washington, a stern young man in a polka-dot shirt who handled Israel's membership in the

Inter-American Development Bank, reported that the Israeli ambassadors in Latin America put about half their time into servicing the needs and wishes of the local Jewish community—which could also be a source of funds, especially travel money for local students and labor leaders and VIPs who were to tour Israel as guests of the government. Like other Christian countries, Latin American states presented the Israeli missions with disadvantages from long traditions of anti-Semitism, and more important advantages from a combination of familiarity with and curiosity about the land of the Bible. There was also an interest in receiving technical assistance not from a Great Power that might exact a price for it at any moment but from this peripheral state that could not force anybody to do anything.

Israel made a major investment in technical assistance for Latin America, supplying the Organization of American States with a larger number of expert consultants than came from any of the European states. Courses were taught in Spanish at Israeli universities and technical institutes for the benefit of these students, and the embassies casually kept in touch with them after their return. "In each country," Livnat observed, "you have by now a club of at least two or three hundred people who have been trained in Israel."

The flow of "experts" is steady and heavy. "We have," Livnat said, "a kind of Mafia of development, two thousand people who have worked abroad. You find them wherever you look.† In the Amazon, you find an expert working with the peasants on agriculture; in Peru, you find an archaeological expert who illuminated the walls of the temple in Jerusalem and is now illuminating the ruins of Cusco. When we get good results, we help ourselves. You must not expect returns on this investment in political terms, but in Latin America we have created an excellent image of Israel. Despite severe pressure from the nonaligned bloc, the Latin American nations did not sever relations with us when the Africans did."

It can be argued that this reservoir of goodwill for Israel has been helpful everywhere, and accounts for the relatively slight impact of the drumfire of anti-Israel resolutions in the United Nations and its specialized agencies. Timor remembered a visit to Nepal, a country that consistently votes to denounce Zionism in the General Assembly. One of his calls was on the Agriculture Minister, who came to the door of his office grinning broadly and called, "Shalom!" He had spent a year in training on an Israeli kibbutz, and remembered it happily. . . .

† Including the United States, where the Ford Foundation has sponsored an Israeli technical team to help black communities in Louisiana grow rice, and the Labor Department has given the Israelis a contract to help the Navajos organize kibbutz-like rural cooperatives.

3

Planning a Foreign Service for Israel, Walter Eytan, principal of the Public Service College of the Jewish Agency, had expected to draw on Jews around the world, but in the end the only significant contributions were from the British Isles—most notably Abba Eban, an all-but-unique triple first from Cambridge, fluent in Arabic and Hebrew as well as English and French. In any event, most participation from the Diaspora had been cut off by the decision that the work of the Foreign Ministry would be conducted in Hebrew. (And the second language was to be French, marking the full rejection of the hated mandatory power. The Ministry of Foreign Affairs was one of the first organs of Israeli government to move to Jerusalem, in 1953. It was and is housed in a collection of temporary tin-roofed one-story buildings, identified on their walls with some Hebrew words and, in French, MINISTÈRE DES AFFAIRES ÉTRANGERS.)

"There was a nucleus of people in the political department of the Jewish Agency," said Deputy Director General Hanan Bar-On, a lean man with a lined face, bright blue eyes, long ears, working in a tiny cream-colored office partitioned off from his secretary, an oriental throw rug on the vinyl tile floor, flowers on all the surfaces. "But we had to create a Foreign Service from scratch. We didn't have anybody to teach us, we didn't know a thing. The people who got high posts abroad were drawn from the leadership of the community, highly cultured veterans of the struggle for independence on the political side.

"It was not a *career* question. People moved into diplomacy because it was a necessity, it was the field in which you did your service. That was the major preoccupation of everybody—nurturing this creation. They were a tightly knit group, everybody knew everybody else. The Foreign Minister [Sharett] and the Director General [Eytan] were involved with everybody, for better or worse. They knew who had to be watched, who not— which is not to say their judgments were always right. There was a great deal of freewheeling. Communications were primitive, you had to go through open cables.

"Our ministers were sent out, they didn't find anything when they arrived. They had to find a house, the beginnings of a staff. They didn't know anybody, perhaps they had a few contacts in the Jewish community. But generally speaking, the first Israeli minister was a man from the moon." And the rites and passages of diplomacy were for him a moonscape. As late as 1958, Eytan reported, no chief of mission for Israel had ever served the Foreign Ministry in any post other than chief of mission.

334

By then, there was a Ministry and people rising through it in a career service. How important that service has been in the formulation of Israeli policy is a subject of argument (almost everything related to Israel is a subject of argument). Lewis Brownstein has described foreign policy decision-making in Israel as "highly personalized, politicized, reactive, ad hoc, and unsystematic." Though Eban and Rafael give evidence that cabinets actually voted on foreign policy decisions and that these votes were controlling (something that could happen in few other countries), it seems clear that from the early days of Ben-Gurion through Begin the Prime Ministers have sought to keep control of foreign relations as tightly as possible in their own hands.

In one respect, moreover, the Israeli Foreign Ministry is more politicized than its European peers, for in Europe (and in the British Commonwealth) there is usually a Permanent Undersecretary or Secretary-General, a chief of the Foreign Office, who continues in office through changes in government, while in Israel the Director General (like the American Under Secretary of State for Political Affairs, the highest rank attainable in the U.S. Foreign Service) serves at the pleasure of the Minister, who traditionally finds his own man for the job on taking office.

But to complain as Professor Brownstein does that "foreign affairs has, from the beginning of the Israeli state, been controlled by a very small group of people" is to attack a position that needs no defense. Where would the professor find a contrast? Surely not in the United States, as the populist attacks on the Council on Foreign Relations and the Trilateral Commission so vividly demonstrate. Ben-Gurion in retirement said he distrusted the expert who "does not have to know people," and preferred guidance from a politician's "experience which enables him to know people, to know their capacities, to know their response to a particular policy in a particular circumstance. If, allied to his judgment of people, he can also make a wise assessment of situations, he can go ahead and fix his priorities with confidence whatever the experts say." This is the view of all political leaders, even the domestically oriented Thatchers, Reagans and Mitterrands who would dearly love to have some all-knowing and politically savvy Foreign Minister take this damned cup from their lips. On large decisions, it is also very likely true.

To the accusation that Israeli foreign policy is unplanned, the Ministry would give a cheerful assent. "There is no foreign-policy planning anywhere in the world today," said Pinhas Eliav, Director of the Center for Political Research in the Ministry, a bureau that had the word "planning" in its title when founded. "People have given up on that. Your policy-planning staff in the State Department writes speeches for the Secretary. . . ."

At the beginning, Israeli missions were headed by political figures, there being no Foreign Service from which to draw. Some were distinguished and important Zionist leaders, like Golda Meir, who served as Israel's first ambassador to Moscow (where she had the personal glory but political horror of a wildly affectionate demonstration by twenty thousand Soviet Jews on the occasion of her first attendance at one of Moscow's few surviving synagogues for the first of the High Holy Days in 1948). Much later, Meir as Prime Minister would send to Washington Yitzhak Rabin, Commanding General of the Army, who had no diplomatic experience. But he was a rarity: the young recruits of 1948–53 had matured by then, and virtually all the Israeli ambassadors since 1970 have been Foreign Service professionals, who have lived through the usual alternations of service abroad and service in the Foreign Ministry bureaucracy, and are marked with specific Foreign Ministry attitudes. (In one way, however, the Israeli diplomats seem more closely tied than others to domestic attitudes: when government employees struck for higher wages in late 1982, the Israeli FSOs closed their embassies.)

Three large divisions, each with forty to one hundred people, dominate the Ministry. Technical Assistance organizes and staffs the aid projects. Political Research is essentially a coordinator of intelligence. Information publishes magazines in English, French, German, Spanish, Arabic, Czech and Japanese, arranges and conducts VIP tours for foreigners, sends the Israel Philharmonic and other groups abroad, and keeps the embassies informed of how Jerusalem wants them to answer questions. When the European summit in Venice announced its peace plan in June 1980, the Information office had an analysis of the proposal on the wire to all missions the same night (literally before the European ambassadors in Tel Aviv had seen copies of the plan).

As in other Foreign Ministries, there are geographical bureaus and substantive bureaus, but the geographical divisions are unusual. South Africa is dealt with by the European bureau, Portugal by the Latin American bureau. Though the Information Division has a small section of "Diaspora relations" (sandwiched between "cultural affairs" and "official guests"), there is no bureau of outreach to the Jewish community: that is still done, in theory, by the Jewish Agency. "We want to reach the *non-Jewish* community," said Moshe Arad, a brisk young man who is Assistant Director General for Information.

Eytan's formulation of the Israeli ambassador as envoy extraordinary to the local Jewish community would make the Foreign Ministry a little itchy today. "The cultivation of the local Jewish community, the maintenance of close contact both official and unofficial, is always part of the task of the Israeli Foreign Service Officer," said Bar-On. He shrugged. "It's a Jewish state. The government of Israel always protests, takes note, tries to counteract anti-Semitic manifestations wherever they occur. It can be seen as interference in domestic affairs." From the Foreign Ministry's point of view, this tail can also wag the dog: even before the unfortunate development of the league of pariah states in the 1970s, Israeli horror at apartheid and memories of Afrikaner support for Hitler were suppressed to soothe the fears of the South African Jews. "We could not," said Bar-On, "cut them adrift." In 1982, the government sought cancellation of a conference on genocide, usually a subject dear to Israeli hearts, because the speakers were to include Armenians denouncing Turks, and the Turkish Government had threatened revenge on the forty thousand Jews in Turkey.

Even in Argentina, which stands second only to the Arab states and the Soviet Union in the virulence of its official anti-Semitism, the Israelis have kept a low profile. The Jewish propaganda organs in the United States did not rise to the defense of Jacopo Timerman when the Reagan administration and its allies among the neo-conservatives sought to discredit the leading victim of that anti-Semitism—even though Timerman had chosen Israeli nationality and residence upon his expulsion from his native land.

By far the largest of the Israeli missions abroad, necessarily, is that in the United States. About four hundred employees work at the embassy in Washington and the eight consulates general (New York, Boston, Chicago, San Francisco, Los Angeles, Houston, Atlanta and Philadelphia—no other country has so many consulates in America). They concentrate, said Zvi Brosh, chief of information for the embassy and supervisor of Israeli official propaganda throughout the United States, on public relations rather than the usual consular activities, though trade and tourism are supervised from the New York consulate rather than from Washington. In the PR operation in New York, Israel has separate bureaus for press, information, library, film, speakers, liaison with academics, publishing and radio ("because the people the networks send to Jerusalem," said Moshe Arad, "are interested only in getting on television").

The embassy staff includes, among others, no fewer than seven political officers; a military mission headed by a major general (the highest rank in the Israeli Army); economics counselors seconded from the Treasury (who predict American economic trends for use back home and generate the arguments to make plausible the U.S. political decision that although Brazil, Mexico, Taiwan and South Korea have become prosperous enough to do without American trade preferences and food packages—a decision temporarily reversed in the days of the debt crisis—Israel is still a worthy object of charity); and an agricultural attaché (who arranges research cooperation between U.S. and Israeli government and university stations, helps sell in America as in Europe the out-of-season flowers and avocados and fruits Israeli farmers grow for export, and also promotes Israeli equipment for dry farming in the American West).

But this is in a sense no more than the tip of the iceberg, for the embassy and to a lesser degree the consulates are under orders not to become too visible in grass-roots lobbying. For that purpose there is the American-Israeli Public Affairs Committee (AIPAC), which describes itself as "an *American* organization registered as a domestic lobby. It is supported solely by private donations (not tax-deductible) from individuals. It receives no monetary assistance whatsoever from Israel nor any foreign group." The Israeli embassy and government do not, Brosh said, give AIPAC instructions—just "facts; what they do with the facts is their business." But except for a few days after Begin brusquely rejected Reagan's peace plan in September 1982, nobody on Capitol Hill, where AIPAC spends its annual $1 million budget, can recall occasions when Israel and AIPAC were on different sides of an issue.

The usefulness of AIPAC is especially great when Israel hopes to influence U.S. behavior in the Arab world. It would have been clearly improper, for example, for the Israeli embassy to lobby the Congress to reject President Reagan's plan to sell AWACS aircraft to Saudi Arabia, but there was no formal Israeli interference in American affairs when AIPAC blanketed the country with literature and stalked the halls of Congress to block the proposal. Or at least that was the position in the days of Nixon, Ford and Carter; Ronald Reagan found it a little too subtle, and suggested that domestic political discussion of American foreign policy was not a fit subject for foreign participation (though it was okay for the National Security Adviser to escort a young Saudi prince to meetings with key senators, and for the oil companies to spend tax-deductible dollars lobbying on the Saudi side).

Mossad, the Israeli Secret Service, also plays an unusual role in Israel's representation abroad—especially, again, in the United States. Many of Mossad's reports are designed not for use by the Foreign Ministry or the Defense Department, but for exploitation in the press of foreign countries. Yehuda Horam, director of the bureau that deals with most of Western Europe, had a year's sabbatical leave in 1979 to work at Columbia University and study "aspects of American foreign policy and the influence of domestic factors. My conclusion was that the main factor is the media." Mossad makes itself available to American reporters on a deep background basis to supply information about developments not only in the Arab world and in Europe, but also inside the State Department, the Defense Department and the CIA, all of which the Israelis have well and truly penetrated. The world is full of situations of great concern to Israel—for example, the swap of oil and nuclear technology between Brazil and Iraq, where Israel's only hope of influencing the outcome lies in stirring up the U.S. press.

Israeli ambassadors have some unique chores. The Arab League since 1948 has run a boycott against companies that do business with Israel, requiring at a minimum an affidavit from a supplier to an Arab country that no part in his product is of Israeli manufacture. Where these affidavits are given—outside the United States, where the embassy and AIPAC successfully lobbied through an antiboycott law—the embassy cooperates in organizing trade channels that protect Israeli sales but leave the foreign manufacturer with a fig leaf of apparent conformity with the boycott. There is also an incessant stream of messages from Jerusalem to alert ambassadors to new efforts in United Nations organizations to confer recognition on the Palestine Liberation Organization. The week this tourist visited Australia, Jerusalem had distributed an all-points bulletin about an upcoming meeting of the International Civil Aviation Organization, where the Arabs intended to seek a resolution endorsing "the inalienable rights of Palestinians." ("The PLO has observer status at ICAO," said Ambassador Michael Elizur, "presumably because of its experience in hijacking.") The embassy called the Australian Foreign Ministry, which proclaimed itself thoroughly familiar with the question, and entirely prepared to vote right. But the majority, of course, voted wrong.

4

Israel came into existence with the help of the United States and the Soviet Union, in the teeth of opposition by Britain and without significant assistance from France, which had abstained on the partition resolution. The hope was to stay aloof from Great Power conflict, to gather in the exiles and create homes for the refugees, to make and tend a garden in the Middle East. But the hostility of the surrounding states and the impotence of the United Nations forced the new nation to rely on great allies, and the need for funds to pay the costs of settlement prohibited any effort by Israel to distance itself from the United States. Israel had recognized the People's Republic of China in 1950, but when the Korean War came it withdrew from all contacts with Peking, and voted in 1954 and thereafter to deny the Communists China's seat at the UN.

The key event was the overthrow of Farouk, and the subsequent rise of Nasser, who openly gave Egyptian sanctuary to *fedayeen* terrorists striking at Israeli villages and transportation links. Shared hostility to the Egyptian leader and the return of Churchill (who had Zionist inclinations) made possible a rapprochement between Israel and England; Arab support for the Algerian revolt created an unspoken alliance between Israel and France. Meanwhile, the change in Egypt gave the Soviet Union a new opportunity to break into the Mediterranean. In 1951, the Soviet Union had advocated a Security Council resolution ordering Egypt to permit the passage of Israeli shipping through the Suez Canal; in 1954, it vetoed a similar resolution. Russian arms poured into Egypt and Syria. The United States would not sell arms to Israel, which discouraged the Europeans from doing so. But with Nasser helping the Algerians and openly assaulting Israel ("Egypt has decided to despatch her heroes," a communiqué announced on August 31, 1955, "the disciples of Pharaoh and the sons of Islam, and they will clean the land of Palestine"), Paris made common cause with Jerusalem, supplying tanks and antitank weaponry, and the beginnings of a jet air force.

Britain joined the unspoken alliance after the seizure of the Suez Canal, and at a meeting in Sèvres outside Paris the three Prime Ministers—Eden for Britain, Mollet for France, Ben-Gurion for Israel—worked out the framework of a clumsy conspiracy. And in this most international of all Israeli actions, the diplomats were not involved at all. Abba Eban as ambassador to the UN and to Washington (the jobs were then joined) learned about the invasion of Sinai from his American hosts. In the subsequent uproar at the United Nations, there was no coordination among Israel, Britain and France because the Foreign Ministries of all three nations—which would have had to manage such coordination—had never been consulted about the military operations or prepared to manage its diplomatic consequences.

In the aftermath of 1956, Israel became permanently enmeshed in Great Power rivalries. The alliance with Britain ended quickly: the British still had major interests in Jordan and in the Gulf, and Israeli connections were worse than useless in protecting them from Nasserite outreach. The French alliance held, but it was clear enough within the Foreign Ministry that French sympathies with Israel were a function of French troubles in Algeria: if the latter ended, the former would be deeply imperiled. Soon after France made its deal with Ben Bella, De Gaulle wrote in his *Memoirs*, "I put a stop to irregular dealings which had developed between Tel Aviv and Paris on the military plane since the Suez expedition, whereby Israelis had become permanently attached at all levels to French military staffs and services. In particular, French cooperation in the construction of a factory near Beersheba for the transformation of uranium into plutonium—from which, one fine day, atomic bombs might emerge—was brought to an end."

De Gaulle was well ahead of his own electorate in shifting away from the Israeli alliance. Even some years later, Edward Kolodziej notes, "French public opinion . . . resisted any notion of abandoning Israel. . . . Had not Israel stood with France against 'its' Arabs? Now Israel needed help with 'its' Arabs." But France was not the United States; no amount of public sympathy for Israel's cause was likely to deflect French policy. With the Russians arming Egypt and its Syrian ally—in the aftermath of Suez the two had presumably become linked as a United Arab Republic—Israel became entirely dependent on the United States.

The zenith of Foreign Ministry influence on Israeli government policy came in the weeks just before the Six-Day War, when a Cabinet conscious of what would be only a temporary military superiority stayed its hand, watching while Nasser in May 1967 evicted the UN truce supervisors left over from 1956 and blockaded the Straits of Tiran. It was assumed that the Soviet Union was misinformed rather than malicious in its denunciations of a nonexistent Israeli military buildup on the Syrian front (the excuse for Nasser's actions).‡ The Western powers were given time to organize an effective action in defense of the principles of international law that protected Israeli shipping in the Gulf of Aqaba. Only after it became clear that President Lyndon Johnson would not add to his Vietnam troubles by making a show of force in the Straits of Tiran did the Israeli military take matters into its own hands—and even then the diplomats were permitted to offer a pledge of security for the West Bank to King Hussein, who had just signed on as Nasser's ally after years of vituperative hostility, if he stayed out of the war. As late as the fifth day of the war, Israel refrained from attacking the Syrian positions in the Golan Heights, from which Galilean settlements were under steady artillery attack, because the Foreign Ministry feared the total break with the Soviet Union that would (and did) result from a battle in which Russian gunners, part of the force manning the Syrian positions, would be killed.

But the success of the armies doomed the influence of the diplomats. As their representatives in New York entered the minefields of General Assembly resolutions a week after the cease-fire, the Israeli Government proclaimed an end to the division of Jerusalem and the incorporation of the city and its suburbs into Israel. Thereafter, however often the UN resolved to the contrary or the U.S. Government fussed, there could be no status quo ante; and the existing situation being unacceptable, the diplomats would have to create a new situation if the parties were to live in peace.

From the beginning in 1948, Israel took the not unreasonable position that its soldiers had met the soldiers of the Arab states on the battlefields, and if the results of those battles were to be changed on the ground their

‡ The peculiar behavior of the Soviet Union in the Middle East in May 1967 is described in fascinating detail by Theodore Draper in *Israel and World Politics*.

diplomats would have to meet its diplomats. In this context, the existence of the United Nations was perhaps a disadvantage, for in reality Israeli diplomats were forever meeting with Arab diplomats in the grand rooms of the international organizations. But such meetings implied the possibility of an end to the wars through the actions of third parties, by vote of nations not directly concerned (indeed, not particularly interested) in what happened to the peoples of the area. Back at the time of the original partition resolution, Warren Austin, former U.S. senator and permanent representative to the United Nations, was overheard wondering wearily why these Jews and Moslems couldn't settle their differences in a Christian spirit. At best, something of this sort (at worst, something that reflected what John Maynard Keynes, writing about Versailles, described as "the anti-Semitism not far below the surface in such an assemblage") was the only result to be anticipated from the effort to set the Middle East neatly on the path of peace by the decisions of others.

For the Arabs, sitting down with the victors of the Six-Day War meant accepting that they had been vanquished. They had taken so thorough a shellacking in that war that the facts were hard to deny, especially after the Israelis produced a tape recording of a telephone conversation between Nasser and Hussein on the second day, when the Arab leaders (speaking, incredibly, on an unscrambled radio circuit) had agreed to claim jointly that U.S. warplanes rather than Israeli aircraft had destroyed their fighters on the ground. But it was not until after the Yom Kippur War of 1973, when Anwar Sadat had secured something he could claim as a victory, however tenuously, that the Egyptians could meet and negotiate with the Israelis. The Syrians, having experienced the further humiliation of the complete destruction of both civil and military installations between the line to which the Israelis had advanced in 1973 and the cease-fire line drawn by Henry Kissinger, were and are unable to face their conquerors.

Before 1956, the United States had refused to sell arms to Israel. Between Suez and the Six-Day War, it had grudgingly allowed the purchase of a certain quantity of "defensive" weapons. After 1967, the United States had reluctantly replaced the French as the supplier of those arms the Israelis could not, in their rapidly expanding machine-tool industry, make for themselves. Month after month, the Egyptians expended across the Suez Canal the ammunition the Russians gave them, and the Israelis responded with air raids into Egypt using American planes. The superpowers became in a sense responsible for the survival of their clients. The cease-fire after the 1973 war was a joint Soviet–U.S. venture, with Henry Kissinger negotiating the terms in Moscow, and it was made to work only by Kissinger's "shuttle diplomacy," the exploitation of a personal presence that on each visit demanded by inference some gesture toward narrowing the gap between the parties.

There was another side to Kissinger's success: he bought it, as Jimmy Carter later bought the agreement at Camp David. An American Foreign Service Officer of long experience in the Middle East, equally hostile to Arabs and Israelis, describes the principle: "Every year, the United States adds up how much money Israel must spend to have both guns and butter, and we supply the difference between that and their resources so they won't have to make the choice." In effect, the United States pays the entire cost of the Israeli military: aid from the United States constitutes one quarter of the Israeli gross national product. Persuading Menachem Begin to return the Sinai oil fields to Egypt, President Carter promised that any short-fall in oil supplies to Israel would be made up by the United States. Neither Carter nor Begin—nor their advisers in the State Department and the Israeli Foreign Ministry—knew what that pledge meant, financially or operationally, and the terms on which this obligation is to be met still remained to be negotiated as 1982 ended.

A grand total of four employees of the U.S. embassy—two FSOs and two locals—"supervise" the expenditure by Israel of $2.5 billion of U.S. aid, per year. In effect, they write checks. The U.S. embassy in Tel Aviv—a pleasant six-story structure on the beach about half a mile from the disagreeable Fort-Lauderdale-like row of high-rise American hotels—holds only about eighty employees, which is small for a U.S. mission. The post does offer senior FSOs a chance to be near the news. "The first eighteen months I was out here," said Ambassador Samuel Lewis, a large, handsome, elegantly casual man with a round, shining face, "the Secretary of State was here in a negotiating mode seven times, the President was here once, the Vice-President was here once, half the Cabinet members came and about half the Congress, singly or in groups, every general in the U.S. Army and half the admirals, and there were countless visits by special negotiators, first Roy Atherton, then Robert Strauss, then Sol Linowitz. And most of them came here honestly to work."

The ambassador to Israel is one of very few men in the world who can pick up the telephone and get right through to the President of the United States, and he is a personage of surpassing importance to his hosts, all of whom are self-confessed experts on the United States and the exegesis of its statements and silences. Because of the extreme delicacy of the U.S.-Israeli relationship, and because the Near Eastern Affairs Bureau of the State Department is so aggressively pro-Arab, the Spokesman's office in Washington calls in at eleven-thirty each weekday morning (five-thirty in the afternoon in Israel) to check out with the embassy the "guidance" on Israel the Spokesman will use in answering questions from reporters at noon. The daily cable summarizing Israeli press reports is the only one of its kind routed to the White House.

Still, Tel Aviv has never been a particularly cherished post. Israeli food is awful; Hebrew is hard to learn and worth little outside these borders; though you can get heard easily enough back home, the fact is that your principals in Washington will make their decisions about U.S. policy in this area without consulting you (Kissinger especially thought it might actually be harmful to let the U.S. ambassador know what he was doing in his shuttlings). The ceaseless and all but infinite range of informal and quasiofficial contacts between the Israelis and people in the U.S. Government supersedes your function as a conduit of American policy. People are not just friendly; they are eager to spend time with the diplomatic corps. ("I see my colleagues less in Israel than in any post I have ever served in," said the Egyptian ambassador to Tel Aviv, "because the Israelis are so very warm and always want to entertain you.") When there is business to be done with the Israeli Government, the diplomat must drive or have himself driven to Jerusalem, more than an hour away, site of the Knesset [Parliament], the Prime Minister's office, the Foreign Ministry and all but one of the other departments of the Israeli Government, though a series of unanimous UN resolutions in the Security Council has forbidden the absorption of Jerusalem into the State of Israel. (The one department not housed in Jerusalem is the Defense Department, perhaps because of world religious sensibilities, perhaps because before 1967 the situation was too exposed, perhaps because the U.S. military attachés are in Tel Aviv.) "In this country," said the Danish ambassador, speaking for the entire diplomatic corps, "if you can't dictate in the car, you can't survive."

In Washington, a special six-man Office of Israeli and Arab-Israeli Affairs floats just within the bureaucratic borders of NEA (Near Eastern Affairs), functioning essentially as a special secretariat to serve the Seventh Floor. The basic Arab-Israeli "Sit Rep" (Situation Report) is done by the Bureau of Intelligence and Research ("We think it's a little lightweight"), and there are streams of analyses arriving from the CIA. ("The Agency will write analysis for anybody who will read it.") Reports come in floods from the National Security Agency, which monitors the communications of foreigners, and there is stuff to be gleaned from local and foreign newspapers and broadcasts. "A hell of a lot of people in this government are paid to generate paper on Israel. All these guys feel they play a special role, but in fact the paper is all sent to us; we have a special relationship with the Seventh Floor, we find the peg to hang the action memo on." When there is a Special Representative to help with the Israel-Egypt negotiations (the post comes and goes), he is staffed from this Office. Linowitz, when he held the post, short-circuited not only the Office and NEA but the State Department as a whole, maintaining and using an office in the White House itself. It was only as the representative of the President, Linowitz felt, that he could guarantee the necessary access to the heads of state in both Egypt and Israel.

On the Israeli end, a small North American department in the Foreign Ministry exists mostly to keep the Ministry informed of what its own government is doing. "In so many things is Israel oriented toward America," said Michael Elizur, looking back on his six years as director of that office. "Defense, Treasury . . . I had a watching brief, the Ministry would count on me to know, so they would never read in the papers. Cables from the embassy in Washington went directly to the Prime Minister as well as to my desk. A call would come from the Prime Minister's office before I'd had a chance to see it or think about it—'What have you done about this?' I had to sit on so many committees. . . ." The other side of the coin, of course, is the importance of the material on which the diplomat works. "When I was on the Asia desk," Elizur noted, "I could have declared war on the Maldive Islands, and nobody would have known."

What goes wrong here was succinctly stated by a man in the State Department's Israeli office: "These negotiations in the Middle East are really between the United States and Israel." Yet the obvious and interesting fact is that the people with the freedom of motion are the Egyptians—and the easily ascertainable fact is that both their Foreign Service and their top leadership are first-class. Sadat's job in mobilizing the Arab world prior to the Yom Kippur War was the precondition for the effectiveness of the oil boycott and thus of OPEC (from which he then got nothing but *tsouris*). The Egyptian ambassador to Washington, Ashraf Ghorbal, is widely regarded as one of the most astute (and affable) people in town, with considerable discretion in deciding on his activities: he was softening up the American Jewish community, speaking at B'Nai B'Rith meetings and the like, long before Sadat made his pilgrimage to Jerusalem. (Plaques thanking Ghorbal for his appearances before Jewish organizations hang in the reception room of his modest embassy; so does a certificate attesting to the fact that Mrs. Ghorbal rode with Richard Nixon once on *Air Force One*.) The Foreign Ministry in Cairo has a Third World flavor—erratic hours, missed appointments, HQ in a run-down old palace, bad housekeeping (but very good Turkish coffee). The people on the upper bureaucratic levels, however, are as linguistically capable, as shrewd, as easily at home in the great world, as their opposite numbers in Jerusalem. And Egypt, as the descendants of Joseph and Moses must know, has an even longer (and maybe even greater) history than Israel. . . .

Jimmy Carter once told Sol Linowitz that what troubled him after meetings with Menachem Begin was his feeling that Begin did not consider the Palestinians to be truly human. It was not an accusation that could have been brought against the Zionist pioneers, the kibbutzim, the Ebans who mastered Arabic even before coming to Israel because it would be the language of their neighbors. The early Zionists did not wish to be Europeans; they were farmers, egalitarians, building a self-image as citizens of an Asian country, eager for ties with the new states of Africa. After all, Jews were not Aryans, either.

This spirit has gone, victim in part of more than forty years of unrelenting hostility from Arab leadership, who bound the former colonies to their side from the time of Bandung—and who after 1973 could dangle before the noses of the poor their oil wealth and the dream that those who followed their example might similarly pick the pockets of the rich. Compelled to live with the logic that the enemy of my enemies must be my friend, the Israelis have made common cause with the cocaine smugglers of Ecuador, the assassins first of Nicaragua and then of Guatemala, the racists of South Africa, the repressive entrepreneurs of Taiwan. Except for the Taiwan decision (a preference for Nationalist over Communist China is surely legitimate by human rights criteria), these choices of friends would have been intolerable to the early Zionists.

Zionist morality has been victim also, one fears, of the population flows that brought to Israel so large an underclass of Jews from North Africa and Arabia, for whom the hated oppressor of their people's history was not the Crusader or the Cossack or the Nazi or the Cagoulard, but the Moslem, for whom the idea of a Jewish state but a secular government was an unnecessary subtlety.

Nothing has put the United Nations into such deserved disrepute as the series of General Assembly resolutions labeling Zionism as a form of racism. The first of these happened on Moynihan's watch, when he was U.S. permanent representative to the United Nations, and in addition to fighting it he sought to understand why the Arabs were insisting on this absurd and contemptible form of words. "What mattered [to the Arabs]," he concluded, "was that the Israelis looked down upon them. They were prepared to hit back with any charge that came to hand." The distressing fact is that the Israelis, not least at the Foreign Ministry, *do* look down upon the Arabs, as the Americans look down upon the Russians, the Ibo upon the Yoruba, the Japanese upon the Koreans, the Russians upon the Poles, the French upon everybody. The stuff of horror is in these attitudes, as Lebanon demonstrated, and the tragedy is that Zionism was born free of them.

There is no disposition in this corner to sit in judgment on Israel or its policies. To the distant observer, there is obvious truth in King Hussein's 1967 comment that Israel could have territory or peace, but not both.

Closer to the scene, the definitions become crucial: what territory? what peace? Obviously, there are many who would make a graveyard of Israel, and call it peace. The founders of the state wished to be judged by special, high criteria of selflessness and democracy, but those founders are gone now, as dead as Washington and Jefferson. Their successors are entitled to live by the normal rules, and to a recognition that their neighbors have not let them do so.

What must be noted, however, is the unwilled, dangerous and mutually disliked trope toward dependence on the United States. Israel started by identifying with the Asians; then sought to identify with the Africans; then made common cause as much as it could with the West Europeans (where the Jewish state could count on the all but unquestioning support of a Germany still reeling from the guilt of the Holocaust). From before the founding of the nation, Israeli diplomats had lived with personal knowledge of the hostility of the State Department to the idea of a Jewish state in the Arab Near East: it was a nightmare, not a dream of the Foreign Ministry that Israel would become a client of the United States. But it happened: worse, it has been accepted.

Pinhas Eliav, Director of the Center for Political Research, a short, bald man in an embroidered skullcap, an Israeli FSO since 1949, delivered himself in 1980 of an overview of the world as seen from Jerusalem:

"The micro-situation of Israel in the Arab world is not bad. They are quarreling with each other. They have money, but nobody likes them for it. And if God forbid there should be another war, we can take them. The peace process with Egypt is irreversible. In the micro-situation, trends are good for Israel.

"But the macro-situation is bad. The Europeans will throw over Israel for a few small favors from Bahrain. Only the American-Israeli relation is unique. A country that is the biggest in the world to Israel has been like a twin brother. The relationship has a level above which it will not attain, and a level below which it will not fall. We exchange secret information. Never an open alliance like England or France. It's like the Heine song—'Don't Meet Me on High Street.' But never will there be an abandonment like we got from England and France, and are about to get from Germany."

But if Israel is to be a nation like any other, and the United States has become, as the academics say, "an ordinary country," then the normal rules of international relations must apply. The first of these rules, the necessary basis for policy, is "Never say never." It is not Israel's fault that the Reagan administration came to power with the foolish idea that the Arabs and Israelis could be persuaded (actually *forced*: "They will have to see") that their parochial quarrel should be put aside in the face of the Soviet menace. Having thus stressed the one issue on which Arabs and Israelis could unite—that their quarrel with each other was much more real and more important than any damned theoretical nonsense about Soviet imperialism—the United States came into 1982 as no one's brother in the Middle East.

The success of Israeli arms in Lebanon probably eased American problems in that part of the world, for it seemed to deprive the Arabs of an alternative. If the Israelis could destroy a Soviet-supplied Syrian Air Force and still the surface-to-air missiles and knock out the T-72 tanks, there was simply no point in cultivating the Soviet Union. Only those whose policies enabled them to purchase American arms would be able to feel secure in the world. Thus, while the 1973 war had produced an oil embargo and a united Arab League, the 1982 war left the Arabs reluctant to take steps that might antagonize the United States—and compelled to face the fact that the Lebanese wanted armed Palestinians out of their country at least as much as the Israelis did. By mid-1983, the Arabs were being further compelled to face the even more awkward fact that Syria had never recognized the independent existence of Lebanon.

A year after the invasion of Lebanon, it appeared that Begin and his allies among the Sephardim had gained the objectives of their policy. The northern border was safe; the Palestinians of the West Bank were in despair, their leadership cadre draining out to other countries in hopes of a better future for their children; Arafat was cut off from his own resources; Hussein had declared himself irrelevant. Once again, the Israelis had been lucky in their enemies. Sensible policy for the Arabs would have been to arrange—or at least to pretend—an unconditional rapprochement with the Americans. There are, after all, significant actors in American corporate and governmental leadership who believe that the world of the Gulf is more important than Israel to the American future. By appearing to lose interest in Israel in the early stages of such a rapprochement, the Arabs would have reason to hope that the Americans would lose interest later.

But the Saudis and the Syrians found it more comfortable to have an enemy against whom recalcitrant members of their own society could be roused—and Yasir Arafat found it convenient to ride around in the luxurious 707 the Saudis had outfitted for him, playing the big man in Bulgaria while teen-age Palestinian girls fell prey to hysterical hopelessness on the occupied West Bank. By refusing PLO consent to representation by Hussein in negotiations with Israel, the "rejectionists" assured the absorption of Judea and Samaria into Begin's Biblical Israel. That game is over now—if not forever, at least for the generation already adult. "No longer," wrote Larry Fabian of the Carnegie Endowment in spring 1983, "is there any refuge behind the wondrous vagaries of U.N. Security Council Resolution 242, ever closer to becoming a famous anachronism as it relates to the West Bank."

But Fabian also points out that the U.S. commitment to the partition of Palestine was undertaken on behalf of *both* Jews and Arabs, that the United States can no more back away from "autonomy" for the West Bank than it can from the security of Israel within partitioned borders. The "facts on the ground" that the Begin government may create with its settlement program cannot destroy that commitment, and the refusal of the PLO and its allies to claim the commitment cannot excuse the United States from honoring it. For most Israelis, including virtually all the Begin government, such American interference in what they consider their security affairs is worse than presumptuous. But there are in the Foreign Ministry career bureaucrats who see quite clearly that if the United States is to support the Israeli claim to the Mediterranean littoral of Palestine, in perpetuity, it cannot renege on its old pledges to the Palestinian Arabs. The first task of Israeli diplomacy in the next years must be convincing the rest of the Israeli Government that America cannot accept, though it cannot prevent, an Israeli annexation of the West Bank.

For both Americans and Israelis, it is a source of sentiments ranging from discomfort to agony that Israel should be in a position where its future is controlled by what is acceptable to the United States. As Anwar Sadat demonstrated—for his trip to Jerusalem was regarded as folly by the State Department—the diplomacy that can bring peace to the Middle East must be that of the residents: agreements reached because Kissinger or Carter or Shultz needs them eventually add more questions than they answer. The hope for American policy in this unhappy area is that both Arabs and Jews have so much to gain and so little to lose by mutual recognition that there can be no violent cure for their grievances and anxieties. One awaits, not very optimistically, the regional diplomacy that will make that truth acceptable.

V

Purpose

12

DIRECTIONS

> Every city is in a natural state of war with every other, not indeed proclaimed by heralds, but everlasting.
>
> —Plato

> More important was the bottom line: all three of us wanted peace.
>
> —Jimmy Carter on Camp David

> Moscow is a political center, where all reactions are political, and that's what diplomacy is all about.
>
> —Vladilen M. Vasev,
> minister-counselor, Soviet
> embassy, Washington

So many trees, and you promised us a forest.
Well. We will try.

1

What nation-states want in their relations with each other are:
1. to live in peace and develop their own political, legal and economic institutions as they see fit;
2. to supplement the output of their own economies with goods and services unavailable in their geographical situation or so expensive to produce locally that importing them is the only rational procedure. This category includes not only bananas in the United States, soybeans in Germany and

oil in France, but also road-building machinery in Mali, steel in Colombia and computer software in the Soviet Union;

3. like Rodney Dangerfield, a little respect. This includes the opportunity to extend national protection in some sense to citizens (especially diplomats) and to investments located in the jurisdiction of another state.

These goals are easier to state than to reach. Since the beginnings of settled civilization, the occupants of the cities and the farms have had to contend with incursions by nomads and human predators who are not bound by their rules. The question of what constitutes a nation-state has never been settled to everyone's satisfaction, and boundaries have always been fluid. Very few nations—nearly all of them islands—are truly "natural" entities. All the others have borders that reflect political developments and the results of past wars rather than geographical, linguistic or cultural limits.

Within the memory of middle-aged men, it was still considered reasonable if not admirable behavior for nation-states to covet their neighbors' territories—Nice and Savoy for Mussolini; all eastern Europe as *Lebensraum* for Hitler; Manchukuo and then the whole co-prosperity sphere for Japan; the northern provinces of Turkey and Iran, eastern Poland, Bessarabia, Karelia and the Kuriles for the Soviet Union (which got all of them except the first pair); Singapore and Papua and Brunei and Timor and chunks of the Philippines and God knows what else for Indonesia. Even now, the peace of the world is threatened by Iraqi and Israeli and Somali and Guatemalan and Moroccan and Libyan and Venezuelan territorial ambitions, not to mention continuing border disputes between Chile and its eastern and northern neighbors, between India and Pakistan, Peru and Bolivia, India and China, China and the Soviet Union, Greece and Turkey. One of these days, the Mexicans will doubtless come clamoring for the return of Texas and California.

Language groups are the most natural kin for political organization, but from the beginning national boundaries have been drawn to include people who speak different languages, and to separate people with a common tongue. To this day, there are international tensions derived from the presence of Arabic-speaking populations in Iran, Hungarian-speaking populations in Romania, Tamil-speakers in Ceylon, Albanian-speakers in Yugoslavia, Chinese-speakers in Malaysia, Vietnam and Indonesia. Among the advantages of the European Community for the Danes has been an increase in Danish leverage on Germany to improve the treatment of the Danish-speaking minority in Schleswig-Holstein.

In the broad view, history is the tale of large population movements and cultural aggrandizements: Egyptians, Hittites, Greeks, Romans, the Central Asian tribes moving both east and west, the Arabs, the Norse, the Europeans *tout court* moving across the plains to consolidate their grip on the American continent and on Siberia, across the waters to impose their manners and morals and means of production on the entire globe. This last movement still has an air of finality to it, but so did Turkish occupation of the Balkans as late as the seventeenth century. No doubt European cultural dominance is guaranteed in much of the Americas and in the Antipodes, where the European migrants have largely displaced the natives. It is by no means clear, however, that in the conflict between tradition and "modernization" in the Near East and Africa and Asia, the education in European ways so forcefully imposed in the nineteenth and early twentieth centuries must be the winner.

Religious movements have long impinged on the development and relations of the nation-states—proselytizing Romans, Jews, Christians, Moslems, Buddhists have all at one time or another placed the pursuit of truth far above the pursuit of peace. The fissiparous religions—Christianity with its Arians and Manicheans and Orthodox and Catholic and Protestant, Mohammedanism with its Sunni and Shi'ite and lesser offspring—have produced conflicts beyond the control of diplomacy or the comprehension of the unconverted. The Middle East and Ireland, indeed, still suffer from the desperation of these antagonisms. Secular faiths that can be adapted to national purposes—National Socialism in Germany, the Socialism of the Fascisti in Italy, Shintoism in Japan, Russian Communism —couple two dangers at once, though it should be noted that Russian Communism is a deeply conservative faith and nationalist-racist despite rather than because of its sacred texts.

Even the activities of trade, superficially a clear benefit to all the parties, have become occasions for the expression of hostility and the drive for dominance. Denying potential enemies or just plain "others" access to resources that might strengthen them is not a strategy invented by Caspar Weinberger but a tactic followed from the days of the Medes and the Persians. The Japanese sought to heighten the value of silk in the nineteenth century as the English had sought to keep up the price of wool in the fifteenth, by restricting access to the technology (it is not for nothing that the Lord Chancellor sits on a woolsack). Long before Mahan, the British and the Dutch competed for control of the seas to gain for themselves and deny to others access to wealth in foreign parts; even longer before Clausewitz, the Greek city-states lived as though war were simply an extension of diplomacy by other means. In the eighteenth century the French financier Colbert designed a system to strengthen the state by stimulating exports and controlling imports, thereby increasing the nation's store of gold. Substituting foreign exchange for gold, and making such policy adjustments as they are compelled to make, the Japanese have simply followed his example.

Part of this history is now at an end. The technology of modern warfare is such that war as a policy is now practical only in situations where the party being attacked (or his friends) cannot rain the newest means of destruction on the attacker. Even the little wars with limited means have become destructive beyond the possibilities of national gain: the armaments mount, but war avoidance becomes a higher goal than victory. In the civil wars, the implacable ideologues must rely increasingly on adolescent warriors, for whom the destruction of their parents' world is a psychological imperative as well as a revolutionary target. The menace of war remains a tool in the diplomat's kit, but increasingly the remedy for the most deeply felt international injustice is seen to reside in strategies that will not require fighting and death.

Still, international relations are always in large part competitive, and the price of losing is high. To secure the goals of peace, prosperity and respect in a world of states, nations feel compelled to form alliances. Such alliances are always more or less uncertain; as George Washington pointed out, nations may have permanent interests but they do not have permanent friends. History teaches that while individuals may indeed be loving, loyal, truthful and trustworthy, governments are none of these.

In the time of the monarchies, which takes one through Abdul-Aziz ibn-Saud, efforts were forever being made to solidify alliances through marrying oneself or one's heirs to the offspring of the rulers of other kingdoms. The device of choice, however, was always the written treaty, sometimes secret, sometimes public or partly public, by which the contracting parties agreed to take certain actions (or refrain from certain actions) if their opposite numbers got in trouble with somebody else. The existence of chains of these treaties brought World War I cascading onto Europe; the negotiation of a single treaty between Hitler's Reich and the Soviet Union in August 1939 started the tank treads rolling toward World War II.

In the nature of things, alliances are multilateral but antagonisms are bilateral; allies are then pulled into the dispute. And alliances shift because today's antagonist can give a nation-state more than today's ally. Hitler was prepared (temporarily, but Stalin didn't know that) to award to the Soviet Union the little Baltic States that had broken free after World War I, and eastern Poland, and as much of Finland as it could grab. What *Ostpolitik* in West Germany expresses is an understanding that the reunification of Germany requires the consent of the Soviet Union, not of the United States; what keeps the attitude in check is widespread understanding that the price for that consent is likely to be much higher than West German society will ever wish to pay. (And the East

Germans are a proud people. "They used to say," reports one of the men who opened the U.S. embassy in East Berlin, " 'West Germany is all right, but it was easy: they had the Americans. Look what we've done—and we've had the Russians.' ") The danger to the Soviet Union of social revolution in Poland or Czechoslovakia is that the Russians' identification with today's hated tyrants would lead any popularly acceptable successor to swing political alliances toward the United States. The danger to the United States of social revolution in Latin America or Saudi Arabia is that the Americans' identification with today's hated tyrants would lead any popularly acceptable successor to swing political alliance toward the Soviet Union.

What happened in the first four years of the Iranian Revolution is most remarkable politically, perhaps, in the Islamic Republic's ability to continue wishing a plague on both the great houses. The sophisticates who whooped with joy at the ascent of Khomeini made great fools of themselves. ("Contrary to the superficial reports in the American press about his attitude toward Jews, women and others," Richard Falk of Princeton wrote in the spring of 1979, "Khomeini's Islamic Republic can be expected to have a doctrine of social justice at its core: from all indications, it will be flexible in interpreting the Koran, keeping the 'book of research' open to amendment and adaptation," etc.) But they were right in their insistence that the theocratic state would not seek to move into the opposite camp, which would have been normal behavior.

The world has been far more bipolar in the years since World War II than at any previous time, the antagonists having so enormous a preponderance of the ultimate weaponry. Conditions of communication and transportation have made it all but impossible for nations to opt out of all alliances, as the United States sought to do throughout its first century and a half. The heroic efforts of the self-proclaimed "nonaligned" states that called themselves a Third World could not lead down the track the United States had pioneered in the nineteenth century because these states wanted not to be left alone but to be helped by both sides. (The Iranians could be antagonistic in both directions because at the start they needed no help.) Old antagonisms between supposedly nonaligned states lead them willy-nilly to seek protection from one alliance or the other.

2

Bipolarity is what the Chinese call "hegemonism" and the newspapers call the Cold War. That this is an unfortunate way to run the world has been apparent to many people for a long time, and for twenty years there has been an occasionally lively debate on who should be "blamed" for it. "Revisionist" history has influenced American policy—especially in the first two Carter years—and affected the attitudes of political figures and FSOs. Myself, I find certain truths to be self-evident, to wit:

Both the United States and the Soviet Union came out of the war with serious misperceptions of each other and of the rest of the world.

Nations find it hard to believe that the friend of their enemy can be their friend. They find it even harder to believe that the enemy of their enemy is a bad lot. In the United States, then, the war years were years of Uncle Joe Stalin and the fatuities of Joseph E. Davies' *Mission to Moscow*. When it was found that the freed Russian POWs were afraid to go back to the Soviet Union, it was assumed they were all fascists, everyone was too embarrassed to let the facts get out, and tens of thousands of Russians were forced into cattle cars that took them straight to the Gulag.

The fact that the Russian Revolution had, like its predecessors, turned nationalist was welcomed in the United States even by those who knew enough history to remember what the French Revolution had done to Europe after it turned nationalist. The dissolution of the Comintern was considered proof that the Soviets had dropped the old Trotskyite nonsense of world revolution (in earnest of which, Stalin had arranged to have Trotsky axed to death in Mexico). In any event, Stalin had promised at Yalta and Tehran that the countries where the Russian armies were in occupation would be permitted to choose their own governments by free elections, it being generally understood that no government actually *hostile* to the Soviet Union would be tolerated. The United States had been immensely generous to the Soviet Union in the war; Russia would have been overrun without the American equipment and supplies. Americans thought Soviet-American relations would benefit from Russian gratitude for that help for a long time to come.

The leaders of the Soviet Union knew about the rest of the world only that the working class everywhere, except maybe in the United States, was waiting eagerly for Russian help to liberate it from its oppressors (this is what the Comintern delegates had been saying all those years); and that the immense achievements of the Red Army in the war against Hitler had given Russia parity with the United States on the world scene. There is reason to believe that the Russians did not fear free elections in the countries on their borders, because they were confident that the Communist parties would sweep them. When their friends were trounced in Bulgaria (which seemed the safest of all the neighbors), the Soviet leaders decided they could not possibly permit elections in Poland (the most dangerous). They had an understanding with Churchill that they would have a free hand in their "sphere of influence"; they were encouraging the local Communist parties to play the democratic game in France and Italy, and in China they were supportive of General Marshall's mission of reconciliation between Chiang Kai-shek and Mao Zedong. The Russians were thus astonished, then annoyed, finally frightened at Western pressure on them to permit elections in lands on their borders.

It never occurred to the leaders of the Soviet Union that the United States thought its contribution to victory in the war was greater than that of the Russians: the American homeland was unscarred, and American forces in Africa, Italy and France had beaten a German army smaller and less ferocious than what Hitler had sent into Russia. It never occurred to the leaders of the United States that the Soviet Union, a power without a navy or a homegrown air force, would consider itself entitled to share decision-making authority in Japan, the Mediterranean, the Persian Gulf and Southeast Asia.

The Russians reached out for a vote on the Allied Control Commission in Japan, for a dominant role in the control of the Straits in Turkey, for continuation of the wartime condominium over Iran, for inheritance of the Italian trusteeship in Libya (in retrospect, they should have been granted the joy of this particular worm, but American policy-makers were not cynical enough to see that). At every turn, the United States moved to block Russian ambition, going so far as to send the battleship *Missouri* into the Straits on a mission of mercy (delivering the body of an eminent Turk who had died in the United States) after the Russians had growled at the Turkish Government and threateningly renounced the two nations' nonaggression pact.

Soviet economists, like many in the West, believed that once the stimulus of war production was gone the American economy would sink again into a Great Depression, and that the only salvation for the United States was a vast program of imperialist export. In seeking a continuation of American aid to Russia after the end of the war, then, the Soviet leaders regarded themselves not as suppliants but as useful partners. Harry Truman, who had gone bankrupt in the haberdashery business and understood the proper attitude of the borrower applying to the lender, was outraged by Molotov's insouciance in agreeing to accept immense credits the United States had no intention of giving. Molotov departed his meeting with the President (which had been mostly about Poland) complaining that nobody had ever spoken to him as Truman did, a piquant comment for those who have read about Stalin's enjoyment in terrorizing his intimates.

The Soviet Union had been counting on German reparations to remedy some of the devastation the war had brought to their industrial plant. American field commanders faced with the task of maintaining order in occupied Germany were aghast at the problems that would result if the population saw its future means of livelihood being trucked off to the East. Moreover, the United States had already, after World War I, gone through the experience of pumping money into a war-damaged German economy so that its allies could take money out the other end in reparations, and was not prepared to see history repeat. Even reparations from current production would have to be limited to what was left over after the Germans had exported enough to pay for the imports necessary to sustain a low but bearable standard of living.

Cut off from Lend-Lease, which Truman had closed down with the end of the European war, denied reconstruction credits, frustrated in their reach for industrial equipment from the Ruhr, driven from Iran, denied a special role in the Turkish Straits, frozen out of any role in the Allied occupation of Japan, hectored about their refusal to permit the creation of freely elected and potentially hostile governments in Eastern Europe, deeply conscious of a strategic military imbalance which left American bombers potentially armed with nuclear weapons not far from Russian borders, the Soviet leaders more or less panicked. They remembered what Americans had forgotten: British and French support for the whites in their Civil War, American and Japanese expeditionary forces in eastern Siberia, the Polish effort to seize the Ukraine.

The Russians consolidated their control over the areas occupied by their forces, repressing all non-Communist political activity; they leaned heavily on Turkey, pressing not merely their claim to a special role in the administration of the Straits but also claims by the "Georgian and Armenian republics" of the USSR to much of eastern Turkey; they intensified (through the still friendly agency of Yugoslavia and through Bulgaria) their assistance to the left-wing Greek rebels against the British clients who then ruled in Athens. In Western Europe they made what turned out to be a more cautious attempt than State Department analysts had feared to spend their assets in Italy and France, withdrawing the local Communist parties from coalition governments in those countries and stimulating industrial strikes.

In 1948, with the ouster of Eduard Beneš and the murder of Jan Masaryk in Prague, with the actions taken to debase the German currency (which had been unitary, permitting the Russians to print money in the East Zone and spend it in the West), and then with the Berlin blockade that followed the Allied decision to institute a separate currency in the West Zones, the Soviets clamped down the line of demarcation in Europe which has come to be regarded as a permanent boundary on that continent. In the 1970s, they were willing to sign a treaty with a "basket" guaranteeing political rights to domestic dissenters because they were so eager to get a piece of paper recognizing the permanence of that line. But they and their friends did not respect the rights (the fast track to prison in Eastern Europe in the 1970s was membership in a "Helsinki Watch" group of the kind provided for in the treaty), and history obviously will not respect the line.

All this should be seen against a geophilosophical background. Russia and the United States had been the great expansionary powers of the nineteenth century. By the early years of the twentieth century, following the halfhearted venture into colonialism in Puerto Rico and the Philippines, American political expansionism had pretty much run its course. Russian ambitions had been frustrated by growing German strength in the West (where Marx had sarcastically described the Czars' ambitions as a line from Stettin to Trieste, roughly what Stalin achieved before Tito caught wise); by the astonishing emergence of Japan in the East; by British and French willingness to link with the infidel in the Crimean War and then by British manipulations in Afghanistan and India (the "Great Game") to the south. Territorial aggrandizement was part of the heritage of a revolutionary state that had adopted internationally the policies of the Czars— as domestically it had sought to follow the industrialization plans of the last Czarist governments and the distribution to all Russians of the culture and luxuries of the old aristocracy.

Stalin at Yalta quite simply negotiated for expansion of the Russian "spheres of influence." The United States had never accepted this idea as a legitimate principle of international relations (U.S. domination of Latin America was seen as a geographical fact decreed by God rather than as a "sphere of influence"), and placed entirely different interpretations on the documents. George Kennan's doctrine of containment—of meeting outward Soviet pressure with a midcentury version of the cordon sanitaire, eventually NATO, SEATO, CENTO, ANZUS, Alliance for Progress— was an equally simple response. This was what the Russians expected, and they were prepared to live with it as a fact of life.

For Stalin, there was a corollary to the Truman doctrine: whenever the United States receded, the Russians would advance. He was appalled when the United States, having explicitly left South Korea on the other side of the perimeter of its stated vital interests, reacted so violently to the North Korean invasion of 1950. Similarly, Stalin's heirs felt betrayed in 1979 when Jimmy Carter—having said nothing as Soviet forces built up slowly and obviously under the eye of American satellites, as signals that the Russians found developments in Afghanistan "intolerable" were delivered through various means over a period of months—insisted on making the Russian invasion of that country a watershed event in bilateral relations.

This is not of course to *blame* the United States for the invasion of Afghanistan or of Korea, or for the chill of the Cold War. The vast literature of revisionism that seeks to make American policy the source of Russian-American tension rests mostly on a crazy theory of American need for trade with Eastern Europe to avoid economic depression. The documents cited in support of the theory tell a little about the pseudosophistication of a cotton-goods manufacturer named Will Clayton, who as Assistant Secretary of State toward the end of the war uttered the bits of half-understood economic theory that are forever being quoted. But in fact, American industry right after the war had no interest whatever in making investments abroad (the Marshall Plan was necessary because private capital wouldn't flow even to Western Europe), and the United States was a "closed economy" from which less than 4 percent of gross national product was exported. The notion that it would be good *for the economy of the United States* to rebuild the economic capacity of Germany and Japan —far more important exporters than the United States before the war— would have looked just as lunatic to the architects of American foreign policy in the 1940s as it looks today.

In any event, we are dealing during the early years of the Cold War with a paranoid, highly militarized, theological society in the Soviet Union and an optimistic, demobilized, essentially liberal American society eager to get about the business of driving cars and building homes and making babies. The notion that the latter was responsible for setting the scorpions in the bottle is really too ludicrous for rational people to take seriously.

3

Bipolarity has various unfortunate effects on both the composition and the conduct of foreign policy. The Great Powers forget that lesser powers also want peace and security, and profitable trade, and a little respect; they begin to measure their bilateral relations as though the controlling factor were the "side" the lesser nation has chosen in the central struggle. There is a tendency to impugn the patriotism of leaders in foreign countries who have chosen to sup with the Devil rather than pray with God; so intelligent an observer as Dean Rusk once said that the government of the People's Republic could not be recognized as the government of China because "it is not Chinese." Changes are judged by their effect on a "global balance": the need for the newly independent former colonies to distance themselves from the former mother countries which were allies of the United States gave American policy-makers a negative view of the emerging states and gave the Soviet Union feelings of deep satisfaction about the course of history.

Bipolarity conduces to zero-sum games, in which one cheers the crop failures or recessions on the other guy's turf, or the wars between his clients, as benefits to the cause. Participants in such games dangerously lose their ability to see the world as others see it. They also yield almost instinctively to every chance to blame an opposing state for anything that goes wrong, internationally or domestically, poisoning their own political discourse.

Bipolarity also gives top political leadership the false idea that it understands the situation and should take the reins of decision into its own hands. Among the truly cardinal rules of historic diplomacy was the insulation of the head of state from personal involvement in the give-and-take that necessarily occurs in negotiations. Heads of state who insisted on conducting foreign policy in their own persons—a Teddy Roosevelt, a Kaiser Wilhelm II—were regarded as flakes, and the results of their efforts were spotted with large discolorations of folly. But as the Kings of France and England had met on the field of the cloth of gold when those two powers bestrode the Western world, Roosevelt and Stalin (with Churchill seeking his place between them) had to meet to "cement" the wartime alliance; and Eisenhower and Khrushchev had to meet to create "the spirit of Geneva."

Few brief incidents in recent history have had so thoroughly harmful an effect as the meeting between Kennedy and Khrushchev in Vienna in 1961. Believers in bipolarity (Kennedy had said in his inaugural address that "Communist domination in this hemisphere is not negotiable"), both used the occasion to stress how risky it would be for the other to mess with his expanding vital interests. Khrushchev moved on to saber rattling over Berlin and the construction of the Wall, and then to the attempt to place nuclear-tipped IRBMs in Cuba. He stressed as a central point in Soviet foreign policy a right—nay, a duty—to help "liberation" movements throughout the world. Kennedy called up part of the National Guard to bolster the Army and demonstrate that America meant business; he went to Berlin, looked at the Wall, and declared himself a Berliner; he targeted American security assistance to "counterinsurgency" forces, bonding the United States more closely to some most unsavory governments. When the Carter administration made respect for human rights the touchstone of aid in Latin America, political leaders there were bewildered, for much of what they were now being denounced for they had begun under the tutelage of Kennedy's "hard-nosed" advisers. It came naturally to them—politically, Latin America has always been a sinkhole—but they had become proficient at it only when the gringos showed them how.

Usually, meetings of heads of state generate more subtle problems. It is unthinkable that such eminences should meet and not agree on *something*. The best casuistry of each nation is then employed to ensure that the two powers jointly issue some sort of communiqué (which in any decently prepared meeting is written before the high contracting parties actually speak to each other), and real disagreements are papered over by fine phrases—or by what passes for fine phrases in the barbarous language of such diplomacy. The result down the road will often be heightened antagonism when everyone discovers the meaningless nature of the phrases. Khrushchev blew up the 1960 summit, not because the Russians had just learned about the U-2 (they had known about these spy planes for a long time, though the discovery that the pilot carried what could have been assassination weaponry was unsettling), but because the yield from the first summit had been so small that it seemed worth seeking a larger propaganda benefit from outrage. More long-lasting damage was done by the deliberate obfuscation Kissinger and Dobrynin developed to make possible the interim strategic arms agreement between Ford and Brezhnev in Vladivostok.

In the European Community, where a decision-making device is in place, regular meetings of high-level government officials up to the head of state probably make sense. In other contexts, such meetings misstate the nature of international contacts, which are by definition arm's-length relationships. Propaganda values are all very well in their place, but if there is no system for "incurring obligations," the propaganda creates expectations that turn destructive when frustrated.

There are and should be few occasions when the intervention of high-level officialdom is desirable in international relations. The conduct of American foreign policy has not recovered from the precedents set by Henry Kissinger, whose modus operandi was dictated by a personal fear and hatred of bureaucratic procedure. From the point of view of a democratic society in which leaders change with the tides of public opinion, there is something subtly but significantly wrong with the notion that the heads of state or even the Foreign Ministers should know each other personally. The much greater continuity of bosses in the authoritarian societies warps the relationships. What is necessary is that the bureaucracies understand each other, that the permanent undersecretaries (which the United States lacks) have made enough contact with their opposite numbers to have a view on how relations will proceed. The traditional Foreign Service system, the clubbiness of the diplomatic colonies in the capital cities, admirably serves that purpose. Summit meetings do not.

The advantage of high-level meetings is reputed to be that they "force decisions." But the decisions thus forced may be chosen for reasons that have nothing to do with their necessity: they may be simply the agreements that can be reached, or can seem to be reached, at this moment. Their utility for the participants is often domestic: the weight of international agreement is brought to bear on a discontented legislature to gain acceptance of policies that might otherwise be refused. If these decisions are wrong, the errors are more difficult to reverse because of the prestige that has been invested in them. And on these exalted levels errors are more likely, because the principals signing the communiqué cannot in the nature of things be very well informed about the ramifications of what they are signing.

There are dangers in *any* involvement of a head of state with a foreign representative for other than ceremonial purposes, because he probably will not understand the code words that have become the envelope concealing reality. Karen Elliott House in *The Wall Street Journal* reported the mischief Reagan did to the Reagan Plan for Palestine when he told a Saudi prince that "confederation" (implying to the Saudi but not to the President an independent Palestinian state) could be "one of the options" in the relations between the West Bank and Jordan. But that sort of thing happens all the time, to all Presidents; one doesn't hear much about it only because so many people are employed to cover a President's ass.

Obviously, the need is to move the other way, to place decision-making on the lowest level consonant with the national importance of the decision. The first benefit of such procedures would be a deep discount in the influence on decisions of both Soviet-American rivalry and domestic publicity, for the bureaucrat is directly concerned with neither. The second benefit would be the establishment at the center of the process of someone who does in fact understand the situation, if not the exogenous forces playing on it. Perhaps most important, reduction of the level at which decisions are made will greatly ease the often necessary task of correcting mistakes. The only way to avoid the dangerous rigidity of decisions taken with high-level approval after full bureaucratic process is to eliminate wherever possible both the high-level approval and great chunks of the process.

No doubt there are numerous occasions when the international implications of some decision being taken for purely domestic reasons should be called to the attention of Agriculture or Commerce or Energy, Ex-Im Bank or OPIC, the SEC, CAB, Federal Reserve or the Maritime Administration, even Health and Human Services, Labor or Interior. And there are other occasions when the State Department must be made to take into account the domestic importance of arrangements being worked out with foreigners. But the great majority of these expressions of interdependence can and should be managed informally, without the rituals of interagency or interdepartmental groups, the endless process of "signing off" that takes so high a proportion of the time of so many people in the State Department and the other agencies. Somebody in one department of government must be given authority to make the decision, personal responsibility for consulting as widely as he thinks necessary (and no further), and a date certain for delivery of the decision—without "options."

Such apparently procedural changes would have profound substantive results. Commodity credits, for example, are the responsibility of the Agriculture Department, which had decided that it would be on all counts a bad idea to devote half its annual allocation to Polish loans in 1980–81. The State Department insisted, and eventually everyone was sorry. Similarly, the Comptroller of the Currency took a dim view of leaning on the banks to extend additional loans to Poland in the fall of 1980, and the State Department intervened. In both cases, State spoke with the authority of the Executive Office, which should never have been involved at all. These matters were within the competence of Agriculture and Treasury: the conclusions they had reached had been based on technical criteria; if after consulting the State Department they still thought they were right, as they did, they should have had the authority to proceed, like the expert from the Meat Inspection Service who denies a USDA stamp to an Australian meat packer whether the embassy likes it or not.

On the other hand, relations between the United States and Canada, and to a lesser degree relations between the United States and the European Community, have been irritated by the insistence of the Justice Department that American laws prohibiting price-fixing can be extended to foreign companies operating in foreign parts. The question whether such efforts should be made was primarily a question of international relations, and should have been left to State, which proved powerless against the public-relations sanctity of the word "antitrust" in the United States.

Turning over decisions to lower-level officials in the departments most intimately concerned will require that both presidential and congressional fingers cease to itch to interfere in matters which they do not understand. Dean Rusk observed that the proper answer to most questions at a Secretary of State's press conference would be "I don't know." It is an even more correct and appropriate reply in the President's press conferences. No doubt the buck stops on the desk in the Oval Office, but it doesn't have to get there so often.

Congressional oversight can be accomplished without incessantly summoning Secretaries and under secretaries or even assistant secretaries to appear with congressmen and senators before the television cameras, and without the present essentially punitive attitude toward people and programs that characterizes so much of what goes on in hearing rooms.

Though the principle of protecting the foreign and civil service staffs must be maintained—political figures must continue to take responsibility even if they have delegated authority: see what happened in the McCarthy years when they did not—the Congress can be and essentially is kept informed through contact by staff assistants with the bureaucratic levels of the departments.

And congressional policy intervention must be restricted to matters of budget, broad direction and organizational procedure. Perhaps the greatest legislative triumph of the Ford administration in foreign policy was the agreement by the Congress to vote up or down on the entire collection of tariff schedules that would emerge from the Tokyo Round of negotiations in the General Agreement on Tariffs and Trade. The resulting treaty pleased nobody very much, and more items than anyone wished to see were left open for additional haggling and process at GATT. But without that treaty, the protectionist pressures that mounted through the world recession of 1980–82 would have been uncontrollable—and there could have been no treaty if the Congress had retained its power to eliminate this item or that as a service to individual members' constituents and contributors.

On the other side, one of the great disasters in international relations in the 1970s was the Jackson-Vanik amendment which conditioned American agreement to most-favored-nation status for Soviet trade on Russian willingness to open the gates to Jewish emigration. Nobody can intelligently estimate how different relations between the Great Powers would have been had the symbols of trust represented by most-favored nations and expanded trade been put in place by Nixon and Kissinger, but it does seem reasonable to believe that their deterioration would not have been so drastic or damaging.

The Congress is also capable of pure, motiveless mischief. In 1977, economic pressures had compelled a 5.5 percent limit on increases in salaries for federal government employees. The Congress extended this rule to foreign nationals employed at U.S. embassies—without mentioning whether the limit applied to dollars or to local currencies. Obviously, in countries with 30 percent and higher inflation, a 5.5 percent raise calculated in the local currency would quickly produce impoverishment; and in countries with currencies appreciating against the dollar (which was the case with many currencies in 1977–78), a 5.5 percent raise calculated in dollars would mean in effect a pay cut. The State Department's lawyers ruled that by failing to specify a currency Congress had forbidden increases of more than 5.5 percent in *either* currency. The Department got around the rules by farming out work previously performed by embassy employees, reclassifying jobs, and simply disobeying the legal counsel's version of the rules.

But it takes no great wit to think of better uses for the time employed in this process.

4

Since 1973, the bloodbaths of the world have come as the result of civil wars in Iran, Nicaragua, Chad, El Salvador, Ethiopia, Cambodia, Lebanon, the Philippines, Pakistan, Guatemala, Syria, Angola; cruel tyrannies in Uganda, Cambodia, the Central African Empire, Chile, Argentina; aggressions by Somalia against Ethiopia, the Soviet Union against Afghanistan, Vietnam against Cambodia and China against Vietnam, Iraq against Iran, Syria and Israel against Lebanon, Indonesia against East Timor, Yemen against North Yemen, Turkey (much provoked) against Cyprus, Algeria by proxy (the Polisarios) against Morocco, Argentina by accident almost (the Falklands) against Britain. This is quite an impressive record for a decade that most people in the United States and Europe would consider a time of peace. The total direct casualties are counted in the millions; the lives violently disrupted run into the tens of millions.

To say that these killings were a failure of diplomacy is either tautological or meaningless. Some of the civil wars are egged on by foreigners, but most are indigenous, reflecting either a class struggle or the failure of a nation-state to extend the feeling of nationality to all its tribes (a condition that also plagues such economically developed nations as Belgium, Italy, Canada, Spain, Yugoslavia and arguably the Soviet Union and the United States, without civil war). Most of the other conflicts reflect, as so often in history, an overdeveloped nationalism. Henry Kissinger has written that "credible threats or credible promises" are "the instrumentalities [sic] of diplomacy." One need not agree with this formulation (which leaves out the entire range of cooperation, which is in practice the daily mode of diplomacy) to see that even on these extreme terms diplomacy may be entirely insufficient to douse the flames of frenzied nationalism—especially at times when this last refuge makes so strong an appeal to endangered scoundrels like the generals who governed Argentina.

Historically, nations did "win" wars, with considerable profit to their populations. But it is a striking fact about the period since World War II that nations with few exceptions have not gained by armed aggression. The attack on Goa won Goa for India at virtually no cost, Senegal has painlessly absorbed what had been The Gambia, and Libya will probably show benefits from its annexation of northern Chad, reputedly rich in uranium deposits. There have, moreover, been two instances where the side that was attacked has come out ahead after winning the war—the Turks in

Cyprus and the Israelis on the West Bank in 1967. Israel also may have "won" its war in Lebanon, if winning is defined as a shift of Lebanon from the Syrian to the Israeli "sphere of influence," though the books are still far from closed on that horror story. But Indonesia's rape of East Timor, Vietnam's assaults on Laos and Cambodia, Egypt's invasion of Yemen, Somalia's attack on Ethiopia, Tanzania's conquest of Uganda, Argentina's venture on the Falkland Islands, North Korea's attempt to take over South Korea, and especially Iraq's invasion of Iran—all these have been irrationally costly to the aggressor.

Unfortunately, the great exception is the Soviet Union. Four times since World War II—in East Germany in 1952, Hungary in 1956, Czechoslovakia in 1968, and Afghanistan in 1979—the Russians have thrown major armed force against indigenous resistance to their empire. On all but the first of these occasions, invading troops were sent across internationally recognized borders. It can be argued that the end result in Afghanistan is still uncertain, but dispassionate analysis of the situation in that miserable land argues that the cost to the Russians in terms of military losses, UN votes, the reduced propaganda value of the Olympic Games and inconvenience in the grain market add up to considerably less than the strategic benefits from victory in the Czars' "Great Game" and profits from cheap access to what are probably considerable mineral resources. Meanwhile, the Russians have hung onto the spoils of World War II: the Karelian peninsula of Finland, the Baltic States, Eastern Poland, Bessarabia, Sakhalin and the lesser islands to the north of Japan, not to mention the captive states in the Eastern bloc.

It must also be recognized that while the Russian people suffered horribly in the war against Hitler, the Communist Party leadership did not. They personally lived very well throughout the war, they achieved hero status they had by no means enjoyed before, and having gone into the war period semi-pariahs to be controlled by a cordon sanitaire, they emerged at the head of one of the two Great Powers. The contempt with which the leaders of nations normally regard the population they lead—in all countries, West or East, North or South; it is the nature of government—has been heightened in the Soviet Union by a political doctrine justifying the most brutal repression against anyone whose activities seemed to block the asserted purposes of the state.

Paranoid about the prospect of a world combining against them (as the world pretty much did in the 1919–1921 period), conscious that the Soviet Union is the only country in the world surrounded by hostile Communist powers, cosseted by a theology proving that history is on their side, the Russian leaders could—they really could—make reflexive use of the immense armed force at their disposal to bludgeon their way out of a tight corner. Though it is not true that "the forces of Communism march only one way," as ardent Communists and ardent anti-Communists both insist —the Russians removed their troops without compulsion from Ataturk's Turkey and Sadat's Egypt—a doctrine that one must have none but friendly states on one's borders easily extends to the proposition that those states must have friendly neighbors. We have seen in Afghanistan how the Soviet Union can react to the prospect that a once-dominated neighbor might move to greater independence. Because the theory of government in the Soviet Union insists on the identity of economics and politics—which saddles friendly neighbors with political distortion of the information needed by economic decision-makers—the chance that satellite nations will seek to escape steadily increases with the passage of time, and the chance that newcomers will voluntarily enter the Soviet orbit steadily declines.

Thus it continues to be necessary for other nations to confront the Soviet leadership with a near-certainty that the use of armed force outside their borders will be rebuked. This implies a price in terms of the allocation of resources to defense beyond anything democratic societies have been prepared to pay. The availability of nuclear deterrent—"more bang for the buck," as the vulgar philosophizers of military strategy said in the Eisenhower days—made it seem possible to buy the likelihood of such rebuke at considerably lower cost than would otherwise have to be paid. But proclaiming a doctrine that Soviet conventional aggression would be met with nuclear retaliation merely ensured that over time the Soviet Union would acquire a nuclear arsenal powerful enough to immobilize its potential antagonists.

The result, as Henry Kissinger pointed out in a speech in Europe in 1979 (two years after his departure from office), has been the end of any plausible plan to defend Europe under an American "nuclear umbrella." The United States clearly will not endanger its own society by launching intercontinental ballistic nuclear weapons against the Soviet Union when the Soviet Union can strike back. The answer to this dilemma, suggested by the West Germans (rather carelessly) and adopted by both the Carter and Reagan administrations, was to equip NATO forces in Europe with their own nuclear weaponry, so that an attack across borders by the Soviet Union could be greeted by a purely *European* nuclear response. But American fingers would remain on the trigger—memories even in our frantic time are not quite short enough for anyone East or West to accept the idea of German fingers on a nuclear trigger—and the notion that these weapons could be used to insure the restriction of a nuclear war to European soil is neither attractive to the Europeans nor convincing to anyone except, unfortunately, Defense Secretary Weinberger and President Reagan.

In the Soviet-American balance, any nuclear force large enough to provide an assured second-strike capability (how easily one falls into this barbarous jargon) will also be large enough to threaten a first strike against an adversary's weaponry. Hence the ratchet effect that moves the arms race to ever higher levels of expenditure. Successive American administrations have failed to face the fact that a doctrine of Mutual Assured Destruction is incompatible with the defense of Western Europe through the first use of nuclear weapons. And, of course, the whole thing is a charade, anyway, because the entire purpose of these weapons is deterrence: once they are used, the game is over for too large a proportion of mankind.

The question, then, is always and everywhere the challenge set by Robert McNamara to his whiz kids in the Defense Department in the 1960s: How much is enough? And the answer at some point must be, Less than you think. Never has Lord Salisbury's warning been so clear, that if you trust the generals, nothing is safe. At some point in this imitative world, someone must have the courage to say to his adversary, You are wasting your money. When your weapons systems and your civil defense procedures and your abstract military doctrines are all in place, you will be no safer than if you did not have them, and we will be in no greater danger for lacking them.

Thus there is a danger—as Pierre Elliott Trudeau (of all people) pointed out to the Second Special Session on Disarmament in June 1982—in the antinuclear movements, the Ground Zeros and freezes. Because the Russians believe they manipulate these outpourings—and to some extent, they do—their success in influencing the military posture of the democracies may convince the Soviet military that they have won a vital advantage through political means when in fact the advantage that has been conceded to them is fundamentally trivial. Strangely, the panic-mongerers on the right become the partners of the disarmers in promoting this danger, insisting that there is some significant "window of vulnerability" and asserting, as President Reagan himself insisted in a careless moment, that the Soviet has a meaningful nuclear advantage. Even Kissinger, grousing about the refusal of the Defense Department to accept the implications of its own decision to diversify American nuclear might through a range of land, air and sea delivery systems, wound up worrying about the resulting imbalance between Soviet and American land-based capability.

One can imagine a decision to use tactical nuclear weapons to repel a Soviet attack on Western Europe. Any such decision could be made, however, only by the Europeans themselves, who would have to watch the nuclear explosions on European soil. It is hard to know which is more unlikely—the attack, or the decision to repel it with tactical nuclear arms. Clearly, expenditures designed to make such an attack impossibly costly *without* nuclear reprisals are a far more intelligent way to establish the security of Europe. The lessons of the fighting between Israel and Syria in June 1982 would seem to be that such defense can rely on the technical superiority of conventional Western arms, especially but not exclusively in the air, without expenditures as great as those previously regarded as essential.

In any event, the foundation of arms-reduction negotiations between East and West must be the recognition that the nuclear deterrent deters nuclear attack, and that an attack with conventional forces would have to be rebuked conventionally. Russian willingness to use chemical weapons against enemies who cannot return the favor—certainly through surrogates in Yemen, Ethiopia and Southeast Asia, and probably directly in Afghanistan—argues strongly that the capacity to reply in kind to a Soviet nuclear attack must be maintained. But the forces in being are surely sufficient for that.

The scenario of Soviet forces "surgically" taking out the Minutemen and then demanding U.S. surrender because American counterforce is gone—that is video-game stuff, significant mostly because it gives Soviet planners reason to fear that Americans are planning something of the sort. With Pershing missiles, yet—six minutes from Moscow. When the Pershings are installed—and the Russians in response have violated the 1962 Kennedy-Khrushchev agreement by installing equivalent IRBMs in Cuba —will the United States or Europe be more secure? Is there any serious reason to believe that the retaliatory capabilities of the British and French submarines—especially after the British have their Trident missiles—are insufficient to prevent a Russian nuclear attack on European cities?

Diplomacy enters into this sort of thing in three ways. Negotiations on arms control must in the end be conducted at least partly by diplomats, because they are the negotiators. (The military on both sides are by no means happy with this situation. A famous story that may even be true tells of a Russian general approaching his American counterpart during a break in the SALT talks to warn that some of the facts and figures on Soviet arms which the Americans had used to buttress their arguments were inappropriate for a meeting with civilians present: the Russian diplomats had not been cleared to hear such secrets.) Diplomats are required by the top leadership who must eventually accept arms-control treaties because military advisers see the world in a fundamentally useless zero-sum way, where each gain for an adversary is necessarily a loss for the home team. (The argument that Soviet gas sales to Western Europe would be dangerous because they would give the Russians hard currency to buy European technical goods is a very pure example of military thinking projected onto a nonmilitary problem. The European rejection of this jejune approach should have been definitive; American persistence in it, with the clear implication that the United States knew better than Europeans what would be good for Europe, was a tragic misjudgment that did more damage to the Atlantic alliance than the Russians could have hoped to do by withholding gas supplies.) Finally, diplomats cannot be kept out, for they are fighting for their professional as well as their personal lives: once war comes, their functions and careers are much devalued.

Most American and European opposition to Western nuclear armament reflects incomprehension of the world or cowardice or Communist influence. Those seeking to restrain Soviet expansion must keep their powder dry whether literary intellectuals like it or not—but they need not turn their societies into powder kegs. Let the Russians do that, if their paranoia requires it: they will not be the gainers, over time.

In general, military matters require the intervention of the President, because he is the commander-in-chief, and also because *any* contact with the military forces of a foreign power means an infringement on the organization of that society. One cannot allow the Defense Department to decide the recipients or the extent of military sales abroad. Such sales would seem one of the few areas where an independent board, with terms longer than the President's, should have authority to permit or deny. Nothing could be worse than the present system in which a Kissinger uses armaments as a reward, a Carter refuses them as a punishment, and then a Reagan permits them as good business.

Nuclear weaponry and the negotiations for its control are, however, inescapably the concern of the chief executive. The military cannot advocate settling for second best; the diplomats, as Kissinger shrewdly observes, tend to become obsessed with what is "negotiable"—i.e., within the negotiating frame of the adversary—rather than what is desirable. (On the other hand, Carter and Vance suffered a major humiliation in Moscow when they rejected the advice of their diplomats and abandoned negotiability as a criterion in the search for drastic, sudden disarmament.) By establishing an Arms Control and Disarmament Agency outside the State Department, the Nixon administration hoped to secure a structure blending scientific and military expertise with diplomatic skill; then Kissinger decided he had to do it himself, anyway.

Even during the days of the Carter administration, when all the posts were in the hands of people who really believed in disarmament, arms-control negotiations were more complicated inside the U.S. Government than in either the bilateral or the multilateral fora. SALT II proved unsalable mostly because nobody felt much enthusiasm for it. That the Russians were not very enthusiastic, either, seems to be demonstrated by the timing of their Afghanistan adventure, which was certain to destroy any chance that the Senate would accept the treaty. What is important at bottom in the nuclear negotiations is the certainty of no first use and the retention of capability for riposte; and both sides have a stake in that.

Even more troublesome than the East-West nuclear negotiations are the nonproliferation agreements that must be worked out both in an international framework and as part of commercial contracts to supply nuclear power installations and fuel to nations that could relatively easily develop the capacity to use these peaceful reactors for the production of weaponry. Again, the diplomats' desire to reach agreement leaves them either ineffective or dangerous in the negotiations they should be able to conduct—which is especially sad because these negotiations offer benefits to both sides, and diplomats are at their best in such conditions. Perhaps the most disheartening failure of the 1970s was that of the International Nuclear Fuel Cycle Evaluation Conference, which wound up with the scientists convincing the politicians that there was no way to prevent the generation of plutonium from enriched uranium fuel. Current appearances to the contrary notwithstanding, the poor countries of the world will need nuclear power if they are to approach even their most modest developmental goals.

Thomas Schelling has suggested that wise heads of government in Less Developed Countries should react to the offer of nuclear weapons with the answer, " 'Not yet—let me think about where to put them.' . . . Ownership of nuclear weapons poses embarrassing questions for a head of state," Schelling continues. "Does he trust his senior officers sufficiently to put his weapons in military hands? Can he dare to display his distrust by keeping them from the military? Would he have to provide them to the competing military services or can he elevate one service as the sole nuclear force? Could he, as Secretary McNamara could not in the early 1960s, get enthusiastic military acquiescence in electronically safeguarded presidential control? And could he in some future war—a contingency that has to be considered possible, else why nuclear weapons?—let an army be surrounded, immobilized, even captured, as suggested by the final stages of the October War, without authorizing some use of these supposedly awesome weapons? And what use might that be? And if he withheld the weapons, wouldn't he then regret having possessed them?

"It must furthermore be exceedingly difficult to get a president, defense minister, minister for nuclear power, and chief of armed forces to sit together around a table and acknowledge that they may shortly be on opposite sides of a coup or civil war, or evacuating in disorder, and that they would therefore be wise not to encumber themselves with as competitive a prize as a nuclear arsenal.

"I wish there were evidence that some heads of government shared my misgivings. . . ." Giving the heads of state of the nonnuclear powers some sense that, as Schelling argues, "the weapons are far more dangerous than they are worth"—that's a task for diplomatic persuasion in the years ahead. Unlikely as its accomplishment may be, the job should certainly be tried.

5

Finally, there is the question whether a nation stands for something besides the interests of the inhabitants—an interesting and difficult question, obscured by universal hypocrisy. Islamic fervor appalls the United States in Iran but delights it in Afghanistan. Political repression is abominable in Cuba or Poland but not in Morocco or the Philippines or South Korea or Taiwan or Zaire. Anti-Semitism blights the Soviet Union but not Argentina, and is of course entirely understandable in Saudi Arabia. Persecution of indigenous minority tribes is vile in Nicaragua and Laos but none of our business in Brazil or Sri Lanka. Communism may after all be what the Chinese need. Jimmy Carter, who really cared about what happened to people in the abstract, went to Iran to praise the Shah; George Bush, who does think it matters that private enterprise is unshackled, went to the Philippines to praise a President who consistently uses the power of the state to assure that the profits of industry siphon off to his extended family.

Yet the United States does have a philosophical position and an operational strategy for realizing the benefits of that position. The philosophy is minimal interference by the state or other large bureaucratic organizations with the power of human imagination (a power that includes "technology" but also a great deal more) to work changes in society for the enhancement of the general welfare. The strategy is what Justice Oliver Wendell Holmes, Jr., in a much disliked and highly ethnocentric but entirely accurate phrase once called "the marketplace of ideas." We argue from our experience and also from observation elsewhere that the greatest good for the greatest number will arise from maximizing the freedom and opportunities of individuals, including the opportunity to form private groups. This attitude may include an encompassing curiosity, even an occasional infatuation with remote and vastly different societies operating on entirely different principles. But American affinities in the end are for those nations that profess a similar philosophy.

The desire to be morally correct at all times has its dangers. "The statesman who sincerely believes himself to be defending righteous action in a just cause," Grant Hugo writes, "is still guilty of cant if he is more concerned with his own virtue than with the predictable and concrete results of his action."

Still, it is not sentimentality but an expression of self-esteem to base a foreign policy on such affinities. Obviously, the United States should seek correct—even friendly—relations with everyone, saving only perhaps the handful of vicious leaders forming vicious states (Pol Pot's Kampuchea, Amin's Uganda, Mobuto's Zaire, Duvalier's Haiti). But grants or concessional loans to help develop an economy—or (especially) military assistance—should surely be restricted to those nations with which we are pleased to be closely identified.

"Countries have Cabinet meetings when I come to visit," said Patricia Derian, a lean, blue-eyed League of Women Voters leader from Mississippi whom Carter made Assistant Secretary for Human Rights. "If I make a speech in Iowa and mention a situation in a country, they hear about it. Countries are like adolescents entering a dance—their pimple is showing like a lighthouse, they're sure everybody is thinking about nothing but their inadequacies." And that's fine—or was fine, when Pat Derian was doing it, listening to the press and the nongovernmental organizations rather than the calls to ideological warfare. The United States exposes its own misbehaviors all the time; it is fitting and proper that we should do it to others, too.

There will be occasions when it is necessary to give military help to governments we detest, especially in countries that border on Soviet satellites and can thus become the victims of direct and all but irreversible aggression; but we should be seen to be holding our noses as we do so, and should not seek or offer any special signs of friendship. If the military assistance requires training programs, they should of course include (as Russian programs include) a substantial dollop of political indoctrination, stressing the desirability of free elections, freedom of information, freedom of assembly and the like.

Since the 1960s, unfortunately, the United States has been afflicted with a knee jerk of counterinsurgency. Greatly overestimating the efficiency of Communist-sponsored dictatorships, the Kennedy administration feared that a country once "lost to the free world" would remain forever in an enemy camp, progressively isolating the United States and its friends. Under these circumstances, any combination of Argentinian tyrants or Indonesian crooks or Pakistani thugs or Congolese medicine men would be preferable to the acolytes of amateur Leninism who were pressing upon them. At that time, moreover, the Viet Cong were pioneering a new short-form scheme for successful revolution, destroying the economic and cultural as well as the social infrastructure—burning the crops, destroying the bridges, dynamiting the power pylons, shooting the schoolteachers and doctors, meanwhile extorting sustenance from the peasantry, and terrorizing any who might seek to help the authorities. To the challenge, "You can't protect your friends," the first response was an insistent "Oh yes, we can." When that failed, the response became, "Maybe not; but you can't protect your friends, either"—and the full horrors of the Vietnamese and Central American civil wars were loosed upon the world's newspaper readers and television viewers.

But the world changed. Soviet-style economies did poorly in Cuba, Guinea, Vietnam, Guyana, Benin, Congo (Brazzaville)—everywhere, indeed, except in the enclaves where U.S. oil companies drew exports from the ground to sustain improvements in the local standard of living provided by imports. Chinese Communism did even worse, and those who modeled their development procedures on some variant of the Chinese example—most notably Nyerere's Tanzania—became basket cases. While nobody could ever talk the head of a one-party state out of his belief in the superiority of one-party systems, the challenge to the United States from the Soviet example receded throughout the Third World. In the nations suffering insurgency, moreover, the revolutionary tactic of destroying the economy to save the poor ultimately denied the rebels that popular support the romantic left always assumes they have. The landlord and the moneylender and the oligarchic government are all awful, but mostly they are awful in a rather remote way: they don't destroy the crops, or dynamite the pylons that bring the great novelty of electricity that makes the television set entertain the people in the local bar. People come to feel they prefer the Devil they know.

Where the Russians did achieve direct influence their presence soon became noisome. Soviet ambassadors to the Third World tend to be *apparatchiks*, ward politicians who speak no language but Russian and clump about at parties with KGB men at their elbows, translating and not infrequently instructing. Like the American contingents, the Soviet embassy staff tends to be larger than what is needed to perform the work. They almost always live in compounds of their own, rarely send their children to any schools but the compound school, and socialize primarily with each other except for formal gatherings. They are particularly unpopular with the ambassadors from the other Eastern-bloc countries, whom they push around, and who respond by bad-mouthing big brother at the local Foreign Ministry—something they are tempted to do in any event, to assert the ego-enhancing fiction that their nation's policy is not dictated from Moscow.

Bertrand de Jouvenal likes to tell the story of the return from Moscow of Georges Bidault, then French Foreign Minister, after one of the early four-power meetings. A French railroad worker ran along the platform as the train slowed down, calling through the window: "M. le Ministre! M. le Ministre! Is it really true there is a workers' paradise in the Soviet Union?" A central difference in the European scene over the past generation has been the all but total disappearance of the notion that the Soviet Union is a workers' paradise. Even people who recognize the degree to which this change has altered the diplomatic opportunities of the two Great Powers in Europe tend not to see that a similar process of disillusionment has been at work in the Less Developed Countries. To foreigners —even to heads of non-Russian Communist parties—the Soviet Union no longer has a heroic image, and its foreign policies no longer seem to serve in any way any interest beyond that of the Russians themselves.

One of the more peculiar aspects of the Reagan attitude toward the Soviet Union was its insistence that the Russians were in train to take over the world, at a time when Sweden was recalling its ambassador to protest the incursion of Soviet submarines and Khomeini was ordering members of the Iranian version of the Communist Party to turn themselves in for arrest, when Berlinguer was announcing on behalf of the Italian Communist Party that the October Revolution no longer had anything to teach the working class, when from France to Australia socialist governments were expelling Russian "diplomats" in quantity to reduce the effectiveness of Andropov's KGB, when a summit meeting of Comecon countries had to be canceled because the Soviets could not force their view of the correct agenda on their satellites. Of the "nonaligned," only the basket cases like Cuba, the militarily dependent like Ethiopia and South Yemen and Syria, and the cynically naive like Mrs. Gandhi can now be counted on to accept Russian bona fides on any international issue. Not since the 1930s has the Soviet Union been so isolated in the world community—and not since Harry Truman, or maybe Calvin Coolidge, has a U.S. President found the Red Menace to be such a clear and present danger.

People also think less well of America than they did, and for equally good reason. Through the instrument of the CIA, the United States arrogated to itself—in Iran and Guatemala and Laos, Italy and Greece and Egypt, Brazil and Peru and Chile and others—a "right" to direct the internal affairs of other nations for the interests of the United States, and by means inconsistent with any expressed American principles. Arriving in markets where they had not sought sales before, American multinational corporations escalated the endemic bribery until the relatively discreet brothel of political life in the poor countries (and some not so poor, like Italy and Japan) became a roaring whorehouse. Some sold shoddy or dangerous products and many cheated on their taxes. In nations receiving official aid, U.S. Government representatives pushed the locals around impatiently in the interests of efficiency. Junketing congressmen misbehaved in public. Americans as corporations and as individuals do not act that way at home (at least not often), and this was reasonably well understood —but it was also irrelevant from the point of view of people living outside the American homeland and exposed to the excesses of the visiting pitchmen, foremen and firemen.

The claim that the United States acted on motives grander than self-interest was further undermined by the inherent complexity of issues that Americans insisted on regarding as simple. It takes no great analytical capacity to recognize that the first "human right" of the poor devil in Calcutta is enough to eat; he will sacrifice most of his other rights relatively gladly for the assurance of that one. On a less obvious level, however, questions of the "human rights" of the members of a sacral community arise if an iconoclast must be protected in his right to a dissent that violates a central taboo. It seems entirely natural to Americans that the right of the individual supersedes the authority of the group, but even if this were true (and as an American I believe that within limits it is), there is no general agreement on what costs are thereby imposed, how they are to be paid, or who is to pay them.

Cultural diffusion destroys cultures; this too is part of "the marketplace of ideas." While some cultures are clearly incompatible with the rational socioeconomic organization required to cope with the population increase that follows upon the introduction of modern medicine, the frictions created by cultural destruction can generate so great a heat that nothing is accomplished except destruction.

In point of fact, Marxism-Leninism is even more exigent than American pluralism in its demand for "modernization." But Communist movements have been far more tolerant of the persistence of emperor worship ("the cult of personality")—in the Soviet Union itself, in North Korea, in Cuba, or in Guinea (where the poster on every wall shows the monstrous fool Sékou Touré in military dress with the legend, POWER—ALL POWER—TO THE PEOPLE). Though the United States is seen as the status-quo power, and in many ways in many countries the perception is obviously correct, the ideology presented by America to the world remains far more uncompromisingly revolutionary than anything offered by the antagonists of the United States in either the Eastern bloc or the Third World. In societies where people know only one chief, the message of pluralism is immensely destabilizing.

6

American foreign policy must balance between the need to contain Soviet expansionism, to eliminate the danger of nuclear war, to offer rewards
for those (and so far as possible only for those) who run the risks of moving toward its pluralist ideology. Executing this policy, the United States
must inculcate some understanding of what it is about not only among
those independent actors who must be allies in the venture if the policies
are to produce results, but also within American society itself. There is
sufficient consensus for the support of pluralism in American society to
sustain a consistent foreign policy if American political leadership will
keep its purposes in mind.

In foreign as in domestic policy, the first requirement is a high enough
time horizon to permit the intelligent measurement of short-run costs
against long-term benefits, short-term benefits against long-run costs. The
future being strictly indeterminate, the stronger and more "realistic" arguments always seem to be on the side of those who claim the short-term
benefits and avoid the short-run costs. The emphasis on the short term is
made worse by the absence of historical perspective in American culture
and in the operation of the State Department. "You need," Anthony Lake
said wistfully while Director of Policy Planning, "the human being who
remembers that something like this happened fifteen years ago, so he
knows what questions to ask the file." That person has been reassigned,
and nobody thinks of asking him.

No administration since Dwight Eisenhower's has had the kind of internal cohesion that made possible a consistent concern for the more
remote future—a tribute to Eisenhower's essentially nonpolitical, "Presidential" status, but also to the recent experience of great success in ventures like the Marshall Plan, where the presumably remote payoff on a
relatively substantial short-term cost had come quickly into view. But part
of the price for this cohesion was the sacrifice of the State Department's
institutional memory. "You have to remember," said Frank Meehan, "what
happened to the China school, all the people who said the right thing
at the wrong time." And even in the Eisenhower days, the United States
committed idiocies like imposing quotas on imported oil in what a spokesman for Texaco would later call a "drain-America-first" policy. (Of course,
Texaco in the Eisenhower days was one of the strongest advocates of import quotas, which raised the price Texaco could charge for its Texas and
Louisiana production; the worry about draining America came only later,
when congressional investigators were inquiring why Texaco didn't run its

Gulf platforms flat out to help ease the crunch of 1974.) It was Eisenhower, too, who fell into the trap of using the relatively inexpensive nuclear deterrent as the means of preventing a conventional attack—a posture that could not be viable over time.

Today the mix of foreign and domestic consequence falls heavily on many decisions, and it is difficult to lift the time horizons higher than the date of the next congressional elections. This is less damaging in the particular than most observers think: the one positive element in the series of economic summits has been every leader's increased understanding of his partners' domestic problems. It is today acceptable (more or less) for nations to have trade policies, agricultural policies, monetary policies and energy policies that conflict with their announced foreign policies. The task of the expanded diplomatic missions in the democratic countries is to establish separate contacts with the Ministries and the legislative pressure groups that affect international relations by their domestic demands. As problems rise to the surface, they get negotiated out separately, in bilateral meetings, multilateral fora—and intragovernmental committees. All this is messy (pluralism in action), and leaves diplomats incessantly engaged in plucking little burrs from under saddles—but, after all, they are paid to do some work. "All diplomats suffer," George Kennan writes, "from what we might call the domestic-political distractions of their official masters." It comes with the territory.

What cannot be tolerated for long is the situation that arises frequently in the United States, where separate foreign policies are enunciated by the Secretary of State, the National Security Adviser, the Secretary of Defense, the ambassador to the United Nations, and roving "special ambassadors" based in the White House. The Secretary of State need not have the primacy in "crisis management" that Alexander Haig claimed for himself in the early days of the Reagan administration, but he must have control over the day-to-day business.

A first obvious reform is an end to the Office of International Security Affairs in the Defense Department—now a separate State Department urging military substitutes for diplomatic policy all over the globe—to be matched by the abolition of the Bureau of Politico-Military Affairs in the State Department, which serves mostly as a bureaucratic control on ISA. (Associated with that reform might be a law forbidding the Secretary of Defense to travel outside the boundaries of the United States, except for large meetings of allied defense ministers.)

A second reform would be the return of the National Security Adviser's staff to Bundy dimensions: a dozen people, all more or less expert, most (maybe all) drawn from outside government service, performing liaison functions to improve the efficiency of the process by which decisions are definitively assigned to departments or taken to the President.

A third would be the subordination of the Central Intelligence Agency to the Secretary of State, with any surviving "operations" division hived off to the Defense Intelligence Agency to be coordinated with military rather than political policies under the direct control of the President.

A fourth would be restoration of the State Department's complete control over the U.S. Mission to the United Nations, and the end to the anomalous cabinet status now enjoyed by this one ambassador.

In foreign policy as in other areas of American governance, the proper role of Congress is oversight and budgetary control, with a special function relating to the employment of armed force which is implied in the legislature's exclusive power to declare war. But budgetary control is a blunt tool, and in conditions of modern technology wars are declared only after it is too late to stop them. Oversight and its attendant publicity are still the best means of asserting legislative concern about the conduct of foreign policy: nothing so refines the attitudes and behavior of an executive authority (in government or large corporations) as the thought that what is done today will be in the newspapers tomorrow. And there is only one justification for secrecy: that an antagonistic foreign government does not know what the United States is doing. Surely there can be no justification for the ludicrous spectacle of the Congress and the President publicly fighting over the purposes and the funding of "covert" operations in Nicaragua. To the extent that the nation's foes have the information, the public (and the nation's friends) must have it, too. For the foundation of Justice Holmes' "marketplace of ideas" is and must be a shared basis of information: there can be no effective pluralism without it.

In general, the aim within the State Department should be devolution: ambassadors should have greater authority to commit the United States in nonbudgetary matters, and where opposing claimants seek American support the Department should encourage the ambassadors to the contesting states to work out something between themselves, with supporting services from the appropriate regional bureau. Overburdening the desks of the senior people in the Department secures neither coordinated policies nor intelligent consideration of alternatives. From the deputy-assistant-secretary level on up, and to an only slightly lesser degree below that level, people at the State Department work literally sixty to seventy hours a week, of which literally forty to fifty are simply wasted on matters that should be decided in other bureaus or departments, or at the desk or ambassador level, or more quickly, or not at all. Petty tyrannies are unpleasant, but if they remain petty they do less harm than immobility. Of course, there will be mistakes and embarrassments, but it seems unlikely that their frequency will increase greatly from the present stream of gaucheries—and, as already noted, lower levels of decision-making permit easier reversals of course if the decision turns out to be a mistake. Moreover, the press is less likely to learn about it, or to take an interest if the news leaks out. Nobody can get his story on the front pages by detailing the goofs of a desk officer.

Chou En-lai told Henry Kissinger that if John Foster Dulles had been willing to shake his hand in Geneva in 1954, the history of the world might have been different. There is just enough truth in this sort of statement to keep it alive and resonant in the corridors of history: China today has at least as much reason to regret its support of the Vietnamese Communists as the United States has to regret its opposition, and may have had an inkling of that in 1954. But at bottom, nearly if not quite all the time, policies are determined by real interests rather than by personal relations. The international lineup after the Argentine invasion of the Falkland Islands was unusually revealing: France, with island properties in the Western hemisphere, was vigorously pro-British; also Germany, with its hostage to fortune in West Berlin; and Guyana (one of the two South American nations on the Security Council at the time, Guyana voted consistently against the Argentines), which sees two thirds of its territory coveted by Venezuela. The leaders of the opposition to British recapture of the islands were Panama, looking to reclaim the Canal Zone, and Cuba, lusting for Guantánamo; Venezuela, anticipating its claim on Guyana; Peru, coveting parts of Chile; Guatemala, hoping to swallow newly independent Belize; Libya, with designs on Tunisia and Chad; China, with Hong Kong on its borders; and Indonesia, waiting to reclaim Brunei and the rest of New Guinea if a moment comes when no one is looking. All this was highly predictable by specific situation, entirely unpredictable by ideology or political logic.

Indeed, specifics—geographical specifics—still play an overwhelming role in international relations. The pieces of land that have started wars for millennia are still fought over—Palestine, Cyprus, the Western Sahara, the Shatt-al-Arab, the Himalayan passes, the Chaco. Argentina's claim on the Falklands goes back to 1833, which is earlier than the United States' claim on Texas or California, or the Soviet claim on Vladivostok. I had occasion to remark to a Danish diplomat during the course of work on this book that the great accomplishment of Europe in the years since 1945 was the permanent withdrawals from this list of bits of land that have caused millions of deaths in the last thousand years: Alsace-Lorraine, Schleswig-Holstein, the South Tyrol, the Benelux triangle, Savoy. . . . "You are assuming," he said conversationally, "the continued division of Germany"—and of course I was.

Still, what has been learned in Europe, very much the hard way, is that real interests lie on the side of peaceful resolution of disputes rather than forceful conquest. Given the continued European domination of the world's modes of thought, the idea has taken root in the regional organizations that grew up first to supplement the United Nations and then to replace it when there is serious business to be done. The first principle of the Organization of African Unity is the sanctity of borders, even the borders drawn most foolishly by the ignorant colonial powers of the nineteenth century. The recurrent fly-bitings on Latin American boundaries are dealt with surprisingly effectively by the Organization of American States, usually with only a few dead from careless bombing. ASEAN—the Association of South East Asian Nations—has had an even more remarkable record, especially in taming what had been a territorially aggressive Indonesia. If there is a plausible resolution of the Israeli-Arab confrontation, it must include the construction of a Middle East geographical organization that is not religiously oriented, and accepts in its membership an Israel that has honestly joined in a general renunciation of the use of force.

The United States is blessed with the absence of any specific geographical quarrels—the Mexicans have one, but they can't do much about it. The running sore in its relations with its neighbors is immigration. The long-term problem economically is reliance on returns from prior investments to pay for imports now running heavily (in 1983, at a rate of 1.5 percent of gross national product) in excess of exports. The other side of the same coin is the immense value of those investments, which serves as a cushion for the very large dollar debt piled up in the 1960s and 1970s. The long-term problem politically has greatly diminished in recent years as the inability of the Russian and Chinese systems to harness their nations' energies efficiently has increasingly sapped the vitality of their societies and blunted their drive toward international dominance. Of course, the United States has not been able to maintain what was in truth a hegemony over the world in the 1950s, but the incessant clamor about the "loss of American influence" conceals the fact that most of that influence the United States had no particular reason to want.

To the extent that "détente" means a shared hegemony with the Soviet Union—and this is what the Russians have always had in mind—the United States should have no interest in it. To the extent that the word implies a shared willingness to let other people work out their own problems—and this is what "détente" did mean in Europe, which is why the concept retains its appeal there—it should continue to be one of the structural supports of American foreign policy. The other nations of the world are right to be skeptical that either of the Great Powers really intends the independence of others. American foreign policy in the years ahead must be built on support for international as well as domestic pluralism; American diplomats must work to make that support both apparent and real.

Better organization would help a little. Less neuroticism about America's role in the world would help a lot.

NOTES

CHAPTER 1: ISOLATIONS

p. 3   Bismarck: Lamar Cecil, *The German Diplomatic Service, 1871–1914,* Princeton University Press, Princeton, N.J., 1976, p. 227.

p. 10   wife: Hernane Tavares de Sá, *The Play Within the Play: The Inside Story of the UN,* Knopf, New York, 1966, p. 141.

p. 11   Capen: Daniel J. Boorstin, *The Americans: The Democratic Experience,* Random House, New York, 1973, p. 565.

Lenin: George Kennan, *Russia Leaves the War,* Princeton University Press, Princeton, N.J., 1956, p. 501.

Stimson: Henry Stimson and McGeorge Bundy, *On Active Service in Peace and War,* Harper & Bros., New York, 1948, p. 170.

p. 12   Yost: Charles Yost, *The Conduct and Misconduct of Foreign Affairs,* Random House, New York, 1972, p. 143.

Cleveland: Harlan Cleveland, *The Obligations of Power,* Harper & Row, New York, 1966, p. 11.

Benton: Te-kong Tong, *United States Diplomacy in China, 1844–1860,* University of Washington Press, Seattle, Wash., 1964, pp. 29, 30.

p. 13   Coolidge: L. Ethan Ellis, *Republican Foreign Policy, 1921–33,* Rutgers University Press, New Brunswick, N.J., 1968, p. 44.

aloof: John A. S. Grenville and George Berkeley Young, *Policy, Strategy and American Diplomacy: Studies in American Foreign Policy, 1873–1917,* Yale University Press, New Haven, Conn., 1966, pp. 125–26.

p. 14   Richard Gardner: Robert D. Murphy, Chairman, *Commission on the Organization of the Government for the Conduct of Foreign Policy* (henceforth, *Murphy Commission*), Government Printing Office, Washington, D.C., 1975, Vol. 2, Appendix A, p. 280.

p. 15   Rafael: Gideon Rafael, *Destination Peace: Three Decades of Israeli Foreign Policy,* Stein & Day, New York, 1981, p. 21.

p. 16 Grew: Charles E. Bohlen, *Witness to History, 1929–69*, W. W. Norton, New York, 1973, p. 111.

p. 17 Thayer: Charles W. Thayer, *Diplomat*, Harper & Bros., New York, 1959, p. 15.
beating: Robert Blum, *Drawing the Line*, W. W. Norton, New York, 1982, p. 82.

p. 19 Dickins: Ian Nish, *Japanese Foreign Policy, 1869–1942*, Routledge & Kegan Paul, London, 1977, p. 16.

p. 19 fn Yanaga: Foster Rhea Dulles, *Yankees and Samurai*, Harper & Row, New York, 1965, p. 154.

p. 19 Bayard: Alexander De Conde and Armin Rappaport, eds., *Essays Diplomatic and Undiplomatic of Thomas A. Bailey*, Appleton-Century-Crofts, New York, 1969, p. 57.
Mr. Dooley: Ross Gregory, *Walter Hines Page, Ambassador to the Court of St. James's*, University Press of Kentucky, Lexington, Ky., 1970, p. 42.

p. 20 Bismarck: Cecil, *German Diplomatic Service*, p. 240.
Kennedy: Richard Betts, *Soldiers, Statesmen and Cold War Crises*, Harvard University Press, Cambridge, Mass., 1977, p. 139.

p. 21 Yarmolinsky: Adam Yarmolinsky, *Organizing for Interdependence: The Role of Government*, Aspen Institute for Humanistic Studies Program in International Affairs, Aspen, Colo., 1976, p. 6.
White House Commission: *Murphy Commission*, p. 185.

p. 22 Ball: George W. Ball, *The Discipline of Power*, Atlantic Monthly–Little Brown, 1968, p. 103.

p. 23 Brenner: Michael Brenner, "Carter's Bungled Promise," *Foreign Policy* 36, p. 89 and pp. 95–96.
Alsop: Stewart Alsop, *The Center: People and Power in Political Washington*, Harper & Row, 1968, p. 254.

p. 24 Cuban oil refineries: Phillip C. Jessup, *The Birth of Nations*, Columbia University Press, New York, 1974, p. 290.

p. 25 Kennan: Blum, *Drawing the Line*, p. 90.
Schulzinger: Robert Schulzinger, *The Making of the Diplomatic Mind*, Wesleyan University Press, Middletown, Conn., 1975, p. 61.
Acheson: Dean Acheson, *Present at the Creation*, W. W. Norton, New York, 1969, p. 35.

p. 26 Murphy: Robert D. Murphy, *Diplomat Among Warriors*, Doubleday, Garden City, N.Y., 1964, p. 70.
Abrikossow: George Alexander Lensen, ed., *Revelations of a Russian Diplomat: The Memoirs of Dmitri Abrikossow*, University of Washington Press, Seattle, Wash., 1964, p. 138.

CHAPTER 2: LIFE AMONG THE NATIVES

p. 27 Harr: John Ensor Harr, *The Professional Diplomat*, Princeton University Press, Princeton, N.J., 1969, pp. 206–7.
Bright: Milton Katz, *The Things That Are Caesar's*, Knopf, New York, 1966, p. 69.

p. 27   Roosevelt: John Franklin Campbell, *The Foreign Affairs Fudge Factory*, Basic Books, New York, 1971, p. 114.

p. 28   Dawes: De Conde and Rappaport, eds., *Essays of Thomas Bailey*, p. 53.
Nicolson: Harold Nicolson, *Diplomacy*, Harcourt Brace, New York, 1939, p. 119.
Durrell: Lawrence Durrell, *Mountolive*, Faber, London, 1963 (paper), p. 119.

p. 29   Venetian historian: Donald E. Queller, *The Office of Ambassador in the Middle Ages*, Princeton University Press, Princeton, N.J., 1967, p. 7.
treatise: Garrett Mattingly, *Renaissance Diplomacy*, Houghton Mifflin, Boston, 1955, p. 218.
Gregory VII: Queller, *Office of Ambassador*, p. 10.
Vishinsky: Bohlen, *Witness to History*, p. 286.

p. 30   Canning: Nicolson, *Diplomacy*, p. 88.
Plumb: J. H. Plumb, *In the Light of History*, Houghton Mifflin, Boston, 1973, p. 184.

p. 31   Rafael: Rafael, *Destination Peace*, p. 75.
cover: John Stockwell, *In Search of Enemies*, W. W. Norton, New York, 1978, p. 45.

p. 32   Nicolson: Nicolson, *Diplomacy*, p. 183.
Gonzaga: Mattingly, *Renaissance Diplomacy*, p. 71.

p. 33   Japan: Ernest Satow, *A Diplomat in Japan*, Lippincott, Philadelphia, 1921, p. 67.
Nicolson: Harold Nicolson, *The Evolution of Diplomacy* (originally *Diplomatic Method*), Collier Books, New York, 1962 (paper), p. 46.
Commines: ibid., p. 52.

p. 34   Queen Victoria: *State Department Centennial History*, 1978, p. 6.
Taft: Walter V. Scholes and Marie V. Scholes, *The Foreign Policies of the Taft Administration*, University of Missouri Press, Columbia, Mo., 1970, p. 19.

p. 35   Nicolson on Franklin: Thayer, *Diplomat*, Introduction, p. x.
chamber pot: Elmer Bendiner, *The Virgin Diplomats*, Knopf, New York, 1976, p. 78.
Einstein: Abba Eban, *An Autobiography*, Random House, New York, 1977, p. 168.
Franklin on Adams: Bendiner, *Virgin Diplomats*, p. 244.

p. 36   Briggs: Ellis Briggs, *Farewell to Foggy Bottom*, David McKay, New York, 1964, p. 288.

p. 37   Villadiego: Queller, *Office of Ambassador*, p. 152.
Nasser: George Brown, *In My Way*, St. Martin's Press, New York, 1971, p. 138.

p. 38   Wriston: Henry Wriston, *Diplomacy in a Democracy*, Harper & Bros., New York, 1956, pp. 22–23.

p. 39   fn Mattingly: Mattingly, *Renaissance Diplomacy*, pp. 62, 50, 274–75.

p. 40   parking tickets: *The Economist*, July 4, 1981, p. 58.

p. 41   Ayatollah: Barry Rubin, *Paved with Good Intentions: The American*

Experience in Iran, Oxford University Press, New York, 1980, p. 111.

p. 44 American wine: *Foreign Service Act,* 94 STAT 2128.

p. 45 Kennedy: Harr, *Professional Diplomat,* p. 358.

p. 46 Frankel: Charles Frankel, *High on Foggy Bottom,* Harper & Row, New York, 1969, p. 177.

p. 47 tools: Campbell, *Fudge Factory,* p. 60.
Galbraith: J. K. Galbraith, *Ambassador's Journal,* Houghton Mifflin, Boston, 1969, p. 129.

p. 49 fn Draper: Theodore Draper, *American Communism and Soviet Russia,* Viking Compass, New York, 1960 (paper), p. 239.

p. 52 Harr: Harr, *Professional Diplomat,* p. 206.

p. 53 Rockhill: Scholes and Scholes, *Foreign Policies,* p. 22.

p. 54 hardships: Christopher Plimmer, Chairman, *Report of the Review Committee on Foreign Service Administration,* New Zealand Government (draft), October 1977, par. 10, 2.
Le Carré: John Le Carré, *A Small Town in Germany,* Pan Books, London, 1959, p. 60.

p. 55 Franks: Geoffrey Moorhouse, *The Diplomats: The Foreign Office Today,* Jonathan Cape, London, 1977, pp. 251–52.

CHAPTER 3: INFORMING

p. 61 Stalin: W. Averell Harriman and Elie Abel, *Special Envoy to Churchill and Stalin,* Random House, New York, 1975, p. 377.

p. 62 Hoveyda: Rubin, *Good Intentions,* p. 187.

p. 63 Louisiana Purchase: Walter Lippmann, *United States Foreign Policy: Shield of the Republic,* Atlantic Monthly–Little Brown, Boston, 1943, p. 14.

p. 64 Berrill Report: Sir Kenneth Berrill, Head, *Review of Overseas Representation: Report by the Central Policy Review Staff* (henceforth, *Berrill Report*), Her Majesty's Stationery Office, London, 1977, pp. 116, 117.

p. 67 Harriman: W. Averell Harriman, *America and Russia in a Changing World,* Doubleday, Garden City, N.Y., 1971, p. 8.

p. 68 Eban: Eban, *Autobiography,* p. 592.

p. 69 Herridge: Dean Acheson, *Grapes from Thorns,* W. W. Norton, New York, 1971, pp. 231–32.

p. 70 Bohlen: Bohlen, *Witness to History,* p. 347.
Galbraith: Galbraith, *Journal,* p. 116.
Kissinger: Henry A. Kissinger, *White House Years,* Little Brown, Boston, 1979, p. 686.

p. 71 Pearl Harbor: Bohlen, *Witness to History,* p. 111.

p. 72 Cleveland: Foster Rhea Dulles, *Prelude to World Power,* Macmillan, New York, 1965, p. 70.
Field: Murphy, *Diplomat,* p. 7.
Moynihan: Daniel Patrick Moynihan with Suzanne Weaver, *A Dangerous Place,* Atlantic Monthly–Little Brown, Boston, 1978, p. 41.

p. 73 Sandinistas: Constantin Meng, "Central America and Its Enemies," *Commentary*, Aug. 1981, p. 32.

Abrikossow: Lensen, ed., *Memoirs of Abrikossow*, p. 91.

p. 74 Berchem: Cecil, *German Diplomatic Service*, p. 240.

Murphy: Murphy, *Diplomat*, p. 15.

p. 75 telegraphic traffic: Arthur Schlesinger, Jr., *A Thousand Days: John F. Kennedy in the White House*, Houghton Mifflin, Boston, 1965, pp. 409–10.

Barnes: Hugh de Santis, "Conflicting Images of the USSR: American Career Diplomats and the Balkans, 1944–46," *Political Science Quarterly*, Fall 1979, Vol. 94, No. 3, p. 475 @ 488.

Galbraith: Galbraith, *Journal*, p. 187.

p. 76 Smith: Gerard Smith, *Doubletalk: The Story of SALT I*, Doubleday, Garden City, N.Y., 1980, esp. pp. 376–77.

Valeriani: Richard Valeriani, *Travels with Henry*, Houghton Mifflin, Boston, 1979, p. 361.

ambassador to Britain: David J. Blum, "After Years of Checkbook Politics, Choice for British Envoy Gets His Wish," *The Wall Street Journal*, Apr. 21, 1981, p. 36.

p. 77 Bismarck: Cecil, *German Diplomatic Service*, p. 237.

Wilhelm II: ibid., p. 212.

Nicolson: Nicolson, *Diplomacy*, p. 109.

Thayer: Thayer, *Diplomat*, p. 243.

Beck: Telford Taylor, *Munich: The Price of Peace*, Doubleday, Garden City, N.Y., 1979, p. 149.

Gromyko: Herbert Feis, *From Trust to Terror*, W. W. Norton, New York, 1980, p. 143.

Hay: Kenton J. Clymer, *John Hay: The Gentleman as Diplomat*, University of Michigan Press, Ann Arbor, 1975, p. 152.

p. 78 Koreans: Raymond A. Esthus, *Theodore Roosevelt and Japan*, University of Washington Press, Seattle, 1966, p. 108.

Washington: Raymond Aron, *The Imperial Republic*, Prentice-Hall, Englewood Cliffs, N.J., 1974, p. xxix.

p. 79 Shah: Mark Hulbert, *Interlock*, Richardson & Snyder, New York, 1982, pp. 148 et seq.

p. 80 Buckley: William F. Buckley, Jr., *United Nations Journal: A Delegate's Odyssey*, Anchor Books, Garden City, N.Y., 1977 (paper), p. 123.

CHAPTER 4: PERSUADING

p. 82 Kissinger: Henry A. Kissinger, *Years of Upheaval*, Little Brown, Boston, 1979, p. 1088.

dangers: Nicolson, *Diplomacy*, pp. 119, 120.

p. 85 Hungarian payment: *Settlements of Claims, Treaties and Other International Acts*, Series 7569, GPO, Washington, D.C., 1973, p. 7.

p. 90 Catherine: Nicolson, *Diplomacy*, p. 106.

Monts: Cecil, *German Diplomatic Service*, pp. 244–45.

p. 93 British ambassador: Humphrey Trevelyan, *Middle East Revolution*, Gambit, Boston, 1970, p. 137.

p. 94 Chehab: Thayer, *Diplomat*, p. 29.

navy captain: Robert McClintock, *The Meaning of Limited War*, Houghton Mifflin, Boston, 1967, pp. 108–9.

ambassador: Thayer, *Diplomat*, p. 33.

p. 95 table tennis: Kissinger, *White House Years*, p. 709.

p. 96 American commissioners: Te-kong Tong, *U.S. Diplomacy*, p. 36.

consul on Harris: Dulles, *Yankees and Samurai*, p. 102.

Stimson: Ellis, *Republican Foreign Policy*, p. 257.

Morrow: ibid., pp. 246–47.

p. 97 Bunker: Frances Fitzgerald, *Fire in the Lake*, Vintage, New York, 1973, p. 490.

p. 98 Winant: Murphy, *Diplomat*, pp. 231–32.

p. 99 "magots": George Kennan, *The Decline of Bismarck's European Order*, Princeton University Press, Princeton, N.J., 1979, p. 89.

Henderson: Telford Taylor, *Munich*, p. 265 fn.

Japanese: Satow, *Diplomat in Japan*, p. 155.

p. 100 Hammarskjöld: Brian Urquhart, *Hammarskjöld*, Knopf, New York, 1972, p. 256.

p. 101 Malmesbury: Nicolson, *Evolution of Diplomacy*, p. 110.

CHAPTER 5: THE FOREIGN AGRICULTURAL SERVICE

p. 102 Socrates: *The Economist*, May 29, 1982, p. 71. I haven't been able to find the quote in my Jowett, either; but the English have earned the right to have their Greek tags respected.

p. 120 Hammarskjöld: Brian Urquhart, *Hammarskjöld*, p. 374.

CHAPTER 6: PASSPORTS TO DIPLOMACY

p. 127 Maggi: Nicolson, *Diplomacy*, p. 106.

Kennan: Campbell, *Fudge Factory*, pp. 139–40.

p. 129 British procedures: "Recruitment to the Administrative Grades of the Diplomatic Service," *Hansard*, Jan. 24, 1978, pp. 39614–15.

p. 136 Eytan: Walter Eytan, *The First Ten Years: A Diplomatic History of Israel*, Weidenfeld & Nicolson, London, 1958, pp. 204, 205.

secret: Schulzinger, *Diplomatic Mind*, p. 108.

Grew: ibid., pp. 108–9.

p. 137 *Foreign Service Act*: 94 STAT 2074.

British announcement: *Appointments in Administration*, HMSO, London, 1977, p. 23.

p. 137 fn vetting: Andrew Boyle, *The Climate of Treason*, Hutchinson, London, 1979, p. 398.

political affiliations: *Foreign Service Act*, 94 STAT 2075.

"Saving Provisions": ibid., p. 2168.

p. 138 standards: Thayer, *Diplomat*, p. 235.

State Department: Schulzinger, *Diplomatic Mind*, p. 70.

p. 139   Mark Twain: Waldo Heinrichs, "Bureaucracy and Professionalism in the Development of American Career Diplomacy," in John Braeman, Robert H. Bremner, and David Brody, eds., *Twentieth Century American Foreign Policy*, Ohio State University Press, Columbus, Ohio, 1971, p. 119 @ 142–43.

p. 140   "wreckognized": Scholes and Scholes, *Foreign Policies*, p. 17.
Timeo Danaos: Richard D. Challener, *Admirals, Generals and American Foreign Policy, 1898–1914*, Princeton University Press, Princeton, N.J., 1973, p. 105.
Ecuador: ibid., p. 109.
Adee: David McCulloch, *The Path Between the Seas*, Simon & Schuster, New York, 1977, p. 340.

p. 141   Roosevelt: Henry F. Pringle, *Theodore Roosevelt, a Biography*, Harcourt Brace, New York, 1931, pp. 489, 490.

p. 142   quaint: Heinrichs, in Braeman et al., *Foreign Policy*, p. 138.
Adee: Dana Munro, *The United States and the Caribbean Republics, 1921–1933*, Princeton University Press, Princeton, N.J., pp. 6–7.
Carr appointment: George Kennan, *Memoirs, 1925–1950*, Atlantic Monthly–Little Brown, Boston, 1967, p. 89.
Schulzinger on Carr: Schulzinger, *Diplomatic Mind*, p. 47.

p. 143   Heinrichs on Carr: Heinrichs, in Braeman et al., *Foreign Policy*, pp. 133–34.

p. 144   Scruggs: Grenville and Young, *Politics, Strategy*, p. 147.

p. 145   White: Schulzinger, *Diplomatic Mind*, pp. 17, 18.

p. 146   Wriston: Wriston, *Diplomacy*, p. 36.
Foreign Service Act: 94 STAT 2085.
Satow: Sir Ernest Satow, *A Guide to Diplomatic Practice*, Longmans, Green, New York, 1917, Vol. I, p. 1.
Harlan: Schulzinger, *Diplomatic Mind*, p. 45.

p. 147   Carr: ibid., p. 51.
list: Heinrichs, in Braeman et al., *Foreign Policy*, pp. 146–47.
Wilson: Martin Weil, *A Pretty Good Club*, W. W. Norton, New York, 1978, p. 47.

p. 148   professional diplomats: Schulzinger, *Diplomatic Mind*, pp. 8, 41.
State Department exam: Nicolson, *Diplomacy*, p. 256.
Thayer: Thayer, *Diplomat*, p. 7.

p. 149   First Assistant: Satow, *Diplomat in Japan*, pp. 30, 18.
language examinations: Nicolson, *Diplomacy*, p. 207.
Kirk: Kennan, *Memoirs*, pp. 113–14.

p. 152   Kennan: ibid., p. 149 fn.
Acheson: Acheson, *Present at Creation*, p. 127.

p. 153   Rowe Committee: Harr, *Professional Diplomat*, p. 63. The words quoted are Harr's paraphrase, not the committee's.
Nixon: Campbell, *Fudge Factory*, p. 117.

p. 154   NORC data: Harr, *Professional Diplomat*, p. 63.
Acheson: Campbell, *Fudge Factory*, p. 121.

p. 156   Herter Commission: The Committee on Foreign Affairs Personnel, *Personnel for the New Diplomacy*, Carnegie Endowment for International Peace, Washington, D.C. 1962, pp. 2, 3.

p. 156 Laise: "From the Director General," *Department of State Newsletter*, Aug./Sept. 1977, No. 193.

p. 157 Foreign Service personnel: *Berrill Report*, p. xiii.

CHAPTER 7: TRAINING, ASSIGNMENT AND PROMOTION

p. 158 master's thesis: *13. Jahrbuch des Diplomatische Akademie Wien*, 1977–8, Vienna, pp. 117, 118.

p. 160 scholar: Victor T. LeVine, *The Cameroon Federal Republic*, Cornell University Press, Ithaca, N.Y., 1971, p. 45.

p. 160 fn the Nsaw and the Bamoun: Willard Johnson, *The Cameroon Federation*, Princeton University Press, Princeton, N.J., 1970, p. 44.

p. 161 Fonlon: ibid., p. 291.

p. 162 announcement: *Note à l'Attention des Candidates à l'I.R.I.C.*, translation by the author.

p. 163 Dembinski: Ludwik Dembinski, *Une Expérience de Formation et de Recherche en Relations Internationales en Afrique*, IRIC, Yaoundé, 1979 (mimeo), p. 2, translation by the author.

p. 168 apprenticeship in Britain: "The Staffing of a Global Service: Personnel Policy and Practice in the Diplomatic Service" (A Note by the Chief Clerk at the Foreign and Commonwealth Office), *Hansard*, Jan. 24, 1978, p. 39614 @ 39617.

p. 171 code: Schulzinger, *Diplomatic Mind*, pp. 82, 183.

p. 172 Shaw: Heinrichs, in Braeman et al., *Foreign Policy*, p. 199.

p. 173 economic studies: *FSI Handbook*, Department of State, Washington, D.C., 1978, p. II-C-11.

courses: ibid., pp. II-C-4, 5.

courses: ibid.

Area Studies: ibid., p. II-E-2.

Kerala: School of Area Studies, *South Asia*, Oct. 31–Nov. 11, 1977, p. 10.

Church: Latin American Studies, p. 8.

p. 176 *Foreign Service Act*: 94 STAT 2099.

p. 181 sinologist: "Staffing of a Global Service," *Hansard*, Jan. 24, 1978, p. 39617.

p. 192 Whitehead: Alfred North Whitehead, "The Aims of Education," in Martin Mayer, *The Schools*, Harper & Bros., New York, 1961, p. 327.

CHAPTER 8: ORGANIZING A GOVERNMENT FOR THE CONDUCT OF FOREIGN RELATIONS

p. 195 Pickering: Gerard H. Clarfield, *Timothy Pickering and American Diplomacy, 1795–1800*, Missouri University Press, Columbia, Mo., 1969, p. 33.

p. 196 Commission: *Murphy Commission*, pp. 40–41.

p. 197 fn official order: Jessup, *Birth of Nations*, p. 5.

p. 198 Huntington-Wilson: Scholes and Scholes, *Foreign Policies*, pp. 15–16.

p. 198   Knox's wines: ibid., p. 8. The cost of a similar cellar today would be considerably more than $10,000.

Knox's habits: ibid., pp. 8–9.

p. 199   code-cracking: David Kahn, *The Code-Breakers*, Macmillan, New York, 1967, pp. 356–60.

gentlemen: Stimson and Bundy, *Active Service*, p. 188.

p. 200   Cleveland: Dulles, *Prelude*, p. 118.

p. 202   Czech brewery: Joan Hoff Wilson, *American Business and Foreign Policy, 1920–1933*, University of Kentucky Press, Lexington, Ky., 1971, p. 118.

p. 203   bankers: Munro, *Caribbean Republics*, p. 12.

White comment: ibid., p. 9.

Hoover: Ellis, *Republican Foreign Policy*, p. 259.

p. 204   Stimson and Jefferson: Stimson and Bundy, *Active Service*, p. 178.

"Not on your life": ibid., p. 182.

tariffs: ibid., p. 162.

p. 205   trade adviser: Munro, *Caribbean Republics*, p. 7.

p. 206   Kottman: Richard N. Kottman, *Reciprocity and the North Atlantic Triangle, 1932–1939*, Cornell University Press, Ithaca, N.Y., 1968, pp. 217–19.

p. 207   Hay, Knox and Huntington-Wilson: Challener, *Admirals, Generals*, p. 69.

p. 208   Adee: ibid., pp. 147, 73, 265.

p. 209   notion not true: *see* Dana G. Munro, *Intervention and Dollar Diplomacy in the Caribbean, 1900–1921*, Princeton University Press, Princeton, N.J., 1964.

Morgan bank: Challener, *Admirals, Generals*, p. 271.

Knox: Scholes and Scholes, *Foreign Policies*, p. 53.

State steps out: Challener, *Admirals, Generals*, p. 268.

Solicitor: ibid., p. 53.

p. 210   Byrnes: James F. Byrnes, *Speaking Frankly*, Harper & Bros., New York, 1947, p. 244.

p. 211   country committees: ibid., p. 245.

Byrnes quote, et seq.: John Lewis Gaddis, *The United States and the Origins of the Cold War, 1941–1947*, Columbia University Press, New York, 1972, pp. 285, 347.

Marshall: Betts, *Soldiers, Statesmen*, p. 95.

p. 212   Kennan military policy: Thomas H. Etzold and John Lewis Gaddis, eds., *Containment: Documents on American Policy and Strategy, 1945–1950*, Columbia University Press, New York, 1978, pp. 121–22.

p. 214   NSC Memorandum: ibid., p. 387.

Etzold: ibid., p. 22.

Bloomfield: Lincoln Bloomfield, "Planning Foreign Policy: Can It Be Done?" *Political Science Quarterly*, Vol. 93, No. 3, Fall 1978, p. 369 @ 374.

p. 215   Bloomfield conclusions: ibid., pp. 384–85.

p. 216   Acheson: Dean Acheson, *This Vast External Realm*, W. W. Norton, New York, 1973, p. 206.

Collins: Betts, *Soldiers, Statesmen*, pp. 97–98.

p. 216 Lord Salisbury: Yost, *Conduct and Misconduct*, p. 107.

p. 217 Macmillan: Harold Macmillan, *At the End of the Day*, Harper & Row, New York, 1973, p. 357.

Acheson: Acheson, *Present at Creation*, p. 214.

Kennan: Etzold and Gaddis, *Containment*, p. 125 fn.

p. 224 Frankel: Frankel, *Foggy Bottom*, pp. 174–75.

p. 225 Galbraith: Galbraith, *Journal*, p. 212.

Galbraith: ibid.

p. 226 hierarchy: Graham Martin, "Organizational Imperatives," in Smith Simpson, ed., *Resources and Needs of American Diplomacy*, American Academy of Political and Social Science, *Annals*, Vol. 380, Nov. 1968, p. 16 @ 18–19.

p. 227 Bundy: *Murphy Commission*, Vol. 2, Appendix A, p. 36.

Rourke: Francis Rourke, *Bureaucracy and Foreign Policy*, Johns Hopkins University Press, Baltimore, Md., 1972, p. 5.

p. 228 Bernstein: Barton J. Bernstein, "The Cuban Missile Crisis: Trading the Jupiters in Turkey?" *Political Science Quarterly*, Vol. 95, No. 1, Spring 1980, p. 97 @ 101, 103, 103 fn.

Kissinger: Henry A. Kissinger, *American Foreign Policy*, W. W. Norton, New York, 1969, p. 20.

p. 230 arms sales: Andrew J. Pierre, "Arms Sales: The New Diplomacy," *Foreign Affairs*, Winter 1981/82, Vol. 60, No. 2, pp. 266, 276.

Galbraith: Frankel, *Foggy Bottom*, p. 11.

p. 232 cryptography: *Murphy Commission*, p. 122.

CHAPTER 9: ORGANIZING A COUNTRY

p. 239 Kennedy: Schlesinger, *A Thousand Days*, pp. 430–31.

Chatfield: Christopher Thorne, *The Limits of Foreign Policy: The League and the Far Eastern Crisis of 1931–33*, Putnam's, New York, 1973, p. 398.

p. 241 Johnson NSC: Lyndon B. Johnson, *The Vantage Point*, Holt, Rinehart & Winston, New York, 1971, p. 65 fn.

President's policies: George Ball, *Diplomacy for a Crowded World: An American Foreign Policy*, Atlantic Monthly–Little Brown, Boston, 1967, p. 199.

general's star: Vernon Walters, *Silent Missions*, Doubleday, Garden City, N.Y., 1981, pp. 109–10.

p. 242 Acheson comments: Acheson, *External Realm*, p. 252.

Jackson Subcommittee: Campbell, *Fudge Factory*, p. 269.

Kennedy habit: Yost, *Conduct and Misconduct*, pp. 138–39.

p. 243 Rostow: W. W. Rostow, *The View from the Seventh Floor*, Harper & Row, New York, 1964, p. 39.

Betts: Betts, *Soldiers, Statesmen*, p. 153.

p. 245 Brzezinski: "Brzezinski on National Security Advisers," New York *Times*, Jan. 6, 1982, p. A19.

p. 247 marketing and sales: Ichak Adizes, "The Internal Conflict Over Foreign Policy," *Wall Street Journal*, Dec. 22, 1981, editorial page.

Equally jejune, of course, is Professor Adizes' notion that marketing and sales should be "struggling" against each other.

p. 250 Fred Greenstein, "Eisenhower as an Activist President," *Political Science Quarterly*, Vol. 94, No. 4, Winter 1979–80, p. 575 @ 592.

Eisenhower: Dwight David Eisenhower, *Mandate for Change*, Doubleday, New York, 1963, p. 478.

p. 254 postal clerk: Joseph Kraft, quoted in Bernard Cohen, *The Press and Foreign Policy*, Princeton University Press, Princeton, N.J., 1963, p. 45.

photographers: William H. Sullivan, *Mission to Iran*, W. W. Norton, New York, 1981, p. 19.

p. 255 Cohen: Cohen, *The Press*, p. 13.

p. 256 public affairs programs: *Murphy Commission*, p. 109.

p. 257 polling: ibid., p. 111.

p. 258 Washington: James Flexner, *George Washington and the New Nation, 1783–1793*, Little Brown, Boston, 1970, p. 217.

p. 259 expurgated version: letter of Attorney General Edward H. Levi, in *Murphy Commission*, p. 244.

House motion: James Flexner, *George Washington: Anguish and Farewell*, Little Brown, Boston, 1972, p. 265.

House leaders: ibid., pp. 273–74.

p. 260 XYZ affair: Alexander De Conde, *The Quasi-War*, Scribner's, 1966, p. 72.

p. 261 Jefferson: Flexner, *Washington and the New Nation*, p. 405.

p. 262 Senator Allen: Frederick Merk, *The Oregon Question*, Harvard University Press, Cambridge, Mass., 1967, p. 380.

platform: Donald Bruce Johnson and Kirk H. Porter, *National Party Platforms, 1840–1972*, University of Illinois Press, Urbana, Ill., 1975 (5th ed.), p. 4.

Polk: Merk, *Oregon Question*, pp. 382–83.

p. 263 Moore: *Murphy Commission*, p. 248.

p. 264 commitment: Edward A. Kolodziej, "Congress and Foreign Policy," in Harvey C. Mansfield, Sr., ed., *Congress Against the President*, Academy of Political Science, *Proceedings*, Vol. 32, No. 1, p. 167 @170.

p. 266 agreements: Edward A. Kolodziej, "Formulating Foreign Policy," in Richard M. Pious, ed., *The Power to Govern*, Academy of Political Science, *Proceedings*, Vol. 34, No. 2, p. 172 @ 183–84.

p. 267 House staffs: ibid., p. 188.

p. 269 "Too few": David K. Willis, "Dealing with Congress," in Simpson, *Resources and Needs of American Diplomacy*, p. 112 @ 114.

CRS report: Joseph T. Kendrick, *Executive-Legislative Consultation on Foreign Policy*, House Foreign Affairs Committee Print, GPO, May 1981, pp. 4, 2.

p. 270 Theodore Roosevelt: Charles L. Mee, Jr., *The End of Order: Versailles 1919*, E. P. Dutton, New York, 1980, p. 14.

ethnicity: Nathan Glazer and Daniel P. Moynihan, *Ethnicity*, Harvard University Press, Cambridge, Mass., 1975, p. 24; cited in Charles McC. Mathias, "Ethnic Groups and Foreign Policy," *Foreign Affairs*, Vol. 59, No. 5, Summer 1981, p. 975 @ 979.

p. 271   Theodore Green: Jessup, *Birth of Nations*, p. 4.
John Marshall: John G. Tower, "Congress Views the President: The Formulation and Implementation of American Foreign Policy," *Foreign Affairs*, Vol. 60, No. 2, Winter 1981–82, p. 229.
Huntington: Samuel Huntington, "Strategic Planning and the Political Process," *Foreign Affairs*, Jan. 1960, Vol. 38, No. 2, p. 287.

p. 272   Edward S. Corwin, *The President: Office and Powers, 1787–1957*, New York University Press, New York, 1957, p. 200.

CHAPTER 10: ORGANIZING A NUMBER OF COUNTRIES

p. 273   Sorel: Georges Sorel, *Reflections on Violence* (tr. T. E. Hulme and J. Roth), Collier Books, New York, 1961, p. 212.
WIPO: *U.S. Participation in the UN*, Report by the President to the Congress for the Year 1976, GPO, 1977, p. 276.

p. 274   preamble: Jean Monnet, *Memoirs*, Doubleday, Garden City, N.Y., 1978, p. 357.

p. 285   whined: European Documentation, *The Agricultural Policy of the European Community* (1978 ed.), Brussels, 1979, p. 29.

p. 297   Roosevelt: Acheson, *Present at Creation*, p. 73.
FAO: Charles Wolf, Jr., "A Theory of Non-Market Failures," *The Public Interest*, No. 55, Spring 1979, p. 114 @ 127.

p. 298   UNESCO's future: Henry Tanner, "UNESCO to Fight Gap Between Rich and Poor," New York *Times*, No. 25, 1982, p. A6.

p. 299   Levy: Marion Levy, *Modernization: Latecomers and Survivors*, Basic Books, 1972, p. 46.

p. 300   Russian ships: Tavares de Sá, *Play Within Play*, p. 276.

p. 301   Lippmann: Urquhart, *Hammarskjöld*, p. 206.

p. 303   Hazzard: Shirley Hazzard, *Defeat of an Ideal*, Atlantic Monthly–Little Brown, Boston, 1973, pp. 97, 98.
UN Secretariat: Moynihan, *Dangerous Place*, pp. 85–86.

p. 304   UN study: Wassily Leontief et al., *The Future of the World Economy*, Oxford University Press, New York, 1977, p. 69.
annual report: Moynihan, *Dangerous Place*, p. 253.

p. 306   social aspect: Tavares de Sá, *Play Within Play*, pp. 197, 198.

p. 307   Truman: Thomas M. Campbell and George C. Herring, Jr., eds., *The Diaries of Edward R. Stettinius, 1943–46*, Franklin Watts, New York, 1975, p. 404.
Hiss: ibid., p. 416.

p. 308   Acheson: Acheson, *Present at Creation*, p. 450.
Thant: Katz, *Things That Are Caesar's*, pp. 63–64.

p. 309   Dulles and Lodge: Murphy, *Diplomat*, p. 367.

p. 315   Lall: Arthur Lall, "The Superpowers, the UN and Disarmament," in Alvin Z. Rubinstein and George Ginsburgs, eds., *Soviet and American Policies in the UN*, New York University Press, New York, 1971, p. 48 @ 61.

CHAPTER 11: THE ISRAELI FOREIGN MINISTRY

p. 318 Gromyko: Theodore Draper, *Israel and World Politics*, Viking-Compass, New York, 1968 (paper), p. 5.

Arendt: Hannah Arendt, *Imperialism*, Harcourt Brace, New York, 1970 (paper), p. 170.

p. 320 fn Emir Feisal: John Maynard Keynes, "Dr. Melchior," in Keynes, *Essays and Sketches in Biography*, Meridian Books, New York, 1956 (paper), p. 216.

p. 320 fn Sykes-Picot: Harry N. Howard, *Turkey, the Straits and U.S. Policy*, Johns Hopkins University Press, Baltimore, Md., p. 34.

p. 320 French actions: *see* Introduction and Conclusion, in William I. Shorrock, *French Imperialism in the Middle East: The Failure of Policy in Lebanon, 1900–1914*, University of Wisconsin Press, Madison, Wis., 1976.

p. 321 British mandate: Jessup, *Birth of Nations*, p. 259.

p. 324 Nehru: Eytan, *First Ten Years*, p. 167.

p. 325 Icelandic ambassador: Eban, *Autobiography*, p. 97.

Syrkin: Marie Syrkin, "How Begin Threatens Israel," *The New Republic*, Vol. 185, No. 11, Sept. 16, 1981, p. 27.

p. 326 Rafael: Rafael, *Destination Peace*, p. 7.

p. 330 Eytan: Eytan, *First Ten Years*, p. 9.

p. 332 Eytan: ibid., pp. 179–80.

p. 335 Brownstein: Lewis Brownstein, "Decision-Making in Israeli Foreign Policy," *Political Science Quarterly*, Vol. 92, No. 2, p. 259 @ 260.

small group of people: ibid., p. 261.

Ben-Gurion: *Ben Gurion Looks Back, Talks With Moshe Pearlman*, New York, 1970, p. 122.

p. 340 Egyptian heroes: Anthony Eden, *Full Circle*, Houghton Mifflin, Boston, 1960, p. 575.

De Gaulle: Charles de Gaulle, *Memoirs of Hope, Renewal and Endeavor*, Simon & Schuster, New York, 1971, p. 266.

p. 341 Kolodziej: Edward Kolodziej, *French International Policy Under de Gaulle and Pompidou: The Politics of Grandeur*, Cornell University Press, Ithaca, N.Y., 1974, p. 489.

p. 341 fn Soviet behavior: Draper, *Israel and World Politics*, pp. 52–58.

p. 342 anti-Semitism: Keynes, *Essays and Sketches*, p. 229.

p. 346 Moynihan's watch: Moynihan, *Dangerous Place*, p. 194.

p. 348 Fabian: Larry L. Fabian, "Red Light, West Bank," *Foreign Policy 50*, Spring 1983, p. 53 @ 65.

CHAPTER 12: DIRECTIONS

p. 353 Plato: *Laws* 626a; cited in Michael Grant, *The Ancient Mediterranean*, Scribner's, New York, 1969, p. 9.

Carter: Jimmy Carter, *Keeping Faith*, Bantam Books, New York, 1983, p. 356.

NOTES

p. 357 Falk: Richard A. Falk, "Khomeini's Promise," *Foreign Policy* 34, Spring 1979, p. 28 @ 32.

p. 368 Kissinger: Kissinger, *Years of Upheaval*, p. 1191.

p. 374 Schelling: Thomas Schelling, "Thinking About Nuclear Terrorism," *International Security*, Vol. 6, No. 4, Spring 1982, p. 61 @ 76, 77.

p. 376 Hugo: Grant Hugo, *Appearance and Reality in International Relations*, Columbia University Press, New York, 1970, p. 29.

p. 381 Kennan: George Kennan, *Foreign Policy and the Professional Diplomat*, p. 149.

INDEX

ABOUT THE AUTHOR

MARTIN MAYER was born in New York City in 1928. His parents, Henry and Ruby, were both lawyers, and his father is still in active practice at the age of eighty-seven. In 1947, Martin Mayer was graduated from Harvard, where he studied mostly economics, music and duplicate bridge. After assorted jobs on a business newspaper, a scholarly magazine of the labor movement, a fact-detective magazine and *Esquire*, he set up shop as an independent writer in 1954.

In the years since, Mr. Mayer has written twenty books, three of them novels, plus several unpublished studies for foundations and several hundred articles and reviews. His major reportorial books include *Wall Street: Men and Money, Madison Avenue U.S.A., The Schools, The Lawyers, About Television, The Bankers* and *The Builders*. He has also written *Emory Buckner*, a biography of a lawyer, and a book of recent history and economic analysis, *The Fate of the Dollar*.

For twenty-three years, Mr. Mayer was music critic of *Esquire* and wrote a number of musical profiles for the New York *Times Magazine, Harper's*, and others. He continues to review musical performances for *Opera* in England and *Musical America* in the United States. One of his novels, *A Voice That Fills the House*, has an operatic subject, and he collaborated with Sir Rudolf Bing on the first volume of his memoirs. *The Met*, Mr. Mayer's history of the Metropolitan Opera, commissioned by the Metropolitan Opera Guild, is currently in press.

Mr. Mayer was married for thirty years to the late Ellen Moers, a critic and scholar of comparative literature. They had two sons, Thomas, now a lawyer, and James, a research chemist. In 1980, he married Karin Lissakers, then deputy director of the Policy Planning Staff at the State Department, whom he met while working on this book. The book is dedicated to their daughter, Fredrica.